54504A

SO-AHA-605

99BB
$11⁰²

LANGUAGE
ACQUISITION
AND
LANGUAGE
BREAKDOWN

LANGUAGE ACQUISITION AND LANGUAGE BREAKDOWN

Parallels and Divergencies

EDITED BY

Alfonso Caramazza
and
Edgar B. Zurif

THE JOHNS HOPKINS UNIVERSITY PRESS
BALTIMORE AND LONDON

Copyright © 1978 by The Johns Hopkins University Press

All rights reserved. No part of this book may be
reproduced or transmitted in any form or by any means,
electronic or mechanical, including photocopying,
recording, xerography, or any information storage and
retrieval system, without permission in writing
from the publisher.

Manufactured in the United States of America

The Johns Hopkins University Press, Baltimore, Maryland 21218
The Johns Hopkins Press Ltd., London

Library of Congress Catalog Card Number 77–4789
ISBN 0–8018–1948–2

Library of Congress Cataloging in Publication data
will be found on the last printed page of this book.

To the memory of Eric Lenneberg

CONTENTS

PREFACE

Few psychologists read both the developmental psycholinguistic literature and the literature on aphasia. Fewer still do research in both areas—so few that many, if not most, such researchers have papers appearing in this volume. The reason for the limited size of this set is not difficult to understand. Historically, research has become diversified and specialized. The study of cognition, once mainly within the purview of philosophy, is currently undertaken by investigators representing such diverse disciplines as cognitive psychology, linguistics, psycholinguistics and developmental psycholinguistics, aphasiology, computer science, and philosophy. Analyses of language and language use have therefore taken different forms, each discipline contributing in its own characteristic fashion.

Attempting to straddle even two of these disciplines is a difficult matter. There are practical problems in gaining data from both nursery schools and the neurological wards of hospitals. And there are differences in perspective. Thus, developmental psycholinguistics is comfortable with mentalism; aphasiology much less so. The former uses mental constructs in describing the form and manner in which a child internalizes linguistic knowledge; the latter, rooted in a neurological tradition, tends to seek brain-behavior relations and to study language for its lesion-localizing value. Yet, given that both disciplines focus upon language that differs from the adult norm, it seemed heuristically valuable to look over the barriers and to compare notes. More specifically, our intention was to explore whether informal observations of correspondences between levels of language mastery and stages of language dissolution were fortuitous or whether they permitted a common generalization and a genuine theoretical synthesis.

Accordingly, the contributors to this volume were asked to examine their research findings for parallels and divergencies between patterns of language acquisition in children and patterns of language breakdown under conditions of brain damage. They were given one general guideline: to attempt to determine whether the linguistic forms acquired latest in development are the most vulnerable in aphasia and whether those learned earliest are the best retained. They were asked, that is, to determine whether or not aphasia is a regressive phenomenon.

This possibility is usually referred to as the regression hypothesis and is variously associated with Ribot, Jackson, Freud, and most recently, Jakobson.

This hypothesis has exerted a great deal of intellectual appeal in the history of aphasia research. The problem with it, however, as we discovered when confronting our own data and reading the replies of the other contributors, is that it simply does not bear close scrutiny.

To be sure, the phrase "development in reverse" is descriptive in the sense that complexity is often a factor in both acquisition and aphasia. Comprehension for syntactically complex sentences, for example, develops late and is most vulnerable in aphasia. And there are other examples. But to our knowledge, where there is correspondence, it can be maintained in most instances only at a superficial level. The two groups—children and aphasics—usually employ different strategies, face different obstacles, and show different degrees of awareness of their problems.

If there is an exception, it is likely to be at the level of segmental speech perception. Thus, just as the preverbal infant seems especially tuned to the acoustic parameters of speech without appreciating their functional significance, so too the adult who suffers brain damage may find his capacity to classify speech sounds categorically vitiated, while his capacity to distinguish among such sounds on the basis of their relevant acoustic parameters may be spared. Perhaps it is no accident that we find the best support for the regression hypothesis at the level of speech perception. At this level the differences between the child's and the aphasic's extralinguistic, conceptual knowledge seem least intrusive. As the articles in this volume make abundantly clear, however, phenomena that fit the regression hypothesis in more than a superficial fashion are far outnumbered by phenomena that do not.

Furthermore, for the regression hypothesis to truly apply, even should one or another aspect of language performance be held in common by a given developmental stage and a particular aphasic syndrome, there is the problem of assigning the various syndromes to steps on a scale of regression. It is relevant here that the neural capacity for language does not appear to be neurologically undifferentiated; that is, brain damage does not appear to lead simply to an across-the-board reduction in language—the more extensive the damage, the greater the reduction. Rather, the site of the lesion is of extreme importance in determining the form of the syndrome. More to the point, these different clinical forms resist alignment with levels of language acquisition. For example, developmentally, semantic intentions seem to appear in advance of their adequate syntactic expression. But it does not follow from this that the telegrammatic aphasic, whose speech can at least be understood, is at a more regressed stage than the aphasic whose speech, although marked by a variety of complex grammatical forms, contains indefinite noun phrases, incorrect lexical insertions, and even neologisms.

Yet, because there are more differences between normal child and aphasic language than there are similarities makes it even more pressing that comparisons be continued. By more completely charting the differences and similarities, we will be better able to determine the manner in which earlier mental structures become integrated and transformed into complex hierarchical structures.

This volume grew from a symposium organized by Howard Gardner for the meeting of the Academy of Aphasia held in 1974. The participants in this symposium were Alfonso Caramazza, Jill de Villiers, Jean Berko Gleason, and Eric Lenneberg, with Harold Goodglass as discussant. All have contributions appearing in this volume.

Both the symposium and this printed enterprise were supported by National Institutes of Health grants 11408 and 06209 to the Aphasia Research Center, Department of Neurology, Boston University School of Medicine.

I
SPEECH PERCEPTION AND
SPEECH PRODUCTION

The chapters in this section, although each is concerned with phonological aspects of language, vary considerably in terms of the issues explored, the experimental methodology, and most importantly, the level of explanation sought by the authors. Chapters 3 and 4, by Ingram and Holmes, take a primarily linguistic approach in order to explicate the structure of a deviant system, whereas chapters 1 and 2, by Blumstein and Tallal, are more deeply embedded in a psychological tradition, and deal with basic mechanisms that may underly the perception of speech sounds.

Ingram and Holmes share a common concern when they ask whether deviant language can be characterized in terms of earlier forms of development, but they differ in the substantive issues they address. Holmes's chapter is devoted to an analysis of the type of impairment in phoneme-grapheme correspondence rules that may be associated with acquired dyslexia in adults and developmental dyslexia in children. Ingram, on the other hand, compares the phonemic structure of fricatives and affricates in normal and linguistically deviant children. The data base in these two chapters is production errors that are analyzed as deviations from intended targets. Both authors

conclude, as do others in later chapters in this volume, that, while there are intriguing similarities between a deviant system and early forms of language development, such similarities may be accidental, and, to quote Ingram, deviant systems are "more than just delayed systems."

The chapters by Tallal and Blumstein focus on abnormal language functioning to reveal general mechanisms that may underly the perception of language. Thus, Tallal explores the possibility that developmental dysphasia results from an inability to process information that incorporates rapidly changing acoustic spectra (e.g., stop consonants). She goes on to relate this claim to the hypothesis that one of the specialized functions of the left hemisphere is to process information of just this type. On the basis of her extensive experimental work she concludes that developmental dysphasia is a consequence of impaired perceptual processing. An obvious corollary is that the processing of rapidly changing acoustic information is a central component in a hierarchical system of language perception and comprehension.

Blumstein also suggests that language functioning and language acquisition are hierarchically organized. But she deals with a different level of perception, being concerned with the relation of identification to discrimination of speech and with the mechanisms that underly these processes. To this end, she brings forth evidence to suggest that speech discrimination is based on the functioning of property (feature) detectors for ranges of acoustic stimuli —detectors that may be prewired as part of man's biological apparatus.

I

THE PERCEPTION OF SPEECH IN PATHOLOGY AND ONTOGENY

Sheila E. Blumstein

INTRODUCTION

Much discussion about the nature of human language has focused upon the dichotomy between language as a product of man's biological endowment and language as a product of learning. It is clear that language reflects the essential role of both nature and nurture, for language cannot be acquired normally when a child sustains brain damage (Eisenson 1972) or when he is deprived of normal linguistic or social environmental stimulation (Brown 1958; Fromkin, Krashen, Curtiss, Rigler, and Rigler 1974). Nevertheless, what is far from clear is the extent to which and in what manner the linguistic system is predetermined by biological endowment or is shaped by experience.

It has been known since at least 1863, with the publication of the work of Paul Broca, that the left hemisphere of the brain is specialized for language. Thus, 99% of right-handed aphasics have damage restricted to the left hemisphere (Zangwill 1962). Evidence implicating the specialization of the left hemisphere for language in adults has also been obtained using various controlled procedures: aphasialike symptoms are produced by the injection of sodium amytal in the left carotid artery (Wada and Rasmussen 1960); auditory-evoked potential differences are obtained between the two hemispheres upon presentation of language stimuli (Wood, Goff, and Day 1971); right-ear advantages are obtained for language stimuli under conditions of dichotic listening (Kimura 1961); and anatomical asymmetries have been found between the upper surface of the right and left temporal globes (Geschwind and Levitsky 1968).

Moreover, recent evidence suggests that a lateralized predisposition for language is present even in neonates. Specifically, greater auditory-evoked responses have been demonstrated over the left hemisphere for speech stimuli

This work was supported in part by United States Public Health Service grants NS 07615 to Clark University and NS 11408 and NS 06209 to Boston University School of Medicine. Special thanks to Kenneth N. Stevens, Harold Goodglass, and Vivien Tartter for their helpful suggestions and critical comments on an earlier draft of this paper.

3

in infants ranging from 1 week to 10 months old (Molfese 1972; Molfese, Freeman, and Palermo 1975). In addition, Witelsohn and Pailie (1973) found anatomical differences in neonates ranging in age from 1 day to 3 months similar to those demonstrated by Geschwind and Levitsky (1968) in adults.

Although the specialization of the left hemisphere for language seems to be predetermined by biological factors, the question still remains, what is it that is "special" about the left hemisphere? Largely as a result of the study of aphasia, the language-dominant hemisphere has been considered to be uniquely specialized for the more symbolic aspects of language, such as syntax and semantics. However, semantic and syntactic analysis may not be the sole linguistic process to be specifically located in the left hemisphere. In fact, recent results from evoked-potential research in normal adults (Wood et al. 1971; Dorman 1972) and dichotic listening studies in normal adults (Shankweiler and Studdert-Kennedy 1967; Studdert-Kennedy and Shankweiler 1970) and adult aphasics (Oscar-Berman, Zurif, and Blumstein 1975) suggest that the perception of speech and its underlying phonetic features seem to be processed more efficiently by the left hemisphere.

It is the object of this chapter to consider the results of recent research on the perception of speech in language pathology and language development. The evidence presented from each area bears directly upon the nature of speech specialization and phonological processing. Taken together, this research presents compelling evidence in support of the biological predisposition for the linguistic system in man.

Any attempt to establish a relationship between the nature of the processes of perception in development and those in pathology must be made with extreme caution. The adult aphasic is an individual who had a fully acquired and normally organized linguistic system and who then sustained brain damage that affected the normal processing of this completed system. In contrast, the infant is a developing organism, one whose linguistic system is at best only partially developed or incompletely organized. Consequently, any correspondence between the performance of aphasics and infants on perception tasks does not necessarily imply that the aphasic represents an ontogenetically earlier stage of language processing or that the perceptual processes in pathology and development are the same. Nevertheless, such correspondences may reveal important evidence suggestive of the types of process that seem to underlie speech perception in man.

PHONEME DISCRIMINATION
AND COMPREHENSION IN APHASIA

The comprehension of language is based upon the integration of both psychological and linguistic dimensions. To understand a sentence correctly it is necessary, at the very least, to apprehend the phonological structure, relate it to the meaning of individual words, integrate the words in relation to the syntactic frame in which they belong, and consider the full sentence in its social context. In nearly all forms of aphasia, patients demonstrate some form of language comprehension deficit. Nevertheless, only recently have investigators attempted to parcel out the contribution of these various dimensions to auditory language comprehension. One obvious candidate for study has been phonological perception. If the phonological form of a word or utterance is incorrectly perceived, remaining analysis of the signal in terms of its semantic content or syntactic form may be in error. In fact, Luria has suggested that a selective deficit in phonemic hearing, i.e., an inability to discriminate minimal phonological contrasts, forms the basis for the comprehension deficit in one common form of aphasia, Wernicke's aphasia. As Luria (1970) states, "We have every reason to believe that the basic defect in temporal [Wernicke's] aphasia is the disturbance of auditory analysis and synthesis which leads to the loss of phonemic hearing, and, as a secondary result, to the disturbance of all functions which are dependent upon this physiological function" (p. 127).

Clinically, patients suffering from this form of aphasia have fluent speech that is typically empty, in the sense that little if any semantic information is conveyed. This is especially striking in light of the quantity of verbal output of these patients. Often their speech is interspersed with neologisms that conform to the phonological structure of the language but that nevertheless are not a part of the lexicon of the language. Moreover, the language comprehension of these patients is usually severely impaired. They often have difficulty understanding names of objects, simple or complex sentences, or simple commands.

Although a deficit in phonological processing may contribute to disorders of language comprehension, it seems unlikely that this impairment alone could be the basis for the profound comprehension deficit of these patients. Moreover, it is unclear to what extent disorders in phonological processing may exist in other forms of aphasia. Consequently, we (Blumstein, Goodglass, and Baker 1977) attempted to systematically investigate phonological discrimination ability in aphasics. We had three goals in mind: (1) to determine if Wernicke's aphasics have a selective disorder in discriminating minimal phonemic contrasts; (?) to determine if such an impairment could account for their comprehension deficit; and (3) to ascertain the vulnerability of phonological discrimination in aphasic patients with dominant-hemisphere lesions. To this end, a discrimination test was devised consisting of two parts: discrimination of real words and discrimination of nonsense syllables. The nonsense syllables were designed to reflect the same phonological relations present in real words and to differ from real words only by an absence of meaning. The use of nonsense syllables seemed to us to provide a more sensitive measure of phonemic hearing, since the only cue available to the subject for discrimination was the sound structure of the test item. With real words, meaningfulness of necessity interacted with phonological distinctions.

The phoneme discrimination task was designed to test the patient's ability to apprehend minimal phonological contrasts. These contrasts are based on the notion that the phoneme is defined in terms of a bundle of distinctive-feature attributes. Thus, the phoneme /p/ can be characterized in several linguistically relevant dimensions; for example, /p/ is a stop consonant [+ obstruent], it is produced with closure at the lips [+ bilabial], and vocal chord vibration does not begin until after the release of the consonant [− voice]. The phoneme /b/ shares both manner of articulation [+ obstruent] and place of articulation [+ bilabial] with /p/, but in contrast, it is characterized by vocal cord vibration simultaneous to the release of the consonant, i.e., [+ voice]. In using a distinctive-feature framework, the type of phonological contrast and the phonological distance between phonemes can be systematically investigated. In this particular study, the phoneme discrimination contrasts considered consisted of the distinctive-feature values of place of articulation, and voice and place for the stop consonant series /p/, /t/, /k/, /b/, /d/, /g/. Both one- and two-syllable stimuli were used, contrasting in initial and final position for one syllable words (e.g., 'pit' vs. 'kit'; 'tip' vs. 'tick') and initial and medial position for two-syllable words (e.g., 'pony' vs. 'bony' and 'sopping' vs. 'sobbing'). The subject's task was to press a button marked Yes if the two stimuli were the same, one marked No if they were not.

Twenty-five aphasic patients served as subjects. Patients were assigned to one of four diagnostic groups on the basis of a composite aphasia examination including psychological, language, and neurological tests. Patients with anterior left-hemisphere lesions were assigned to two groups: those with good comprehension (Broca's aphasics) and those with impaired comprehension (mixed anterior group). The speech output of Broca's aphasics is characteristically nonfluent. Function words, such as articles and connectives, and grammatical markers, such as plurals and tense endings, are commonly omitted, resulting in so-called telegraphic speech. In addition, these patients often produce both phonetic and prosodic distortions. Comprehension is usually intact or mildly impaired. The speech output of the mixed anterior group is similar to that of the Broca's aphasics, but unlike them, the mixed anterior group has a moderate-to-severe language comprehension deficit. The remaining population was drawn from patients with posterior left-hemisphere lesions. These patients were also divided into two groups: patients with predominantly temporal lobe lesions (Wernicke's aphasics) and patients who represented several other diagnostic categories (residual group). As indicated earlier, the speech output of Wernicke's aphasics is fluent but empty, and language comprehension is severely impaired. Patients in the residual group represented other aphasic categories, such as anomics (patients with naming difficulties) and conduction aphasics (patients with fluent speech, moderate to good comprehension, but severe repetition difficulties).

Figure 1.1 shows the performance of the four aphasic groups on the task of

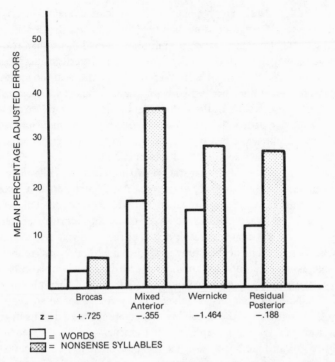

Fig. 1.1 Performance of four aphasic groups on the task of phoneme discrimination. The z-scores listed below each group represent the mean performance of the group on the auditory comprehension subtest of the Goodglass-Kaplan battery (see text). Positive scores indicate good comprehension; negative scores, poor comprehension.

phoneme discrimination. The comprehension scores listed below each group are based on the mean z-score performance of the subjects on the comprehension subtests of the Goodglass-Kaplan test battery (Goodglass and Kaplan 1972). Note that the Broca's aphasics have the best comprehension, followed in descending order of comprehension facility by the residual posterior group, the mixed anterior group, and finally the Wernicke's aphasics.

There are two important results illustrated in this graph: (1) in all groups the perception of real words was better than the perception of nonsense syllables and (2) perhaps more important, the Wernicke's aphasics, the group with the most severe comprehension deficit, were not the most impaired in phoneme discrimination. Both of these results suggest that phoneme discrimination is not selectively impaired in Wernicke's aphasics in comparison to other aphasic groups, nor does it seem to be the basis for the comprehension deficit of these patients. Firstly, if the poor auditory comprehension of Wernicke's aphasics is caused by poor phoneme discrimination, then one might expect the performance of these patients to be *less* affected by the shift from real words to nonsense syllables; that is, all phonological discriminations should be impaired, regardless of the meaningfulness of the test item. The fact that for all groups nonsense-syllable discrimination was significantly more difficult than real-word discrimination suggests that all were employing similar performance strategies on these tasks. Secondly, although the Wernicke's aphasics had the most severe comprehension deficit, they performed better than the mixed anterior group on the test of nonsense syllables. Thus, disturbances of phonemic hearing do not seem to be limited to patients with temporal lobe damage, and more importantly, a disturbance in phonemic hearing does not seem to be sufficient to account for the severe comprehension deficit of these patients.

Further analysis revealed that the posterior aphasics (Wernicke's and residual), unlike the anterior aphasics (Broca's and mixed anterior) seem to have a subtle deficit in the discrimination of place contrasts in comparison to voice or voice and place contrasts. Nevertheless, this impairment certainly cannot account for the comprehension deficit of the Wernicke's aphasics.

In general, the results of this study suggest that, although discrimination of speech sounds may be impaired to some degree in aphasia, this impairment cannot be the basis for comprehension deficits in any of the aphasic groups studied. A failure to find a selective deficit in discrimination of speech sounds however, does not rule out the possibility that comprehension deficits in aphasia in general and in Wernicke's aphasics in particular may be attributable, at least in part, to an inability to use phonological attributes in a linguistically meaningful way. That is, it is one thing to be able to ascertain the presence or absence of differences between speech sounds and quite another to use a particular phonological attribute to represent the meaning of a given word in contrast to another. A deficit in this latter case should result in difficulty in assigning a label to a particular speech sound or in the inability to point reliably to an appropriate picture given the test item auditorily. In a subsequent study, we attempted to directly compare the aphasic patient's ability to discriminate phonological contrasts with his ability to use these same contrasts in a linguistically meaningful way.

THE PERCEPTION OF VOICE-ONSET TIME IN APHASIA

Studies on the perception of consonants in normal adults indicate that the perception of such phonetic categories as *voice* and *place of articulation* is based upon a set of distinctive acoustic and phonetic attributes. Articulatorily, voicing distinctions (e.g., [p-b], [t-d], [k-g]) in initial prestressed position are signaled by different times of onset of vocal cord vibration in relation to the release of the consonant. In the time interval between consonantal release and voicing onset, aspiration is produced by the egressive flow of air. A delay in vocal cord vibration and concomitant aspiration produces a voiceless aspirated

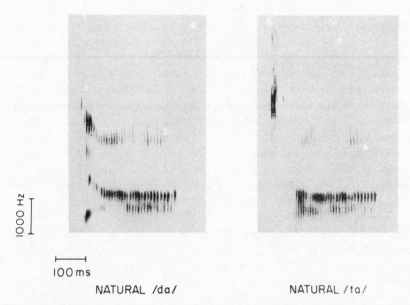

Fig. 1.2   Wide-band spectrograms of the naturally produced syllables /da/ and /ta/ for a male speaker.

consonant (e.g., [tʰ]), while simultaneous voicing at the release of closure or vocal cord vibration before release of the closure produces a voiced consonant (e.g., [d]). Acoustically, the voiceless consonant is characterized by a delayed onset of the first formant relative to the higher formants and the occurrence of a harmonic source only after the formant transitions are essentially completed.* The higher formants are excited by a noise source rather than a periodic source during the time interval when F1 is absent (see figure 1.2). For voiced stops, F1 begins simultaneously or slightly after the onset of the higher formants, and a harmonic source is present throughout (see figure 1.2). This timing relation between glottal pulsing and consonantal release has been called *voice-onset time*, or VOT (Lisker and Abramson 1964, 1967).

The perception of voice-onset time as a cue to voiced-voiceless contrasts has been investigated by synthesizing acoustic continua ranging systematically along this dimension. Results of these studies indicate that the perception of voice-onset time changes is not continuous. Rather, when subjects were asked to identify or label stimuli from the continua, they labeled them consistently as one phonetic value and then suddenly, usually at a particular stimulus item, changed category values. The identification responses of a typical subject can

---

* A formant is generally defined as a concentration of spectral energy in a narrow-frequency region of a speech signal. These peaks are numbered consecutively from the lowest to highest frequency range. Thus, F1 represents energy at the lowest acoustic energy range, F2 represents the next higher range, and so on.

be seen in figure 1.3. Note that the subject heard stimuli ranging from a VOT of −20 (i.e., 20 msec of voicing prior to the release of the consonant) to +25 msec (i.e., a 25-msec delay of vocal cord vibration relative to the consonantal release) as a [d], and from +30 msec−+60 msec VOT as a [t]. When asked to discriminate differences between stimuli taken from the same continua, subjects could only reliably discriminate those stimuli that belong to different phonetic categories; those stimuli that were labeled as the same phonetic category could not be reliably discriminated. Figure 1.4 shows the discrimination function for the same continuum and same subject illustrated in Figure 1.3. This subject could only discriminate stimuli with a VOT of +20 (labeled by him as [d]; see figure 1.3) from +40 (labeled by him as a [t]). Comparisons between stimuli lying within the [d] range, e.g., VOT 0 and VOT +20, or within the [t] range, VOT +40 and VOT +60, could not be discriminated. The term *categorical perception* has been applied to this phenomenon whereby subjects can discriminate only those contrasts that they identify as belonging to different phonetic categories, despite the fact that the acoustic differences between all stimuli are equivalent (at least along one acoustic dimension) (Liberman, Harris, Hoffman, and Griffith 1957; Liberman, Cooper, Shankweiler, and Studdert-Kennedy 1967).

Results of these studies are particularly important since they are not restricted to the English language. The voicing dimension is found in nearly all languages, and although the phonetic boundaries along this dimension are not identical, subjects speaking different languages perceive the VOT continuum categorically (Abramson and Lisker 1970; Lisker and Abramson 1970).

The question we (Blumstein, Cooper, Zurif, and Caramazza 1977) were concerned with investigating was what effect brain damage had on the perception of the voicing dimension, a nearly universal feature of human language. To this end, a synthetic continuum varying in voice-onset time was constructed by means of a computer-controlled parallel resonance synthesizer made available at Haskins Laboratories. The stimuli signaling the phonetic categories [da] and [ta] ranged in VOT from −20 to +80 in 10 msec steps. Negative values indicate that the first formant and periodic pulsing began prior to the release of the consonant, i.e., before the onset of the second and third formants, and positive values indicate that the first formant and periodic pulsing began after consonantal release. A VOT value of 0 indicates that glottal pulsing began simultaneously with consonantal release.

Subjects took two tests, an identification test and a discrimination test. In the identification test, subjects were required to identify each stimulus presented auditorily by pointing to the appropriate printed card, *da* or *ta*. In the discrimination test they were asked to determine whether stimulus pairs presented were the same or different by pointing to a card marked Yes if the pair members were identical and No if they were not. The different pair members were distinguished from each other by a VOT of 20 msec. Twenty-four subjects participated in this experiment: four control subjects taken from the medical and orthopedic services of the Boston Veterans Administration Hospital; four right-brain-damaged subjects; and sixteen aphasic patients.

The identification and discrimination functions for one of the normal control patients can be seen in figures 1.3 and 1.4. Note the close correspondence between this subject's identification and discrimination functions. All the normal patients performed similarly on both tasks.

The performance of the right-brain-damaged group was equivalent to that of the normal control group. Identification and discrimination functions for one of these subjects can be seen in figures 1.5 and 1.6. The normal performance of the right-brain-damaged subjects on the identification and discrimination of voice-onset time is crucial, as any deficits on these tasks manifested by the left-brain-damaged aphasic patients can now be attributed to the effects of damage to the dominant-language hemisphere rather than to a general lesion effect.

The performance of the aphasic patients on these tasks was characterized by three distinct patterns. In the first, patients performed normally on both identification and discrimination tasks. In the second, patients performed normally on the discrimination task but were unable to identify the test stimuli reliably. The identification and discrimination functions of such an aphasic are presented in figures 1.7 and 1.8. Note that even though this subject's identification function

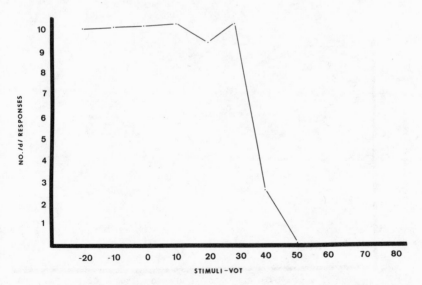

Fig. 1.3   The identification function for a voice-onset time continuum for a normal control subject. The abscissa represents the stimulus values of the continuum ranging from −20 msec to +80 msec VOT. The ordinate represents the total number of d-responses (maximum is 10).

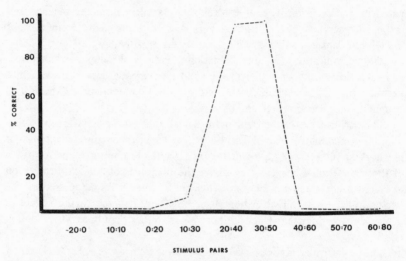

Fig. 1.4   The discrimination function for a voice-onset time continuum for a normal control subject, the same subject as in figure 1.3. The abscissa represents the stimulus pairs presented. Each pair was distinguished by a VOT of 20 msec. The ordinate represents the percentage of correct different responses.

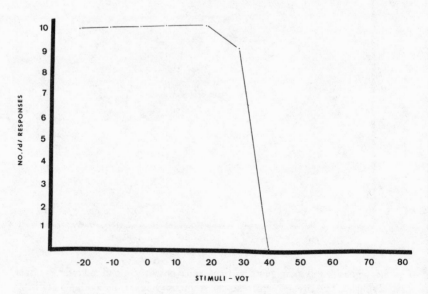

Fig. 1.5   The identification function for a right-brain-damaged nonaphasic patient. See legend for figure 1.3.

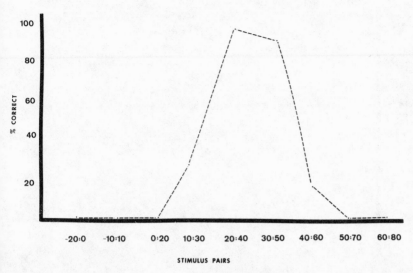

Fig. 1.6 The discrimination function for a right-brain-damaged nonaphasic patient, the same subject as in figure 1.5. See also legend for figure 1.4.

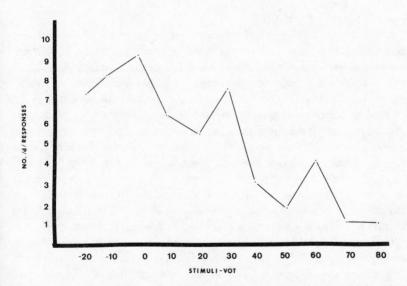

Fig. 1.7 The identification function for a left-brain-damaged aphasic patient. See legend for figure 1.3.

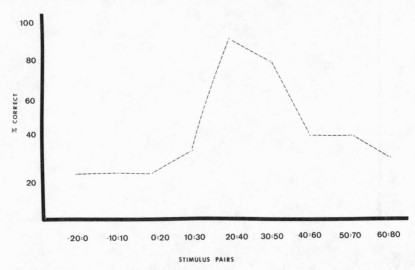

Fig. 1.8   The discrimination function for a left-brain-damaged aphasic patient, the same subject as in figure 1.7. See also legend for figure 1.4.

does not indicate a distinction between the [d] and [t] categories, his discrimination peaks correspond to the phoneme boundaries typically found in normal English-speaking subjects. This was true of all patients found in this group. The third group of aphasics is represented by abnormal functions both for identification and discrimination. The performance of such a patient is represented in figures 1.9 and 1.10.

Thus, the results of this study demonstrate an important relation between identification and discrimination of a speech acoustic continuum. If a subject is able to identify reliably the stimuli along this continuum, he is also able to make consistent discrimination judgements; no cases were found in which a patient was unable to discriminate but was able to label the same stimuli. In addition, and perhaps of even greater significance, discrimination ability was reflected by peaks at the phoneme boundaries *even* for subjects who were unable to label the stimuli. These results suggest that there are two levels of phonological processing—a more primitive prelinguistic discrimination level that reflects the functioning of a set of property detectors sensitive to certain parameters of the acoustic signal, and a linguistic level that makes use of this information to "encode" or classify the stimuli along a linguistically relevant dimension. Categorical perception was originally defined (Liberman et al. 1967) in terms of the predictability of peaks of discrimination from the derived labeling functions. The results of this study suggest that the relation between identification and discrimination is in fact reversed; that is, discrimination ability underlies phoneme perception, and the use of linguistic categories as discrete phonemic entities is based upon the system's ability to discriminate

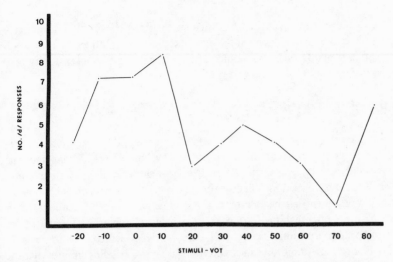

Fig. 1.9   The identification function for another left-brain-damaged aphasic patient. See legend for figure 1.3.

differences along a particular acoustic dimension. Thus, the aphasic's impairment reflects an inability to maintain a stable configuration or category label despite the fact that the aphasic retains the ability to make phonological discriminations. Yet, one can question how such discriminations so neatly reflect the category labels used in the linguistic system. It has been suggested here that this discrimination ability reflects the sensitivity of property detectors to ranges of acoustic stimuli. It may well be that it is this limited set of properties

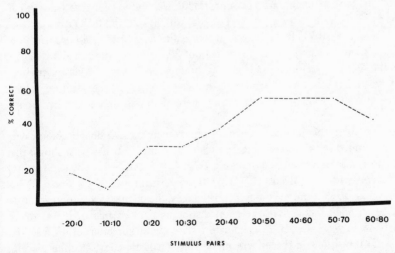

Fig. 1.10   The discrimination function for another left-brain-damaged aphasic patient, the same as in figure 1.9. See also legend for figure 1.4.

to which the system is sensitive that defines the linguistically significant categories ultimately used in natural language. Recent research from infant speech perception supports such a view and further suggests that such sensitivity may be part of the biological endowment of the human organism.

INFANT SPEECH PERCEPTION

In recent years a series of studies has been reported in the literature investigating speech perception in infants (see review by Morse 1974). Two paradigms have been used to investigate infants' discrimination ability. Both measure habituation-dishabituation effects after repeated presentation of auditory stimuli, one measuring heart-rate, and the other high amplitude nonnutritive sucking rate. After habituation occurs as a result of repeated presentation of the same auditory stimulus, a novel stimulus is presented. An increase in heart-rate or high-amplitude sucking rate relative to a baseline implies that the infant has discriminated the stimulus change. In contrast, no change or a decrement in either response measure implies that no discrimination difference has been perceived.

In one of the first studies conducted (Eimas, Siqueland, Jusczyk, and Vigorito 1971) 1- and 4-month-old infants were tested for their ability to discriminate voice-onset time differences. Results indicated that both groups of infants were able to discriminate 20 msec differences in voice-onset time only when these discriminations corresponded to distinct linguistic categories, i.e., they were able to discriminate VOT values of +20 and +40, values that to the adult distinguish the phonetic categories of [ba] and [pa]. In contrast, the infants were unable to discriminate 20 msec differences that belonged to the same adult linguistic category, i.e., [ba] with a −20 and 0 VOT or [pa] with a +60 and +80 VOT. Moreover, absolute differences in voice-onset time between stimulus pairs, that is, differences of 20, 60, or 100 msec, had little effect on the subjects' performance. What was of importance was whether the particular voicing values represented the same or different phonetic feature values. Similar results using both synthetic and natural stimuli were found by Trehub and Rabinovitch (1972).

The ability of infants to make discriminations across phonetic boundaries is not limited to the voiced-voiceless phonetic contrast. It has been shown that infants can perceive place distinctions, as [b]-[g], signaled either by two formant synthetic patterns (Moffitt 1971) or by three formant patterns (Morse 1972). Moreover, as with the voice-onset time studies, the infants' perception seems to be based upon linguistically relevant distinctions. In particular, it was found that infants were able to discriminate differences in direction of 45 msec F2 and F3 transitions in three formant syllables (acoustic cues signaling place of articulation dimensions) but that they demonstrated different discrimination functions for the same F2 and F3 transitions presented in isolation (Morse

1972; Eimas 1974). In this case the stimuli no longer contained the complete set of acoustic attributes that appear in speechlike stimuli, namely, the steady-state vowel formants.

What is remarkable about these findings is that the discrimination ability of infants reflects that of normal adults; that is, infants not only discriminate across phonetic categories and fail to do so within phonetic categories, but their crossover boundaries for place as well as for voice are similar to those found in adults. This discrimination ability and the correspondences to the adult phonetic boundaries suggest that these abilities could not have been acquired within the first month after birth simply through experience and interaction with the linguistic environment. Rather, innate biological mechanisms have been postulated to account for the infants' discrimination capacity.

To be sure, it is unlikely that the infant is born with a fully developed phonological discrimination ability. Rather, it seems undeniable that some exposure to or interaction with the linguistic environment is necessary in order for this capacity to be developed and ultimately realized in language perception. However, the exact role of the linguistic environment in the development of perception is still unclear. In some recent experiments, it has been difficult to demonstrate discrimination ability in infants for those phonetic categories to which they were not exposed in their native language. In particular, English infants showed small but nonsignificant discrimination peaks between prevoiced and voiced phonetics categories, a phonemic contrast that does not exist in English (Eimas et al. 1971; see also Moffitt 1971). In contrast, Kikuyu infants were able to make such discriminations reliably (Streeter 1974); a prevoiced distinction is phonemic in this language. To be sure, more research must be done to determine the relation between nature and nurture in the development of phonological perception.

Although it is clear that the infant has the capacity to discriminate acoustic signals that represent phonological contrasts, it is probably not the case that these contrasts have a linguistic or functional significance. Thus, similar to the aphasic's performance, the infant's discrimination ability need only reflect a capacity to perceive differences between acoustic parameters. Presumably, at a later stage of development, the infant is able to consistently classify these contrasts into functional categories; that is, he develops the capacity to classify, or encode, the discrimination categories into linguistically relevant dimensions. It is this latter stage that characterizes the acquisition of the phoneme system of a language (see Jakobson 1968).

A more striking example of the dichotomy between discrimination and phoneme usage has been reported in a study by Garnica (1973). Garnica attempted to replicate an earlier study by Shvachkin (1973) in which Russian children between the ages of 10 and 21 months were purportedly able to choose various objects designated by nonsense monosyllables distinguished by minimal phonological contrasts. Garnica found that the performance of her subjects ranging in age from 1.5 to 1.10 years was extremely variable and did not reflect an ability to reliably choose nonsense objects based on certain phonological contrasts. These results seem to contradict the results found in infant perception, for if infants can discriminate phonetic categories, then why are young children as old as a year and a half unable to do this task? It would seem that the problem for them is not one of discriminating, but rather of assigning a stable phonological configuration to a particular nonsense object; that is, simply labeling or naming a figure. Thus, the perception of speech sounds seems to be based upon the integration of two distinct levels of processing. The first and more basic is a prelinguistic level in which selective differences between auditory stimuli may be discriminated. The second level may be properly termed *linguistic*, since the acoustic categories derived from the prelinguistic level are used to distinguish functionally different speech sounds within the linguistic system. It is only when these two levels are integrated that the comprehension of names of objects may be fully realized.

PROPERTY DETECTORS FOR SPEECH

The hypothesis that the discrimination ability evidenced in aphasics, infants, and normal adults reflects the sensitivity of the human organism to a limited range of acoustic parameters is based upon the assumption that the human organism is incapable of using any array of acoustic stimuli for speech sounds but, rather, is constrained in some definable way to perceive only a finite set of properties. Similar constraints have been suggested for the production of speech sounds. Clearly, there are limitations on the types of sounds used in speech production. Certain articulations are beyond the capabilities of the human vocal tract. For example, it would be physiologically impossible for the tip of the tongue to touch the uvula to produce a lingual–uvular place of articulation. It has been suggested, however, that the limited set of speech sounds used in natural language is based upon more fundamental considerations, considerations that are based upon the relation between articulatory parameters and their acoustic consequences. In particular, it has been shown that small changes in some articulatory configurations produce substantial changes in the acoustic output, whereas similar changes in other articulatory configurations have little effect on the attributes of the acoustic signal (Stevens 1972). The consequences of this relation are that only a limited set of articulatory configurations produces stable acoustic patterns, with distinctive properties. It has been suggested that it is those configurations that produce stable patterns which form the basis for the finite set of speech sounds used in natural language and, moreover, that it is the complex interface between the production and perceptual constraints of the system that defines the full range of phonological properties found in human language.

To date, this hypothesis can be tested only by indirect behavioral measures. One such measure is the selective adaptation paradigm. Studies conducted with this paradigm have shown that the perception of an acoustic continuum can be systematically altered by the repeated presentation of a particular stimulus (Eimas and Corbitt 1973). For example, the repeated presentation of [ba] affects the perception of a voice-onset time continuum in such a way that subjects now assign fewer responses to the voiced end of the continuum. Such effects occur regardless of whether the continuum shares the same place-of-articulation value of the test stimuli, e.g., [ba] = [pa] continuum with [ba] as adapting stimulus, or does not share the same place-of-articulation value, e.g., [da] = [ta] continuum with [ba] as adapting stimulus. It has been suggested that these results reflect the fatiguing of neural feature detectors sensitive to voice-onset time parameters. Thus, the repeated presentation of a voiced consonant decreases the sensitivity of those detector mechanisms that normally fire to short voice-onset parameters of the signal, i.e., voiced consonants (or to some property or set of properties that varies concomitantly with voice-onset time).

The selective adaptation paradigm is similar to the habituation paradigm used with infants (see above). It is important to note that, unlike the adaptation shifts in both the labeling and discrimination functions reported in the adult data, the repeated presentation of the same stimulus to establish habituation in infants resulted in discrimination peaks similar to those reported for adults in the *unadapted* state. This is presumably because the discrimination comparisons presented to the infants have not been sufficiently small to reflect such adaptation effects. For example, voice-onset time discriminations typically presented to infants are 20 msec in comparison to 5 msec differences presented to adults.

Although no direct evidence is available from electrophysiological studies to support the hypothesis that the perception of speech is in fact dictated by a set of feature detectors sensitive to a limited set of properties defined by both auditory and articulatory constraints, there have been some interesting electrophysiological studies conducted with animals that bear on this question, albeit by analogy only. Recent investigations with the frog (Frishkopf, Capranica, and Goldstein 1968), the squirrel monkey (Wollberg and Newman 1972), and some species of birds (Konishi 1970) have shown that these animals do in fact possess complex auditory feature analyzers that are in some sense matched to the characteristics of their respective vocal repertoires. In particular, it has been shown that within the auditory systems of these animals there are single units that fire selectively to certain characteristics of the particular species' mating call. Moreover, it has been shown that in the cat (Nelson, Erulkar, and Bryan 1966), the monkey (Katsuki, Suga, and Kanno 1962), and the bat (Suga 1972), particular features of complex auditory stimuli appear to be detected and processed by neuronal cells structured to respond to a particular set of physical characteristics. The characteristics to which the systems respond may be fairly "abstract" pattern detectors; that is, they may be sensitive to rising or falling patterns across the time domain independent of the particular frequency range of the test stimuli (Whitfield 1967).

Returning now to the perception of speech in humans, what types of detector might we expect to find? First, it has been suggested that the range of property detectors for speech is constrained by the limitations of possible vocal tract configurations (Stevens 1972, 1975). Moreover, the auditory system is capable of extracting certain gross properties of the acoustic signal. In this way, the property detectors may be said to be sensitive to patterns of speech stimuli. Such patterns might include sudden onset of acoustic energy in contrast to gradual onset of energy distinguishing the two major articulatory classes of consonant and vowel; the rate of spectral changes characterizing various manners of articulation; and the direction and extent of rapid spectrum changes signaling various places of articulation (Stevens 1975). With a limited set of such detectors, the major acoustic distinctions utilized in human speech can theoretically be derived.

Much research is of course necessary to test the validity of these hypotheses. Research in speech perception in pathology and ontogeny may help provide answers to some of the theoretical issues raised here. For example, the suggestion that most aphasics are able to discriminate normally the sounds of speech suggests that either the discrimination capacity is such a basic function of the dominant left hemisphere that deficits are manifest only in those patients with severe left-brain damage, or that it is a basic capacity of the human auditory system and, as a consequence, is affected only by severe brain damage to both the left and right hemisphere. Thus, research in aphasia may help determine which aspects of perception are uniquely specialized for language and which aspects are part of man's general auditory capacity. Research in ontogeny may provide valuable information concerning the basic perceptual capacity of the infant as well as the role of nurture on the development of these capacities. The suggestion that there exist innate detectors sensitive to ranges of acoustic patterns does not deny the potential importance of learning. It may well be that certain phonetic contrasts are dependent upon the prior activation of simple detector mechanisms before they themselves are "learned": for example, the perception of retroflexive stop consonants, a place of articulation contrast found in the Dravidian languages, seems to depend upon acoustic properties derived from both the dental stop consonant and the velar stop consonant (Stevens and Blumstein 1975; see also Jakobson 1968). Such a contrast would presumably be a difficult discrimination for neonates.

The perception of speech is such a fundamental part of our general linguistic capacity and yet, we are only beginning to have some understanding of the nature of this process. Research in pathology and ontogeny provides a view of the nature of speech perception unavailable in studies with normal adults. It is only with the integration of the results of research in these various areas that we may begin to better understand the complex process of speech perception in man and ultimately the nature of human language.

REFERENCES

Abramson, A. S., and Lisker, L. 1970. Discriminability along the voicing continuum: cross language tests. In *Proceedings of the Sixth International Congress of Phonetic Sciences*, pp. 569–73. Prague: Academia.

Blumstein, S.; Goodglass, H.; and Baker, E. 1977. Phonological factors in auditory comprehension in aphasia. *Neuropsychologia* 15:19–30.

Blumstein, S.; Cooper, W.; Zurif, E.; and Carmazza, A. 1977. The perception and production of voice-onset time in aphasia. *Neuropsychologia* 15:371–83.

Brown, R. 1958. *Words and things*. New York: Free Press.

Dorman, M. 1972. Auditory evoked potential correlates of speech sound discrimination. *Status Report on Speech Research* 29/30:111–20.

Eimas, P. D. 1974. Auditory and linguistic processing of cues for place of articulation by infants. *Perception and psychophysics* 16:513–21.

Eimas, P. D., and Corbit, J. D. 1973. Selective adaptation of linguistic feature detectors. *Cognitive Psychology* 4:99–109.

Eimas, P. D.; Siqueland, E. R.; Jusczyk, P.; and Vigorito, J. 1971. Speech perception in infants. *Science* 171:303–6.

Eisenson, J. 1972. *Aphasia in children*. New York, Harper & Row.

Frishkopf, L. S.; Capranica, R. R.; and Goldstein, M. H., Jr. 1968. Neural coding in the bullfrog's auditory system: a teleological approach. *Proc. IEEE* 56:969–80.

Fromkin, V.; Krashen, S.; Curtiss, S.; Rigler, D.; and Rigler, M. 1974. The development of language in Genie: a case of language acquisition beyond the "critical period." *Brain and Language* 1:81–107.

Garnica, O. K. 1973. The development of phonemic speech perception. In *Cognitive development and the acquisition of language*, ed. T. E. Moore, pp. 215–22. New York: Academic Press.

Geschwind, N., and Levitsky, W. 1968. Human brain: left-right asymmetries in temporal speech region. *Science* 161:186–7

Goodglass, H., and Kaplan, E. 1972. *The assessment of aphasia and related disorders*. Philadelphia: Lea & Febiger.

Jakobson, R. 1968. *Child language, aphasia, and phonological universals*, trans. A. R. Keiler. The Hague: Mouton.

Katsuki, Y. N.; Suga, N.; and Kanno, Y. 1962. Neural mechanisms of the peripheral and central auditory systems in monkeys. *J. Acoust. Soc. Amer.* 34:1396–1410.

Kimura, D. 1961. Cerebral dominance and the perception of verbal stimuli. *Canad. J. Psychol.* 15:166–71.

Konishi, M. 1970. Comparative neurophysiological studies of hearing and vocalizations in songbirds. *Z. Vergl. Physiologie* 66:257–72.

Liberman, A. M.; Cooper, F. S.; Shankweiler, D. P.; and Studdert-Kennedy, M. 1967. Perception of the speech code. *Psychol. Rev.* 74:431–61.

Liberman, A. M.; Harris, K. S.; Hoffman, H. S.; and Griffith, B. C. 1957. The discrimination of speech sounds within and across phoneme boundaries. *J. Exp. Psychol.* 54:358–68.

Lisker, L., and Abramson, A. 1964. A cross-language study of voicing in initial stops: acoustical measurements. *Word* 20:384–422.

——. 1967. Some effects of context on voice-onset time in English stops. *Language and Speech* 10:1–28.

——. 1970. The voicing dimension: some experiments in comparative phonetics. In *Proceedings of the Sixth International Congress of Phonetic Sciences*, pp. 563–7. Prague: Academia.

Luria, A. R. 1970. *Traumatic aphasia*. The Hague: Mouton.

Moffitt, A. R. 1971. Consonant cue perception by twenty- to twenty-four-week-old infants. *Child Develop.* 42:717–31.

Molfese, D. 1972. Cerebral asymmetry in infants, children, and adults: auditory evoked responses to speech and noise stimuli. Ph.D. dissertation, Pennsylvania State University, University Park.

Molfese, D. L.; Freeman, R. B., Jr.; and Palermo, D. S. 1975. The ontogeny of brain lateralization for speech and nonspeech stimuli. *Brain and Language* 2:356–68.

Morse, P. A. 1972. The discrimination of speech and non-speech stimuli in early infancy. *J. Exp. Child Psychol.* 14:477–92.

——. 1974. Infant speech perception: a preliminary model and review of literature. In *Language perspectives:Acquisition, retardation, and intervention*, ed. R. L. Schiefelbusch and L. L. Lloyd, pp. 19–53. Baltimore: University Park Press.

Nelson, P. G.; Erulkar, S. D.; and Bryan, J. S. 1966. Responses of units of the inferior colliculus to time-varying acoustic stimuli. *J. Neurophysiol.* 29:834–60.

Oscar-Berman, M.; Zurif, E.; and Blumstein, S. 1975. Effects of unilateral brain damage on the processing of speech sounds. *Brain and Language* 2:345–55.

Shankweiler, D., and Studdert-Kennedy, M. 1967. Identification of consonants and vowels presented to left and right ears. *Quart. J. Exp. Psychol.* 19:59–63.

Shvachkin, N. Kh. 1973. The development of phonemic speech perception in early childhood. In *Studies of child language development*, ed. D. A. Ferguson and D. I. Slobin, pp. 91–127. New York: Holt Rinehart and Winston.

Stevens, K. N. 1972. The quantal nature of speech: evidence from articulatory-acoustic data. In *Human communications: a unified view*, ed. E. E. David, J. Denses, and P. B. Denes. New York: McGraw-Hill.

——. 1975. The potential role of property detectors in the perception of consonants. In *Auditory analysis and the perception of speech,* ed. G. Fant and M. A. Tathan, pp. 303–30. London: Academic Press.

Stevens, K. N., and Blumstein, S. E. 1975. Quantal aspects of consonant production and perception: a study of retroflex stop consonants. *J. Phonetics* 3:215–33.

Streeter, L. 1974. Language perception of two-month-old infants shows effects of both innate mechanisms and experience. *Bell Telephone Technical Memorandum,* #1125–5.

Studdert-Kennedy, M.; and Shankweiler, D. 1970. Hemispheric specialization for speech perception. *J. Acoust. Soc. Amer.* 48:579–94.

Suga, N. 1972. Analysis of information bearing elements in complex sounds by auditory neurones of bats. *Audiol.* 11:58–72.

Trehub, S. E., and Rabinovitch, M. S. 1972. Auditory-linguistic sensitivity in early infancy. *Develop. Psychol.* 6:74–77.

Wada, J., and Rasmussen, T. 1960. Intracarotid injection of sodium amytal for the lateralization of cerebral speech dominance: experimental and clinical observations. *J. Neurosurg.* 17:266–82.

Whitfield, I. 1967. *The auditory pathway.* London: Edward Arnold.

Witelson, S. F., and Pallie, W. 1973. Left hemisphere specialization for language in the newborn: neuroanatomical evidence of asymmetry. *Brain* 96:641–6.

Wollberg, Z., and Newman, J. D. 1972. Auditory cortex of squirrel monkey: response patterns of single cells to species-specific vocalizations. *Science* 175:212–4.

Wood, C.; Goff, W.; and Day, R. 1971. Hemisphere differences in auditory evoked potentials during phonemic and pitch discrimination. *Science* 173:1248–51.

Zangwill, O. L. 1962. Dyslexia in relation to cerebral dominance. In *Reading disability*, ed. J. Money, pp. 103–14. Baltimore: Johns Hopkins Press.

2

AN EXPERIMENTAL INVESTIGATION OF THE ROLE OF AUDITORY TEMPORAL PROCESSING IN NORMAL AND DISORDERED LANGUAGE DEVELOPMENT

Paula Tallal

INTRODUCTION

Language is dependent upon the normal development of all those mechanisms that are utilized in the perception, production, and comprehension of speech. One of the major goals of studying language development is to better understand the various sensory, perceptual, and cognitive mechanisms that interact in the development and maintenance of language functions. Although we are still a long way from realizing this goal, there are certain processes that have been demonstrated to be critical to normal language development. For example, there must be adequate reception of the physical acoustic aspects of the speech signal. One need only observe the immense difficulties experienced by congenitally deaf children attempting to learn language in the absence of a normal acoustic input to appreciate how important normal auditory sensation is to language development. However, even after the acoustic input has been adequately detected, it must still be processed and then comprehended as meaningful speech. As a result of recent technological advances, the study of the mechanisms involved in the acoustic processing of speech has become an exciting area of research. The investigation of one aspect of acoustic processing, temporal analysis, and its role in speech perception forms the basis of this chapter.

There are several ways to approach the study of the temporal processes involved in speech perception. I have chosen to investigate the interrelation between the development of the mechanisms of auditory temporal processing and speech perception, in children with normal and disordered language development. The studies reported here are based on the hypothesis that if

The work reported in this chapter was supported by grants from the American Association of University Women and the Grant Foundation. I would like to thank Malcolm Piercy for his help and supervision.

certain aspects of acoustic processing are critical to normal speech perception, and hence to language development, then failure to develop these specific acoustic processes normally should result in retarded language development. This hypothesis can be investigated by comparing the development of the acoustic processing abilities of language-disordered children to those of children with normal language development. However, such an hypothesis must be examined with caution. Merely pinpointing specific perceptual deficits in children with retarded language development does not necessarily indicate that the perceptual deficits are "causal" or even related to the language disorder. Since we know that a child can have multiple, relatively isolated handicaps, we cannot merely assume that one handicapping condition is necessarily related to another. The onus should be on the investigator to show specific correlations between one dysfunction and another before suggesting that two or more functions are interrelated.

Although the method of study I propose poses certain difficulties, it avoids others that are perhaps more serious. For example, the development of functions in normal children and the breakdown of similar functions in adults who have sustained specific brain lesions have been compared. However, it has been demonstrated that there are major differences between the organization and functions of the developing brain and the adult brain. It also has been shown that the recovery of function after insult to the brain differs markedly depending upon age; the younger the brain, the more recovery or "redevelopment" of function may be expected (Lenneberg 1967). Therefore, studies that attempt to demonstrate parallels and divergencies between the acquisition of language in the child and the breakdown of language in the adult who has sustained brain injury must contend with the intrinsic differences that exist in the brain at different ages. Furthermore, the differences between mechanisms that might be involved in developing a function and those involved in maintaining the developed function must be considered. The investigation of functions in normally and abnormally developing children of the same age may eliminate, at least in part, some of these major difficulties. This approach may yield information concerning the acoustic mechanism involved in speech perception that might be difficult to substantiate using other research approaches.

DEVELOPMENTAL LANGUAGE DYSFUNCTIONS

Definition

Some children fail to develop normal language functions at the usual age. Such language retardation is often attributable to peripheral impairments such as deafness (elevation of sensory threshold), malformation of the vocal apparatus, or paralysis of the speech musculature. In addition, language may fail to develop as a consequence of general mental subnormality, severe personality disorder, early infantile autism, or acquired childhood aphasia in which there is known postnatal brain lesion to the areas that subserve language in the adult.

However, when all children with language retardation attributable to such known causes are excluded, there still remains a group of children who fail to learn to speak at or near the expected age. In 1964 Benton argued for the existence of "developmental aphasia" as a distinct clinical syndrome. He defined developmental aphasia as, "the condition in which a child shows a relatively specific failure of the normal growth of language functions. The failure can manifest itself either in a disability in speaking with near normal speech understanding or in a disability in both understanding and expression of speech. The disability is called a 'specific' one because it cannot readily be ascribed to those factors which often provide the general setting in which failure of language development usually is observed" (p. 44). Furthermore, Benton reported that in some cases of developmental aphasia there is evidence to implicate early damage to the central nervous system as a causative factor, while in other cases no evidence of cerebral disease of trauma can be found. He also reported that there is evidence to suggest that the basis of developmental aphasia is a "high-level deficit" of auditory perception.

The term *developmental aphasia* is at present, basically a definition by exclusion; that is, it describes those factors that are not involved in the syndrome rather than those that are.

It is unfortunate that Benton and others have chosen to use the term *aphasia* to describe this childhood language syndrome, since implicit in this term is an analogy to adult language disorders resulting from known cerebral damage to the areas of the brain that subserve language. It is mere conjecture, however, to assume a similar functional basis for this childhood language disorder given our present knowledge of this syndrome. Until more is known about the primary causes of this specific language dysfunction, I do not think a specific term to describe it should be coined. Furthermore, as more precise information about this group of children is obtained, it is possible that subgroups within the syndrome will become apparent.

For the purposes of this chapter, however, I refer to this developmental language syndrome as *developmental dysphasia*. *Dysphasia* is used as a general descriptive term implying impairment or delay to, rather than total loss of, language function. The term is not intended to imply any specific etiology of the dysfunction; it is intended to take account of the diversity of the symptoms that can occur in different children with this specific language dysfunction, or even within an individual child over a period of time.

The terms *developmental dysphasia, dysphasia,* and *developmental language dysfunction* are here used interchangeably. Childhood-acquired aphasia and adult-acquired aphasia, are described as such.

When discussing other authors' work, however, I use the terms they have chosen to describe the group of language-impaired subjects in their studies.

Background Literature

Clinical descriptions of children with specific developmental language dysfunctions have often indicated the existence of auditory perceptual deficits. Benton, in his original (1964) definition of the syndrome *developmental aphasia*, reported that there was evidence to suggest that the basis of the disorder is a high-level deficit of auditory perception. However, the exact nature of this perceptual disorder was unclear.

The difficulties of the dysphasic child in the auditory modality were originally thought to result from a peripheral hearing loss. Ewing (1930) had shown that six of ten aphasic children in his study had raised thresholds for certain high frequencies (high-tone deafness), thresholds that he hypothesized were sufficiently high to account for difficulty in discriminating speech sounds. However, we now realize that a characteristic of developmental dysphasics is an inconsistent response to sound. Benton (1964) noted that developmental aphasic children may "turn off" human sounds but respond to animal or environmental sounds. Furthermore, such children may respond to soft sounds, but not to loud ones. As audiometric techniques have improved (for example, the development of evoked-response audiometry, in which a conscious response is not required from the subject [Rapin and Graziani 1967]) it has become apparent that the degree of peripheral hearing loss in dysphasic children is not sufficient to explain the severity of their language impairment.

Mark and Hardy (1958) suggested that the inconsistency of the aphasic child in responding to sound might be explicable in terms of a history of poor reinforcement contingencies for auditory perceptual responses. This may have resulted in the child's learning to "inhibit" responses to certain auditory stimuli.

Although psychological theories of this type may be useful in explaining the outcome of poor auditory perceptual functioning in dysphasic children, they do not add to our understanding of the nature of the underlying perceptual impairment. Many workers have focused their attention directly on the nature of auditory perception in developmental dysphasics. In particular, interest has centered on the role of auditory sequencing and auditory memory in this childhood language disorder.

As early as 1937, Orton pointed out that in children with speech and reading problems arising from suspected organic disturbances, it is the recall of sounds in proper temporal order that seems to be at fault. Since Orton's time, reports have continued to stress the difficulty that dysphasic children seem to have in perceiving temporal order. Monsees (1957) stressed the possible importance of temporal sequencing deficits in developmental aphasics. Hardy (1965) described the aphasic child's difficulties with what he called "auding," or "the integrative functions in the brain's management of auditory information," and suggested that such difficulties may result in the inability to distinguish between similar-sounding words. Eisenson, in two particularly informative articles on developmental aphasia (1968, 1972), described the types of perceptual impairment that have been observed in most aphasic children. These include: (1) defective capacity for storing speech signals (McReynolds 1966); (2) impairment of speech generalizations in contextual utterances; and (3) impairment in processing sequences of speech events at the normal rate at which they occur. These precise clinical observations have provided a basis for the experimental investigation of the perceptual abilities of dysphasic children.

Lowe and Campbell (1965) studied children whom they classified as "aphasoid" using the methods originally employed by Efron (1963) in the study of the perception of temporal order in adult aphasics. In this experiment, aphasoids were compared with normal children, matched according to age, on their ability to judge "succession" (auditory fusion, the inter-sound interval [ISI] at which two stimuli are heard as two sounds rather than one sound). They were also tested on their ability to judge temporal order. Two different 15 msec pure tones (400 Hz. and 2,200 Hz.) were presented in rapid succession with brief ISIs, and subjects were required to indicate which of the two tones occurred first.

No significant difference between the two groups' performances was demonstrated on the succession task. Compared with normal controls, however, the aphasoid subjects were significantly impaired in their ability to indicate which of two tones presented in rapid sequence occurred first. The normal controls made correct temporal order judgements at between 15 msec and 80 msec (mean = 35.8 msec). The aphasoids required intervals of 55 msec to 700 msec (mean = 357 msec) to achieve the same level of performance (75% correct) as the controls. Lowe and Campbell concluded that a malfunction in temporal ordering might be a major factor in the communication difficulties of aphasoid children.

Aten and Davis (1968) carried out an extensive study of the perception of nonverbal and verbal auditory sequence in children whom they classified as having "minimal cerebral dysfunction' (MCD). Children with one or more definite "signs" of central nervous system disorder were included in the MCD group. Evidence of central nervous system disorder included abnormal electro-encephalogram readings, seizures, head injuries, and bilateral hematomas.

Aten and Davis's tests of nonverbal auditory perception included (1) sequencing rhythmically presented pure tone patterns and (2) judging the duration of pure tone sound bursts by selecting a short, medium, or long plastic block corresponding in length to the duration of the tone. The tests of verbal perception included (1) serial memory span for nonsense syllables, digits, and words and (2) verbal reproduction of multisyllabic words presented sequentially, scrambled sentences, and paragraphs.

The results of these verbal and nonverbal tests demonstrated that the MCD group, in general, performed less well than the control group as evidenced by shorter perceptual memory spans and reduced number of stimuli accurately reproduced. The perception of the nonverbal auditory stimuli varying in rhythm and duration was most significantly impaired in the MCD group. This evidence supported Aten and Davis's hypothesis that the perception, storage, and reproduction of sequential auditory stimuli is disturbed by cerebral dysfunction.

Griffiths (1972) reported a study in which developmental aphasic and normal children were tested for their ability to reproduce nonverbal rhythmic patterns. Rhythmic patterns were tapped in 4/4, 6/8, and 3/4 time on a tambourine, within the child's range of vision, at the rate of approximately two crotchets (quarter notes) per second. The subjects were required to produce an immediate repetition of the pattern on another tambourine. Although the aphasic children reproduced the simplest patterns as well as the control subjects did, which indicates that they understood the task, they were markedly impaired in reproducing the more complex rhythmic patterns. Griffiths suggested that difficulties in temporal ordering of auditory stimuli, discrimination of relative duration, or reduced memory span could be responsible for the impaired performance of the developmental aphasic children on this task.

Monsees (1968) studied the ability of children with "expressive" language disorders and normal controls to: (1) repeat isolated phonemes presented over a loud speaker (thus eliminating visual cues), (2) perform a Same-Different judgment between two nonsense syllables (Templin Sound Discrimination Test, Templin 1957); (3) "blend" a sequence of phonemes into a word (for example, p + ai = pai (pie); and (4) repeat a sequence of phonemes in the order of their presentation.

The results showed no significant difference between the abilities of the children with or without "expressive" language disorders to imitate isolated phonemes. The performance of the language-impaired group, however, was significantly inferior to that of the controls on all other tasks studied. This study provides evidence that the previously reported inability of aphasics and other language-impaired children to report the temporal order of nonverbal auditory stimuli could also apply to verbal stimuli.

Poppen et al. (1969) reported that aphasic children exhibit similar impairment in both the auditory and the visual modality on sequencing tests. Hence, they suggested that these children have a *general* sequencing impairment that may underlie their language impairment. However, it should be emphasized that such a conclusion could correctly be drawn only if the visual stimuli and the auditory stimuli in the sequencing tests studied had been presented in the same manner, either both spatially or both temporally. This was not the case in the experiments reported by these authors. Therefore, the modality specificity of the sequencing disorder of aphasic children remains to be established.

Rosenthal and Eisenson (1970) reported the results of studies in which aphasic and normal children were compared in their abilities to resolve the temporal order of sounds that differed from one another in acoustic features, particularly emphasizing speech versus nonspeech characteristics. Subjects were required to indicate which member of a pair of auditory stimuli occurred first when the order of stimulus presentation was varied randomly. Six stimulus pairs were studied: pure tone noise (T.N.); high tone–low tone (T_1T_2); vowel /a/-affricate /tʃ/ (V.A.); vowel /a/-vowel /i/ (V_1V_2); fricative [s]-fricative [sh] (F_1F_2); and fricative [sh]-affricate [ch] (F_2A). These stimuli were selected in order to contrast certain features of auditory signals, such as speech versus nonspeech and frequency versus temporal information. Natural speech signals were used as stimuli in this experiment.

The results of these studies indicate that the aphasic group was impaired on all tasks studied in comparison with the normal subjects. However, this difficulty was not associated with simple speech-versus-nonspeech dimensions. Both the easiest (V.A.) and most difficult (F_2A) pairs were speech stimuli. Whereas the aphasic subjects were able to report the order of presentation of V.A. pairs with ISIs of only 64 msec, they required 650 msec to perform to the same level of accuracy with F_2A pairs. In contrast to normal subjects, the aphasics had greater difficulty ordering pairs whose members could be differentiated only by analyzing temporally coded features than ordering those that could be distinguished by frequency cues. Rosenthal concluded that the nature of the auditory disorder of aphasic children may be characterized as inefficiency in auditory temporal analysis.

Interestingly, it has also been reported that some types of specific reading disorders may result, at least in part, from the inability to analyze the acoustic-phonetic components of written language that are essential in learning to read. More specifically, it has been noted that dyslexic children are impaired in their sequential processing abilities (see Bakker 1971 for review).

Sequential processing abilities of patients with acquired communicative disorders have also received a great deal of experimental attention. Efron (1963) hypothesized, on the basis of his studies on temporal order perception of aphasic adults, that "We should not look upon the aphasia's as a unique disorder of language, but rather as an inevitable consequence of a primary defect in temporal analysis—in placing a 'time-table' upon incoming data" (p. 418). Since 1963, several other authors have investigated the sequencing abilities of adult aphasic patients in an attempt to understand further the exact nature of the sequencing disorder and, particularly, its relationship to the language impairment. Swisher and Hirsh (1972) provide an excellent review of this literature.

We can conclude from the literature that temporal order imperception certainly appears to be concomitant with some communication disorders, both developmental and acquired. However, whether or not this perceptual disability is a primary impairment in such disorders, is specific to the auditory modality, or is positively correlated with the degree of language impairment is not resolved by the present literature.

Thus, although the results of these studies demonstrate that auditory temporal analysis is impaired in patients with some developmental or acquired communicative disorders, they do not indicate precisely which aspects of temporal analysis are impaired or more importantly, exactly how such a perceptual impairment relates, if at all, to the communicative disabilities of these patients.

In our own series of studies reported in this chapter, therefore, our goal was twofold: (1) to investigate in more detail the temporal processing abilities of patients with communicative disorders and (2) to relate patterns of perceptual abilities directly to patterns of language abilities.

AN INVESTIGATION OF TEMPORAL PROCESSING ABILITIES OF CHILDREN WITH AND WITHOUT DEVELOPMENTAL COMMUNICATION DISORDERS

Hirsh (1959) investigated experimentally the perception of auditory temporal order by normal adult subjects. He pointed out that the perception of temporal order of two stimuli presupposed two more primary perceptual processes: (1) before a listener can perceive the temporal order of two different, successive stimuli he must first perceive these two stimuli as discrete sounds rather than as a single fused sound; and (2) after a listener has perceived two different, successive stimuli as discrete sounds, he must discriminate these two sounds as being different from each other before he can perceive and hence report their temporal order.

Each of the studies investigating auditory perception of temporal order by dysphasic children concluded that a sequencing disorder might underlie the language impairment of these children. However, these experiments, like those that investigated the perception of temporal order by normal and aphasic adults, failed to ensure that subjects could (1) perceive the two elements in the sequence as separate rather than fused and (2) discriminate and/or identify two signals as different from each other when they were combined and presented rapidly in sequence. Therefore, further studies of the temporal processing abilities of children with developmental dysphasia were needed before the precise nature of temporal processing disorders in language dysfunction could be more fully understood.

General Experimental Design

In designing perceptual experiments in which children with known language impairments are to be subjects, there are technical problems to be taken into consideration. Because these methodological techniques can have such an important influence on the results of experiments, the precise methods used in our studies will be discussed in detail in the following sections.

Heterogeneity of Children Diagnosed as Developmental Dysphasics

One of the difficulties of analyzing and comparing the results of previous experiments is the lack of homogeneity both within and between groups used in different experiments. Our inadequate understanding of developmental dysphasia makes the selection of subjects difficult and to some extent arbitrary. Each author uses his own criteria for including a subject in an experimental group, so comparisons between experiments must be of a provisional character.

It is probable, therefore, that there is more value in systematically studying a large range of perceptual capabilities in a single group of developmental dysphasics, selected according to rigorous criteria, than in studying fewer capabilities in a larger, less homogeneous group. For this reason, the same group of dysphasic and control subjects was used in all of the experiments reported in this chapter (except for the final experiment, which is a developmental study). In this way the dysphasic subjects were not only compared with their matched normal controls within each experiment, but they could also be used as their own controls for comparisons between experiments.

Subjects were nine boys and three girls aged 6:8 to 9:3 years from the John Horniman School for Aphasic Children and 12 healthy primary school children who had been matched with the dysphasic children in respect of age, sex, and nonverbal intelligence. The dysphasic children were selected from the twenty children attending the school according to the following criteria: (1) formal neurological diagnosis of developmental aphasia; (2) normal hearing on standard audiometry; (3) absence of peripheral disturbance of verbal articulation, such as cleft palate, dysarthria, etc.; and (4) absence of obvious emotional disturbance. These children were also free from other signs of neurological dysfunction, although this was not a criterion for selection. It may well be that absence of such signs was a criterion used in the original diagnosis of developmental aphasia. The nonverbal intelligence quotient (I.Q.) for the group was assessed by the administration of Raven's Coloured Progressive Matrices (Raven 1965). The mean score for the group was above the 90th percentile, and the range was from the 50th to the 95th percentile. Further clinical details of each dysphasic child participating in these experiments have been reported in previous publications (Tallal and Piercy 1973a, 1973b).

Experimental Method

When investigating subjects with language impairments, it is important to establish that the results obtained from experimental tests are not significantly affected by the subject's ability to understand the test instructions or by his capacity to produce an appropriate response. In operant conditioning, a specific response to a stimulus is learned as a consequence of systematically reinforcing correct responses. It has been reported that the use of operant-conditioning techniques is a successful means of consistently eliciting required nonverbal responses from language-deficient patients (McReynolds 1966, 1967; Bricker and Bricker 1970).

In order to understand the sequencing deficit of dysphasic children more fully, it seemed necessary to move away from previous methods that require subjects merely to indicate which member of a rapidly presented sequence pair occurred first.

It was necessary, therefore, to devise a method that would enable the subject to report in detail exactly what he perceived in each stimulus pattern, in a non-verbal manner. At the same time the method should be easily demonstrable without the need for verbal instruction or verbal response. It should be flexible enough to allow several different aspects of perception to be investigated by changing only one variable at a time while holding all others constant.

A nonverbal operant-conditioning method was designed to meet all of these requirements. It was designated the repetition method. In each experiment reported on here, whether auditory or visual, verbal or nonverbal, this same general experimental method was used. In each experiment two different stimuli (1 and 2) were used in combination. Subjects' responses were made by pressing either of two identical Perspex panels, which were mounted side by side on a metal response box.

The testing procedure for the Repetition method is summarized in table 2.1. Subjects were initially trained to associate signal 1 with one response panel and signal 2 with another response panel. Training was continued using these two signals presented randomly one at a time, until a criterion of 20 correct responses in a series of 24 consecutive stimuli was reached ($p < 0.001$ Binomial Test) or a total of 48 trials was given. If, and only if, the criterion was reached were subjects presented with two signals presented successively, separated by a 428 msec inter-sound-interval (ISI), and trained to respond to each of the four possible two-element stimulus patterns (1-1, 1-2, 2-1, 2-2) by pushing the panels in the correct order in which they had been presented. For each subject the method was demonstrated 4 times by the experimenter. This preceded 8 training trials in which knowledge of results and correction of errors were given. Following the 8 training trials with knowledge of results, 24 trials without knowledge of results were given. Next, subjects were tested on these same two-element stimulus patterns, but in this series ISIs of 8, 15, 30, 60, 150, and 305 msecs were used. Each subject received a total of 24 two-element patterns, 4 at each ISI, with a random order of presentation of the different intervals. Subjects then were tested for a third time on two-element stimulus patterns, but this time with ISIs of 947, 1466, 1985, 3023, 3543, and 4062

Table 2.1

Experimental Design for the Repetition Method

Name of Subtests	Number of Signals Presented for Trial*	ISI (msecs)	Number of Trials	Signal* Duration (msecs)	Number of elements in Stimulus Pattern	Task
1. Detection of stimulus	1	—	10	75†	1	motor response to tone 1
2. Detection of stimulus 2	1	—	10	75†	1	motor response to tone 2
3. Association	1	—	to criterion	75†	1	discrimination between tone 1 and tone 2
4. Sequencing (ISIs constant)	2	428	24	75†	2	motor response to stimulus pattern
5. Sequencing (ISIs short)	2	random (8–305)‡	24	75†	2	motor response to stimulus pattern
6. Sequencing (ISIs long)	2	random (947–4062)	24	75	2	motor response to stimulus pattern
7. Serial memory (3 elements)	2	428	16	75 & 250	3	motor response to stimulus pattern
8. Serial memory (4 elements)	2	428	12	75 & 250	4	motor response to stimulus pattern
9. Serial memory (5 elements)	2	428	10	75 & 250	5	motor response to stimulus pattern

* In the auditory experiments the two signals used were two different complex tones. In the visual experiment the two signals used were two different colored light flashes.
† In the auditory experiment, the training and testing procedure was also carried out with stimulus tone durations of 125, 175, and 250 msecs.
‡ In the visual experiment (30–305).

msecs. Again each subject received a total of 24 two-element patterns, 4 at each ISI, with a random order of presentation of the different intervals. Tests of serial memory were also included. In these tests the same two stimuli were used, and the procedure was the same as for the previous tests, except that the stimulus patterns were longer. The ISI was constant at 428 msecs for these tests. These binary stimulus patterns consisted of three, four, or five elements, comprising random combinations of the two previously used stimuli. In all tests, subjects were required to wait until all stimulus items had been presented before responding. Subjects were tested first on two-element patterns and last on five-element patterns. If a subject failed to reach criterion on any pattern length, he was not tested on the remaining longer pattern lengths.

Reinforcements

At the beginning of each session each subject was given a white card and shown that correct responses on the panels would result in his winning brightly colored self-adhesive stickers, of several sizes and shapes, which he could select and stick on his card to make a picture throughout the testing session. This method proved to be an effective reinforcer for young children and had a low rate of satiation. Subjects were given between one and six colored stickers for every 1 to 6 trials on a variable schedule. Subjects never received reinforcement directly following an incorrect response.

Experiments

Nonverbal Auditory Perception in Developmental Dysphasic and Normal Children

Experiment 1. It was previously suggested that further research into the exact nature of developmental dysphasics' impairment in the perception of temporal order was needed before the role of this impairment in the language dysfunction of these children could be confidently assessed. The purpose of this experiment was to reexamine the auditory-sequencing abilities of developmental dysphasic subjects.

The sounds used as stimuli in this experiment were two 75 msec complex steady-state tones composed of frequencies within the speech range. Tone 1 had a fundamental frequency of 100 Hz. and tone 2 of 300 Hz. Stimuli were generated by a Speech Synthesizer linked to a Modular One computer, directly recorded onto a Uher 4200 stereo tape recorder and played back to the subject at a comfortable listening level.

The subjects and the experimental method (Repetition Method) described in detail above, in the section on General Experimental Design, were used in this experiment. Tests of serial memory were not included. Furthermore, because a subject may be able to perceive the elements of a temporal sequence but unable to reproduce a corresponding motor pattern, a Same-Different Method was also used in this experiment. The response box was turned through 90° to avoid confusion between the Same-Different and the Repetition Methods. In the Same-Different Method, subjects were initially presented with two tones separated by a 428 msec ISI and trained to press the top panel if the tones were the same as each other and the bottom panel if they were different. As in the Repetition Method, training continued until the criterion of 20 of 24 consecutive trials was reached. Then the same series of 24 two-element sequences with the shorter ISIs (8–305 msec), as were presented in the Repetition Method were again presented, and the subject indicated whether the two tones were the same or different. Half the subjects in each group performed the Repetition task first and half performed the Same-Different task first.

Results using the Repetition Method demonstrated that all the dysphasics and all the matched controls were able to reach criterion ($p < 0.001$, Binomial Test) both on the initial association task in which the two stimulus tones are presented in isolation and on the sequencing of the two-element patterns separated by 428 msec ISI. However, when the interval between the two tones was *decreased*, the dysphasic children's performance was markedly impaired in comparison with that of the controls. Whereas the control subjects were able to reproduce two-element patterns at or above criterion at the shortest ISI (8 msec), this criterion was not met by the dysphasic children at intervals less than 305 msec. However, when the interval between the two tones was *increased* up to 4 seconds, placing demands on short-term memory, the dysphasics, like the controls, performed above criterion.

The Wilcoxen Matched Pairs Test was used to compare the performance between the two groups on tests involving two-element patterns. It was found that at ISIs at or above 305 msec there were no significant differences between the performance of the two groups. However, significant differences between groups ($p < 0.01$) were found for all ISIs of less than 305 msec.

Results for the Same-Different Method show a similar pattern of impairment. Both groups reached criterion on the discrimination between the two tones ($p < 0.001$, Binomial Test) with an ISI of 428 msec. However, when the interval between the tones was *decreased*, the control subjects remained virtually errorless at all intervals, while the dysphasics required at least 305 msec to perform the task to criterion. When the interval between the two tones was *increased* up to 4 seconds, the dysphasics, like the controls, continued to perform above criterion.

The Wilcoxen Matched Pairs Test again showed that with ISIs at or above 305 msec there were no significant differences between the performance of the two groups. Significant differences between the performance of the two groups were again found for all ISIs of less than 305 msec, at at least the 1% level of

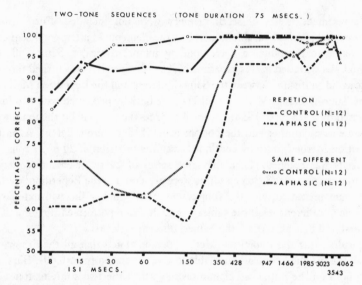

Fig. 2.1 The percentage of correct performances by dysphasic and control subjects on tests involving two-element patterns for the Repetition and the Same-Different Methods.

confidence. The performance of the dysphasics and the controls on tests involving two-element patterns, comparing the Repetition and the Same-Different methods, is illustrated in figure 2.1.

It is noteworthy that correct performance on the Same-Different task requires discrimination of the two tones, but not identification of the *order* in which they occur. Nevertheless, the ISIs at which the dysphasics failed to reach criterion (less than 205 msec) were the same for both the Repetition Method, which does require perception of order, and the Same-Different Method, which does *not* require perception of order. These results strongly suggest that dysphasic subjects are unable even to *discriminate* between two complex tones presented rapidly in sequence. Accordingly, previous authors' observations that dysphasics exhibit impairment of auditory perception of temporal order may be explicable in terms of a more primary failure to discriminate between acoustic signals that are presented rapidly in succession.

Experiment 2.   In experiment 1 it was demonstrated that a group of developmental dysphasic subjects were not only impaired in perceiving the order of rapidly presented auditory stimuli but were also equally inferior, with rapid presentations, in the discrimination of sound quality. In that experiment, demands on the rate of auditory processing were varied by altering the duration of the interval (ISI) between two tones in sequence, while holding constant the duration of the tones themselves. This procedure demonstrated that developmental dysphasics were impaired in the ability to respond correctly to auditory stimuli that were presented at rapid rates. However, the role of the other components of the stimulus pattern, in particular the duration of the stimulus tones, remained unexplored.

The purpose of the second experiment was, therefore, to provide more detailed information concerning the exact nature of the dysphasic children's defect in responding correctly to rapidly presented auditory stimuli. The effect of altering the duration of the tones in the stimulus patterns on the performance of the dysphasic and normal control children was examined.

In this experiment an identical testing procedure to that described for experiment 1 was used except that (1) only the Repetition Method was used, (2) with the two-element patterns only the ISIs between 8 msec and 428 msec (8, 15, 30, 60, 150, 305, and 428) were used, and (3) three different tone durations were employed: 125 msec, 175 msec, and 250 msec. The training and testing procedure was repeated three times for each subject, once for each of the stimulus tone durations studied. The serial memory tests (described in detail in the section on General Experimental Design) were also given with 75 msec, and again with 250 msec, tone durations.

The results of this study permit some further comment on the nature of the dysphasics' auditory impairment. Although the dysphasics' performan was worse than that of the controls on most auditory tasks studied, this inferiority is directly related to the rate of presentation of the stimulus items. When this rate was reduced, either by increasing the duration of the stimulus tones themselves or by increasing the interval between tones, the dysphasics' performance improved significantly (figure 2.2).

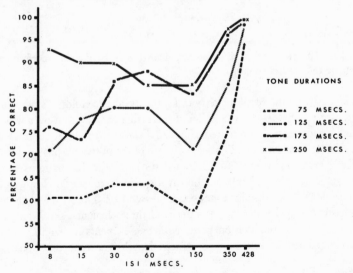

Fig. 2.2   The effect of tone duration on dysphasics' performance on two-element patterns.

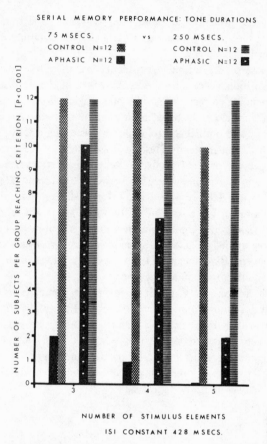

Fig. 2.3   The effect of stimulus duration on the serial memory performance of dysphasic and control subjects.

Similarly, on the serial memory tasks, the dysphasic children's performance significantly improved as a function of increasing the duration over which the stimulus patterns were presented. Figure 2.3 shows that with tones of 75 msecs duration (ISI constant at 428 msec) only two of the twelve dysphasics were able to reach criterion (p < 0.001, Binomial test) on stimulus patterns of three elements in length, and only one on any longer pattern length. However, when the duration of the stimulus tones was increased to 250 msec, ten of the twelve dysphasics reached criterion on patterns of three elements, seven on patterns of four elements, and two on patterns of five elements in length. All of the controls reached criterion on all pattern lengths for tone durations of 250 msecs.

It is suggested, therefore, that for developmental dysphasics, the time available for acoustic processing is critical to performance. Accordingly, previously reported impairment of auditory sequencing and memory in dys-phasics may well be attributable, at least in part, to a more primary inability to discriminate between stimulus elements presented at rapid rates.

It is noteworthy that the dysphasics remained inferior to the controls on auditory serial memory tasks involving sequence of four or five elements even when ISI and tone duration were maximal. Two possibilities may be considered. Dysphasics may require disnroportionately more time to process more elements. Alternatively, dysphasics may have a specific defect of auditory memory that is additional to their defect in discriminating rapidly presented auditory infor-mation. It is strongly suggested, however, that any future investigations of the abilities of developmental dysphasics, using stimuli that are presented to the auditory modality, should take account of the rate at which stimuli are presented.

Nonverbal Visual Perception in Developmental Dysphasics and Normal Children

Experiment 3. Evidence has been reported which suggests that in addition to auditory sequencing deficits, dysphasic children may also be impaired in their perception of temporal order in the visual modality (Doehring 1960; Furth 1964; Stark 1966, 1967; Furth and Pufall 1966; Winthrow 1964; and Poppen et al. 1969).

There are theoretical as well as clinical reasons for investigating whether the perceptual impairment that was demonstrated in experiments 1 and 2 for developmental dysphasics is specific to the auditory modality or is of a more general nature. Hypotheses that are concerned with the possible neurological basis of developmental dysphasia would differ substantially depending on whether or not the disorder had been shown to be modality specific or a more general perceptual deficit. Furthermore, therapeutic techniques that have been designed for use with modality-specific disorders differ from those designed for use with more pervasive perceptual disorders. Thus, the purpose of this experiment was to investigate perception by dysphasics and control subjects of temporal order in the visual modality, using the same subjects and testing procedure as were used in experiments 1 and 2.

In this experiment both the Repetition (including tests of serial memory) and the Same-Different methods, which were described for the previous auditory experiments, were used, however, (1) the two stimuli were light flashes of two different shades of green, (2) the stimulus duration was constant at 75 msec, and (3) intervals between flashes of less than 30 msecs were not studied owing to limitations of the apparatus. Stimuli were generated by a computer tape triggering two photocell beams that flashed the appropriate colored light behind a center Perspex panel mounted on a small metal box. Both lights were flashed in the same location. The paper computer tape, which

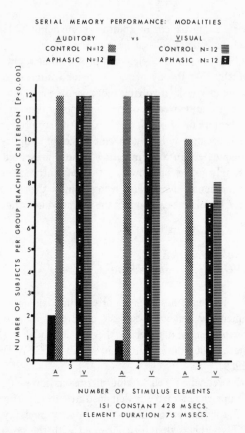

Fig. 2.4   The serial memory performance of dysphasic and control subjects in the auditory and visual modalities.

was used to trigger the photocell beams to flash the appropriate colored lights, was punched directly from the tape used to generate the tone patterns used in the auditory experiments. Therefore, the same series of stimuli were used in the two experiments, with tone 1 being replaced by color 1 and tone 2 by color 2.

The result showed that no significant differences between the performance of the dysphasics and their matched controls could be demonstrated for any of the tests presented in the visual modality, regardless of the method of response used, the ISI employed, or the length of the stimulus patterns. The dysphasic subjects in all cases performed as well as the control subjects on visual tasks involving both rapid nonverbal perceptual processing and nonverbal serial memory. This sharp contrast to the performance of the same subjects on identical tests presented to the auditory modality is illustrated in figure 2.4.

Other reports have suggested that dysphasic children do have difficulty in sequencing visual as well as auditory material. However, it is noteworthy that in the other studies the methods used differed in two important respects from the methods used here: (1) in the other experiments, visual sequences were presented both spatially and temporally, whereas in this experiment the visual sequences were presented only temporally, in the same location; and (2) a delayed response technique was used in some of the other experiments, whereas in this experiment subjects were instructed to respond as soon as the stimulus pattern was completed. It is possible that methods used previously made demands on verbal mediation which, in consequence, placed the dysphasic children at a disadvantage when compared to normal control children.

However, it is important to emphasize that the children in the dysphasic group were required to have normal nonverbal intelligence as measured by the Raven's Coloured Progressive Matrices (Raven 1965). As this test has a particularly high visual loading, it could be argued that this criterion resulted in the exclusion of dysphasic children with visual perceptual impairment. Therefore the finding that the developmental dysphasics who participated in this study were unimpaired on these visual tasks can only be generalized with reservation until further studies with language-delayed children can be undertaken.

Verbal Perception in Developmental Dysphasics and Normal Children

Experiment 4. The relevance of the defect of rapid auditory processing of nonverbal material to the speech disabilities of developmental dysphasics remains to be established. Recently, as the result of the development of the speech sound spectrograph, considerable advancement in our understanding of the normal processes underlying speech perception has been made. The sound spectrograph provides a means of analyzing the acoustic characteristics of speech sounds (phonemes) in terms of a display of frequency by intensity, as recorded over time (Koenig, Dunn, and Lacy 1946). The use of this instrument to investigate the acoustic cues underlying the perception of speech sounds led to a realization that there is not a simple one-to-one relationship between the acoustic signal and the speech sound perceived, as had previously been thought. More precisely, it was discovered that listeners do *not* receive an acoustic representation of specific phonemes in sequential patterns that are perceived as particular words. Since 1946, researchers have attempted to understand exactly what relationship does exist between the acoustic signal and the phonemes that are perceived.

Liberman et al (1967) reviewed the conclusions that have emerged from this line of research. In brief, they reported that the acoustic cues for notionally successive phonemes were so intermingled that the identification of specific definable segments that correspond to discrete phonemes was impossible. In some instances, different acoustic signals gave rise to the same perception. In other instances, identical signals were differently perceived.

Spectrograms showed that phonemes were composed of several formants. Liberman et al. (1967) defined a formant as "a concentration of acoustic energy within a restricted region. Three or four formants are usually seen in spectrograms of speech. Formants are referred to by number, the first being the lowest in frequency, the second, the next higher, and so on. A formant transition is a relatively rapid change in the position of the formant on the frequency scale" (p. 434). Liberman et al. showed that these formants transmit acoustic information about several phonemes at once. That is, the acoustic cues of phonemes are said to be "restructured" and transmitted in parallel order, not in sequence, through the formant transitions.

This restructuring of the acoustic information is a function of phonemic context. For example, the formant transitions of the phoneme /b/ differ according to whether it is followed or preceded by the vowels /æ/ or /I/ or any other phoneme. In addition, the formant transitions of the syllable /bæ/ differ according to whether the syllable is in the initial, medial, or final position of the word. Furthermore, the acoustic signal has also been found to differ from speaker to speaker, depending on the size and shape of the vocal tract and the speaker's age and sex (Ladefoged and Broadbent 1957). There appears, therefore, to be an apparent lack of invariance between the acoustic signal and the perceived phonemic message (Liberman, Delattre, and Cooper 1952).

Liberman has defined the variance or restructuring of the acoustic cues underlying phonemes as "encoding." Furthermore, he has pointed out that some phonemes appear to be more encoded than others. Consonants seem to be highly encoded, whereas vowels are unencoded. That is, analysis of spectrograms have shown that vowels, unlike consonants, do not appear to be restructured. There is a one-to-one relation between the acoustic signal and the perception of particular vowels, and it is possible to identify the specific acoustic segments corresponding to specific vowels, since they do not show the variance that is typical of most consonants.

The major auditory cue for synthesized vowels has been shown to be the steady-state frequencies of the first three formants that remain constant over the entire length of the stimulus and have a relatively long duration, approximately 250 msec (Fry et al. 1962). However, for the stop consonants the essential auditory cue is the rapidly changing spectrum provided by the second and third formant transitions. These are not only transitional in character, but they also occur over a relatively short duration, approximately 50 msec (Liberman et al. 1957).

In experiments 1 to 3 it was demonstrated that developmental dysphasics, unlike normal children, are incapable of correctly responding to nonverbal auditory stimuli presented at rapid rates, but they can adequately respond to the same stimuli at slower rates of presentation. It was also shown that this defect occurred even when perception of sequence was not required and that, on comparable tasks in the visual modality, dysphasics performed as well as normal children. In experiment 2, it was demonstrated that, provided the duration of the stimulus elements was at least 250 msec, developmental dysphasics performed as well as matched controls on a motor representation of two- and three-element patterns at all ISIs studied.

On the hypothesis that impaired rate of auditory processing may be primary to developmental dysphasia, it was predicted that (1) developmental dysphasics would *not* show impairment in discriminating steady-state synthesized vowels /ɛ/ and /æ/ of the same duration (250 msec) as the nonverbal tones they discriminated normally in experiment 2; and that (2) developmental dysphasics would show impaired discrimination of synthesized stop consonants—vowel syllables /ba/ and /da/—which have the same total duration of 250 msec but which incorporate an abrupt transitional component of only 43 msec in duration, which is critical for discrimination (see Tallal and Piercy 1975, for a detailed description of these synthesized stimuli).

This hypothesis was tested by using the same subjects and procedures as were used in the previous experiments, while substituting synthesized vowels in one case and synthesized stop consonants in another for the previously studied complex nonverbal tones. Both the Repetition Method and the Same-Different Method were used in this experiment. ISIs greater than 428 msec were not studied. Half of the subjects performed the tasks with the vowel stimuli first and the other half performed the tasks with the stop consonant–vowel stimuli first.

In the previously reported experiments, it was demonstrated that, compared with normal children, developmental dysphasics are impaired in their ability to respond correctly to rapidly presented nonverbal acoustic signals. The present experiments were concerned with synthesized verbal stimuli, and the results closely parallel those obtained with nonverbal auditory stimuli. When 250 msec steady-state vowel stimuli were used, the performance of dysphasics was inferior to that of controls only on stimulus patterns of five elements, which also provoked inferior performance by dysphasics when 250 msec nonverbal stimuli were used. On two- or three-element patterns, dysphasics performed as well as controls in discriminating 250 msec stimuli regardless of ISI and regardless of whether stimulated vowels or nonverbal sounds were used. The dysphasics' discrimination of vowel stimuli did not differ significantly from their discrimination of nonverbal auditory stimuli of the same duration in any of the tasks studied. Clearly, the dysphasic children's discrimination performance does not deteriorate simply as a consequence of changing from nonverbal to verbal auditory stimuli when both are steady-state in character.

The results with synthesized consonants are entirely different. On all tasks studied, the dysphasics' discrimination of consonant stimuli was significantly inferior to both their discrimination of vowel stimuli and their discrimination of nonverbal auditory stimuli of the same duration (figure 2.5). Furthermore, on all tasks in which consonant stimuli were presented, dysphasics' performance

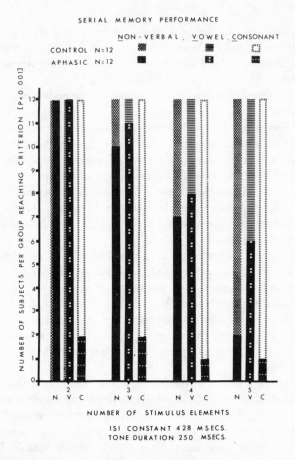

Fig. 2.5 The serial memory performance of the dysphasic and control subjects with stimulus patterns comprising (1) complex tones, (2) steady-state vowels, and (3) stop consonant–vowels.

was significantly inferior to that of their controls, irrespective of whether the Repetition Method or the Same-Different Method was employed.

These results with synthesized verbal stimuli add support to the hypothesis that developmental dysphasia results from impaired auditory processing and thus is not a specifically verbal defect. The consonant stimuli have been described as having the same duration as the vowel stimuli (250 msec). However, it must be remembered that the formant transitions were completed after 43 msec and that the remaining 207 msec consisted of steady-state formants that did not differ between the two consonant stimuli. The discriminable part of the two consonant stimuli, therefore, lasted only 43 msec, and it is notable that the dysphasic children (unlike the normal children) were unable to discriminate nonverbal auditory stimuli, of even 75 msec durations when ISIs were brief.

According to this working hypothesis, then, it is the brief duration of the formant transitions that prevents dysphasic children from discriminating stop-consonant stimuli.

The Perception of Brief Vowels and "Extended" Stop Consonants by Developmental Dysphasics and Normal Children

Experiment 5. In the previous experiment, it was demonstrated that, unlike normal children, developmental dysphasic children are incapable of processing 250 msec synthesized stop consonant–vowel syllables comprising an initial 43 msec transitional period but that they can adequately process 250 msec steady-state synthesized vowels. However, it remains unclear whether the inability of dysphasics to discriminate stop consonants results from (1) the brief duration of the transitional period or (2) an inability to process transitional stimuli irrespective of their duration. The purpose of the present experiments was to distinguish between these two possibilities. Experiment 5a is concerned with perception of vowel-vowel (V-V) syllables without a transitional component but with components of the same duration as the consonant-vowel (C-V) syllables used in the previous experiments. Experiment 5b is concerned with the perception of C-V syllables similar to those used previously but containing a transitional component that is synthetically *extended* in time. A detailed description of these synthetic stimuli is given in Tallal and Piercy (1975).

Since the purpose of these experiments was to investigate in more detail dysphasics' failure to discriminate stop consonants, only the results of the Same-Different judgments will be reported here. The results using the Repetition Method with V-V and "extended" C-V syllables did not differ from those using the Same-Different Method and have been reported in detail in a previous publication (Tallal and Piercy 1975).

The results of experiment 5a using synthesized V-V syllables are identical with those reported previously using synthesized C-V syllables with 43 msec transitions. The same subjects who failed to reach criterion with the C-V syllables also failed to reach criterion with the V-V syllables. In other words, the discrimination ability of developmental dysphasics remained equally poor when the transitional components of the consonant stimuli were replaced by steady-state components of the same brief duration. It may therefore be concluded that one factor limiting the dysphasics' ability to discriminate verbal stimuli is the *duration* of the acoustically discriminable characteristics of the stimuli, regardless of whether these are steady-state or transitional.

The results of experiment 5a do not, however, preclude a further possibility. In addition to the constraint placed on their auditory processing by speed, dysphasic children might also have selective difficulty in processing transitions as such, independently of their duration. The results of experiment 5b would seem to resolve this issue. In this experiment, which used consonants with extended transitions, the results were identical with those obtained in previous experiments in which steady-state vowels or nonverbal stimuli of the same duration (250 msec) were used. In all of these cases, the developmental dysphasics performed as well as the controls. It appears, therefore, that these dysphasic subjects are not impaired in their ability to process transitional acoustic information, provided that the transitions are of relatively long duration.

These experiments with developmental dysphasic children and normal control children began with a study of their ability to discriminate, order, and serially recall complex nonverbal tones. These studies demonstrated that, in comparison with normal matched controls, dysphasic children are impaired in their ability to respond correctly to auditory (but not visual) stimuli that are presented in rapid succession. Further experiments suggested that this perceptual impairment was unrelated to whether or not the acoustic stimuli were verbal or nonverbal but, rather, depended on the demands made on rapid acoustic analysis. Thus, dysphasic children were selectively impaired in their ability to discriminate between stop consonant–vowel syllables whose discriminable components were both brief and transitional. The two studies reported in experiments 5a and 5b strongly suggest that it is the brevity rather than the transitional character of this component of stop consonants that causes the dysphasics' inability to discriminate these phonemes.

The finding that the majority of dysphasic children, who were unable to discriminate between stop consonants with standard duration formant transitions, were able to discriminate between these same speech sounds when the duration of the formant transition was extended is of both theoretical and clinical importance. It has been reported that the abrupt frequency change of the formant transitions in stop consonants is a critical characteristic of this class of speech sounds (Liberman et al. 1957). It has also been reported that extension of the duration of the formant transitions within stops results in a change in the class of speech sounds perceived (stop consonants become liquid consonants, such as /l/ and /r/). However, it must be stressed that the normal control children (8:6 years old) participating in the studies reported here continued to identify the "extended" phonemes used in these experiments as the intended stop consonants. Therefore, the effect on normal speech perception of extending the duration of the formant transition of stop consonants, as well as the limits of such extensions for the various formants, is an interesting area for further investigation.

It is also important to note that only two durations of formant transitions have been investigated here. For experimental efficiency in answering the immediate question at hand, the duration of the standard transitions was more than doubled. However, that does not necessarily indicate that dysphasics actually require such long duration transitions. It will be important to establish exactly how extended the formant transitions must be before dysphasics can accurately discriminate these stop consonants.

Before we can begin to establish the applicability of this finding to therapeutic use, it will be important to determine whether dysphasic children discriminate these "extended" stops phonetically, in a manner similar to that in which normal subjects discriminate this class of phonemes, that is, categorically (see Liberman et al. 1957 for a discussion of categorical perception), or whether they use nonverbal acoustic mechanisms to make this distinction. We are presently testing dysphasic children with these "extended" stop-consonants to determine if they are perceiving them in a categorical manner. These and other methods used in the study of normal speech perception should help to establish the possible value of "extended" synthetic speech as a therapeutic tool for use with language-disordered subjects.

An Investigation of the Normal Development of Rapid Auditory Processing

Experiment 6.   On the basis of the results of the previously reported studies, it was hypothesized that an auditory-specific and rate-specific perceptual impairment may be sufficient to explain the failure of dysphasic children to develop normal language proficiency at or near the expected age. However, dysphasic children differ in their degree of language impairment, and many of them eventually attain near-normal language function. Accordingly, it is possible that this language syndrome results, not from a permanent disability, but from delayed development of a specific auditory perceptual process that is prerequisite to the normal acquisition of language.

The temporal resolving power of the auditory system of normal adults has been a topic of research interest since the early 1900s and continues to be investigated (Wallach et al. 1949; Hirsh 1959; Halliday and Mingay 1964). However, the normal development of rapid auditory processing and its possible interaction with normal language development has yet to be investigated.

The following experiment was undertaken for the purpose of (1) studying the development of rapid auditory processing in normal children and (2) making a comparison between the rapid auditory processing abilities of developmental dysphasic children and normal children of various ages.

If developmental dysphasia does result from a developmental lag in the auditory processing rate, such a study should provide information on the magnitude of the dysphasics' retardation. Furthermore, a comparative study of the development of rapid auditory processing in children who are developing language normally and those who are not should provide information concerning the interrelation between normal perceptual development and normal language acquisition. The Repetition Method, which was previously used in the dysphasia studies, was employed in these experiments. Tests of serial memory were not included.

In a preliminary experiment, young children were tested for their ability to discriminate between the previously described 75 msec complex tones. These are the same two tones that were used in Experiment 1, with dysphasic children. The discrimination-training procedure that has been described as the Repetition Method was used in this preliminary study. It was established that children younger than 4:6 years old could not reach criterion (p < 0.001, Binomial Test) using this procedure. For this reason, 4:6-year-old children were the youngest subjects to participate in this developmental study.

The following age groups were used in this experiment: 4:6-year olds, 5:6-year olds, 6:6-year olds, 7:6-year olds, 8:6-year olds, and adults. Each of these six groups comprised twelve subjects, six males and six females. The subjects, except for those in the adult control group, were all attending a Cambridge primary school. The adult control subjects were nonacademic staff from Cambridge University, England.

The subjects in each age group (except the adults) were selected on the basis of birth date and nonverbal intelligence. Children who were assessed as having either very low (I.Q. < 80) or very high (I.Q. > 115) intelligence were excluded from the study. Four subjects in each group, two males and two females, were assessed as having low-average nonverbal intelligence (I.Q. 85–95); four as having average nonverbal intelligence (I.Q. 95–105); and four as having high-average nonverbal intelligence (I.Q. 105–115). Children were within two months of their "half-birthday" at the time of testing. Where applicable, children with reading ages more than a year and a half below their chronological age (Schonell Test, 1942) were also excluded from the developmental study, as were children with speech impediments and children with elevated thresholds on standard audiometric tests.

The results of this developmental study showed that in general, performance on all the tasks studied improved with age, regardless of stimulus conditions or rate of stimulus presentation. However, the results show that the degree of improvement with age differed between the various stimuli conditions that were studied.

By the age of 6:6 years, the normal subjects were performing as well as adult controls on nonverbal two-element auditory patterns with long duration ISIs (947–4062 msec). However, the ability to perform as well as adults on these same stimulus patterns, but with shorter intervals (8–428 msec), was not achieved until the age of 8:6 years.

These studies demonstrate that performance on the nonverbal auditory tasks is age-dependent. More specifically, the ability to respond correctly to nonverbal auditory stimulus patterns that are presented very rapidly lags by as much as two years behind the development of the ability to respond correctly to those same auditory patterns when they are presented more slowly.

On the basis of these results, it can be concluded that the ability to respond correctly to nonverbal auditory signals, which are presented rapidly in succes-

sion, develops progressively with age and reaches an asymptote by the age of
8:6 years.

The comparisons between the abilities of developmental dysphasic children
and normal children of various ages to respond correctly to rapidly presented
auditory signals were made in order to ascertain whether or not the dysphasic
children's pattern of performance was similar to that of any group of younger
normal children.

Figure 2.6 illustrates the performance of the dysphasic subjects on the
nonverbal two-element auditory patterns as compared with that of the normal
subjects for each ISI studied. This figure shows that the shape of the curve
representing the performance of the dysphasics is more like that of the 6:6
and 7:6-year-old subjects than that of the 5:6 or the 4:6-year-old subjects.
Nonetheless, the number of errors made by the dysphasic subjects on the
auditory patterns comprising the short ISIs (8–305 msec) was significantly
greater (p < 0.01 Mann-Whitney U Test) than even those made by the 4:6-
year-old group. In contrast, the dysphasics made significantly fewer errors
(p < 0.01 Mann-Whitney U Test) than the 4:6-year-old group on these same
patterns comprising the long ISIs (947–4062 msec). The dysphasics' performance was age-appropriate for all ISIs of 428 msec or greater.

In conclusion, the results of the present experiment indicate that the overall
pattern of performance of the dysphasic children is *not* similar to that of any
of the groups of normal subjects that were studied, regardless of age. Whereas
the dysphasic children, as reported previously, proved able to respond as well

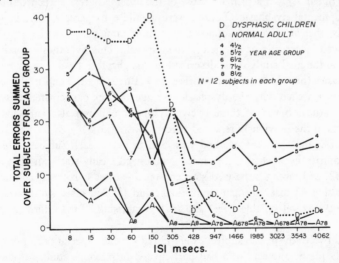

Fig. 2.6 The total number of errors made by each age group of normal subjects,
as compared to developmental dysphasic subjects, on two-element auditory sequences
presented at various rates. The tone duration was constant at 75 msec. The rate of
presentation of the stimuli was determined by the inter-sound-interval (ISI).

as normal children of their same mean age (8:6 years) on the nonverbal auditory patterns that were presented at relatively slow rates, their performance was significantly inferior to that of even the youngest group of children studied (4:6 years) when the same patterns were presented more rapidly.

It is, of course, still possible that the dysphasic children's development of rapid auditory processing is so grossly delayed that it reflects the development of even younger children than were able to participate in these studies. In order to investigate this question further, it is suggested that a longitudinal study of the performance of dysphasic subjects using these tasks be conducted.

There is a dearth of information concerning the interaction between normal auditory perceptual development and normal language acquisition. Nonetheless, the development of basic auditory perceptual skills, such as those investigated in this study, may be critical to normal language acquisition. Comparative investigations of the development of specific aspects of auditory perception in children who are and are not developing language normally may serve to increase our understanding as to which aspects of the acoustic signal are most intimately involved in speech perception.

The Relation between Speech Perception Impairment and Speech Production Impairment in Children with Developmental Dysphasia

*Experiment 7.** If a primary cause of the observed gross speech disorder of developmental dysphasic children were a failure to perceive certain speech sounds, then it might be supposed that these same speech sounds would be produced incorrectly or omitted in their speech. This hypothesis was investigated in the final study to be described in this chapter. Twelve developmental dysphasics (nine boys and three girls aged 7:1 to 9:5 years) and twelve control children matched with the dysphasics for age and sex participated as subjects in this study. Seven of these twelve dysphasic children also participated as subjects in the previously reported perceptual studies.

The Same-Different Method was used to assess each subject's ability to discriminate between: (1) 250 msec synthesized steady-state vowels (/ɛ/ and /æ/); (2) 250 msec synthesized stop consonant–vowel syllables (/ba/ and /da/) comprising 43 msec formant transitions; and (3) 250 msec synthesized stop consonant–vowel syllables (/ba/ and /da/) comprising 80 msec formant transitions.

All twelve dysphasic subjects were tested on these speech perception tests. The dysphasic subjects who had participated in previous studies using these same stimulus pairs were retested on these tasks at the time of the present study.

---

* In collaboration with Rachel Stark and Barbara Curtiss.

The developmental study demonstrated that normal children of the average age of the control subjects in this study (8:6 years) were all able to discriminate adequately between the three stimulus pairs used in this study. Therefore, these control subjects did not participate in these perceptual tests.

The twelve developmental dysphasic children and twelve matched control children were tested for their ability to imitate (1) isolated steady-state vowels such as /ε/ and /æ/ (these are not the same as vowels in word context, since such vowels rarely reach the steady-state spectral pattern we are talking about here); (2) stop consonants in consonant-vowel syllables, e.g., /bε/, /dε/; (3) stop consonants in consonat-vowel-consonant nonsense syllables, e.g., /bεk/, /dεg/; and (4) stop consonants in clusters, e.g. /blε/, /prε/, which were produced by the examiner. Secondly, subjects were required to produce the names of objects that were pictured individually on cards. Single-syllable words comprising stop consonants in the initial and final position ('bed,' 'cup'), as well as words comprising primarily vowels ('eye,' 'ear') and diphthongs and nasals ('knife,' 'nose'), were pictured. All subjects' responses were recorded on magnetic tape and later transcribed phonetically by two independent listeners, who were unaware of the subjects' perceptual abilities.

The results of these dysphasic children's performance on the perception tests are presented in table 2.2. All twelve dysphasic subjects reached criterion (p < 0.001, Binomial Test) on the Same-Different discrimination of the steady-state vowels /ε/ and /æ/. However, only five of the twelve dysphasic subjects

Table 2.2

Ability of Dysphasic Children to Reach Criterion on Tests of Perception of Steady-State Vowels and of Stop + Vowel Syllables with a 43 msec Formant Transition and an 80 msec Formant Transition

| | | Stop + Vowel Syllables | |
| | | 43 msec transition | 95 msec transition |
Subject	Vowels		
V.C.	+	+	+
P.C.	+	+	+
V.P.	+	+	+
W.P.	+	+	+
D.X.	+	+	+
S.L.	+	−	+
C.D.	+	−	+
V.S.	+	−	+
T.L.	+	−	+
C.B.	+	−	+
J.W.	+	−	−
K.M.	+	−	−

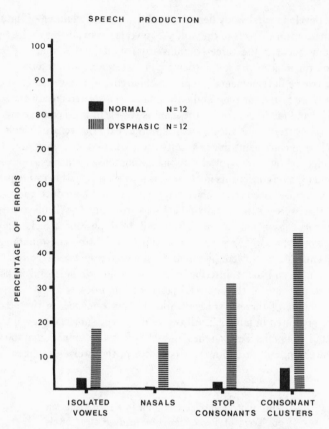

Fig. 2.7   The speech production performance of dysphasic children in comparison to normal subjects on isolated vowels, nasals, stop consonants, and consonant clusters.

reached this criterion on the discrimination of the stop consonant–vowel syllables /ba/ and /da/, using the standard 43 msec formant transitions. When the duration of the formant transitions of the stop consonants was extended by means of a speech synthesizer, ten of the twelve dysphasic subjects in this study were able to reach criterion on this discrimination.

Figure 2.7 shows the performance of the dysphasic children in comparison to the control children on these speech production experiments. The data were analyzed in terms of the overall percentage of errors made on isolated vowels, nasals, stop consonants, and stop consonants in clusters that occurred in the speech sample. This figure shows that the control children were able to produce isolated vowels, nasals, stop consonants, and consonant clusters equally well. There is no significant difference between the control groups' ability to produce any of these speech sounds. However, whereas the dysphasics' production of isolated vowels is within normal limits, just as their perception of these speech sounds has previously been shown to be, their production of stop consonants both singly and in clusters is grossly impaired. Stop consonants are those speech sounds that standardly incorporate the most rapidly changing acoustic spectra and have previously been shown to be indiscriminable by these same dysphasic children. The relationship between speech perceptual impairment and speech production impairment becomes even clearer, however, when the errors of the individual dysphasic children are examined.

Of the group studied in the perceptual experiments, five of the twelve subjects were unimpaired in their discrimination of stop consonants, regardless of the duration of the formant transitions. The remaining seven subjects were unable to discriminate these phonemes adequately with the standard 43 msec

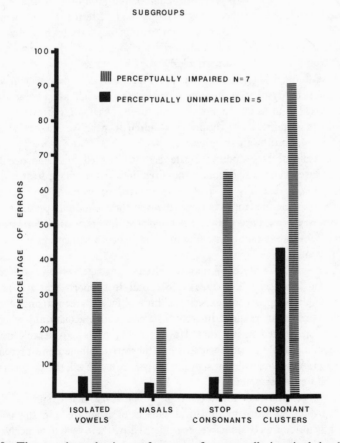

Fig. 2.8 The speech production performance of perceptually impaired dysphasics in comparison to perceptually unimpaired dysphasics on isolated vowels, nasals, stop consonants, and consonant clusters.

transitions. The speech production performance of the dysphasic children has, therefore, been analyzed in terms of their perceptual capabilities.

In figure 2.8, the speech production abilities of the five dysphasics who were perceptually unimpaired on these tests are compared to those of the seven children who were perceptually impaired on these tests. As in the perceptual tests, the unimpaired group performed as well as normal control subjects on the *production* of isolated vowels and stop consonants. They were also normal in their production of nasals, although the perception of nasals has not as yet been investigated. It was only when the production of stop consonants in clusters was required that their production performance was significantly impaired.

In comparison, the perceptually impaired group of dysphasics did significantly less well than the perceptually unimpaired group on all four measures of speech production studied. Furthermore, their pattern of impairment again matched what might be expected from their perceptual abilities, that is, the production of isolated vowels and nasals was significantly less impaired than that of stop consonants and particularly stops in clusters.

These findings suggest that the speech production impairment of at least a subgroup of dysphasic children mirrors their speech perceptual abilities. Those speech sounds incorporating rapid spectral changes, critical for perception, are most difficult for dysphasic children to perceive and are also most often misproduced by these children.

The results of these studies indicate that the observed gross language impairment of developmentally dysphasic children does not result, at least primarily, from a specific inability to analyze the verbal or *linguistic* components of language. Rather, the language impairment of these children appears to reflect their primary inability to analyze the rapid stream of acoustic information that characterizes speech and is essential to normal speech perception and language development.

The results of a study of these children's language comprehension using the Token Test (see Tallal 1975) also appear to support such a hypothesis. These children appear to experience little difficulty recognizing common, familiar words, that are quite different from one another acoustically when these words are presented in isolation. However, they have considerable difficulty in responding to these same words when they are combined and presented in succession. As the demand on acoustic analysis is increased, the performance of these children deteriorates.

This is certainly not intended to imply, however, that dysphasic children have no difficulty with grammatical aspects of language. On the contrary, their difficulties are considerable, as evidenced by their very poor performance on part 5 of the Token Test. It is suggested, however, that these difficulties stem, at least in part, from the auditory perceptual inabilities of these children, and hence their abnormal experience with language as a whole.

TEMPORAL PROCESSING, SPEECH
PERCEPTION, AND HEMISPHERIC ASYMMETRY

It is generally agreed that the human brain is functionally asymmetric. One of the most basic assumptions related to hemispheric asymmetries is that the left cerebral hemisphere is predominantely involved in language processing for most normal people. The dichotic stimulation technique has been used to show that when two different acoustic signals are presented simultaneously to a listener, one to each ear, most normal listeners are more accurate in perceiving verbal stimuli when they are presented to the right ear than when they are presented to the left ear. Kimura suggested that the right-ear advantage (REA) for dichotically presented verbal material indicates that this material is being processed in the left hemisphere (see Kimura 1967 for a discussion of this phenomenon).

Numerous studies have utilized the dichotic stimulation technique for investigating mechanisms of speech perception in more detail (see Berlin and McNeil, forthcoming, for review). Verbal dichotic stimulus material, in the form of complete phrases as well as individual speech sounds, has been used in an attempt to understand how speech is distinguished from nonspeech and why it is processed in the left hemisphere of the brain. Using new computerized techniques that allow for synthesizing speech while selectively controlling the various acoustic variables, it has been demonstrated that not all classes of speech sounds produce an equally strong REA when they are presented dichotically. Cutting (1973) demonstrated that the largest REA was produced when stop consonants b, d, g, p, t, k were presented in pairs dichotically, while liquids (such as /l/ and /r/) produce a less strong REA, and steady-state isolated vowels (such as /ɛ/ and /æ/) did not produce a right-ear advantage. The magnitude of the right-ear advantage for dichotic presentation has been directly related to the degree of verbal encodedness; in other words, the degree to which speech sounds undergo context-dependent acoustic variation (Studdert-Kennedy and Shankweiler 1970; Haggard 1971). Furthermore, the degree of encodedness of classes of speech sounds has also been shown to be related to the extent to which these sounds are perceived categorically, that is, the degree to which two acoustically different speech sounds, identified as belonging to the same speech category, can be discriminated (see Studdert-Kennedy et al. 1970, for review).

Interestingly, highly encoded phonemes are also characterized by very abrupt changes in frequency over time. Thus, the magnitude of the REA that Cutting described for stop consonants, liquids, and vowels, in addition to corre-lating with the degree of encodedness of these classes of speech sounds also correlates with the rapidity of frequency changes in these speech sounds. Fujisaki and Kawashima (1970) demonstrated in a series of elegant experiments that the degree to which vowels were perceived categorically depended on their duration. Whereas relatively long-lasting isolated steady-state vowels, which are the kind most often used in speech perception experiments, were shown not to be perceived categorically, the same vowels *were* perceived categorically if they were very brief in duration (about 20 msec) or presented in a fixed phonemic context. These experiments indicate that the degree of lateralization of speech may be related to the duration over which the critical acoustic aspects occur within certain sounds, and hence the rate at which they must be processed. Recently, Halperin et al. (1973) were able to demonstrate a REA for nonverbal dichotically presented tone sequences containing abrupt changes in frequency or duration. However, despite these few excellent studies, the majority of evidence continues to favor the hypothesis that the REA indicates that specific verbal material must be processed in the left hemisphere and that this laterization results from processing that occurs beyond the level of acoustic analysis (Liberman 1973).

The recent finding that developmental dysphasics are unable to discriminate speech sounds that incorporate rapidly changing acoustic spectra, but can discriminate these same speech sounds when the duration over which the critical acoustic information occurs is extended (Tallal and Piercy 1975), indicates that the rate at which acoustic information must be processed in time may be a critical feature of speech processing. In that normal listeners were able to identify the "extended" stop consonants accurately, it seemed that these speech sounds might provide a useful means of looking again at the question of the role of rapid acoustic analysis in the REA observed with dichotic stimulation, and in categorical perception.

We are presently investigating the effect on normal adult speech perception of extending the duration of the formant transitions within stop consonants. Studies of categorical perception and dichotic perception using standard duration (40 msec) as well as extended duration (80 msec) transitions within stop consonants are presently underway. These studies indicate that functions that have previously been considered to reflect specifically phonetic analysis, such as categorical perception and the REA for dichotic presentation, may actually be reflecting analysis at the acoustic level of speech processing, which is directly related to the rate of change of acoustic information within certain speech sounds.

The results of our studies with children with and without normal language development indicate that the processing of rapidly occurring acoustic information is critically involved in the development and maintenance of language. Several other authors have arrived at a similar conclusion using different experimental techniques—namely, that the dominant hemisphere must play a primary role in the analysis of rapid temporal acoustic information, and hence speech, which required such acoustic analysis, is also lateralized to this hemisphere (Efron 1963; Lackner and Teuber 1973). The results reported here strongly support this hypothesis. It is to be hoped that these new techniques will be a useful means of further delineating the role of auditory temporal processing in the perception and misperception of speech.

REFERENCES

Aten, J., and Davis, J. 1968. Disturbance in the perception of auditory sequence in children with minimal cerebral dysfunction. *J. Speech Hearing Res.* 11 (2):236–45,

Bakker, D. J. 1971. *Temporal order in disturbed reading: developmental and neuropsychological aspects in normal and reading-retarded children.* Rotterdam: Rotterdam Univ. Press.

Benton, A. L. 1964. Developmental aphasia and brain damage. *Cortex* 1:40–52.

Berlin, C. I., and McNeill, M. R. Dichotic listening. In *Contemporary issues in experimental phonetics*, ed. N. Lass, forthcoming.

Bricker, W. A. and Bricker, D. D. 1970. A program of language training for the severely handicapped child. *Except. Child.* 37 (2):101–11.

Cutting, J. E. 1973. Parallel between degree of encodedness and the ear advantage: evidence from an ear monitoring task. *J. Acoust. Soc. Amer.* 53:368 ff.

Doehring, D. G. 1960. Visual spatial memory in aphasic children. *J. Speech Hearing Res.* 3:138–49.

Efron, R. 1963. Temporal perception, aphasia, and déjà vu. *Brain* 86:403–24.

Eisenson, J. 1968. Developmental aphasia: a speculative view with therapeutic implications. *J. Speech Hearing Dis.* 33:3–13.

———. 1972. *Aphasia in children.* New York: Harper & Row.

Ewing, A. W. G. 1930. *Aphasia in children.* London: Oxford Univ. Press.

Fry, D. B.; Abramson, A. S.; Eimas, P. D.; and Liberman, A. M. 1962. The identification and discrimination of synthetic vowels. *Language and Speech* 5 (4):171–89.

Fujisaki, H., and Kawashima, T. 1970. Some experiments on speech perception and a model for the perceptual mechanism. *Annual Report of the Engineering Research Institute, University of Tokyo* 29:207–14.

Furth, H. G. 1964. Sequence learning in aphasic and deaf children. *J. Speech Hearing Dis.* 29 (2):171–7.

Furth, H. G., and Pufall, P. B. 1966. Visual and auditory sequence learning in hearing-impaired children. *J. Speech Hearing Res.* 9:441–9.

Griffiths, P. 1972. *Developmental aphasia: an introduction.* London: Invalid Children's Aid Association.

Haggard, M. P. 1971. Encoding and the REA for speech signals. *Quart. J. Exp. Psychol.* 23:34–45.

Halliday, A. M., and Mingay, R. 1964. On the resolution of small time intervals and the effect of conduction relays on the judgment of simultaneity. *Quart. J. Exp. Psychol.* 16:35–46.

Halperin, Y.; Nachshon, S.; and Carmon, A. 1973. Shift of ear superiority in dichotic listening to temporally patterned nonverbal stimuli. *J. Acoust. Soc. Amer.* 53:46–50.

Hardy, W. G. 1965. On language disorders in young children: a reorganization of thinking. *J. Speech Hearing Dis.* 30 (1):3–16.

Hirsh, I. J. 1959. Auditory perception of temporal order. *J. Acous. Soc. Amer.* 3:759–67.

Kimura, D. 1967. Functional asymmetry of the brain in dichotic listening. *Cortex* 3:157–78.

Koenig, W.; Dunn, H. K.; and Lacy, L. Y. 1946. The sound spectrograph. *J. Acoust. Soc. Amer.* 17:19–49.

Lackner, J. R., and Teuber, H.-L. 1973. Alterations in auditory fusion thresholds after cerebral injury in man. *Neuropsychologia* 11:409–15.

Ladefoged, P., and Broadbent, D. E. 1957. Information conveyed by vowels. *J. Acoust. Soc. Amer.* 29:98–104.

Lenneberg, E. 1967. *Biological foundations of language.* New York: John Wiley & Sons.

Liberman, A. M. 1973. The specialization of the language hemisphere. In *The neurosciences: third study program.* Cambridge, Mass.: M.I.T. Press.

Liberman, A. M.; Delattre, P. C.; and Cooper, F. S. 1952. The role of selected stimulus variables in the perception of the unvoiced stop consonants. *Amer. J. Psychol.* 65:497–516.

Liberman, A. M.; Cooper, F. S.; Shankweiler, D. P.; and Studdert-Kennedy, M. 1967. Perception of the speech code. *Psychol. Rev.* 74:431–61.

Liberman, A. M.; Harris, K. S.; Hoffman, H. S. and Griffith, B. C. 1957. The discrimination of speech sounds within and across phoneme boundaries. *J. Exp. Psychol.* 54:358–68.

Lowe, A. D., and Campbell, R. A. 1965. Temporal discrimination in aphasoid and normal children. *J. Speech Hearing Res.* 8:313–4.

McReynolds, L.-V. 1966. Operant conditioning for investigating speech sound discrimination in aphasic children. *J. Speech Hearing Res.* 9:519–28.

———. 1967. Verbal sequencing discrimination training for language-impaired children. *J. Speech Hearing Dis.* 32 (3):244–56.

Mark, H. J., and Hardy, W. G. 1958. Orienting Reflex Disturbances in central auditory or language handicapped children. *J. Speech Hearing Dis.* 23 (3):237–42.

Monsees, E. K. 1957. Aphasia in children: diagnosis and education. *Volta Review* 59:392–414.

———. 1968. Temporal sequence and expressive language disturbance. *Except. Child.* 35:141–7.

Orton, S. 1937. *Reading, writing, and speech problems in children.* New York: W. W. Norton.

Poppen, R.; Stark, J.; Eisenson, J.; Forrest, T.; and Wertheim, G. 1969. Visual sequencing performance of aphasic children. *J. Speech Hearing Res.* 12:288–300.

Rapin, I., and Graziani, J. 1967. Auditory-evoked responses in normal, brain-damaged, and deaf infants. *Neurology* 17:881–94.

Raven, R. C. 1965. *Coloured progressive matrices.* London: H. K. Lewis.

Rosenthal, W. S., and Eisenson, J. 1970. Auditory temporal order in aphasic children as a function of selected stimulus features. Paper presented at the 46th Annual Convention of the American Speech and Hearing Association, New York City.

Schonell, F. J. 1942. *The Schonell reading test.* London: Oliver & Boyd.

Stark, J. 1966. Peformance of aphasic children on the ITPA. *Except. Child.* 33:153–8.

———. 1967. A Comparison of the performance of aphasic children on three sequencing tests. *J. Comm. Dis.* 1:31–34.

Studdert-Kennedy, M., and Shankweiler, D. 1970. Hemispheric specialization for speech perception. *J. Acoust. Soc. Amer.* 48:579–94.

Studdert-Kennedy, M.; Liberman, A. M.; Harris, K. S.; and Cooper, F. S. 1970. The motor theory of speech perception. A reply to Lane's critical review. *Psychol. Rev.* 77:234–49.

Swisher, L., and Hirsh, I. J. 1972. Brain damage and the ordering of two temporally successive stimuli. *Neuropsychologia* 10 (2):137–51.

Tallal, P. 1975. Perceptual and linguistic factors in the language impairment of developmental dysphasics: an experimental investigation with the token test. *Cortex* 11:196–205.

Tallal, P., and Piercy, M. 1973a. Defects of non-verbal auditory perception in children with developmental aphasia. *Nature* 241 (5390):468–9.

———. 1973b. Developmental aphasia: impaired rate of non-verbal processing as a function of sensory modality. *Neuropsychologia* 11:389–98.

———. 1974. Developmental aphasia: rate of auditory processing and selective impairment of consonant perception. *Neuropsychologia* 12:83–94.

———. 1975. Developmental aphasia: the perception of brief vowels and extended stop consonants. *Neuropsychologia* 13:69–74.

Templin, M. C. 1957. *Certain language skills in children*. Minneapolis: Univ. of Minnesota Press.

Wallach, H.; Newman, E. B.; and Rosenzweig, M. R. 1949. Precedence effect in sound localization. *Am. J. Psych.* 62:315–36.

Wilks, S. S. 1935. The likelihood test of independence in contingency tables. *Ann. Math. Stats.* 6:190–6.

Withrow, F. B. 1964. Immediate recall by aphasic, deaf, and normally hearing children for visual forms presented simultaneously or sequentially in time. *Asha* 6:386.

3

THE PRODUCTION OF WORD-INITIAL FRICATIVES AND AFFRICATES BY NORMAL AND LINGUISTICALLY DEVIANT CHILDREN

David Ingram

INTRODUCTION

What constitutes deviance in the language of a child with a language disorder can be directly examined in comparative studies with normal children. So far, most studies attempting this approach have focused on syntactic development (see Menyuk 1964; Lackner 1968; Morehead and Ingram 1973; Ingram 1974a). These studies demonstrate two different approaches to the problem. The first three compared general grammatical characteristics, whereas the fourth concentrated on a specific grammatical construction. Neither approach, however, has been attempted in the area of phonological development.

Despite a lack of comparative work, there have been a series of papers separately analyzing the phonological development of both normal and linguistically deviant children. The more noteworthy analyses of individual normal children include studies by Stampe (1969), Moskowitz (1970), Menn (1971), Waterson (1971), Kornfeld (1971), Smith (1973), Ingram (1974b), and Ferguson and Farwell (1975). These have contributed to a growing knowledge about the normal process. At the same time, there have been a series of recent studies analyzing the phonological systems of deviant children, e.g., Haas (1963), Compton (1970, 1975), Pollock and Rees (1972), Oller et al. (1972), Oller (1973), Edwards and Bernhardt (1973), and Lorentz (1972, 1974). Basically, these are children who would traditionally be classified as having a functional articulation disorder. Together, these analyses provide a general picture of deviant phonology that can be compared with what is known about normal acquisition.

This comparison was attempted in Ingram (1976), based on findings about normal and deviant acquisition from several sources, including those mentioned above. From that comparison, the following conclusions were drawn about deviant phonology:

1. *Deviant children have systematic phonological systems.* Most of the words they produce can be described by a set of phonological processes that simplify adult words.
2. *Most of the phonological processes found in deviant speech are also found in normal children's speech.* These include processes that reduce consonant clusters to a single member, delete final consonants, make fricatives into stops, and delete unstressed syllables.
3. *Occasionally, deviant children use phonological processes that are not found in normal children or that occur in them with much less frequency.* More needs to be known about normal processes before it can be said with certainty that certain processes used by deviant children are unique to them.
4. *Certain phonological processes persist in the speech of deviant children* and occur together with those more characteristic of later development. For instance, normal children have a process that deletes final consonants in their words. This process usually drops out very early in development. In some deviant children, however, it may persist in their system, while other improvements occur (see Renfrew 1966). Consequently, such a child might show CV syllables with well-developed initial consonants. This would not occur in a normal child.
5. *Because of the above finding, a deviant child's phonology is more than just a delayed system.* It is deviant in that it may result in a system unlike that of a younger normal child.

Besides these findings, two other aspects of deviant language that require further empirical investigation were noted. First, deviant children have a deficit in using a large number of homonyms and in using speech sounds contrastively, owing, in the more severe cases, to phonetic instability. Second (see Edwards and Bernhardt 1973), deviant children show more phonological processes than normal children at a comparable level of development.

These findings present a general picture of the nature of deviant phonology. It is necessary, however, to obtain more information on the development of specific phonological patterns. This chapter reports on the acquisition of English fricatives and affricates in word-initial positions by both normal and linguistically deviant children. These sounds have been selected because they constitute the most frequently mispronounced sounds in English (see summary of research in Winitz 1969). The study is restricted to the initial position

Table 3.1

English Fricatives and Affricates Occurring Word Initially

Class	Labiodental	Dental	Alveolar	Alveopalatal
Fricative				
voiceless	/f/ foot	/θ/ thumb	/s/ sun	/š/ shoe
voiced	/v/ vest	/ð/ there	/z/ zoo	
Affricate				
voiceless				/č/ chair
voiced				/ǰ/ juice

because fricatives and affricates show both a different and a delayed development there as compared to their use at the end of words (see Ferguson 1973). The five findings mentioned above on deviant phonology constitute hypotheses derived from the comparison.

PREVIOUS INVESTIGATIONS

One difficulty in studying the development of fricatives and affricates is that they are acquired over a long period of time. Data from children at different ages must be obtained. Unfortunately this kind of data is not readily available from most current studies on phonological development—a situation that is inherent in the methodology that has been used in most research on child phonology.

Children's phonological acquisition has been dominated by two basic methods of study. These are *diary studies* and *large-sample studies*. Both of these are geared toward providing an overview of all the sounds a child (or children) uses. Consequently, they are usually deficient in sufficient information on more specific sounds. In diary studies, it is difficult to know whether the child is typical of other children in his acquisition of individual sounds. Also, because these studies are usually conducted over a short period of time, they do not observe the sounds to their point of acquisition; several diaries would have to be compared to ascertain general patterns. With large-sample studies, each sound is commonly tested in only one word (e.g., Templin 1957). Since children are selected from a cross section of ages, these studies provide age norms for the acquisition of sounds. These norms, however, are somewhat questionable, since a child's ability to produce a sound may vary according to the word in which it is tested (see Ingram et al. 1975). By grouping data, they also fail to provide information about each child's individual system.

The results from large-sample studies can be used to provide a general picture of the acquisition of sounds at different ages. Two of the most extensive studies of this kind were conducted by Wellman et al. (1931) and by Templin (1957). Wellman et al. examined the productions of 205 children who were between 2 and 6 years of age, using a naming task, that is, children had to name or identify pictures. Wellman studied 480 children between the ages of 3 and 8, testing each sound once per child with an imitation task. Table 3.2 provides the percentages of correct productions on initial fricatives and affricates from both studies.

Since the studies differ in several respects, table 3.2 is only a gross comparison of the two. It does, however, provide an indication of the improvement of production across several years. Each used 75% as a criterion of acquisition. These are circled on the chart and show some correspondence between ages of acquisition.

Table 3.2

Percentage of Children Using Correct Production of English Fricatives and Affricates for Different Ages

Sound†		Age (in years)								Test words*
		2	3	3:5	4	4:5	5	6	7	8	
/f-/	W	53	(85)		92		100	100			fan, fish, feet, feeding, fence, four, five
	T		(88)	90	93	97	92	100	100	100	feet, forth
/v-/	W	0	58		72		(84)	70			vest, vase
	T		12	30	40	47	55	(80)	88	98	vacuum cleaner, valentine
/θ-/	W	20	36		51		(76)	89			thumb
	T		27	28	48	60	67	(85)	90	97	thinning, thumb
/ð-/	W	7	39		49		(79)	89			this, that
	T		23	32	57	60	62	(83)	97	98	those, there
/s-/	W	7	51		64		(77)	74			six, saw, scissors, Santa Claus
	T		70	(85)	77	80	78	77	92	97	seat, silk
/z-/	W	14	61		73		(87)	78			zipper
	T		30	55	62	72	65	67	(90)	95	zipper
/š-/	W	7	46		74		(88)	96			shoes, sugar
	T		53	72	(75)	88	87	87	95	98	ship, shoes
/č-/	W	21	59		72		(88)	92			choo, chair, chickens
	T		50	60	72	(75)	82	88	98	95	chip, cherry
/ǰ-/	W	29	74		(81)		90	82			jump, jar, jug
	T		53	58	(85)	87	92	95	97	97	jumped, jump

SOURCE: Wellman et al. (1931) and Templin (1957). Seventy-five% was used by both to determine ages of acquisition. These are circled for each study.

* The first words for Templin were for children between 3 and 5 years old, and the latter for those from 6 to 8.

† W and T here indicate figures and examples used in Wellman et al. and Templin, respectively.

Table 3.2 provides some interesting trends that can be studied more closely in further investigation. /f-/ is by far the earliest fricative to appear, being acquired by age 3. Age 4 shows the acquisition of the alveopalatal /č-/, /š-/, and /ǰ-/. The dentals and the voiced labiodental and alveolar fricatives reach criterion between the fifth and sixth year. /s-/ provides a curious development. It reached criterion early in the Templin study, but not until age 5 for Wellman et al. This can be explained by considering how rigid one is in accepting a production as correct. Children under 3 begin to produce an s-like sound, often around the same time as [f-] appears. This sound is not an adult [s], but is very bladed in articulation (see Moskowitz 1970). Ingram et al. (1975)

recently completed a large-sample study on 73 normal children between 2:0 and 5:11 years of age, concentrating just on initial affricates and fricatives. Using the same criterion as Templin and Wellman et al., /f-/ reached acquisition for the group 2:6–2:11. /č-/, /š-/, and /ǰ-/ were acquired at 4:0–4:5. These are the same as above for /θ-/, /s-/, and /z-/, and the percentages were 63, 63, and 50 for the oldest children, the 5:6–5:11 group. This late appearance of /s-/ can be attributed to the fact that three transcribers were used in the study, each making fine phonetic transcriptions. Templin was the only transcriber in her study, and she did not use a tape recorder. Due to the noisy conditions in which she tested, she was forced to do a broad transcription. Results like these demonstrate that /s-/ is not as easy an acquisition as one might expect owing to its wide occurrence in languages of the world. The alveopalatals precede it in articulatory proficiency.

While correctness is one aspect of interest, two other areas of importance will be the focus of this paper. These are the substitutions (or phonological processes) that are used by children in attempting to produce fricatives and initial affricates, and the way these sounds are acquired as a class. The latter refers to how the child may produce these sounds at any time in his development. For instance, if the child makes one fricative into a stop consonant, will this affect other fricatives also? These questions will be asked of the data to be presented from normal and linguistically deviant children.

The most comprehensive study to date on the acquisition of fricatives by young normal children is that of Ferguson (1973). Ferguson examined fricatives in all word positions, using data from both diary and large-sample studies. He also included recent findings on the perception of fricatives. All of these data were discussed in terms of hypotheses on acquisition by Jakobson (1968). The following conclusions from his study are relevant to the study of these sounds in initial position: (1) early in development, words with fricatives tend to be avoided, even if the child has acquired one or more individual fricatives; (2) fricatives are acquired one at a time, and it does not appear that a new feature will spread to all the fricatives simultaneously; and (3) there are three systematic ways that children simplify fricatives. Each of these substitutions is given below with examples.

1. To tighter closure, to stops or affricates, e.g., [ð] → [d]
2. To looser closure, to glides or liquids, e.g., [v] → [w]
3. To acoustically similar fricative, with loss of stridency or place of articulation, e.g., [θ] → [f]

He also noted that tighter closure was especially characteristic of fricatives in an initial position.

While Ferguson discusses the order in which substitutions occur, he does not draw any conclusions concerning the order in which the above processes may occur. Some of Jakobson's observations deal with order as well as the common ways these sounds are simplified. Regarding the first process, he states that "the child first changes fricatives to the corresponding stops *f* to *p*, *s* to *t*" (p. 52). He suggests that the closure process precedes the other processes. As for affricates, he says that "before the child acquires affricates, he substitutes either corresponding stops or fricatives for them, e.g., *t* or *s* for *ts*, and *p* or *f* for *pf*" (p. 56). These two observations predict at least two simplifying stops for affricates, one of closure, and a second of loose closure. This implies that children will use Ferguson's processes 1 and 2 in that order.

Although several of the recent phonological analyses of deviant children include discussions on fricatives and affricates, the only study that has directly addressed this question is a recent brief report by Farwell (1972). She collected phonological data from three linguistically deviant children and compared their use of these sounds with Templin's findings on normal children. In addition, she compared their substitution patterns with those found for normal children by Snow (1963) and Olmsted (1971). Farwell concluded that the deviant children showed very similar patterns of acquisition to those of younger normal children. These results are similar to the second finding reported above.

This brief summary of selected studies reporting on the acquisition of fricatives and affricates reveals some general patterns of acquisition. These sounds develop in predictable ways (with allowances for individual variation) across several years. Both /f-/ and /s-/ are early, although /s-/ may be articulatorily deficient for several years after its first appearance. Alveopalatals develop next, reaching accurate articulation by age 4. The last sounds acquired are the voiced stridents /v-/ and /z-/ and the dentals /θ-/ and /ð-/. Early in their development, children will avoid words with fricatives and affricates in them. Once attempted, the sounds are simplified by phonological patterns. An early process is to tighten the closure of the articulation, which is followed by a loosening of the closure. There may also be changes of the place of articulation (toward an alveolar position) and of stridency (e.g., θ → f). These observations provide a basis for further study of the development of fricatives and affricates in both normal and linguistically deviant children.

METHOD

To examine the phonological processes used with fricatives and affricates as individual sounds and as a class, it is necessary to have data in individual children. Information of this kind is usually found in diary or observational studies. The present study examined the development of these sounds in fifteen normal and fifteen linguistically deviant children. The data from normal children are taken from several diary studies that have appeared over the years as shown in table 3.3.

Table 3.3

Name, Sex, Age, and Investigator(s) of Fifteen Normal Children Examined for Fricative/Affricate Production

Child	Sex	Age	Investigator
1. Ruth C.	F	0:7–3:4	Chamberlain and Chamberlain (1904–5)
2. Hildegard	F	0:8–1:11	Leopold (1947)
3. (no name)	F	1:0–1:10	Pollock (1878)
4. E.	F	1:1–1:5	Nice (1917)
5. Jennika	F	1:3–2:3	Ingram (unpublished diary)
6. Daniel	M	1:4–2:1	Menn (1971)
7. (no name)	F	1:6–1:11	Humphreys (1880)
8. Mollie	F	1:6–2:0	Holmes (1927)
9. G.	F	1:11	Jegi (1901)
10. Ruth H.	F	2:0	Hills (1914)
11. Erica	F	2:0	Moskowitz (1970)
12. Mackie	M	2:2	Albright and Albright (1956)
13. A.	M	2:3–2:11	Smith (1973)
14. Anthony	M	2:4–2:6	Weir (1962)
15. Daphne	F	2:4	Bateman (1916)

These diaries vary greatly in both the richness of data in general and the information on fricatives/affricates in particular. Ironically, some diaries can be good on other aspects of phonology yet poor in data on fricatives and affricates (e.g., Velten 1943)—or vice versa (e.g., Hills 1914). The sources in table 3.3 vary in their data on fricatives and affricates from poor (Chamberlain and Chamberlain 1904–5) to adequate (Menn 1971) to rich (Smith 1973).

The data on deviant children came from fifteen children who have been studied in recent years in eight observational studies. The information on these children is displayed in table 3.4.

The quality of the data from these studies is varied as it is for normal children. In the study by Oller et al. (1972) there are few linguistic forms provided, so the information on fricatives and affricates must be taken from their rules. The Lorentz and Applegate studies deal directly with these sounds, so their data is quite useful. The matching between these children and the normal ones is not precise. Both groups represent children who have not completed their acquisition of initial fricatives and affricates.

From each diary or observational study, information was extracted on each of the nine English word-initial fricatives and affricates (see table 3.1). Using the results from Ferguson (1973) as guidelines, the following questions were asked concerning each sound: were adult words attempted that included the adult sound, and if not, what substitution was used? What was the direction of change in the use of phonological processes across the three patterns described by Ferguson? Finally, what variations might occur between alternate substitutions used by the child at any single period?

Table 3.4

Name, Age (if known), and Investigator of Fifteen Deviant Children
Examined for Fricative/Affricate Production

Child	Sex	Age	Investigator
1. Val	M	*	Oller et al. (1972)
2. Jean	F	*	
3. Vince	M	*	
4. Jay	M	*	
5. Curt	M	*	
6. Bernie	M	3:3	Edwards and Bernhardt (1973)
7. Marc	M	3:3	
8. Jennifer	F	4:5	
9. Christina	F	5:3	
10. David	M	4:0	Lorentz (1974)
11. (3 boys)†	M	4:0; 5:6; 8:6	Applegate (1961)
12. Bert	M	4:0–4:4	Cross (1950)
13. Joe	M	4:6	Lorentz (1972)
14. Ethel	F	5:11–6:2	Hinckley (1915)
15. Kevin	M	6:6	Haas (1963)

* Ages not given, but children said to be between 3:8 and 6:0 years old.
† These are handled as one child since all three showed the same pattern.

In order to compare this information on the sounds, each child was given a grid; adult sounds were listed vertically, the ages in years and months horizontally, and the grid itself showed the child's substitutions. (Table 3.5 presents an example of this.) Infrequent or secondary variations were placed in parentheses. A zero ø indicated omission, and *none* was used when the sound was not attempted in the corpus. A blank was left if no information on a sound was available.

RESULTS FROM THE NORMAL CHILDREN

Order of Acquisition

While the observation of the order of acquisition of the selected sounds was not a primary goal of the study, the following facts were found and can be compared to those described in the second section. First, adult words with initial fricatives and affricates did not occur with any frequency among the first words children attempted. That is, the children did not attempt adult initial fricatives until a small phonetic inventory of stops and nasals had been established in their speech. Daniel, for example, did not attempt any adult words with initial fricatives from the age of 1:4 to 1:10 years. This was also true for Jennika in the early months of acquisition. This result agrees with what Ferguson observed in his study.

Second, adult words with /v-/, /z-/, and /θ-/ remained infrequent in the speech of children throughout the first two years. Words with /f-/ and /s-/, however, occurred frequently; these phonemes also proved to be the first sounds to be used. Nine of the fifteen diaries indicated that the /f-/ was acquired during the observation period, and seven reported the acquisition of /s-/. Of the three infrequent sounds, /θ-/, /z-/, and /v-/, only one child was reported to have acquired /z-/; the others were not acquired. Of the remaining sounds, /ð-/ was the most difficult, with none acquiring it. Therefore, /f-/ and /s-/ were the easiest, /θ-/, /z-/, /v-/, and /ð-/ the most difficult. The others, /š-/, /č-/, and /ǰ-/, fell in between, /č-/ being the earliest of the three.

Rate of Acquisition

Another secondary but interesting result concerned the rate at which these sounds were acquired. It was clear that the children gradually acquired the fricatives and affricates over a period of time. Once a sound appeared, it would fluctuate along with earlier substitutions. This was especially clear in the data from A, which proved to be by far the richest on this topic. Table 3.5 summarizes the substitutions that occurred in A's speech for the nine fricatives and affricates from ages 2:2 to 3:9.

Observe, for example, A's acquisition of /s-/. This sound went through a period of substitution by homorganic stops before correct production resulted. Note the two transition periods that took place during this development. First, the tendency to voice initial stops was eliminated, but only gradually, through a period in which both voiced and voiceless stops occurred, until the tendency to voice was finally suppressed. Next fricatives appeared, but this resulted in a period when the affricate [ts] alternated with [ts] and [s], each in approximately equal frequencies. Then [s] became dominant, but some cases of [ts] still occurred. Finally, [s] was used in all adult instances. This gradual appearance is similar to that observed by Brown (1973) in the acquisition of grammatical morphemes. Like grammatical morphemes, fricatives and affricates are not acquired suddenly, but gradually with increasing percentages of occurrence.

Substitution Paths

In recent years, there has been a growing appreciation of the individual strategies children may follow in acquiring a language (e.g., Ferguson, Peizer, and Weeks 1973). Although children have different alternatives available to them, acquisition cannot follow in an indefinite number of ways. A glance at the various substitutions that the children used gave this initial impression. For example, /f-/ was either deleted or replaced by [b], [p], [w], [t], [s], and [h]

Table 3.5

Fricative/Affricate Production by A. from 2:2 to 3:9 years of age

Age	2:2–2:5	2:6–2:7	2:8	2:9	2:10	2:11	3:0	3:1–3:5	3:6–3:8	3:9
/f-/	w	w (f)			f (w)	f				
/v-/	v w throughout; infrequent consonant									
/θ-/	d	d (t)	t			t, s, ts	s (ts)	s		
/ð-/	(d)	d		d						
/s-/	d (ø)	d t	t			t, s, ts	s (ts)	s		
/z-/	(d)	d r	r					z (infrequent)		
/š-/	d	d (t)	t			t, ts	s (ts)	s		
/č-/	d	d (t)	t			ts		s	s, ts, t	ts, č	č
/ǰ-/	d	d	d (dr)			d, dz			dz (infrequent)	

SOURCE: Smith (1973).

by various children. No less than seven possibilities were used for this sound alone. Elsewhere (Ingram 1974c), in the study of a process I referred to as "fronting," I tried to show that individual variations were still within a broader perspective of acquisition. A closer look at the data on fricatives and affricates shows that this is also the case here. When the various substitutions are studied in terms of their order of occurrence, a striking order is observed. The general pattern is: deletion > stopping > continuance. If stopping is occurring, voicing may appear at first and later be suppressed. If continuance appears, two alternatives occur. The first continuants used are sonorants in the form of liquids or glides. These are later followed by obstruents with some friction. These observations confirm the three patterns observed by Ferguson; I add the finding that they occur in a specific order.

Two common processes interact with this general pattern. One is voicing, an assimilation process children use in their early speech forms. This is a tendency to voice obstruents before a vowel. A child who is stopping /s-/ to [t] may also show voicing, resulting in [d-]. The second process is the fronting of alveopalatals; alveopalatals tend to be replaced by alveolar articulations. The affricate /č-/ may undergo both stopping and fronting and become a [d-].

These two processes need to be kept in mind when examining the general pattern mentioned above.

With these various limitations, the child may then follow his own *substitution path* from when a sound is first attempted to when it is acquired. There are various ways that one child's substitution path may vary from another's. A particular child may not need to use all of the possible simplifying processes. For example, here are some of the possible steps a child could follow in learning to produce /f-/, with examples of children who showed each.

	Steps	/f-/	Example
1.	Avoidance of word with /f-/	none	Daniel 1:4–1:10
2.	Deletion of initial /f/	ø	Daniel 1:11–2:1
3.	Stopping and voicing	b	—
4.	Stopping without voicing	p	Mollie 2:1
5.	Continuance as a glide	w	A. 2:2–2:5
6.	Continuance as an obstruent	ɸ	—
7.	Correctness	f	

Some children may find /f-/ an easy sound to produce and completely skip steps 1–5. Others may commence with step 4, without ever deleting or voicing. No child follows every step. As table 3.2 shows in A's speech, however, several steps may occur. The rate may also vary so that a particular step may be very brief in occurrence. The important point is that *the various potential steps show an invariant order*. A child who is substituting [p], will not proceed to [b] or deletion. He will use either a glide or [ɸ]. He may skip both and go directly to [f-], but he cannot step out of the common pattern.

The individual substitution path may also differ in the place of articulation. Here are hypothetical paths for /č-/ with a variation in place, starting from the use of [t].

A'. t → ts → s → š → č
B'. t → ts → s → ts → č

In A', the alveopalatal place appears before affrication. In B', the affrication occurs before the use of an alveopalatal articulation. The two interacting processes of voicing and fronting (as well as possibly others) can occur in different orders in regard to the invariant order of deletions > stopping > continuance (sonorant) > continuance (obstruent) to create different substitution paths. The fact that some of these may be skipped also adds to the variety.

Throughout, however, there are general principles constraining the degree of variation.

Stages of Acquisition

While the above processes show how an individual fricative or affricate is acquired, they do not speak to how these sounds as a *class* develop. In his article,

Ferguson mentioned that each sound appeared to progress in its own way, and that it was not possible to talk about the acquisition of features per se. While this is generally true, it was found that there were five stages in the data for the acquisition of fricatives and affricates.

Stage 1

This stage characterized the speech of the youngest children in the sample. In this stage, fricatives and affricates are avoided throughout the child's system. They are either not attempted or they are deleted from adult words that contain them.

Here are some examples of Stage 1 systems of fricatives and affricates. The left column indicates the adult target sound and the right ones the ways in which the children produced them. Ages are shown at the bottom of each child's system.

Stage 1

	Daniel	Jennika (1)	Hildegard	Daniel (2)
f	none	none	(w)	ø
v	none	none	(w)	
θ	none	none	none	
ð	none	(d)	d	
s	none	(s)	none	ø
z	none	none	none	ø
š	none	(š)	none	
č	none	none	none	ø
ǰ	none	none	d	ø
	1:4–1:10	1:4	1:11	1:11–2:1

At first these sounds were avoided. When the first attempts occurred, they were either deleted, as Daniel (2) did, or else they were used infrequently. The parentheses indicate sounds that do not occur frequently in the child's speech and are consequently of questionable status.

Stage 2

Around age 2:0 the children begin to consistently attempt to produce these sounds. In this stage, fricatives and affricates are consistently attempted, but the predominant substitution is determined by stopping. Alveopalatal articulations do not occur. One or two continuants may appear.

One child, Ruth H., was in a transition period between stages 1 and 2.

Transition to Stage 2

Ruth H.

f	f
v	none
θ	ø, f
ð	ø, d
s	ø
z	none
š	ø
č	t
ǰ	ø, d

2:0

Her system varied between avoiding and deleting these sounds and producing them as stops.

There are two potential substages of Stage 2. The first would be use of stops for all fricatives and affricates. No system like this was observed in the normal data, suggesting that it is common for one or two continuants to appear with the first attempts at these. The second system, which was well documented in the data, is the predominant use of stopping, without any occurrence of palatal articulations. Here are some examples of Stage 2 systems.

Stage 2

	A (1)	Humphrey	A (2)	Ruth C
f	w	w	f	t
v	v, w	b	v, w	
θ	d	t	t	t
ð	d	d	d	z
s	d	t	t	t
z	d	d	r	
š	d	t	t	t
č	d	t	t	t
ǰ	d	d	d	d
	2:2–2:5	1:6–2:0	2:10	1:4

The blanks in Ruth C.'s column reflect the fact that no data was provided one way or the other on the production of these sounds.

Stage 3

This is the stage where a great deal of development occurs in the acquisition of fricatives and affricates. One could say that this is the *active* period of acquisition of these sounds, which commences with virtually no fricatives and ends with most having been acquired. In this stage, the widespread appearance of continuants takes place. Some stops remain, but the system is predominantly one of continuants. The first attempts at palatal articulations appear.

Two of the children, A (3) and Mollie, were in transition between Stage 2 with the use of stops and Stage 3 where continuants occur. Consequently, they showed a great deal of variation.

Transition to Stage 3

	A (3)	Mollie
f	f	f, p
v	v, w	none
θ	t, ts, s	ø, d, s
ð	d	d
s	t, ts, s	t, s
z	r	none
š	t, ts, s	(š)
č	ts	(č)
ǰ	d, dz	(ǰ)
	2:11–3:0	2:1

There are two potential substages to Stage 3—one in which sonorants are used as the first continuants and a later one in which obstruents are used. In this sample, only the latter usage occurred.

Stage 3

	Jennika (3)	A (4)	E (1)	G
f	f	f	f	f
v	none	v, w	none	w
θ	(s)	s	none	
ð	d	d	d	ø
s	(s)	s	s	s
z	none	z	none	s
š	š, s	s	š	š
č	š, c	s	t	č
ǰ	d	d, dz	d	d
	2:3	3:1	1:5	1:11

Jennika (3) is very early in Stage 3. Fricatives and affricates are occurring, as well as alveopalatals, but there is infrequent use of /s-/ and no attempts at /v-/ or /z-/. A (4) has established the use of fricatives, but not yet attempted palatals. G is a good example of a Stage 3 system.

Stage 4

Large-sample studies like those reviewed earlier have shown that certain fricatives and affricates are acquired very late. Children toward the latter stage of phonological development will show a system wherein *most* of these sounds are correct, except for two or three of the more difficult ones, which will continue to be a problem. Since our sample comprised all young children, only one or two of them could possibly be considered at the beginning of Stage 4. In this stage, most fricatives and affricates are acquired. /θ-/, /ð-/, and perhaps /z-/ and /v-/ have yet to be acquired. Occasional distortion of some of the fricatives may occur, especially with /s-/.

Here are examples of two children who might be considered as being at Stage 4, and one child who appears to be in transition.

	Transition	Stage 4	
	Mackie	Anthony	E (2)
f	f	f	f
v	none	v	v
θ	none	θ, (t)	s
ð	d	ð, d	d
s	s	s	s
z	none	none	(z)
š	š	š	š
č	č	č	č
ǰ	ǰ	ǰ, d, dz	ǰ
	2:2	2:4–2:6	3:0

Since these children are so young, it is questionable that their production is as good as the data reported suggests. A recent study (Ingram et al. 1975) examined these sounds in detail in children from 2:0 to 6:0 and found that Stage 4 was more characteristic of children around 4:0 if a strict criterion of acquisition was imposed. The above data have to be considered with that caution.

Mackie appears to be a child who is very good at acquiring fricatives and affricates. He is in transition, however, in that he still avoids producing words with /v-/, /θ-/, and /z-/. Anthony and E (2) show correct production of most of these sounds. Substitutes still occur, but these are restricted to more troublesome sounds.

Stage 5

This would indicate correct production of all of the English fricatives and affricates. The results from Ingram et al. indicate that this does not occur for most children until after age 6, although by that point the troublesome sounds are occasionally being produced correctly. In this stage, correct production is achieved.

RESULTS FROM THE DEVIANT CHILDREN

Order and Rate of Acquisition

While the data from the normal children provided some information on order of acquisition, those from the deviant children were not so clear. The major problem concerns the way acquisition is defined. With the normal children, there were many instances of each sound observed, and the diary-recorder would say that a sound had been acquired when most productions were correct. The studies for the deviant children primarily used elicitation procedures, so that often only one or few instances of a sound were recorded. Acquisition for the latter consequently would be based on only a small number of productions.

In this light, it can be noted that *none of the fricatives or affricates showed widespread acquisition across subjects.* While these sounds are among those most commonly mispronounced by children, it also appears that virtually all were mispronounced in the more severe cases of those examined. The sound that was produced best was /s-/, with five of the fifteen subjects getting it correct. There was no corresponding higher rate for the correct production of /f-/, which was achieved by only two of fifteen, although two others had [f] varying with [p] for it. /z/, /š/, /č/, and /ǰ/ all had three subjects show correct production. There was only one with correct production for /v-/ and none for /ð-/ and /θ-/.

While the normal children also showed avoidance of words with these sounds in the early stages, it was not possible to study this in the deviant data owing to the elicitation approach that was used in most of the studies. The latter does not allow for selective production.

Regarding rate of acquisition, it is first obvious that the deviant children are much slower, given their older ages. Some of the children showed the kind of variation in production observed in A's speech. Since the elicitation procedure elicited only a few words per sound, however, it was not possible to make a definitive comparison in this aspect. The variation that did exist in samples such as Kevin's (which was a spontaneous sample) did suggest that the acquisition of each sound is gradual, as it is in normal children.

Substitution Paths

The deviant children showed substitution paths that were within the limitations of the general pattern and two phonological processes described for the normal children. There were imbalances between the use of certain options; for example, the target sound was rarely deleted. This does not necessarily mean that deviant children never delete, but it indicates that at a certain age these children are producing some substitution. Stopping was a dominant pattern, as was fronting of palatals. Voicing did not appear as a common pattern in the data. Deletion and voicing were two processes that were suppressed by the children in this sample. Since these were not longitudinal samples, it was impossible to see how the substitutions of individual children changed over time.

One striking observation concerns the production of /f-/. Whereas normal children frequently skipped over the process of stopping this sound, the deviant children did not. Six of the children used a stop, and three others showed variation between a stop and a continuant. This suggests the following very tentative hypothesis: *deviant children are likely to use certain simplifying processes that normal children generally skip.* The substitution path for /s-/ by David is another example of this. He substituted [l], using the pattern of continuance (sonorant). Most normal children manage to go from a stop for /s-/ to an obstruent without the need to use a sonorant.

Another divergent aspect of the production of /f-/ was that of two children, Ethel and Kevin, who produced [t], and of Bert, who produced [s]. The use of an alveolar substitution only occurred with one normal child, Ruth C., who used [t]. Interestingly, Ruth C. did this past her third birthday, suggesting that her development of /f-/ was not particularly normal. If so, this would constitute another example of the hypothesis just mentioned and evidence that /f-/ is not as easy for deviant children to articulate as it is for normal ones.

Stages of Acquisition

The systems of productions for fricatives and affricates in the deviant population can be described within the five stages described for normal subjects. The differences found were that deviant children occasionally would show the simplest system possible within each stage.

Stage 1

Since most of the data for the deviant children came from elicitation procedures, it was not possible to observe cases of this stage.

Stage 2

One child, Ethel, showed a system in transition between stages 1 and 2. Compare her system with that of Ruth C., who was also in this transition.

	Ethel
f	t
v	none
θ	ø, t
ð	(ø)
s	t
z	none
š	t
č	t
ǰ	d

5:11–6:1

Recall that there are two potential parts of Stage 2; in one, all the sounds would be made into stops, and in another, most of them would. Referring to these as stages 2a and 2b, respectively, it was noted earlier that 2b was the one found for normal children. For the deviant children, however, 2a was a common pattern. Even the two deviant children who have systems that fall under 2b have aspects suggesting an earlier Stage 2a.

	Stage 2a		*Stage 2b*	
	Applegate's	*Marc*	*Vince*	*Bernie*
f	p	p	h (p)	p
v	b	b	b	b
θ	t	t	t (h)	t
ð	d	d	d	d
s	t	t	t	s
z	d	d	d	d
š	t	t	h (t)	š, s
č	t	t	t	t
ǰ	d	d	d	d
	4, 5:6, 8:6	3:3	?	3:3

These data suggest that not only are processes such as stopping more persistent in deviant children, they are also more *pervasive*.

Stage 3

One of the children, Jean, appeared to be in transition between stages 2 and 3. Notice that her earlier system with stops is more reminiscent of stage 2a than 2b.

Transition to Stage 3

	Jean
f	f (p)
v	v (b)
θ	f (p)
ð	d
s	t
z	d
š	t
č	š
ǰ	ž
	?

Although it was not stated for the normal children, there are actually two possible substages of Stage 3. These would be as Stage 3 is described earlier with the following additions: in *Stage 3a*, virtually none of the continuants used reflect acquisition of the adult model; and in *Stage 3b*, two or more of the continuants used are correct by adult standards. For the normal children, all could be classified as falling into Stage 3b, since by this point each had acquired at least a few of the English fricatives and affricates. Among the deviant children, however, there were two children at Stage 3a, where continuants were used without acquisition of individual sounds.

	Stage 3a			*Stage 3b*	
	David	Kevin	Christina	Val	Jennifer
f	w	t	f (p)	f	f (p) w
v	b	none	b	v	w
θ	w	θ, s, š	š	t (f)	
ð	d	t	d	d	
s	l	θ, s, š	s	s (t, ts)	s
z	none	z	(t)	s (t, ts)	
s	l	θ, s, š	š, s	č	š
c	tl	?	t	č	t
ǰ	dl	?	d	ǰ	d
	4:0	6:6	5:3	?	4:4

Even Christina is on the borderline of Stage 3a.

Stage 4

There were only two children, Bert and Joe, who had Stage 4 systems. Most of their fricatives and affricates were correct except for a small number of troublesome sounds.

	Stage 4	
	Bert	Joe
f	s	f
v	b	b
θ	s	f
ð	z	ð
s	s	s
z	z	z
š	š	š
č	č	č
ǰ	ǰ	ǰ
	4:0–4:4	4:6

Stage 5

None of the deviant children had reached this stage.

DISCUSSION

In the introductory section of this chapter, five conclusions were presented on what constitutes deviant phonology, based on a comparison of the data on normal and deviant acquisition. These conclusions posed as five hypotheses about what would be found in a comparison of normal and deviant acquisition of a specific phonological topic, in this case the development of word-initial fricatives and affricates. The results of the study confirmed these five hypotheses.

With regard to the first one, it was clear that the deviant children had systematic patterns in their speech. This has been found so frequently in studies on deviant speech (see review in Ingram 1976) that it should be accepted as a basic assumption about deviant phonology.

More interestingly, the processes used by the deviant children to simplify fricatives and affricates were by and large the same ones found in the normal data. Deletion, stopping, the use of processes to produce continuants, and fronting of alveopalatals were all found in both groups, One difference was noted, but it was a case in which the normal children used a process (voicing) that the deviant children did not use. The only candidates for possible deviant processes, i.e., ones that deviant children used but that normal children did not, were the production of alveolars for /f-/, and [l] for /s-/. These uses suggest that the third hypothesis presented earlier is also true, i.e., that certain processes occasionally occur that are either not normal or not frequent in normal speech.

The fourth finding was that certain processes persist in the deviant child's speech. This was the case with stopping, which was characteristic of the speech of many of the deviant children. The fact that certain processes persist and co-occur with later ones can be seen in the stopping of /f-/ to [p]. Whereas normal children seem to overcome this early, the deviant children showed its persistence in several cases. Bernie, for instance, was producing [p] for /f-/ at the same time as he was making [s] for /s-/, and [š] and [s] for /š-/.

Because of the persistence of processes in this fashion, deviant systems come out looking different from those of younger normal children. That is, they are more than just delayed systems. They differ in two respects. First, they may have different variations within any stage. Bernie's system, for example, looked different from that of a normal child at Stage 2. The normal children, if they had any continuants at Stage 2, had them for /f-/ and /v-/. Second, the persistence and pervasiveness of processes result in simpler systems at each stage for the deviant children. It was found that two substages were possible for stages 2 and 3. In each case, the deviant children's samples were more representative of the simpler stage, while the normal ones were in the more advanced stage. This indicates that deviant systems are more than the result of delay. The degree of deviation, however, is still within the limits of more general principles of acquisition.

REFERENCES

Albright, R. W., and Albright, J. B. 1956. The phonology of a two-year-old child. *Word* 12:382–90.

Applegate, J. 1961. Phonological rules of a subdialect of English. *Word* 17:186–93.

Bateman, W. G. 1916. The language status of three children at the same ages. *Ped. Sem.* 6:475–93.

Brown, R. 1973. *A first language: the early stages.* Cambridge: Harvard Univ. Press.

Chamberlain, A. F., and Chamberlain, I. C. 1904–5. Studies of a child. *Ped. Sem.* 11:264–91, 452–83; ibid. 12:427–53.

Compton, A. J. 1970. Generative studies of children's phonological disorders. *J. Speech Hearing Dis.* 35:315–39.

———. 1975. Generative studies of children's phonological disorders: a strategy of therapy. In *Measurements in hearing, speech, and language,* ed. S. Singh. Baltimore: University Park Press.

Cross, E. 1950. Some features of the phonology of a four-year-old boy. *Word* 6:137–40.

Edwards, M. L., and Bernhardt, B. 1973. Twin speech as the sharing of a phonological system. Unpublished paper, Stanford University.

Farwell, C. 1972. A note on the production of fricatives and consonant clusters in linguistically deviant children. *Papers and Reports on Child Language Development* 4:93–101.

Ferguson, C. 1973. Fricatives in child language acquisition. *Papers and Reports on Child Language Development* 6:61–85.

Ferguson, C., and Farwell, C. 1975. Words and sounds in early language acquisition. English initial consonants in the first 50 words. *Language* 51. (Citation in text from version in *Papers and Reports on Child Language Development* 6:1–61 [1973].)

Ferguson, C.; Peizer, D.; and Weeks, T. 1973. Model-and-replica phonological grammar of a child's first words. *Lingua* 31:35–65.

Haas, W. 1963. Phonological analysis of a case of dyslalia. *J. Speech Hearing Dis.* 28:239–46.

Hills, E. C. 1914. The Speech of a child two years of age. *Dialect Notes* 4:84–100.

Hinckley, A. 1915. A case of retarded speech development. *Ped. Sem.* 22:121–46.

Holmes, U. 1927. The phonology of an English-speaking child. *Amer. Speech* 2:219–25.

Humphreys, M. W. 1880. A contribution to infantile linguistics. *Transac. Amer. Philol. Ass.* 11:5–17.

Ingram, D. 1974a. The acquisition of the English verbal auxiliary and copula in normal and linguistically deviant children. In *Developing systematic procedures for training children's language*, ed. L. McReynolds. Amer. Speech and Hearing Assoc. Monog. no. 18, pp. 5–14.

———. 1974b. Phonological rules in young children. *J. Child Language* 1:49–64.

———. 1974c. Fronting in child phonology. *J. Child Language* 1:233–41.

———. 1976. *Phonological disability in children.* London: Edward Arnold.

Ingram, D.; Christensen, L.; Veach, S.; and Webster, B. 1975. The acquisition of word initial fricatives and affricates in English by children between two and six. Research Report, Child Language Project, Stanford University.

Jakobson, R. 1968. *Child language, aphasia, and phonological universals*, trans. A. R. Keiler. The Hague: Mouton.

Jegi, J. 1901. The vocabulary of a two-year-old child. *Child Study Monthly* 6:241–61.

Kornfeld, J. 1971. Theoretical issues in child phonology. *Papers from the Seventh Regional Meeting of the Chicago Linguistic Society*, pp. 454–68.

Lackner, J. 1968. A developmental study of language behavior in retarded children. *Neuropsychologia* 6:310–20.

Leopold, W. 1947. *Speech development of a bilingual child: a linguist's record*, vol. 2, *Sound-learning in the first two years.* Evanston, Ill.: Northwestern University Press.

Lorentz, J. 1972. An analysis of some deviant phonological rules of English. Unpublished paper, University of California, Berkeley.

———. 1974. A deviant phonological system of English. *Papers and Reports on Child Language Development* 8:55–64.

Menn, L. 1971. Phonotactic rules in beginning speech. *Lingua* 26:225–51.

Menyuk, P. 1964. Comparison of grammar of children with functionally deviant and normal speech. *J. Speech Hearing Res.* 7:109–21.

Morehead, D., and Ingram, D. 1973. The development of base syntax in normal and linguistically deviant children. *J. Speech Hearing Res.* 16:330–52.

Moskowitz, A. 1970. The two-year-old stage in the acquisition of English phonology. *Language* 46:426–41.

Nice, M. 1917. The Speech development of a child from eighteen months to six years. *Ped. Sem.* 24:204–43.

Oller, D. K. 1973. Regularities in abnormal child phonology. *J. Speech Hearing Res.* 38:36–47.

Oller, D. K., et al. 1972. Five studies in abnormal phonology. Unpublished paper, University of Washington.

Olmsted, D. 1971. *Out of the mouths of babes*. The Hague: Mouton.

Pollock, E., and Rees, N. 1972. Disorder of articulation: some clinical applications of distinctive feature theory. *J. Speech Hearing Res.* 37:451–61.

Pollock, F. 1878. An infant's progress in language. *Mind* 3:392–401.

Renfrew, C. E. 1966. Persistence of the open syllable in defective articulation. *J. Speech Hearing Res.* 31:370–3.

Smith, N. 1973. *The acquisition of phonology: a case study*. Cambridge: At the University Press.

Snow, K. 1963. A detailed analysis of articulation responses of "normal" first grade children. *J. Speech Hearing Res.* 6:277–90.

Stampe, D. 1969. The acquisition of phonetic representation. *Papers from the Fifth Regional Meeting of the Chicago Linguistic Society*, pp. 443–54.

Templin, M. C. 1957. *Certain language skills in children*. Minneapolis: Univ. of Minnesota Press.

Velten, H. 1943. The growth of phonemic and lexical patterns in infant language. *Language* 19:281–92.

Waterson, N. 1971. Child phonology: a prosodic view. *J. Linguistics* 7:170–221.

Weir, R. 1962. *Language in the crib*. The Hague: Mouton.

Wellman, B. L.; Case, I. M.; Mengert, I. G.; and Bradbury, D. E. 1931. *Speech Sounds of young children*. University of Iowa Studies in Child Welfare no. 5.

Winitz, H. 1969. *Articulatory acquisition and behavior*. New York: Appleton-Century-Crofts.

4

"REGRESSION" AND READING BREAKDOWN

Jane M. Holmes

"REGRESSION" AND READING BREAKDOWN

"Regression" as an explanatory principle was proposed in the context of aphasic language disturbance by Jakobson (1968). He advanced the thesis that the dissolution of the phonological system in aphasia took place in an orderly fashion and reflected the sequence of acquisition of the phonological system by children, but in reverse order. This, he felt, was hardly surprising, since "the phonological acquisition of the child and the sound disturbances of the aphasic are based on the same laws of solidarity as the phonological inventory and the phonological history of all the languages of the world." The reference to "all the languages of the world"—all of which do not share the same phonological systems—should make it clear that Jakobson was not saying that the child learns x after y after z and, therefore, that the aphasic loses x before y before z, but that, given a dependent relation between x and y (in this case, the relation of phonological opposition), if the presence of x depends on the presence of y, then the child will learn y first and the aphasic will lose it last. And in the wider context, a language that has y must have x (though it might have neither).

The greater part of Jakobson's monograph deals, as indicated by the title, with the relationship between "child language, aphasia and phonological universals." However, noting that "phonological, as well as grammatical components of language are subject to the same principle of linguistic stratification" (see Liberman 1970), he goes further and proposes that "a component of this morphological or syntactical system (e.g., a part of speech, a case, a verbal category), which with respect to some other component (another part of speech, case, verbal category) proves to be necessarily secondary, arises in

The data presented herein is from the writer's doctoral thesis presented to the Department of Linguistics at the University of Edinburgh, 1973, while the writer was a member of the Medical Research Council's Speech and Communication Unit. Thanks are given to Dr. John Marshall of the Department of Psychology, University of Edinburgh; to Dr. Freda Newcombe, Churchill Hospital, Oxford; and to Miss Catriona Collins of the Society for the Study of Dyslexia, Edinburgh.

children after, disappears in aphasics before, and does not occur in the languages of the world without, the corresponding primary components."

There is now evidence (see the present volume) to show that Jakobson was going too far in applying "regression" beyond the phonological component of language. However, the fact that "regression" has been found to be an inappropriate explanatory principle for the aphasic disturbance of "grammatical" components of language does not necessarily invalidate Jakobson's principle as it applies to other aspects of language ability.

I would like to present other data for which "regression" is an appropriate explanatory principle; to outline the similarity between these data and those of Jakobson; and to suggest why "regression" may be valid for these two sets of data, but not (or, perhaps, less) so for other components of language.

The data I wish to present are the reading responses of two adult males with dyslexia resultant on brain injury, and of four boys diagnosed as developmental dyslexics.

Dyslexia may be defined as a difficulty with reading. This may involve the disruption of a previously learned and well-practised skill as a consequence of brain damage—that is, acquired or traumatic dyslexia—or it may characterize a "difficulty in learning to read despite conventional instruction, adequate intelligence, and sociocultural opportunity" (Critchley 1970)—that is, developmental dyslexia. The difference between the two dyslexias is important. One would not logically expect a breakdown in the *acquisition* of the reading skill by the child to have all the possible ramifications of a breakdown in the *already acquired* reading ability in the adult. Marshall and Newcombe's (1966) case is an illustrative example.

Their adult patient was asked to read single words printed on cards; he "read" such items as *ill, ancient, city,* etc., as "sick," "historic," and "town," respectively. Marshall and Newcombe characterize this type of behavior as "deep" dyslexia, underlining the difference between this type of "semantic" error and those semantic errors in running text that do not change the overall meaning of the text and that are characteristic of good rather than poor readers; they cite Clay (1969), Gill (1970), and Goodman (1969) as evidence for errors like "mother said" for "mother remarked." These latter errors reflect the ongoing linguistic analysis of the written message; the "deep" errors imply the existence of direct links between the visual array and the more central "lexicon," links that presuppose considerable experience with the reading task, thus ruling out this type of error by the child who is learning the skill.

In their (1973) paper on acquired dyslexia, Marshall and Newcombe describe other types of error involving specific visual perceptual problems and "partial failure of grapheme-phoneme correspondence rules." Visual deficiencies have also frequently been implicated as a factor in developmental dyslexia (see Vernon 1971, for review). Generally, however, "visual deficiency" has been operationally defined as performance on psychological tests of visual, perceptual, and/or spatial ability; there is little data on the nature of actual reading errors, with the result that a comparison of the visual perceptual errors of acquired as opposed to developmental dyslexia has still to be carried out.

The investigation to be reported here concerns the role of grapheme-phoneme correspondence rules. In the analysis of the errors made by the men with acquired dyslexia it was felt that their patterns of error were also characteristic of those of children who had difficulty learning to read. Preliminary testing revealed that this was indeed the case, and formed the basis for the more extensive comparison.

The two adult males, J.C. and S.T., sustained severe penetrating wounds to the left temporoparietal region of the brain during the latter part of World War II at the ages of 20 and 24, respectively. The most recent neurological examinations (25 and 26 years after injury) revealed marked impairment in reading, writing, and oral spelling, with, however, average scores on a variety of nonverbal performance tasks. In the case of J.C., spontaneous speech showed no impairment, being fast, fluent, grammatical—and amusing; in the case of S.T., spontaneous speech was reasonably fluent and grammatical, although occasional word-finding and dysarthric difficulties were apparent (see Holmes 1973, for further details).

The four boys were aged between 9 and 13 years and had all experienced difficulties in learning to read. The performance of the boys when attempting to read—their overt spelling of the experimental material, either by sound or by letter name—supports the general finding that the problem for children who are not making progress in learning to read does not lie in the visual identification of individual letters (Doehring 1968; Shankweiler 1964). Compare traumatic dyslexia where specific visual perceptual problems constitute one pole of a continuum (Marshall and Newcombe 1973).

The phenomenon of "developmental dyslexia" is widely considered to reflect a delay in maturation, rather than direct morbidity (Bender 1957; Doehring 1968; Harris 1957; Ilg and Ames 1950; Ingram 1963; Lyle 1969; Lyle and Goyen 1968; Newton 1970; Olson 1973; Schonell 1940; Wechsler and Hagin 1964; Zurif and Carson 1970). Some dyslexic children continue to make errors that are appropriate to an earlier stage in the acquisition of the reading skill; their performance can be regarded as a prolongation of the acquisition process rather than as a deviation from it. This means that the immature strategy (that is, the strategy of the "normal" child at an earlier stage) can still be seen in these children in the context of a more sophisticated vocabulary, which can be compared to that of an adult. This was considered to be the case in the present instance.

The six subjects were required to read over 800 words that were individually typed on plain white cards; each subject took as long as he wished to respond. The words had been chosen to represent a wide range of initial, medial, and final vowel and consonant graphemes. It was considered unnecessary for the subjects to attempt to read connected text, since the major problem for these subjects was already manifest at the level of the word (Shankweiler and Liberman 1972).

Responses were tape-recorded and tran. ribed phonetically. Care was taken to establish the accuracy of the observer's interpretation of the status of responses; subjects were frequently asked to give the meaning of a response or to use it in a sentence. Differences in the phonetic transcription in the text resulted from the differences in the subjects' dialects—those of Liverpool and Belfast, and four varieties of Scottish English.

Before going on to examine the nature of the subjects' errors, some aspects of the task that the would-be reader faces should be noted, and some discussion devoted to the more general relation between reading and listening. The long-standing, and apparently unquestioned, assumption that the sounds of speech are merely the vehicle for language and bear no organic relation to it has been shown by Liberman and his colleagues to be untenable. Liberman, Cooper, Shankweiler, and Studdert-Kennedy (1967) demonstrated that the sounds of speech are typically transmitted in parallel and not in sequence; the segments in the acoustic message do not correspond to the segments in the phonetic message, and in this sense the acoustic signal can be considered a code. Liberman et al. contrast the "code" of spoken language with the "cipher" of written language: "In writing and reading it is possible to communicate phonemes by means of a cipher or alphabet; indeed there appears to be no better way. Spoken or written language differ, then, in that the former must be a complex code while the latter can be a simple cipher." Liberman (1970) has further maintained that the code nature of speech argues for speech being considered an integral part of language, which is commonly seen as a structure that contains successive recodings of linguistic information, the concept of coding being basic to the theory of language.

The code–cipher distinction, as it pertains to spoken and written language, is more apparent than real, however; mature reading ("language for the eye"— I. Y. Liberman 1971) relies just as much on a complex (de)coding process, though in a different way, as speaking and hearing do ("language for the ear"— ibid).

Although "language for the ear" is received in parallel, it is perceived in terms of phonemic categories that are not present as separate units in the acoustic wave but that are abstracted from the input by the language user at a cortical level (the specialized "neural apparatus" of Mattingly and Liberman [1969] perhaps? See also Blumstein, this volume). For the permanent visual record of language, translation from the auditory stimuli to the visual is mediated by this central representation, and it is, for an alphabetically written language, in terms of the phonemic categories that the visual representation is effected. At this point, then, the alphabetically written language might be regarded as Liberman et al.'s (1967) "simple cipher" in that the relationship of "language for the eye" to the centrally represented phonemic categories appears to be closer than that of "language for the ear": the individual configurations of the permanent visual record match the phonemic categories in a (near perfect) one-to-one relation.

But psychological research has shown that reading does not—indeed, cannot—take place on a deciphering basis. Early experimental work demonstrated that we read "par saccades" (Javal 1878) jumping from one fixation point to the next; that perception only occurs at the points of fixation (Erdmann and Dodge 1898)—thus indicating that we sample our visual environment discretely rather than take in information continuously; and that at the point of fixation, a word can be read as easily as a letter, and a short phrase as easily as a word (Cattell 1885)—which suggests that the structure of what is seen interacts with the seeing. More recent work shows that it takes 40 msecs to process just one character (Sternberg 1966) but that a skilled reader can read at 1,000 words, or 6,000 characters per minute (Bower 1970). Clearly, deciphering is not the key to the visual aspect of the reading process.

Decoding, however, may be the key—decoding, that is, on the basis of both "featural" (visual) and "sequential (linguistic) constraints" (Smith 1971), processing the input in "chunks" (Miller 1956), and trading off knowledge as to what must be the structure of the material read (because of the rules of the language in question) against the minimal visual differentiating features across words and word groups—which seems to be precisely what both the acquired and developmental dyslexics, as evidenced by the nature of their errors, are not able to do.

The majority of the errors from all six subjects are "literal," that is, they reflect a "partial failure of grapheme-phoneme correspondence rules" (Marshall and Newcombe 1973). They can be subsumed under the general rubric of "ambiguity" or, in linguistic terms, "context sensitivity." It is a well-known fact of English orthography that the correct phonetic values for graphemes often cannot be assigned in a single, left-to-right pass over the individual letters of a word; the unit of visual-to-acoustic coding is bigger than a letter. For example, the sound-value associated with the *a* in *fan, father,* and *fade,* is influenced by the context in which the letter appears.

The characteristics of English orthography have been described by Venezky (1969). He outlined one regularity as follows: "in the word-final patterns VC*e* (vowel + consonant + *e*), *e* generally indicates the free pronunciation of V. Thus, *mate: mat, mete: met, site: sit, note: not, cute: cut*" (Venezky 1969). This can be stated as a context-sensitive rule: a "primary spelling unit" (a vowel) is to be pronounced as its "free alternant" when followed by C*e*, or PSU → FrAlt./ -C*e*. This statement expresses what I have called "rule of *e*"; errors that can be described in terms of the nonoperation of this "rule" are a standard feature of all six corpora—viz., from J.C., *bike* → [ˈbɪk]; *unite* → 'unit'; from S.T., *lace* → [ˈlas]; *describe* → [dɪsˈkrɪb]; from J.B., *clothes* →

'cloths'; *wage* → 'wag'; from M.C., *code* → 'cod'; *pane* → 'pan'; from T.C., *code* → 'cod'; *unite* → 'unit'; from R.E., *fade* → [ˈfab]; *quite* → [ˈkwɪt].

It is the occurrence in the errors of all six subjects of such regular patterns of failure of the "rules" for grapheme-phoneme correspondence that has given rise to the classification of the errors, a subset of which is outlined below. With few exceptions all subjects produce examples of all the "grapheme-phoneme" types of error. I will, therefore, restrict the data presented here to a few significant examples of each type; full details of the transcription and analysis can be found in Holmes (1973).*

"Rule of *e*" errors have been illustrated above. The regular nature of the assignment of a phonetic realization to *c* and *g* can also be expressed by a "rule": with few exceptions, *c* is pronounced /s/ when followed by *e*, *i*, or *y*, and /k/ in all other contexts; similarly, but with rather more exceptions (see Venezky 1969), *g* is pronounced /dʒ/ when followed by *e*, *i*, or *y*, and /g/ in other contexts. The "ambiguous" nature of these two orthographic symbols creates a problem for the subjects who make errors in both directions. Thus, for *c*: *cactus* → [ˈkastʌs] 'castors'; *certain* → 'carton'; *delicious* → [ˈdɛlɪkʌs]; *insect* → 'insist'; for *g*: *beggar* → 'badger'; *gorge* → (for the adults) [ˈgɔrg] or [ˈkoug, ˈgoug, ˈgɒg] (for the children) 'George'†; *logic* → [ˈlɒgɪ, ˈlɒgɒs, ˈlɒgɪ]; *margin* → [ˈmagən]; *recognise* → [ˈrɛkʌdʒ]; *strange* → 'string'; *strength* → 'strange'.

Ambiguity can also be considered a feature of the so-called silent consonants, which have, in some contexts, no phonemic realization; the subjects attempted to assign a pronunciation nonetheless. Examples include *bristle* → 'Bristol'; *calm* → 'column'; *debt* → [diˈbɛt]; *island* → [ˈɪzlənd]; *listen* → 'Liston' (glossed as "the boxer"); *muscle* → 'musical'; *subtle* → [ˈsʌbtʌɪl].

---

* Several points should be made here:

1. For all subjects there are many instances of responses that sound as if they are lexical items but that are evidently not recognized as such (the subject may not know the meaning when asked, or he may say that there is no such word, or that he "can't get it"). Sometimes an appropriate pronunciation is given before "the penny drops" and he recognizes a lexical item, signaling this recognition by a change in his voice. In the text, nonrecognized items are in phonetic transcription, recognized items are in single quotation marks, e.g., S.T.'s response for *lace*, i.e., [ˈlas], is not *lass* for S.T. at this moment.

2. With respect to the boys it was not the case that they were giving a wrong response, because the correct response was unknown to them; in most cases stimulus words could be shown to be part of their speaking vocabulary.

3. In categorizing the erroneous responses a single response frequently had double or even triple classification as a natural result of the individual item's complexity: for example, M.C.'s response [lʌˈgʌɪdⵏ] for *legible* exhibits erroneous stress placement, choice of incorrect member of the ambiguous *g* pair, and a "visual" error of *d* for *b*.

4. The tendency of all subjects, but particularly of the adults, to respond with genuine (if incorrect) lexical items may result in "regularization" of a response; for example, the postulated pronunciation [*ˈmɪzə] for *miser* will suffice to evoke *misery* for J.C.

† This difference presumably reflects long exposure to the written form of the language, as in the case of the two men before injury, which results in a greater attention to cues like the presence or absence of such things as upper-case letters; these did not worry the children at all.

The *g* can also be "silent," not only alone, as in *design*, but also in clusters, as in *daughter*, or worse, in the *-ough* group (so notorious for the foreigner learning English). It is also relevant to note the salience of *g* as a visual unit, since it is one of the few graphemes with an element descending below the line. Errors from the subjects for such ambiguities include *foreign* → 'forgiven' (twice) and 'forage'; *fought* → 'forget', 'forgot'; *reign* → 'region'; *rough* → 'rug' (twice).

The boys in particular found another "ambiguous" occurrence troublesome, viz., the *ch* cluster; they all gave /tʃ/ for *ch* in those contexts where the correct realization is /k/, e.g., *anchor*, *character*, *monarch*, etc.

In the above examples, with the exception of "rule of *e*," it was the ambiguity of consonant graphemes that prompted the error. The fact that consonant graphemes were involved probably accounts for the ease of recognition of the principle of error, since consonant graphemes are generally thought of as relatively unambiguous: *t*, let us say, still belongs to the phoneme /t/ whether it occurs in *pat*, *top*, or *tin*, although the *t*s are not, phonetically speaking, identical. The possible pronunciations of the vowel graphemes, on the other hand, are numerous: the relationship of the orthographic representation to the phonetic realization is on a one-to-many basis. Accordingly, assigning a phonetic realization to vowel graphemes was very difficult for these subjects.

Errors on vowels were generally of two types. The first type occurs when the subject ignored one element of a vowel group, either the first or the second: *beat* → 'bet'; *quiet* → 'quit'; *shoe* → 'show'; *feather* → 'father'; or based a phonetic realization on a wrong analogy, as in 'breed' for *bread*, [ˈaun] for *own*, 'repair' for *reappear*.

Not only segmental but suprasegmental features can be ambiguous. None of the six subjects appear to have a regular guide to stress placement, particularly in disyllabic words where stress is moved from the appropriate place on the first syllable to the second syllable, and vice versa. Examples include *amuse* → 'Amos', *begin* → 'beggin'' (glossed as "when you ask someone"), *concert* → 'consent', *omit* → '(Mah) omet', *recent* → 'resent', *revise* → 'rivers', *routine* → 'rotten'. (Some readers may argue that at least some of these errors can be attributed to the visual similarity of stimulus and response words. To some extent such a judgment must remain a matter of personal bias.)

It was one of the subjects, J.C., who illumined the nature of the errors and thus of the problem. Presented with *affront*, he said "'often—can't be 'often', there's a *t* in it"; with *crumb*, "the *b*'s not supposed to be there, is it? [ˈkrɒm . . . ˈkrɒmba . . . ˈkrɒmba . . . ˈkrɒm]" (but he puts it there); with *glisten*, "that's [lɪs . . . ˈlɪstən], it's the *g* that's got me puzzled, there's a *g* on it [gəˈlɪstən], but I don't know what the *g* means"; with *once*, "'once' [ɒn . . . ɒns] not 'once', 'once' is *w*, isn't it?"; with *our*, "[ˈawə], not [ˈawə . . . ˈawə] starts with an *h*"; with *persuade*, "[ˈpɜs] this *u* doesn't seem to be there—silly place to put it."

What J.C. seems to be saying, here and elsewhere, is that if a grapheme is there it ought to have a phonetic value, and if not, not. In other words, what he wants to do is to assign a phonetic value to each grapheme on a left-to-right pass. But the ambiguities of English orthography are usually resolved "after the event"; the context that a given item is sensitive to is most often that which follows it. Therefore, to be able to read one has to be able to take in information in chunks, to process it in parallel, both for the information about the grapheme that is available from the following graphemes and for the featural cues that operate over the groups of letters encompassed in each fixation of the eyes (Smith 1971).

But this is the coding that the subjects should be doing in order to read. When these subjects gave an erroneous response, however, a failure of coding occurred; they were operating at the level of the cipher. Descriptively, it is as though cerebral injury in the case of the men, and some as yet unexplained developmental factor in the case of the boys, had resulted in their being unable to "hold in mind" and process the sequence of graphemic items over which linguistic mapping rules operate.

The foregoing comparison of the reading performance of adults and children on the same material has highlighted the fact that the performances are equivalent insofar as the same analysis will account fully and economically for both, and in fact, many of the errors, not just the types of error, are common to both. This equivalence argues for a common theoretical base for the two types of dyslexia, one that should properly be treated within the larger framework of a theory of reading when such becomes available. It also suggests that the brain-damaged adult is operating at the level of the child who has yet to make the crucial step toward full literacy; in this sense the adult may be said to have regressed.

In the historical context this notion, that because of brain damage the adult has regressed to an earlier stage of development, in this case, of reading skill, marks an important shift in emphasis in the consideration of the two dyslexias.

It was the medical fraternity that first recognized the existence of developmental dyslexia—known then as "congenital word blindness" (Hinshelwood 1895, 1900). The early neurologists viewed the deficit in children in the light of their experience with "word blindness" resulting from brain injury in adults. They did note, and laid great emphasis on, the similarity of the reading performances of children to those of adults and consequently attempted to explain the two manifestations of the deficit in the same—neurological—terms. Knowing that word blindness in the adult followed injury to the left hemisphere of the brain and being able with reasonable accuracy to localize the damaged area in the parieto-occipital region, the early workers in this field postulated similar damage to the angular and supramarginal gyrus areas in the child with specific reading disability (see Critchley 1970, for review). The extreme nature of this point of view, then—as now—unsupported by any "hard" pathological findings, was unfortunate in that it provoked a strong reaction in later researchers and led to dyslexia in children being studied as a distinct entity with no reference to the performances of adults.

It seems that we have come full circle and that the emphasis of the early neurologists was wrongly placed. Developmental dyslexia is not (as they thought) like acquired dyslexia; what is interesting is that acquired dyslexia is like developmental dyslexia. Brain lesions take apart what the child is trying to put together.

It is now relevant to ask in what respects the data from dyslexia described here, and Jakobson's phonological data, might be considered to be alike. I would like to propose that they are both, in a sense, "once and for all learned" skills and, beyond a certain point and unlike other aspects of the language hierarchy, are not susceptible to modification with experience.

Take the case of "language for the ear" first. The normal child learns the phonological structure of his mother tongue well within the preadolescent period: articulatory skills are essentially those of the adult by the age of six. Once learnt there is little change in the overall phonological structure of the individual's ideolect. This is a necessary concomitant of the social nature of language. The child is pressured to join the linguistic community; only relatively small deviations from the linguistic patterns of that community can be tolerated in the individual if communication is to be maintained within and between generations. The available evidence suggests that this "once and for all" learning of the phonological structure of language does not obtain equally for the lexical and possibly more general semantic aspects of language, the organization of which is modified in the course of the individual's interaction with his environment. Evidence from neurobehavioral studies (Lenneberg 1967; Perlstein and Sugar 1954), and from psychology (Brown and Berko 1960; Ervin-Tripp 1961; Holmes and Marshall unpublished data; Reiss 1946; Werner and Kaplan 1952) highlights the qualitative change in brain and behavior relations (including language behaviors) that appears to be coincident with the attainment of adult status from a reproductive point of view.

Language behavior is modified in a way that implies a progressive structuring of lexical organization (Anglin 1970), a process that continues to be modified as new experiences require integration within the individual's linguistic capacity. This is not the case for the development of the phonological categories, which, once learnt, do not tolerate significant change.

The evidence from the present study reveals how one aspect of "language for the eye" is like the phonological component of "language for the ear." The grapheme-phoneme correspondence in reading and the phonological component of speaking and hearing are learned once and for all and are mediated by categories of units that tolerate little modification. They both differ from those aspects of language that characterize experience and are thus modified by new experience. This divorce of the "medium" from the "message" is clearly seen in reading. Everyone who has learned to read a foreign language can testify to the distinction between reading as a mechanical behavior and reading with comprehension.

There is a dearth of information speaking specifically to the acquisition of the grapheme-phoneme correspondence level of language in nonliterate adults, but it seems unlikely that learning to read in adulthood, at least at this level, would differ from learning to read as a child, which means that someone who learned to read as an adult and then suffered brain damage could, if conditions so disposed, be a literal dyslexic in the same way as the two adult dyslexics under discussion here. If this is true, it suggests that regression as it applies to the acquisition and dissolution of the phonological system is only accidentally a case of an adult regressing to the state of the child; it is because first-language phonological systems have to be learned at a critical period in development that this impression is formed. The conclusion to be drawn from the literal dyslexia data is that the initial once and for all learning of the skill and the subsequent lack of significant modification explains why regression is applicable at this level of language breakdown and not at other, more central, levels.

REFERENCES

Anglin, J. M. 1970. *The growth of word meaning.* Cambridge, Mass.: M.I.T. Press.

Bender, L. 1957. Specific reading disability as a maturational lag. *Bull. Orton Soc.* 7:9–18.

Bower, T. G. R. 1970. Reading by eye. In *Basic studies in reading,* ed. H. Levin and J. Williams. New York: Basic Books.

Brown, R., and Berko, J. 1960. Word association and the acquisition of grammar. *Child Devel.* 31:1–4.

Cattell, McK., Jr. 1885. Uber die Zeit der Erkennung und Bennennung von Schriftzeichen, Bildern und Farben. *Philosophische Studien* 2:635–50.

Clay, M. M. 1969. Reading errors and self-correction behavior. *Brit. J. Educ. Psychol.* 39:47–56.

Critchley, McD. 1970. *The dyslexic child.* London: Heinemann.

Doehring, D. G. 1968. *Patterns of impairment in specific reading disability.* Bloomington: Indiana Univ. Press.

Erdmann, B., and Dodge, R. 1898. *Psychologische Untersuchungen uber das Lesen, auf experimentaller Grundlage.* Halle.

Ervin-Tripp, S. M. 1961. Changes with age in the verbal determinants of word association. *Am. J. Psychol.* 74:361–72.

Gill, V. 1970. Factors affecting the comprehension of written English texts. Term paper, Department of Linguistics, University of Edinburgh.

Goodman, K. S. 1969. Analysis of oral reading miscues: applied psycholinguistics. *Reading Res. Quart.* 5:9–30.

Harris, A. J. 1957. Lateral dominance, directional confusion and reading disability. *J. Psychol.* 44:283–94.

Hinshelwood, J. 1895. Word-blindness and visual memory. *Lancet* 2:1564–70.

———. 1900. *Letter-, word-, and mind-blindness.* London: H. K. Lewis.

Holmes, J. M. 1973. Dyslexia: a neurolinguistic study of traumatic and developmental disorders of reading. Ph.D. thesis, University of Edinburgh.

Ilg, F. L., and Ames, L. B. 1950. Developmental trends in reading behavior. *J. Genet. Psychol.* 76:291–312.

Ingram, T. T. S. 1963. Delayed development of speech with special reference to dyslexia. *Proc. Roy. Soc. Med.* 56:199–203.

Jakobson, R. 1968. *Child language, aphasia, and phonological universals,* trans. A. R. Keiler. The Hague: Mouton.

Javal, E. 1878. Sur la physiologie de la lecture. *Annales d'Oculistique* 82:242–53.

Lenneberg, E. H. 1967. *The biological foundations of language.* New York: Wiley.

Liberman, A. M. 1970. The grammars of speech and language. *Cogn. Psychol.* 1:301–23.

Liberman, A. M.; Cooper, F. S.; Shankweiler, D. P.; and Studdert-Kennedy, M. 1967. Perception of the speech code. *Psychol. Rev.* 74:431–61.

Liberman, I. Y. 1971. Basic research in speech and lateralization of language: some implications for reading disability. *Status Report on Speech Research,* Jan.–June 1971. Haskins Laboratories SR-25/26. 51–66.

Lyle, J. G. 1969. Reading retardation and reversal tendency. *Child Devel.* 40:833–43.

Marshall, J. C., and Newcombe, F. 1966. Syntactic and semantic errors in paralexia. *Neuropsychologia* 4:169–76.

———. 1973. Patterns of paralexia. *J. Psycholing. Res.* 2:175–99.

Mattingly, I. G., and Liberman, A. M. 1969. The speech code and the physiology of language. In *Information processing in the nervous system,* ed. K. N. Leibovic. Berlin: Springer-Verlag.

Miller, G. A. 1956. The magical number seven, plus or minus two: some limits on our capacity for processing information. *Psychol. Rev.* 63:81–97.

Newton, M. 1970. A neuropsychological investigation into dyslexia. In *The assessment and teaching of dyslexic children,* ed. A. W. Franklin and S. Naidoo. London: Invalid Children's Aid Association.

Olson, M. E. 1973. Laterality differences in tachistoscopic word recognition in normal and delayed readers in elementary school. *Neuropsychologia* 11:343–50.

Perlstein, M. A., and Sugar, O. 1954. Hemispherectomy in infantile hemiplegia. *Arch. Neurol Psychiat.* 73:256–7.

Riess, B. F. 1946. Genetic changes in semantic conditioning. *J. Exp. Psychol.* 36:143–52.

Schonell, F. J. 1940. The relation of reading disability to handedness and certain ocular factors: pt. I. *Brit. J. Educ. Psychol.* 10:227–37.

Shankweiler, D. 1964. A study of developmental dyslexia. *Neuropsychologia* 1:267–86.

Shankweiler, D., and Liberman, I. Y. 1972. Misreading: a search for causes. In *Language by ear and by eye,* ed. J. F. Kavanagh and I. G. Mattingly. Cambridge, Mass.: M.I.T. Press.

Smith, F. 1971. *Understanding reading*. New York: Holt, Rinehart and Winston.

Sternberg, S. 1966. High speed scanning in human memory. *Science* 153:652–4.

Venezky, R. L. 1969. *The structure of English orthography*. The Hague: Mouton.

Vernon, M. D. 1971. *Reading and its difficulties*. Cambridge: at the University Press.

Wechsler, D., and Hagin, R. A. 1964. The problem of axial rotation in reading disability. *Percep. Mot. Skills* 19:319–26.

Werner, H., and Kaplan, E. 1952. The acquisition of word meanings: a developmental study. *Soc. Res. Child Devel. Monog.* 15:84.

Zurif, E. G., and Carson, G. 1970. Dyslexia in relation to cerebral dominance and temporal analysis. *Neuropsychologia* 8:357–61.

II
PROCESSING OF SYNTAX
AND MEANING

The ten chapters in this section offer comparisons between language acquisition and disruption at different levels of description and from different perspectives. These contributions, however, do not lend themselves to a tidily organized sequence of concerns. At best, there is a rough progression to be discerned, from analyses of a limited number of grammatical morphemes, through analyses of more basic intra-sentence relations, to a consideration of a number of nonlinguistic variables; each of these analyses, in turn, being anchored to a certain amount of neurological theorizing.

Goodglass's contribution opens this section and reflects his role of discussant in the symposium from which this volume grew. His chapter summarizes some of the analyses that follow and attempts to account for them within the framework of a tentative physiological model. Chapters 6 and 7, by Berko Gleason and de Villiers, respectively, deal with language production, focusing on linguistic and nonlinguistic variables involved in the production of grammatical formatives—the ability to handle number and tense agreement and the like. In contrast, chapters 8 through 11, by Caramazza and Zurif; Scholes; Whitaker and Selnes; and Lenneberg et al., examine sentence comprehension, especially the ability of children and aphasics to process basic semantic roles.

This ability is analyzed in terms of processes roughly divided as lexical, syntactic, semantic, and in the light of nonlinguistic and physiological variables. This is followed by Zaidel in Chapter 12 with details of the individual language capacities of the two cerebral hemispheres—details that are offered from the unique vantage point of an analysis of the hemispheric disconnection syndrome.

The perspective is shifted yet again in each of the last two chapters of this section. In Chapter 13, Cermak focuses on memory in the service of language, particularly on word retention, and on language in the service of memory. In Chapter 14, Gardner considerably expands the scope of the developmental-dissolution comparison. Language performance is placed in the context of a wide variety of human symbolic behaviors—behaviors as diverse as object naming, sensitivity to metaphor, and sensitivity to artistic style.

What emerges from these varied analyses is that both the child and the adult aphasic are less-than-normal language processors. Yet, the limitations in each population afford some clarity concerning the levels involved in sentence processing and suggest some of the sorts of procedures likely to be engaged when mediating between sound and meaning.

The acquisition of linguistic skills

seems to be governed by both grammatical and semantic complexity and to be characterized by the learning and organization of heuristic strategies. To emphasize the obvious, the procedures the child applies to linguistic data become increasingly regularized and deterministic and correspondingly less reliant on diagnostic indicators such as word order. To be sure, the comparative data from aphasia highlight this orderly progression. But the data gained from brain-damaged adults do more than just fulfill this standard comparative function. They offer insights into language processing that are simply not available from an examination of language development. As the following chapters will make clear, focal brain damage does not run the film of development backward. Nor does it lead to an across-the-board reduction in language. Rather, lesions seem to be quite selective in the manner in which they undermine language.

A problem here, of course, is to determine whether this selectivity reflects distinctions that are made in linguistic theories among components in a grammar. As some contributors emphasize, there is little likelihood of establishing an exact correspondence between physiological and linguistic hierarchies. Yet, even granting this claim, the clinical fact remains that there are specific patterns of sparing and disruption—a fact to which models of sentence comprehension and production should be responsive. In this sense, then, the brain-damaged adult is a deficient language processor, but he is deficient in an instructive fashion.

5

ACQUISITION AND DISSOLUTION OF LANGUAGE

Harold Goodglass

To what extent is the dissolution of language in aphasia a regression along the lines laid down during the individual's acquisition of speech? To pose the question in this way is to ask more than whether there are surface similarities or analogies between the deficit in aphasia and incomplete language acquisition. Rather, it is to ask whether the aphasic is compelled, in some respect, to back-track to earlier learned operations. Such backtracking might be explained in terms of the greater stability of earlier behavior patterns (Ribot's law) or in terms of physiological similarities between the language mechanisms of the child and those of the aphasic. In the course of this paper I shall develop the argument that parallel physiological limitations impose certain parallels in performance.

It is easy to be trapped by the attractiveness of a regression hypothesis into making sweeping analogies between the development and the dissolution of language abilities. One such effort was made by Wepman and Jones (1967) when they proposed, in somewhat tentative fashion, that the varieties of aphasia could be scaled so as to correspond to the stages of development of speech in the child—that is, the major aphasic syndromes could be regarded as steps in a scale of regression.

While few persons would quarrel with placing the global aphasic on a par with the preverbal child, there are serious difficulties with the Wepman-Jones hierarchy as soon as one examines the stages in descending order. The acquisition of syntax by the child is treated as the highest stage of language development. Correspondingly, the aphasic with the highest level of residual language is considered to be the "syntactic" or agrammatic patient, who has a vocabulary of contentives but is deficient in syntax. Yet two stages further along on the Wepman-Jones scale of regression, we find the "pragmatic aphasic," who produces a syntactically organized jargon of both real and neologistic words.

This work was supported in part by National Institutes of Health grants NS 06209 to Boston University School of Medicine and NS 07615 to Clark University.

In fact, looking at a transcript of the speech of a pragmatic aphasic, we find that he is capable of using the perfect tense and such embedded constructions as, "Well all I know is somebody is clipping the kreples." A little later in the same passage we find, "Now this here, I'm confoy here, because the have explained what I don't know." One may wonder how the most advanced—the syntactic—stage of language is functioning in a type of aphasia that is low in the developmental hierarchy, while the least-regressed aphasic syndrome is lacking in syntax.

The best argument against scaling aphasic syndromes in a hierarchy of this type is the evidence from patterns of recovery. The patient with grammatically fluent, but anomic and paraphasic, speech (Wernicke's aphasia) never evolves into a patient with agrammatic speech made up of predominantly contentive words; nor does the reverse pattern of recovery occur. The reason for this is that the nature of the language disorder is a function of the locus of the causative lesion, and the lesion does not migrate during the course of recovery. It is true that the zone of dysfunction may shrink in the aftermath of a cerebral insult, as the edema and associated physiological disruption subside. However, as the language deficit diminishes, the final residuals are determined—not by any developmental hierarchy, but by the site of the permanent destructive lesion and its specific effect on the language system. It is only within one linguistic component at a time, be it syntax, phonology, or lexicon, that we can discern parallels between the order of acquisition and the order of breakdown.

Thus, if we are to find a common explanation for the forms of undeveloped language and damaged language, it will not come from a comparison between aphasic syndromes. Yet there are a group of observations which, I propose, may be tied together to suggest such a common mechanism. These observations involve the changing pattern of acquired aphasia from childhood to adulthood, one that is paralleled by differences between patterns of aphasia in right-handers and left-handers. The basic observation is that acquired aphasia in young children is much more undifferentiated than it is in adults. Instead of selectively impaired articulation in association with anterior lesions and selectively impaired auditory comprehension with posterior lesions, in young children, any lesion in the speech area of the right or left hemisphere is reported (Guttman 1942) to result in a similar uniform reduction in language. This suggests that something approaching equipotentiality of representation of all the elements of language throughout the anatomical speech zones is the condition that obtains in early childhood.

To a lesser extent, the same observation can be made concerning left-handers. The notion that left-handers, like young children, have an unlateralized cerebral organization is widely suggested (e.g., Subirana 1969; Conrad 1949; Hécaen and DeAjuriaguerra 1963). The reasons for this belief are first, that standard aphasic syndromes, well differentiated by site of lesion, are uncommon in left-handers. Hécaen and Angelergues (1965), for example, report that selective impairment of auditory comprehension does not occur in left-handers. Wepman's (1951) experience was that left-handers almost never developed a true aphasia. There is also compelling evidence from the series of Luria (1970); Gloning, Gloning, Haub, and Quatember (1969); Conrad (1949); and Goodglass and Quadfasel (1954) that patients who have a personal or familial pattern of non-right-handedness show, in common with children, a tendency to recover relatively rapidly from aphasia.

All this leads to a suggestion that, in the early stages of language acquisition, each language act recruits neurons over the full spread of the perisylvian language areas bilaterally. During the period in which overt language skill is developing, I suggest that the most compact, rapidly acting systems in the brain survive, while the slower, less efficient components of the neural network drop out of the processing of language. For the vast majority of individuals, it may be further conjectured that these performances are most quickly brought about by activity within the left hemisphere. The evidence that cerebral bilaterality for language has given way to left hemisphere dominance is indirect. By age five, we no longer find reports of acquired aphasia from right hemisphere lesions. Moreover, studies of dichotic listening (Goodglass 1973; Berlin et al. 1973) show no further developmental trend beyond this age.

Within the left hemisphere language zone, however, changes must be continuing, so that, by adulthood, differently placed lesions will be producing different selective deficits consistently across individuals. What is suggested here is that any linguistic operation must engage a certain minimum number of neurons to provide the information-processing capacity to carry out the particular operation. Whether these are recruited over a wide cortical area or in a concentrated one is immaterial to the success of the operation. However, if a sufficient concentration of neurons is available within a restricted zone, those at the periphery will tend to drop out as the brain learns to use the most efficient networks.

Passing from one level of conjecture to the next we may consider the relation of the available neuron pool to the level of linguistic operations that is possible at a given stage of cortical maturation or under given conditions of cortical damage. The principle suggested is that for a linguistic operation of a given complexity there is a corresponding calculating capacity required, in the form of a minimum concentration of available neurons in a certain zone. This implies that the complexity of linguistic operations can be scaled in terms of the corresponding neuronal capacity needed to carry them out. Thus, a given reduction from the normal mature neural substrate, whether through damage or through an incomplete level of maturation, implies that certain high-level operations are deleted from the linguistic repertory. By this line of reasoning, then, there could be a physiological explanation for the observation that young children and aphasics are reduced to using some of the same linguistically primitive forms.

It is unlikely, however, that as Lenneberg, Pogash, Cohlan, and Doolittle point out (in this volume), different levels of linguistic complexity are allocated to different tissue locations. Rather, this formulation has been presented primarily in terms of levels of severity of anterior aphasia, where one is concerned with the reduction from complex to simple syntactic forms. Indeed, several other contributors to this volume—Gleason, Lenneberg et al., Caramazza and Zurif, and De Villiers—have drawn analogies between acquisition and breakdown in the area of syntactic expression and comprehension. If the model is viable in respect to syntactic production, it should be equally applicable to other modalities of language, particularly to auditory comprehension.

Developing this idea a bit further, I would suggest that a scale of linguistic operations available at various levels of severity of aphasia is the best measure of the intrinsic difficulty of such operations, if "difficulty" is defined in terms of the complexity of the neuronal network needed to carry it out. This suggestion contrasts with the usual assumption that complexity can be verified against the developmental progression in the appearance of linguistic operations in children's language.

A purely developmental criterion confounds two concurrent influences, in the following sense: while children acquire linguistic forms in an order that may be partly determined by what their maturing brains can carry out, there is a second factor at work—namely, the fact that the mastery of certain constructions may be a prerequisite for learning others. Lenneberg et al. phrase this very well in referring to the progressive differentiation of relationships that permits new relationships to be established. In addition, some forms are encountered too infrequently by the young child to be incorporated in his early grammar, even though such forms may be linguistically simple.

The adult aphasic, prior to his brain injury, had fully mastered the normal range of grammar; the order in which constructions were acquired during childhood may not, in itself, influence their present level of mastery. Consequently, a given reduction in neural capacity may reduce the aphasic's grammar in a way that more directly reflects the intrinsic complexity of the constructions that have been lost and that is free of artifactual influences determining the order of acquisition.

A number of contributions in this volume present opportunities to examine the differences between operations in which immaturity and organic breakdown produce congruent results and those in which there is a disparity between the typical performance of the young child and the dysphasic. Gleason's data, for example, indicate that the morphophonemic rules governing the use of the syllabic or the nonsyllabic form of the plural, the possessive, and the past tense morpheme are at risk in the speech of 4-year-old children, but not in aphasics. This suggests that from the point of view of linguistic complexity it is as easy to pluralize 'dog' to 'dogs' as 'horse' to 'horses'. The syllabic form of the plural may be acquired later either because it is a special, less frequently encountered case, or because the final sibilant of the stem is identified as the plural morpheme. Once the special case is learned, however, it may entail no greater processing demand than the more frequent case of the nonsyllabic morpheme, so that this dimension of variation is irrelevant to the effect of brain damage. On the other hand, aphasics were found to be similar to children in that the inflections were dissociated in terms of syntactic function (Goodglass and Berko 1960), the possessive ending being more difficult than the phonologically identical plural.

De Villiers's data provide another possible instance of the disparity between factors determining the order of rule acquisition and neurological factors governing the order of rule dissolution. First, De Villiers notes that the order of difficulty of eight grammatical morphemes that can be ranked on a scale was different in Broca's aphasia from their order of acquisition by normal young children. In this instance, it would be of interest to compare those morphemes that correspond in difficulty with the ones that are most divergent in difficulty for aphasics and children. In particular, it would be valuable to examine those that are late-maturing, but relatively resistant to aphasia. If my thesis is to be supported, these morphemes should be syntactically simple but based on prior knowledge of other forms. In other words, cumulative transformational complexity may correspond well to order of learning but not to psychological complexity in adult speech.

It is also interesting to note that when De Villiers examined the grammatical morpheme usage of Wernicke's aphasics, there was no systematic order of difficulty, as had been found in the case of Broca's aphasics. Moreover, there were comparatively few omissions of grammatical morphemes in obligatory contexts. Here is evidence that the systematic dissolution of linguistic rules in aphasia is confined to the particular sphere—syntax, in the case of Broca's aphasia—that is implicated by the lesion.

Caramazza and Zurif's results (this volume) are in general agreement with this principle. It may be noted that syntactic comprehension behaves like syntactic production in that its dissolution in aphasia is comparable to children's data for *anterior aphasics only*. The fact that the utilization of semantic cues is possible with both the impaired and undeveloped language systems suggests that this mode of comprehension requires a simpler neurological substrate than does the processing of syntactic relationships.

The chapters in this volume by both Lenneberg et al. and Caramazza and Zurif deal with variability in performance as a function of the stimulus context. The factors inducing success, however, are of a different character in the two instances. Caramazza and Zurif reported that 4- and 5-year-old children were unable to understand embedded sentences where the absence of semantic constraints made it possible to link the subject of the embedded clause with the predicate of the main clause, as in the sentence "The boy that the girl is chasing is tall." However when semantically constrained, as in the sentence "The apple the boy is eating is red," they selected the correct answer. Caramazza and Zurif justifiably conclude that the correct answer given in the latter case did not really indicate comprehension of the embedding. Rather, the subjects were by-passing the difficult syntactic solution to answer on the basis of the semantic content, using their real-world knowledge.

In the data of Lenneberg et al. it is not the syntactic demand that is responsible for variation in performance. As their meticulous analysis reveals, after physiological "noise" is discounted, cognitive factors related to stimulus structure are responsible for determining success or failure. Weigl and Bierwisch (1970) have argued vigorously that "deblocking" of performance with the help of certain contextual cues is evidence that "competence" remains intact in aphasia. Indeed, it is common experience that increased structure, reduction of the number of alternatives to be searched, introduction of high transitional probabilities, and priming of a response in an impaired modality by practice in an unimpaired modality are all factors that have been found to "deblock" performance, to borrow Weigl's term.

I agree that if a performance can be elicited under some conditions from an aphasic, the latent knowledge of this operation cannot have been totally destroyed. What must be emphasized, however, is that linguistic knowledge is not necessarily either destroyed or intact but that impaired functioning of the substrate, which mediates the knowledge, often makes that knowledge available either erratically or under special conditions only. Thus, there is a totally different principle underlying the variable language performance of Caramazza and Zurif's young children from that which can be cited to explain variability in acquired aphasia. In the first instance, linguistic competence has not been acquired and success may be attained through recourse to nonlinguistic knowledge. In adult aphasia, physiological variation and variation in cognitive or linguistic demands of the stimulus determine recovery or failure or recovery of latent knowledge.

There are of course features of adult aphasia that cannot be reflected either in child language or in childhood aphasia. These are the factors related to factual knowledge and to the automization of overlearned abilities. By factual knowledge, I refer chiefly to the lexicon. When Goodglass, Gleason, and Hyde (1970) examined the comprehension vocabulary of aphasics with the Peabody test, they found it to be in the adult range for all groups of aphasics, although these same patients functioned below the level of 6-year-old children in other auditory tasks. The other factor, automization, is reflected in the retention of certain phrases—such as adverbials of time, e.g., "one year ago" or "one year later"—that have a great deal of internal cohesiveness in the speech of some severely agrammatic patients (Goodglass, Gleason, Bernholtz, and Hyde 1972).

The factor of frequency of usage is always lurking in the background as an explanatory principle that is usually hopelessly confounded with other factors, such as utility and age of earliest exposure. Certainly, frequency of usage is an essential factor in the automization of certain expressions. In respect to individual vocabulary items, frequency plays a central role in both acquisition and recovery of lexical words. We learn from Brown (1974) that frequency of usage plays little if any role in determining the order of acquisition of grammatical morphemes. However, the role of frequency in relation to dissolution and return of function in aphasia may be different. Ludlow (1973) presented data indicating that the order of recovery of syntactic structures by Broca's aphasics corresponds to the frequency of occurrence of these structures in normal conversational samples. By implication, then, within the category of grammatical morphemes there is probably a relationship between vulnerability to aphasia and frequency of daily usage.

In conclusion, we are not yet in a position to array a developmentally derived hierarchy of complexity against a hierarchy determined from the language of aphasics. Each is contaminated by extraneous influences, and a painstaking process of eliminating artifactual influences must be undertaken if a valid scale of linguistic complexity is desired. On the developmental side, we have the problem that the order of prerequisite constructions need not correspond to the order of complexity. In the data from adult aphasics, we have the artifacts produced by overlearning and consequent partial automization of constructions.

REFERENCES

Berlin, C. I.; Hughes, L. F.; Lowe-Bell, S. S.; and Berlin, H. L. 1973. Dichotic ear advantage in children 5 to 13. *Cortex* 9:393-401.

Brown, R. *A first language: the early stages.* 1974. Cambridge: Harvard Univ. Press.

Conrad, K. 1949. Uber aphasische Sprachstorangen bei hirnverletzten Linkshandern. *Nervenarzt* 20:148-54.

Gloning, I.; Gloning, K.; Haub, G.; and Quatember, R. 1949. *Cortex* 5:43-52.

Goodglass, H. 1973. Developmental comparison of vowels and consonants in dichotic listening. *J. Speech Hearing Res.* 16:744-52.

Goodglass, H., and Berko, J. 1960. Agrammatism and inflectional morphology in English. *J. Speech Hearing Res.* 3:257-67.

Goodglass, H.; Gleason, J. B.; Bernholtz, N. A.; and Hyde, M. R. 1972. Some linguistic structures in the speech of a Broca's aphasic. *Cortex* 8:192-212.

Goodglass, H.; Gleason, J. B.; and Hyde, M. R. 1970. Some dimensions of auditory language comprehension in aphasia. *J. Speech Hearing Res.* 13:596-606.

Goodglass, H., and Quadfasel, F. A. 1954. Language laterality in left-handed aphasics. *Brain* 77:521-48.

Guttman, E. 1942. Aphasia in children. *Brain* 45:205-19.

Hécaen, H., and DeAjuriaguerra, J. 1963. *Les gauchers. Privalence manuelle et dominance cerebrale.* Paris: Presses Universitaires de France.

Hécaen, H., and Angelergues, H. 1965. *Pathologie du langage*. Paris: Larousse.

Ludlow, C. The recovery of syntax in aphasia. Paper presented at Academy of Aphasia, Albuquerque, N.M., October 1973.

Luria, A. R. 1970. *Traumatic aphasia*. New York: Basic Books.

Subirana, A. Handedness and cerebral dominance. 1964. In *Handbook of clinical neurology*, ed. P. J. Vinken and G. W. Bruyn, vol. 4. Amsterdam: North Holland Publishing Co.

Weigl, E., and Bierwisch, M. 1970. Neuropsychology and linguistics: topics of common research. *Foundations of Language* 6:1–18.

Wepman, J. 1951. *Recovery from aphasia*. New York: Ronald Press.

Wepman, J. M., and Jones, L. V. 1964. Five aphasias: a commentary on aphasia as a regressive linguistic phenomenon. In *Disorders of communication*, ed. D. McK. Rioch and E. A. Weinstein, vol. 17, Research Publications, Association for Research in Nervous and Mental Diseases. Baltimore: Williams & Wilkins.

6

THE ACQUISITION AND DISSOLUTION OF THE ENGLISH INFLECTIONAL SYSTEM

Jean Berko Gleason

AGRAMMATISM AND CHILD LANGUAGE

Agrammatism is one of the most frequently noted characteristics of the speech of aphasic subjects. The language of aphasics who have sustained lesions in the anterior regions of the left hemisphere associated with Broca's area typically lacks small obligatory function words like articles and prepositions and may only inconsistently display the bound inflectional morphemes representing, in English, number and possession in nouns, person and tense in verbs. The agrammatic aphasic's speech thus consists of short utterances constructed of base lexical forms, produced in the appropriate order, but lacking the grammatical morphemes that further modulate meaning. Agrammatic aphasics are not the only speakers whose language is of this singularly "telegraphic" nature: an utterance like "Baby cry" in a context where most speakers would say "The baby cries" might also be produced by a young child just learning language. In fact, in the early stages of language acquisition, children's utterances are typically composed of short strings of uninflected content words, produced in approximately the right order. Inflectional endings and function words like articles and prepositions do not appear in children's earliest utterances. Thus, on the surface at least, young children's language and the language of adult aphasics contain a number of formal similarities.

Many theorists have suggested that aphasia is a regressive phenomenon, one in which the subject returns to lower levels of linguistic competence. The idea that the disruption of linguistic systems seen in aphasia represents a regression to an earlier, childlike state is expressed in Ribot's rule (1883), which holds that in aphasia the most recently acquired linguistic forms are the most vulnerable and subject to loss, while the earliest-learned forms will be best retained—the linguistic equivalent of the "last hired, first fired" rule. Freud expressed similar sentiments when he wrote *On Aphasia* in 1891:

> In assessing the functions of the speech apparatus under pathological conditions, we are adopting as a guiding principle Hughlings Jackson's doctrine that all these

109

modes of reaction represent instances of functional retrogression (dis-involution) of a highly organized apparatus, and therefore correspond to earlier states of its functional development. This means that under all circumstances an arrangement of associations which, having been acquired later, belongs to a higher level of functioning, will be lost, while an earlier and simpler one will be preserved (1891, p. 87).

In a similar vein, Jakobson (1971), while referring particularly to phonological patterning, expressed the same view: "Aphasic losses reproduce in inverse order the sequence of acquisitions in child language (p. 78).

This formulation holds a great deal of intellectual appeal. At the same time, it may not be sufficiently comprehensive to explain all the linguistic behavior we see in aphasic patients; if aphasia were pure regression, for intance, we might expect aphasic patients to be as content with their own utterances as children are. Quite to the contrary, we have seen patients react with dismay to their own agrammatisms and attempt repeatedly, if unsuccessfully, to correct their utterances (Goodglass, Gleason, Bernholtz, and Hyde 1972). Children's linguistic performance may be a more direct reflection of their linguistic knowledge, while the speech of aphasics may be flawed as a result of diverse forces that affect performance. It is possible that aphasic speech represents not so much a regression to earlier stages as a reordering of priorities and strategies; and that the formal similarities between aphasia and child language stem from different functional bases.

METHODS OF STUDY

One way of comparing aphasic speech with child speech is to examine transcripts of free conversation and look for the presence or absence of the structures under consideration in contexts where they are obligatory. This has been ably demonstrated by Jill de Villiers (see Chapter 7). Another technique, which may yield somewhat different data, is to present both aphasics and children with the same experimental tasks and to compare the results. This has rarely been done, partly because few researchers have sought subjects both in nursery schools and on the neurological wards of hospitals, and partly because of the difficulty of constructing experiments that are appropriate for both groups of subjects. In testing for children's knowledge of the morphological system of English, for instance, it was possible to present them with nonsense words like *wug* and *gutch* and ask them to inflect them. "This is a *wug*. Now there is another one. There are two ____?" (Berko 1958). When we attempted to administer this same Wug test to aphasic subjects we found them unable to deal with nonsense syllables. We therefore constructed a parallel test,* seeking the same information but using real English words (Goodglass and Berko 1960). The data discussed in this paper derive primarily from these two experiments and a more recent intensive study of one Broca's aphasic (Goodglass et al. 1972).

In order to compare children's acquisition and aphasics' loss of English inflectional morphology, we thus have data from two similar, but not identical, experiments. Both experimental procedures attempted to elicit from the subjects their knowledge of a limited subset of the English morphological system. Although there were some other items, we were mainly interested in the inflectional endings of the regular plural, the possessive, the third person of the verb, and the regular past tense; we also asked children to produce the *-ing* of the present progressive, but did not include this form in the aphasics' test since pilot work revealed that aphasics produce this form very frequently and have little difficulty with it.

The regular plural, possessive, and third person endings are identical and phonologically conditioned with the following distribution: /-z/ occurs after stems that end in any voiced sound except /-z -ǰ -ž/, e.g., *plays, hens*; /-s/ occurs after stems that end in /p t k f θ/, e.g., *hops, muffs*; and /-iz/ occurs after stems that end in /s z č ǰ š ž/, e.g., *mazes, hatches*.

The past tense is similarly phonologically conditioned, with the following distribution: /-d/ occurs after all voiced stems except those ending in /-d/, e.g., *played, amazed*; /-t/ occurs after stems ending in /p k f θ s š/, e.g., *hopped, missed*; and /-id/ occurs after /t d/, e.g., *landed, melted*. Unimpaired adult speakers of English "know" these rules in the sense that when confronted with a new word they are able to inflect it without being told how to form the plural or the past tense. For the easiest of these endings, the variant to be used can be determined by the general phonological rules governing permissible phoneme combinations in English. This is true of words that end in most voiced or unvoiced consonants, which must be followed by a similarly voiced or unvoiced inflection. Thus, English phonological rules determine that the plural allomorph added to *bed* must be /-z/ and the plural of *bet* must be /-s/. But for words whose stems end in /l m n r/, or any vowel or semivowel, phonological considerations do not intervene. These are more difficult, because either variant is phonologically possible: words like *hens, hence, purrs, purse*; and *falls, false* all are possible—and, indeed, exist—so speakers must know a particular morphological rule, which is that when phonology permits, the voiced variant forms the inflection. It must be emphasized that what is described here are the

---

* Newfield and Schlanger (1968) also constructed a test using real words that parallel the nonsense items on the Wug test. They administered both the Wug test and the lexical-item version to groups of normal and educable mentally retarded children and demonstrated the generality of our earlier findings as well as the differential in performance between lexical and nonsense items.

regular and productive forms, those that speakers use when faced with a new word. Even though some speakers may have individual words like *learnt* or *burnt* in their vocabularies, the addition of /-t/ is not the pattern that is followed when forming the past tense of new words ending in /-n/. The morphological rule for the addition of the /-iz/ and /-id/ endings is even more difficult, since the /-iz/ is added to one set of stem endings and the /-id/ to another.* Thus, there are three levels of difficulty involved in forming these inflections: at the lowest level, prior rules of English phonology determine which variant is to be used. At the second level, speakers must know that in general the voiced variant is to be used when phonology permits either voiced or unvoiced sounds. At the most complex level, speakers must know to add the /-id/ past tense form to stems ending in /t d/ and the /-iz/ plural to a particular set of six sibilants and affricates, /s š z ž č ǰ/.

One final morphological note, since it has relevance to our findings, is that the possessive, while it is usually formed just like the plural, has an additional zero form, which occurs after plurals that already end in /-s -z -iz/. Thus, the plural of *boy* is *boys*, and the possessive of *boys* is *boys'*, with no difference in pronunciation. This is because another English morphological rule dictates that only one of these inflections can end a word. When the word has already been pluralized, no further inflection is possible. (This is not true for words whose plural is irregularly formed, which means we can have a *children's* hour, but not a *girls-es* hour.) There is no bar to adding a possessive to words that end in /-s -z -iz/ that are not inflections: *horse's, fox's, topaz's*. In order to make a correct possessive of a word ending in an /-s/ the speaker must first determine if it is part of the stem, in which case the possessive ending is added, or if it is a plural, in which case the possessive is the zero form. This, then, represents a fourth level of difficulty, and a problem that normal speakers frequently do not agree on, particularly when the noun in question is a proper noun; for instance, when a family is named *Johns*, there is some disagreement about the formation of the plural possessive of their names.

The basic format for the children's test consisted of showing the children pictures of nonsense animals or of people engaged in unusual activities and reading them a text that omitted the form to be elicited: "This is a man who knows how to *mot*. He did the same thing yesterday. What did he do yesterday? Yesterday he ____?" The children looked at the pictures and provided responses. Items calling for the /-s/ /-z/ and /-iz/ forms of the plural were included, e.g., *bik, wug,* and *gutch*. The third person of the verb and the possessive, which have the same phonological shape as the plural, were also sampled in the /-iz/ form. Similarly the /-t/, /-d/, and /-id/ forms of the past tense were tested, e.g., *rick, spow,* and *bod*.

---

* For a thorough discussion of these allomorphic variations, see Brown (1973, pp. 284–89). The three levels of difficulty described here are those suggested by Brown's work.

The test given the aphasics had the same general format, except for the use of real words. An item for eliciting the plural in /-z/, for instance, also called upon the subject to supply the missing form: "You can't walk around with only one shoe. You need a pair of ____." We were able to construct some items that called for forms that were phonologically identical but functionally different—for instance, the plural: "My upstairs neighbor is a nurse and my downstairs neighbor is a nurse. Both of my neighbors are ____" versus the possessive: "This hat belongs to the nurse. Whose hat is it? It is the ____." In this way we were able to investigate whether the aphasics' difficulties lay more with the phonological or the morphological aspects of inflection; if their difficulty were phonological, performance on both of these items would be similarly impaired, but impairment at the morphological level, that is, with the expression of possession or plurality rather than with pronunciation could lead to different performance on the two items.

The test administered to the children was more difficult than the one constructed for the aphasics because it called upon their abstract knowledge of the morphological rules of English; in order to supply the correct plural of a new word like *tass* it is necessary to have abstracted the general rule that after sibilants and affricates the plural is formed by adding /-iz/. In supplying the plural of *horse* the aphasic subjects could refer to their memory of this plural as well as to more abstract knowledge.

SUBJECTS

The children who took the Wug test were between 4 and 7 years old. They were nineteen preschoolers and sixty-one first graders; a group of twelve normal adults also took the Wug test.

The aphasic subjects who were given the parallel real-word version were twenty-one hospitalized patients, ranging in age from 24 to 65 years. All were diagnosed aphasic, and some had very little free speech. A group of fifteen hospitalized but nonaphasic subjects also took this test.

The single Broca's aphasic who was studied intensively was a 22-year-old male high school graduate who had sustained a wartime gunshot wound in the left fronto-parietal region, resulting in right hemiplegia, right homonymous hemianopsia, and severe nonfluent aphasia.

RESULTS AND DISCUSSION

The inflectional verb form that children produce best, earliest, and most consistently is the progressive, which ends with *-ing*. When asked what a man who knew how to *zib* was doing, 97% of first graders told us he was *zibbing*. The progressive is also the inflectional form most used and preferred by aphasics.

In fact, in response to questions that call for either a past or a future tense (What did you do last week? What will you do when you leave the hospital?) Broca's aphasics will most typically supply a progressive like *workin*. This earliest child form is thus also the best retained aphasic form, and as such gives support to Ribot's rule. There are a number of factors that might contribute to the early acquisition and long retention of the progressive. Its frequent occurrence is obviously important: present tense verbs are more likely to be in the progressive than the indicative aspect. Pervasiveness is a relative factor, since the progressives occur as a past tense and can be used in place of the future tense as well: "He's sailing for France tomorrow." The progressive has other advantages besides frequency and pervasiveness: it is phonologically salient because it occupies a complete syllable, and, it comes in one basic shape. (There is some variation in speakers' use of -*in* or -*ing*, but that is not an allomorphic variation related to the final phoneme of the verb stem, as is the case with the third person or the past.) In addition, the progressive -*ing* is not homophonous with any other form that serves a different function, as is the case with /-s -z -iz/, which can mean plural or possessive or third person of the verb.

These are just some of the factors that might make the progressive tense easy for children to learn and for aphasics to retain: frequency, saliency, pervasiveness, uniqueness of form and function. There may be other factors as well, and we have no way of knowing which of these is the most important, or if children and aphasics rely upon the same set of features. It is possible, for instance, that the aphasics' one-word utterances like *workin'* are not so much progressives as nominalizations. Whatever the case, it looks as if the progressive tense satisfies so many criteria that we might establish for ease of learning or retention that it is bound to succeed on some of them even if we cannot with certainty say which. Where fewer factors are positive, for instance, where there is some phonological complexity, as there is in the regular plurals, possessives, third person verbs, and past tenses, and where the effects of frequency, saliency, and other factors vary, the effect of different forces can be seen, and the aphasics and children perform somewhat differently.

Table 6.1 shows the percentages of correct answers supplied by preschoolers, first graders, and aphasic adults in these nonsense word and real word morphological tests. The responses have been categorized according to the three orders of difficulty described by Roger Brown (1973, pp. 284–9): responses that are determined by English phonology, those that require the knowledge that where a choice exists the inflection is realized as the voiced allomorph, and those that require a special rule for the /-iz/ and /-id/ endings.

It is important to keep in mind that the children's task was more difficult, since they were dealing with nonsense words, while the aphasics' test used real lexical items. Even with this handicap, the preschoolers performed about as well as the aphasics overall, with one or two notable exceptions.

Table 6.1
Performance of Normal Children and Adult Aphasic Subjects in the Production of English Inflections (percentages correct)

Rule / Inflection	Phonologically Determined /-s -z -t -d/ (ex.: books, laughed)			Voicing Rule for Inflections /-z -d/ (ex.: shoes, played)			Special Rule /-iz -id/ (ex.: glasses, melted)		
	4–5 year olds	first graders	aphasic adults	4–5 year olds	first graders	aphasic adults	4–5 year olds	first graders	aphasic adults
Plural	76	97	80	66.7	89.3	78.5	23.7	36.5	79
Possessive	68	88	59.5			51	58	46	34
Past	65.3	78.7	60	36.1	59.1	53.7	23	32	60
Third person of verb			61.7			65	56	52	50

The children's performance on these nonsense forms also reflects the order of acquisition of the inflections in their own speech (Brown 1973). This is particularly true if we look at the simplest cases, where phonological rules determine which morphophonemic variant must be used. In these cases, after the progressive, the best performance was with the plurals, followed by the possessives, the past tense, and finally, the verbal endings for the third person. The differences in the children's performance on the simple inflections are not, however, large. The significant differences are between the simple instances of the inflection and those requiring special knowledge—the difference between adding a simple /-z/ to words like *bug*, where English phonology determines the form, and knowing to add /-iz/ to words like *glass* and other words ending in /s z š ž č j/, that limited subset of sibilants and affricates. Nonsense words that end in vowels, semivowels, or /l m n r/ represent the intermediate level of difficulty; a general voicing rule for inflections decides which variant is to be used. The children's performance on those items was also intermediate.

Thus, when we combined the data on all of the children, we found that 91% of them were able to provide a simple /-z/ to form the phonologically determined plural *wugs*; 79% of them were able to apply the voicing rule and give the correct plural *cras*; only 28% of them could supply the contingent plural *nizzes*. These differences were all significant. A parallel situation existed with the past tenses, where the combined groups of children produced 78% correct responses in giving the past tense of *bing* as *binged* (children, unlike adults, did not follow irregular patterns; only one of eighty-six children said *bang*, while this answer was given by half the adults); only 31% of the children gave the past tense of *bod* as *bodded*. Thus, children at this age appear to be struggling with morphophonemic rules; whether it is plural, possessive, third person, or past, the form that requires the extra syllable /-iz/ or /-id/ is always much harder for them. When we compared the preschoolers with the first graders we found that performance generally improved with increasing age. There was only one exception: with the formation of the possessive of the nonsense word *niz* (This is a *niz* who owns a hat. Whose hat is it? It is the ____?),

Table 6.2

Children's Performance with Possessives

Possessive	% of Correct Answers by Preschoolers	% of Correct Answers by First Graders	Significance Level of Difference
bik's	68	95	.02
wug's	68	81	
niz's	58	46	
biks'	74	99	.01
wugs'	74	97	.02
nizzes'	53	82	.05

Table 6.3

Scores of R.H. in Inflectional Morphology
Test (maximum possible score = 6 in
each category)

	Nonsyllabic		Syllabic	
Plural	/-s -z/	1	/-iz/	3
Possessive	/-s -z/	0	/-iz/	0
Third person Vb	/-s -z/	0	/-iz/	2
Past	/-t -d/	0	/-id/	3

SOURCE: Goodglass et al. 1972.

first graders performed less well than preschoolers. Preschoolers gave 58%
correct answers, and first graders gave 46% correct answers. While this does
not reach significance, it is provocative: with words ending in /-z/ older children
had more difficulty than younger children in forming the possessive. This may
be related to the fact that the possessives of words ending in /-s -z/ represent
a fourth level of difficulty, one in which the speaker must decide if the word is
already inflected and hence takes the zero allomorph or if the /-s/ is part of
the stem, in which case the possessive /-iz/ is added. Younger children may not
have been aware of this complication. The adult controls who took this test
were clearly confused by the plural possessives. A third of them, for instance,
said that the possessive of *wugs* (These are two *wugs*. They both own hats.
Whose hats are they? They are the ____?), was *wugses*. Children all erred in
the direction of omitting obligatory inflections. The possessives were the only
inflections that adult subjects made errors on.

The aphasics' performance on the inflectional items in the lexical word
version of the test differed in several respects. While the children always had
more difficulty with the contingent, extra-syllable allomorph of any inflection
than with its less complex realizations, this was not true of aphasics, who did
not have more difficulty with the extra syllables. In fact, when we looked at
the Broca's aphasics within our sample, we found that they actually did better
with the /-id/ and /-iz/ endings. This can be seen as well in the performance of
the single Broca's aphasic we studied (Goodglass et al. 1972). This patient,
R.H., had much less difficulty with the syllabic form, as can be seen in table
6.3.

As this table shows, he was able to produce only one nonsyllabic form, a
simple plural. By contrast, he was able to produce 3 out of 6 syllabic plurals,
2 third person verbs, and 3 past tenses, all the syllabic variants. He could
produce no possessives at all. This pattern is one that is never seen in children,
yet it is typical of Broca's aphasics. Perhaps the fact that these forms require
an extra syllable makes them more salient for the Broca's aphasics, and thus

easier to retain, while their infrequent occurrence and lack of generality makes them difficult for children to learn. So in this instance the /-iz/ and /-id/ forms are difficult for children because they are rare and phonologically complicated, but easy for the Broca's aphasics because they are salient and take up an extra syllable, and we have an example of two different sets of principles at work, resulting in different performance by aphasics and children. These differences are particularly clear when the comparison is made between children and Broca's aphasics, who are the subjects most likely to be characterized as agrammatic.

The children's difficulties with the inflectional system appear to stem largely from their incomplete grasp of the morphophonemic patterns of English, especially the rarer syllabic endings. The aphasics, on the other hand, especially Broca's aphasics, find the rarer form easier to produce. Where the aphasics have difficulties, they lie in an inability to express entire functions. Of a possible 252 correct answers in each category, aphasics produced 199 correct plurals, 144 correct third person verbs, and 11 correct possessives. A significance test comparing plurals with verbs, verbs with possessives, and plurals with possessives revealed that the differences were all significant at the 0.01 level. The aphasics were significantly better at plurals than with verbs and significantly better with verbs than with possessives.

This can be seen in some of the individual test items, where the same phonological word was called for in different functional form—the plural, two *nurses*, versus the possessive, the *nurse's* hat, for instance. For the plural, the aphasics produced 80% correct answers, while for the possessive, they were only 29% correct, a difference that was significant at the 0.01 level.

In general, the aphasics were much less able to produce possessives than the other inflections. Some of them produced none at all, even in the simplest cases, and it is only with the possessives that there is a significant difference between their performance on the /-s -z/ and /-iz/ forms. The aphasics' performance with the /-iz/ possessives (only 34% correct) was much worse than their performance with any other inflectional form, while younger children were surprisingly better at this form than were older children. Moreover, all of the children were capable of producing at least some simple possessives.

It is difficult to say why aphasics performed so poorly on items calling for possessives, but we have found some clues in ourselves, in our nonaphasic controls, and in some historical grammars of English, (Jesperson 1942, Poutsma 1914). Earlier, it was indicated that the normal subjects who took the Wug test had difficulty forming the possessive of words that end in /-s/. A similar situation occurred when we gave the real-word test to fifteen nonaphasic, but brain-damaged, control subjects on the neurological wards of the Boston Veterans Administration Hospital. These subjects for the most part had right-hemisphere damage. Ten of these subjects performed without error. All five subjects who made errors omitted the possessive /-iz/ from a word ending in

/-s/; three of the five also omitted a simple /-s -z/ possessive. One subject substituted a past tense for the present.

It is clear that nonaphasic individuals find the possessive confusing, particularly where it is to be added to a word already ending in /-s/. As was suggested earlier, this represents a complicated problem because speakers must first decide if the /-s/ is part of the stem of the word or if it is an inflection. If it is the stem, an /-iz/ is added for the possessive; if it is a plural /-s/, the possessive becomes the zero allomorph. Younger children may have been unaware of this complication.

This complication must be added to a larger body of irregular formations. While we have dealt here with the regular, productive rules of English morphology, those rules by no means represent all that speakers know. Even the plural, which seems so simple, has hundreds of irregular forms, which, furthermore, change over time. The word *chicken*, for instance ,was once a plural like *children*, and its singular was *chick*. There was an interim period when speakers were unsure of how to form the plural. Jespersen (2:161) quotes a seventeenth-century grammarian who chides: "nam qui dicunt in singulari *chicken* et in plurali *chickens*, omnino errant." Today *chickens* is the accepted plural; but there are other words, like *gallows*, which may or may not be a plural—no one seems positive. While *gallows* may lie in the grey area of English inflection, there are many other irregular words that competent speakers deal with every day; words that stand for singular objects, but are always in the plural, like *pants* and *pliers*; words that look like singulars, but are always plural, like *police*; even our own field, *linguistics*, has the formal and historical trappings of a plural while functioning as a singular.

Just as no one has yet mapped out adult competence with plurals, no one has described the possessives in all of their intricacies. They begin as more complicated because of the extra rule. Additionally, when a singular noun ends in -s, usage varies, depending on such diverse factors as whether the noun is polysyllabic or not and whether it represents a name from classical or modern times. Speakers are not sure if they should say "Moses' law" or "Moses's law"; nor is there general agreement on how to form the possessive of names like *de Villiers*.

We have no real data on how adults have acquired all of their inflectional knowledge, but our experiments have shown that both aphasic and nonaphasic adults have particular difficulty forming the possessive of words that end in -s, while this is not the case for children just acquiring these forms. One explanation for this is that the adults are confused by the conflicting patterns they have learned, while children have not yet acquired those patterns, and so cannot be misled by them. Our finding that first graders were somewhat worse than preschoolers in forming these possessives lends some support to this view. The fact that both aphasic and nonaphasic adults had difficulty with the same forms further suggests that the aphasics have not regressed to a child-like state but that they have always with them the remains of their previous adult competence. The speech of both young children and adult aphasics can be characterized as agrammatic, and the formal similarities are striking. However, further investigation has revealed qualitative differences in the language functioning of these two groups of subjects. Children are content with their own performance, and their production of inflections proceeds on a developmental scale calibrated along lines of morphophonemic complexity. Agrammatic aphasic adults appear to be aware of the disparity between their "knowledge" of forms and their surface realizations, an awareness that is expressed in dissatisfaction and frequent attempts at self-correction. Morphophonemic complexity is not an important variable for them, but function is. Unlike children, they may be unable to express an entire functional category; we never found children who could make no possessives at all, while we did see aphasics with this problem. Finally, aphasics have the most difficulty with just those forms that prove troublesome for unimpaired adults as well.

REFERENCES

Berko, J. 1958. The child's learning of English morphology. *Word* 14:150–77.
Brown, R. 1974. *A first language: the early stages*. Cambridge: Harvard Univ. Press.
Freud, S. 1953. *On aphasia*. trans. E. Stengel. New York: International Universities Press.
Goodglass, H., and Berko, J. 1960. Agrammatism and inflectional morphology in English. *J. Speech Hearing Res.* 3:257–67.
Goodglass, H.; Gleason, J.; Bernholtz, N. A.; and Hyde, M. R. 1972. Some linguistic structures in the speech of a Broca's aphasic. *Cortex* 8:191–212.
Jakobson, R. The sound laws of child language and their place in general phonology. Reprinted 1971 in *Child language: a book of readings*, ed. A. Bar-Adon and W. Leopold, pp. 75–82. Englewood Cliffs, N.J.: Prentice-Hall.
Jesperson, O. 1942. *A modern English grammar*. Copenhagen: Ejnar Munksgaard.
Newfield, M., and Schlanger, B. B. 1968. The acquisition of English morphology by normal and educable mentally retarded children. *J. Speech Hearing Res.* 2:694–706.
Pitres, A. 1895. Etude sur l'aphasie chez les polyglottes. *Revue de Médicine* 15:873–99.
Poutsma, H. 1914. *A grammar of late-modern English*. Groningen: P. Noordhoff.
Ribot, T. A. 1883. *Les maladies de la mémoire*. Paris: Librairie Germain Baillière.
Spreen, O. 1968. Psycholinguistic aspects of aphasia. *J. Speech Hearing Res.* 11:467–80.
Weinreich, U. 1953. *Languages in contact*. New York: Linguistic Circle of New York.

7

FOURTEEN GRAMMATICAL MORPHEMES IN ACQUISITION AND APHASIA

Jill G. de Villiers

INTRODUCTION

The hypothesis that provided the impetus for a book of this sort requires some justification. Surely it is naïve to search for parallels between aphasia and language acquisition. Primitive speech in the child is a consequence of a lack of knowledge, both conceptual and linguistic, in an immature brain. In the aphasic, there is considerable debate as to whether the brain injury that resulted in a speech deficit has spared underlying knowledge or whether a more drastic curtailment of both conceptual and linguistic information has occurred, but now in a mature brain. Hence learning and relearning probably operate on a very different neural substrate and from different conceptual starting points.

So what is the rationale for comparison? One argument is based on a crude model of the anatomy of any representation of language or other behavior: that the forms acquired early in life have deeper, more protected localization, and later forms are represented more peripherally. In damage to the brain, the early forms are more resistant. Unfortunately, this model of language representation as a growing onion has little to support it anatomically.

There are several other reasons for making the comparison, reasons that do not rely on an anatomical model but that have reasonable psychological principles as their basis. As a starting point for argument, assume that someone has demonstrated a clear similarity in the language of young children and aphasics. Why might this occur? There are four possibilities.

1. The most important variable governing the learning or relearning of a form is the frequency with which it is heard or practiced. Very frequent forms will then have an advantage for both the child and the aphasic.

Preparation of the manuscript was supported by Grant GS 37931 X from the National Science Foundation to Professor Roger Brown.

2. Forms that are acoustically salient will be more easily learned or relearned.

3. Forms that are psychologically complex are acquired later than simpler forms, or a stronger version; perhaps certain forms are not only less complex but are prerequisite to others, both in acquisition and in use. So one would not expect composite forms to survive after or be acquired before their component forms.

4. Both children and aphasics try to economize effort by using essential items rather than redundant forms.

Since objections can be raised to each of these possibilities, imagine there are demonstrated *differences* between children and aphasics:

1. Forms the child hears frequently are not necessarily those an adult uses or hears from other adults. The accumulating evidence on the special nature of parent-child speech would support this (Snow 1972).

2. The relation between acoustic saliency and ease of production in aphasia is not obvious; it is possible that stressed or syllabic forms will be harder to produce.

3. What might be psychologically complex in terms of conceptual development might be easy to produce in adulthood. Rankings of complexity for children and adults could differ markedly. Furthermore, what is logically prerequisite might nevertheless be psychologically inoperative in normal adult production or processing. Parsimony dictates the accretion of several established rules to serve a new function but it is possible that this is not at all the way language is organized. There might instead be several sets of special purpose heuristics for the production of adult speech. (See Bever 1970.)

4. Children and aphasics could differ in their communicative needs; what is dispensible for the child, particularly in the protected environment where all family members share the same presuppositions (Brown 1973), might be crucial for the adult.

This morass of arguments and counterarguments serves to demonstrate that the issue of comparison is not theoretically unmotivated. The question is, can one tell which of the possibilities is correct in any given case? This chapter will explore a well-defined set of data on telegraphic speech collected from children and Broca's aphasics, with the aim of clarifying by example some of the arguments listed above.

TELEGRAPHIC SPEECH

The term *telegraphic speech* has been used as a description of the speech of young children and also of Broca's, or nonfluent, aphasics. It refers to the fact that their speech consists of short sequences of content words, such as nouns and verbs, with the words of primarily syntactical use—prepositions, articles, and auxiliaries—omitted. This is a sensible strategy to get the most essential information across, for in a telegram words cost money. Function words are comparatively more redundant than content words, but they are not devoid of semantic significance; they serve an important role in modulating the meaning of other structures. One notable difference between agrammatic speech and the composition of a telegram is that in a telegram, bound morphemes such as the plural *s* or verb endings are not omitted, but bound morphemes are often absent in the speech of young children and nonfluent aphasics.

Despite the similarity that gave rise to the common label, it is generally agreed that one can recognize differences in transcripts of agrammatic aphasics and young children. Perhaps this difference is a product of the different vocabulary and topics of conversation of the two groups, or the difficulty and hesitation in the aphasic compared to the fluency of the chattering child. However, it is also possible that there are grammatical differences between the two groups, so a closer look is warranted.

ACQUISITION

The grammatical morphemes noticeably absent from telegraphic speech have recently been subjected to a most thorough syntactic and semantic analysis (Brown 1973). Given the methodology and results that Brown's study of acquisition made available, the study of grammatical morphemes proved the ideal candidate for a comparison of acquisition and dissolution.

Brown (1973) collected biweekly samples of speech from three children known as Adam, Eve, and Sarah, from the time the children were about two years old. This continued for eighteen months in the case of Eve and for several years for Adam and Sarah. The transcripts were of natural interaction in the homes between the children and their parents, and occasionally with the investigators. Notes on nonverbal contexts were taken, so much information is recorded in the written transcript. Brown chose, among many other things, to trace the acquisition of a set of fourteen grammatical morphemes that are common in child speech, and make their appearance early. There are other morphemes, such as modals, auxiliaries, other prepositions, and verb tenses, but these are rare in child speech and appear much later. As selected by his criteria, the morphemes are a mixed class: the prepositions *in* and *on*; the verb inflection of the present progressive, *-ing*; the past tense *-ed*; the irregular past tense, e.g., *went*; the third person regular *-'s*; the irregular third person, e.g., *has*; the main verb copula, contractible forms, e.g., I'*m*, they'*re*, that'*s*; and uncontractible forms, e.g., *was*, this *is*; contractible auxiliary of *be* (same forms as main verb copula); uncontractible *be* auxiliary; the possessive noun inflection *-'s*; the plural noun inflection *-'s*; and the articles *a* and *the*.

The groupings are not as arbitrary as they seem. The reader might ask why, for example, the prepositions *in* and *on* are considered as separate morphemes, but the articles *a* and *the* are classed together. Brown argues that the groupings are functional: the articles, for example, are acquired hand-in-hand; it is relatively difficult to distinguish separate contexts of use; and they develop out of an undifferentiated schwa.

The significant methodological contribution to the analysis of spontaneous speech came from Brown's rejection of a simple frequency measure. Instead of merely counting the occurrences of the various morphemes over time, he took into account the occasions when the morphemes would be obligatory in adult speech. This allows for variation in frequency depending on topic of conversation; it provides a measure of what the child *can* say rather than what he *chooses* to say. For example, if we heard the segment "Give me all of the ____," we would expect a plural marking on any following count noun. If we heard "Yesterday I ____," we would anticipate some form of past tense marking on the verb. If it does not occur, we perceive the sentence as deviant. Each such occasion provides a test of the speaker's control of that morpheme; for a given morpheme, the percentage of such contexts that are correctly filled is a measure of knowledge of that morpheme's usage. By this method, spontaneous speech in context has most of the advantages and none of the disadvantages of a deliberately contrived test of language knowledge. It is just unfortunate that many of the larger and more interesting aspects of grammar are less susceptible to this kind of analysis by their very *optionality*.

At the beginning of Brown's study, most of the morphemes were absent from the speech of all three children, but as the children grew older, the morphemes were increasingly often supplied. For any particular morpheme the growth curve was gradual rather than abrupt in form; learning was by no means all-or-none. Neither, however, are the rules governing any one morpheme's use. Since each morpheme has to be learned in many different contexts, the slow process is not an unexpected finding. There exists little evidence that even for a particular context the learning is sudden; that is, it is not the case that the slow growth is due to the gradual accretion of many abruptly acquired rules (Hakuta 1975). Instead, the child often says several identical sentences in a row in which the morpheme under consideration appears and disappears! This fluctuation has not yet, despite repeated attempts, been related to other linguistic or situational variables.

Brown took as his criterion for acquisition of a morpheme its presence in 90% or more of obligatory contexts in three successive speech samples from a particular child. After this level was reached, the percentages did not fall again. Then for each child, the morphemes were ranked in the order in which they reached criterion. Rank order correlations (Spearman's rho) computed among the three orderings revealed a substantial degree of invariance in order of acquisition. For Adam and Sarah, the rho value was +0.88, for Adam and Eve, +0.86, for Eve and Sarah, +0.87.

Here is a remarkable invariance in order of acquisition and a powerful methodological tool for the analysis of spontaneous speech. The problem in comparing children to nonfluent aphasics was that no one had collected large speech samples during the recovery of agrammatic patients, and often recovery is far from complete. Extension to aphasia awaited another demonstration—

Table 7.1

The Order of Acquisition of the Fourteen Morphemes in Brown's Longitudinal
Study and by Both Methods in the de Villiers' Cross-sectional Study

The 14 Grammatical Morphemes	Average Rank-Ordering for the Three Children Studied Longitudinally (Brown 1973)	Rank-Ordering for the Children in the de Villiers' Study	
		by method 1	by method 2
Present progressive	1	2	4
On	2.5	2	2
In	2.5	4	1
Plural	4	2	3
Past irregular	5	5	5
Possessive	6	7	11
Uncontractible copula	7	12	10
Articles	8	6	8
Past regular	9	10.5	7
Third person regular	10	10.5	12
Third person irregular	11	8.5	6
Uncontractible auxiliary	12	14	14
Contractible copula	13	8.5	9
Contractible auxiliary	14	13	13

that the order of acquisition was mirrored in a single transcript at one point
in time.

If the order of acquisition is almost invariant, then taking a single sample
of speech from a child one should be able to predict which morphemes will be
present to criterion and which will not. A cross-sectional study of this sort is
also useful to extend the finding to a wider sample of children. De Villiers and
de Villiers (1973) undertook the same analysis of the speech of twenty-one
children aged between 16 and 40 months, for each of whom transcripts had
been collected in two 1½-hour play sessions about a week apart.

We could not use Brown's criterion for acquisition of 90% presence in
three successive speech samples since we only had one transcript of sufficient
size for each child (average 359 utterances). The data were also too variable and
scanty to modify the criterion for acquisition to 90% presence in three successive
children ranked according to mean length of utterance (MLU) measured in
morphemes per utterance. Therefore, two different procedures were employed
to order the morphemes: (1) the morphemes were ranked according to the
lowest MLU sample at which each morpheme first occurred in 90% or more
of the obligatory contexts, or (2) the percentages for each morpheme were
summed across all the children and averaged, then these mean percentages
were ranked.

Table 7.1 shows the rank orderings of the fourteen morphemes resulting
from the above two methods together with the average order of acquisition

Table 7.2

The Percentage of Each of Eight Morphemes Supplied by Each of Eight Nonfluent Aphasics, with their Subject Averages

Patient	Plural	Articles	Contractible Copula	Uncontractible Copula	Progressive	Third Regular	Past Regular	Past Irregular	Average
A3	99.0	97.3	98.1	98.0	100.0	92.8	95.8	96.6	97.2
A50	97.2	94.0	94.7	96.6	100.0	96.3	93.3	96.5	96.1
A14	98.4	85.6	98.4	97.7	98.0	73.3	82.0	85.1	90.5
A5	95.0	91.4	88.1	94.1	93.5	56.8	90.0	64.9	84.3
A24	98.3	55.6	73.2	47.3	100.0	40.0	66.6	56.1	66.6
A6	98.8	48.4	63.2	73.9	94.4	42.9	51.5	46.4	64.9
A43	98.1	48.8	72.9	20.6	100.0	51.3	22.4	18.8	54.1
A11*	94.0	16.6	—	96.1	100.0	—	0.0	40.0	57.8
Average	97.8	74.4	84.1	75.5	97.9	64.9	71.8	66.3	

* Morpheme averages exclude data from A11.

for Adam, Eve, and Sarah. The rank-order correlations among the three order-ings are as follows: Brown's data and Method 1, +0.84; Brown's data and Method 2, +0.78; Method 1 and Method 2, +0.87. An additional finding was that mean length of utterance was a substantially better predictor of the overall percentage of morphemes supplied by a child (rho = +0.92) than was chrono-logical age (rho = +0.68).

APHASIA

The transcripts used in the study of morphemes in aphasia were from interviews with eight nonfluent aphasics ranging widely in severity. The transcripts were part of a corpus of aphasic speech collected by Howes (1964), and each was at least 5,000 words long and had been coded already for repeti-tions, paraphasias, and cumulative number of words. The interviews were nonstructured and designed to keep the patient talking with as little interruption from the interviewer as possible.

The transcripts differed from those collected from children since notes on nonverbal context were not available. However, the aphasic patients were not usually talking about the immediate physical environment and were much more considerate of the listener's needs than are young children, providing plenty of adverbs of time and quantifiers as reference points for the discourse. There-fore, although all the cues used to define obligation were linguistic ones, there was surprisingly little ambiguity. Ambiguous contexts were not included in the count and averaged only 3.3% of the total number of contexts.

The fourteen morphemes were analyzed in exactly the same way as for the children's transcripts, and thus only omissions in obligatory contexts were tallied, not errors of usage. Errors were few, the majority being number misagreements on the copula, e.g., "The tomatoes was really ripe." Such con-texts were excluded from the count.

It was decided that a minimum sample of ten contexts per morpheme was necessary to assess its difficulty. Despite the large size of the transcripts, only eight of the fourteen morphemes had the opportunity to occur this frequently in most transcripts. Table 7.2 shows the percentages of obligatory contexts filled for this subset of eight morphemes, for each aphasic. All the percentages reflect a sampling of at least ten contexts per morpheme.

Table 7.3 shows the percentages for the six infrequent morphemes for the eight aphasics. It must be remembered that these are based on only a few examples per transcript. The patient A11 had no discernible contexts for the third person regular or contractible copula, and the majority of contexts for the uncontractible copula consisted of the routine greeting "How are you today?" possibly an unanalyzed stereotype. Thus the averages across morphemes in table 7.2 exclude the data from A11, and his personal average is probably exaggerated.

Table 7.3

The Percentages of Each of Six Infrequent Morphemes, Averaged for Aphasic and Normal Subjects (including number of subjects contributing to a percentage)

	On	In	Possessive	Third person Irregular	Contractible Auxiliary	Uncontractible Auxiliary
Aphasics	7	7	7	3	7	7
Average percent supplied	69.9	80.9	77.2	100.0	64.5	63.3
Controls	5	5	5	5	5	5
Average percent supplied	100.0	100.0	100.0	100.0	99.4	100.0

The question the study set out to ask was this: Is there a stable difficulty ordering for these fourteen morphemes that can be compared with the acquisition order? The best that can be done is to assess the degree of consistency across the rankings of the eight morphemes and seven aphasics with complete data. Kendall's coefficient of concordance (W) among the rankings is 0.68, which is significant beyond the 0.001 level. It is clear that the aphasics agree in finding some morphemes more difficult than others. This difficulty ordering is shown in table 7.4 along with the order of acquisition of the subset of eight morphemes. The rank-order correlation coefficient between the two orderings is nonsignificant (tau = +0.25). Evidently dissolution does not parallel acquisition.

Further support for the difficulty ordering in aphasia was revealed when two transcripts taken five months apart from patient A3 were analyzed. This patient recovered substantially during this period, and yet the product-moment correlation between the two sets of data was +0.83 (significant $p < 0.02$).

Table 7.4

Difficulty Ordering for Nonfluent Aphasics Compared to Order of Acquisition from de Villiers and de Villiers (1973), Method 2

Morphemes	Order of Difficulty in Aphasia	Order of Acquisition in Children (de Villiers', method 2)
Progressive -ing	1	2
Plural -s	2	1
Contractible copula	3	6
Uncontractible copula	4	7
Articles a and the	5	5
Past regular -d	6	4
Past irregular	7	3
Third person regular -s	8	8

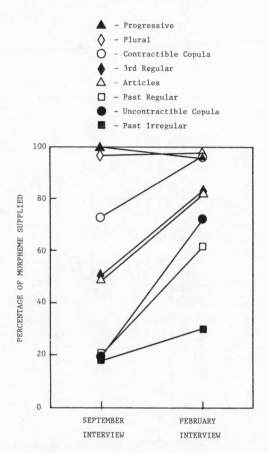

Fig. 7.1   The recovery of A43 over a five-month period, evidenced by increased accuracy for the eight morphemes.

It is evident that the order of difficulty was retained in the recovery of this patient (see figure 7.1).

Five thousand word transcripts were also made available by Davis Howes for five normal controls, matched in age and educational level to the aphasic patients. To obtain comparison data on frequency and accuracy, these transcripts were submitted to the same analysis. The percentages of obligatory contexts filled are shown in table 7.5 for the eight morphemes, and in table 7.3 for the six infrequent morphemes. It is clear that these grammatical elements are supplied quite automatically in normal speech, and the pattern shows no consistency (W = 0.30, nonsignificant).

Is the consistency found for nonfluent aphasics restricted to that subgroup of aphasics? To test this question, seven additional 5,000-word transcripts

Table 7.5

Percentage of Each of Eight Morphemes Supplied by Six Normal Subjects

Subject	Plural	Articles	Contractible Copula	Uncontractible Copula	Progressive	Third Regular	Past Regular	Past Irregular	Average
N1	98.7	99.4	99.1	100.0	100.0	100.0	100.0	98.8	99.7
N2	100.0	99.4	98.5	100.0	96.8	100.0	98.6	100.0	99.2
N3	99.1	95.2	100.0	100.0	100.0	100.0	100.0	94.8	98.6
N5	98.0	99.2	100.0	100.0	100.0	100.0	100.0	100.0	99.7
N11	97.6	99.6	99.0	98.3	100.0	95.8	100.0	86.9	97.2
Average	98.6	98.6	99.3	99.6	99.3	99.1	99.7	96.3	

from fluent aphasics were selected from the corpus (Howes 1964). A sample of one transcript (A38) is given below.

> But I figured that if I defective my my talking see my talking itself I I get my tongue back again to where I can talk from what they say why then it's liable to that will straighten me out again and bring me back to where I can hear something see and until I talk I under talk I got to do the interfering has got to act with me for a while see because it doesn't it won't interfere with me properly now now I hear them talking you know . . . .

Although several of these patients had severe communication problems, they had rather less difficulty with the fourteen morphemes than did the non-fluent aphasics. While it was difficult to keep track of the content, grammatical agreements were remarkably intact. The data are presented in table 7.6. The coefficient of concordance is 0.30, which is nonsignificant. There is little agreement among patients as to difficulty, although there seems to be a special problem with the past irregular. Since this is also a different lexical item, it may reflect a word-finding problem rather than a grammatical failure. There is other evidence that confusions rather than omissions mark the so-called paragrammatism of fluent aphasics apart (Goodglass 1968). Such errors were particularly noticeable in these transcripts in preposition use (see also Goodglass Gleason, and Hyde 1970), which was often odd, as in the following sample: 'His place burned. His place had a tidal wave and he had a thirty thousand dollar place *went up the window*.'

As mentioned, Howes (1964) had already scored paraphasias in these transcripts. Paraphasia refers to the substitution or intrusion of unintended phonemes or words. Some paraphasias resemble the target word in sound (literal paraphasia); others, in meaning (semantic paraphasia). In still other cases the relationship is obscure and the form is called either an unrelated verbal paraphasia if it is a recognizable English word, or a neologism if it is not.

It was decided to check on the possibility that paragrammatism was another manifestation of paraphasia. Do patients with a large number of paraphasias per 1000 words also omit more morphemes from obligatory contexts? The answer is that they do (product moment correlation $r = +0.73$, $p < 0.05$). It appears that the fluent aphasics make paraphasic errors that show up in the selection of both content words and grammatical morphemes. There is no such relation for nonfluent aphasics, but it may be the case that there are unexplored differences in the type of paraphasia between the two subgroups. By counting them together an underlying relationship may be obscured.

It is difficult to interpret the lack of a consistent ordering. Since the fluent patients, like the normal subjects, averaged over 90% correct, it may be a ceiling effect. However, the three nonfluent aphasics who also averaged in this range show a consistent pattern of difficulty ($W = 0.78$, $p < 0.01$) when the concordance is calculated for their data alone. It appears that the difficulty

Table 7.6

Percentage of Each of Eight Morphemes Supplied by Seven Fluent Aphasics

Patient	Plural	Articles	Contractible Copula	Uncontractible Copula	Progressive	Third Regular	Past Regular	Past Irregular	Average
A38	95.3	99.2	100.0	99.0	94.8	91.3	95.0	75.3	93.7
A29	97.5	96.6	100.0	93.8	100.0	100.0	94.9	85.2	96.0
A59	80.0	98.9	99.0	100.0	71.7	100.0	64.0	96.0	88.7
A39	99.4	98.9	100.0	99.4	100.0	100.0	100.0	98.0	99.4
A40	100.0	99.3	100.0	100.0	95.3	93.3	97.5	91.1	97.1
A37	98.2	97.4	96.6	98.4	95.7	91.6	98.0	93.2	96.1
A35	98.0	97.2	98.4	94.3	92.5	90.9	87.9	76.9	92.0
Average	95.5	98.2	99.1	97.8	92.9	95.3	91.0	88.0	

with grammatical morphemes is neither as marked nor as consistent in the fluent patients. The interpretation offered is that their paragrammatism is a form of paraphasia.

Table 7.7 displays summary data for all the subjects discussed: five normals, seven fluent and eight nonfluent aphasics. It is worth noting that rate of speech distinguishes the subgroups of aphasia, while overall number of paraphasias does not. There is also a difference between normals and nonfluent aphasics in the number of contexts for the morphemes per thousand words. We will return to this frequency decrease at a later point.

DISCUSSION

We can now turn to the possibilities discussed at the beginning of this chapter as possible explanations for the invariant but distinct orderings obtained for acquisition and dissolution of the grammatical morphemes.

Frequency

The argument might be made that frequency is the variable determining both orderings, but the frequency of use changes between childhood and adulthood in such a way as to account for the differences. Brown (1973) estimated the frequency of use of the fourteen morphemes from samples of speech of the three pairs of parents in conversation with their children. The purpose was to test the hypothesis that the frequencies with which particular morphemes are modeled in parental speech account for the order in which those morphemes are acquired. There was a rather stable frequency profile across the three sets of parents, even with regard to different allomorphs of a single morpheme such as the plural.

Brown first performed the simplest check possible on the hypothesis: does the frequency ranking correlate with acquisition order? The rho value was +0.26, which is nonsignificant. There is no simple relation, then, between parental frequency and order of acquisition. Brown also looked at the MLU stage at which the different children acquired a particular morpheme. For example, Adam acquired full use of the present progressive when his utterances were between 2.0 and 2.5 morphemes long, whereas Sarah acquired the same morpheme when her utterances were 2.5 to 3.0 morphemes in length. The question was asked, could it be that Adam's parents used the present progressive more frequently in absolute terms than Sarah's parents, hence hastening its acquisition for Adam? This was true for the present progressive, but not for other cases having this property. Thus, absolute frequency differences also failed to account for variation in the acquisition points. Frequency in parental speech, therefore, fails as a predictor of the order of acquisition.

Table 7.7

Data on Rate of Speech Paraphasias, Paraphasias and Filled Pauses, Percentage of Morphemes, and Contexts for Fourteen Morphemes per 1000 Words of Transcript for all Subjects

Normals	Rate of Speech: Words per Minute	Paraphasias per 1000 Words	Paraphasias and Filled Pauses per 1000 Words	Percentage of 8 Morphemes Supplied	Contexts per 1000 Words for 14 Morphemes
N1	101.6	0.7	5.5	99.7	159.4
N2	131.9	0.2	2.9	99.2	182.2
N3	116.5	0.7	5.9	98.6	163.8
N5	159.3	0.3	5.1	99.7	164.7
N11	150.1	0.2	8.7	97.2	178.6
Fluent aphasics					
A39	165.1	1.8	11.1	99.4	179.0
A40	148.4	1.6	14.7	97.1	124.4
A29	184.2	6.3	24.5	96.0	152.1
A38	175.1	11.8	39.6	93.7	163.0
A59	64.4	13.4	17.7	88.7	126.4
A37	112.8	13.7	36.5	96.1	160.0
A35	211.4	21.3	37.3	92.0	169.4
Nonfluent aphasics					
A3	59.0	12.2	34.8	97.2	153.5
A50	19.4	103.8	209.2	96.1	140.3
A14	13.5	6.6	87.1	90.5	131.7
A5	57.0	8.1	87.2	84.3	103.1
A24	36.0	7.1	19.8	66.6	116.4
A6	21.0	13.8	23.6	64.9	69.9
A43	29.0	13.6	20.3	54.1	118.9
A11	18.3	40.0	66.4	57.8	35.5

Nevertheless, it might still be true that frequency predicts the order of difficulty in aphasia, not necessarily because of the frequency with which the morpheme is modeled, but rather because overall frequency of use might render some morphemes more resistant to disruption than others.

The frequency profiles for the normal adults were remarkably similar: the coefficient of concordance across frequency rankings was 0.84 (p < 0.001). The same degree of invariance was found for the nonfluent aphasic subjects (W = 0.83, p < 0.001), and the two average frequency profiles were highly correlated (r = +0.89, p < 0.01). Not surprisingly, the frequency ranking for these adults in interview situations with other adults did differ from that for parents speaking to children, but not markedly. The only major difference was in the parents' enhanced use of the present progressive, entailing a concomitant increase in the contractible auxiliary, apparently at the expense of the past regular. It is possible that this reflects the situational difference rather than the difference in addressee.

Comparing the adult frequency ranking and the order of difficulty in aphasia revealed a nonsignificant correlation (r) of +0.29. Frequency appears to be no more successful as a candidate for explaining the invariance in aphasia than it was for explaining invariance in acquisition.

Before leaving the discussion of frequency, two findings deserve mention. First, the overall absolute frequency of contexts decreased in aphasic speech, and it decreased with increasing severity of aphasia. Second, the decrease was much more marked for some morphemes than for others. For instance, the contexts for the plural actually went up for the aphasics, a finding that has attracted attention before. Goodglass (1968, p. 198) remarked, "Broca's aphasics tend to find reasons to quantify many more nouns than either fluent aphasics or normals." This is interesting in light of the fact that the plural is one of the best preserved morphemes. In contrast, contexts for the third person regular and past irregular are down by almost 50% from normal frequency, and these morphemes are very poorly preserved. In fact, the product-moment correlation between percentage decrease from normal frequency, and the difficulty of the morphemes, is +0.75 (p < 0.05). It is mysterious that nonfluent aphasics not only fail to supply some morphemes but also apparently have less occasion to try. We shall return to this argument later in the discussion.

Saliency

The second proposal was that acoustically salient forms would be more easily acquired or reacquired than nonsalient forms. Goodglass, Fodor, and Schulhoff (1967) elegantly demonstrated that nonfluent aphasics had significantly more difficulty with functors in an unstressed position in the speech train; for example, an article was omitted more frequently in sentence-initial position than in medial position. They suggested that this lack of saliency, rather than grammatical complexity, was the major source of difficulty in nonfluent aphasia.

If this alone is to account for the present results, it is necessary to demonstrate that the difficult morphemes are more often found in unstressed positions. None of the morphemes is normally stressed in speech the way content words are, but some at least have a potential for stress that others do not—that is, the syllabic forms. On this hypothesis, the progressive, past irregular, articles, and uncontractible copula would be learned first. This is clearly not the case either for children or aphasics. The counterhypothesis is not true either: aphasics do not have any more trouble with syllabic than nonsyllabic forms. Even the grammatically and semantically matched pairs of past tenses and copulas do not show a systematic difference in favor of either the syllabic or nonsyllabic member. Neither could a clear advantage be demonstrated for the syllabic or nonsyllabic allomorphs of the past regular, plural, or third person regular for the aphasics, though the frequency of contexts for syllabic allomorphs was very low.

Complexity

There are at least two ways in which one might order the morphemes by their complexity, independently defined. One method is taken from transformational linguistics; the steps involved in the derivation of the deep structure from the surface structure of a sentence have been taken literally as a model of comprehension, or in reverse, as a model of production. The number of steps is then a measure of the psychological complexity of the sentence. The early experiments on this model looked extremely promising, but Fodor and Garrett (1968) provided a devastating review of its failure as a model of speech processing in adults.

Brown and Hanlon (1970) applied the model to language acquisition, looking at sentence types similar to those used in the adult processing research: negatives, affirmatives, questions, negative-questions, and so forth. Derivational complexity proved useful in predicting which forms would appear before others in child speech.

The authors suggested that the accumulation of knowledge in acquisition might be more closely related to the steps in a derivation than is processing of speech by adults. "In studying first-language acquisition, psychologists have all been concerned with the order in which knowledge is acquired, not yet with the processes the child uses in putting his knowledge to work" (Brown and Herrnstein 1975, p. 474). Presumably once a child has all the composite knowledge required by a construction, there develop heuristics of production and processing that do not involve the initial derivational steps. In other words, adult processing is not a microgenesis of acquisition.

It is an attractive idea that is not without support. For in addition to Brown and Hanlon's paper on the derivation complexity of sentence types in acquisition, Brown (1973) provides evidence that the morpheme acquisition order is highly correlated with derivational complexity (rho = +0.80, p < 0.01). The complexity was assessed by counting the transformations involved in the derivation of each morpheme in the grammar by Jacobs and Rosenbaum (1968). Brown points out that a mere count of transformations is a dubious measure of complexity, for the transformations may not be equivalent in terms of internal complexity. Both Brown and Hanlon (1970) and Brown (1973) use instead cumulative derivational complexity, that is, if one construction involves transformations x and y it will be more complex than one requiring just x or just y. Thus, constructions which do not share transformations cannot be ordered relative to one another.

There were several comparisons Brown (1973) could make using cumulative derivational complexity, namely:

present progressive < contractible auxiliary
present progressive < uncontractible auxiliary
past irregular   < past regular
past irregular   < third irregular
past irregular   < third regular
third irregular   < third regular

All of these predictions were confirmed for acquisition.

The same predictions were tested for the aphasia data. There were 20 such tests possible using only those data representing more than ten contexts for a morpheme. Only 13 of these predictions were confirmed, which is not significantly greater than chance for binary predictions. Derivational complexity does not seem to provide a measure of difficulty in nonfluent aphasia.

A second possible metric of complexity is semantically based. Unfortunately, systematic semantic analyses are not so common as grammars. Brown (1973) integrated the work of many different authors to come up with an index of semantic complexity for each morpheme, and to do so he chose to limit his considerations to the meanings expressed in child language. Rarer instances, such as the use of the hypothetical past tense, as in the subjunctive "If I asked him, he would go," do not occur in child speech until well after the simple past has reached criterion. In searching the literature, Brown isolated the major dimensions of meaning that occur in early child speech. The distinctions *regular/irregular* and *contractible/uncontractible* do not change meaning and were thus disregarded in the analysis. The first of each such pair to reach criterion was considered, since at that point the child could be said to control the meaning underlying that morpheme, and differences between members of a pair are just grammatical or phonological.

The semantic analysis provides an externally based rather than an internal model of complexity, for Brown and other writers consider the stimuli or dimensions that the speaker must take into account in order to use a form correctly. For example, to correctly use the copula in English, a child must learn to make discriminations of number to distinguish *is* and *are*, and of tense to distinguish *is* and *was*. In other languages, he may also have to attend to gender. Surely then, the full use of the English copula must follow correct use of the plural (discriminations of number alone) and past tense (tense alone). Given that there are no dimensions that have been overlooked, cumulative semantic complexity makes the following predictions (Brown 1973):

plural	< copula
past	< copula
plural	< third person
past	< third person
plural	< auxiliary
progressive	< auxiliary
copula	< auxiliary
third person	< auxiliary
past	< auxiliary

For acquisition, these predictions were all borne out, but they are not so successful for predicting difficulty in aphasia. Out of 55 possible tests, there were 27 confirmations, most of which involved the superiority of the plural. Of course, it could be that the analysis of meaning in child speech is inappropriate for adult speech when rarer uses are included. It is not clear, however, how this would upset the predictions based on cumulative semantic complexity as they stand. For example, the hypothetical would be added to the copula as well as to the past tense.

Again it is found that an explanation that is highly satisfactory for acquisition is unsatisfactory when applied to aphasia. Inspection of the transcripts reveals that the aphasics are expressing a much richer set of meanings than the very young child, despite limited means of expression. Nevertheless, more severely affected patients might demonstrate a loss of even basic meanings.

Economy

The argument about economy is perhaps the most intuitively convincing, but it is the hardest to prove. Pick (Spreen 1973) held the opinion that agrammatism was a result of economy of effort, especially in consideration of the labored, difficult articulation of some nonfluent aphasics. Yet dysarthrics with severely impaired articulation often do not show agrammatism (Goodglass, personal communication). Agrammatism does not appear to be a matter of choice. Perhaps, though, redundancy is the controlling variable, even if unconscious. Features of speech that are redundant, that are inessential to communication, would be more disturbed than nonredundant items in aphasia. This is clearly a cogent explanation for the choice of content over function words, for the morphemes discussed here are clearly redundant to the extent that one can define obligatory contexts for them; their absence is noticeable. If a content word were missing, there would frequently be a more severe loss of information, since its possible replacements would be more numerous. Compare the following sentences: "The woman carrying a basket when she fell." "The woman was carrying a when she fell."

Hence we see that redundancy is equivalent to discriminability: if a word or item is highly redundant, its identity can be almost uniquely determined by the surrounding context. A word of low redundancy is less defined by its context. How then to demonstrate that the fourteen morphemes vary in redundancy? It is necessary to prepare a passage of prose or conversation with the various morphemes absent and ask several judges to correct it. There should be a higher consensus of agreement on some morphemes than others, and this, then, is the measure of redundancy.

If the reader has not already realized it, this is the situation I unwittingly set up in scoring aphasics' transcripts. My impression was that the absence of certain morphemes rarely presented ambiguity, while others required a patient search for contextual cues. The plural morpheme was very easy to identify, for in the aphasics' speech it was almost always signalled by a cardinal number. In contrast, the tense markings often required a scan for the sentence subject (for the third person) or an adverb of time to set the scene, often not immediately adjacent to the verb. Goodglass and Hunt (1958) had the opposite opinion about redundancy. They contrasted the plural marking in a sentence such as "My sister lost her glove/gloves." In the absence of context that marking is certainly not redundant. The third person they believed to be highly redundant, as in the sentence "The soldier writes home every day," because it merely signals number and person. In many cases, however, the unmarked verb with a third person subject is ambiguous between past tense and present, for example: "My wife work at a factory." Then a search is necessitated for time indications.

The point is that the morphemes each have a range of redundancy that it is impossible to estimate without analyzing large portions of natural dialogue in many different circumstances. Suppose, for the sake of argument, that my impressions were correct for these transcripts in these circumstances. The plural marker was highly redundant, the tense markings had low redundancy. Table 7.2 indicates that the plural is one of the best preserved morphemes; the tense markings are frequently absent in aphasia. That is the wrong way round for the redundancy argument. Why should the patients omit essential information and provide redundant information? Remember that redundancy is related to discriminability. Contextual cues better signal the need for some morphemes than for others. Neither the patient nor the scorer has a problem with the plural following a cardinal number.

Notice that the argument is closely tied to the issue of semantic complexity, which was also defined in terms of the discriminations a person had to make to use a form correctly. The present argument goes one step further. In speaking, especially without nonverbal props, there are cues, such as adverbs of time and cardinal numbers, which signal that certain meanings are being expressed, and they might serve as automatic cues for agreement in noun and verb inflections. These surface-structure signals can be near to or far from the morpheme in time, and more or less acoustically salient. Hence, unlike simple semantic complexity, this argument allows that any given morpheme can change in its discriminability if other variables, such as distance and acoustic salience, change. But for the present data, it is necessary also to demonstrate that the different morphemes vary in their average discriminability.

This is not a problem likely to engage linguists, with their interest in knowledge rather than performance. One of the major weaknesses of transformational grammar is that it does not spell out the relationship between knowledge and processing. Competence is said to be a *component* of the production/comprehension device and its interaction with memory and attentional strategies is left unspecified.

A more promising approach has been the development of Augmented Transition Network (ATN) computer models (Kaplan 1975; Wanner and Maratsos 1972), which are designed to mimic real sentence processing for adult comprehension. The models are an improvement over earlier accounts (Bever 1970) in that the strategies proposed are not arbitrarily chosen to fit certain demonstrated facts but are components in a coherent model that has greater predictive power. Unfortunately, they are still in an early stage of development, concentrating on the processing of simple sentences in isolation from context. While this is obviously a first step, until the contextual constraints can be specified as parameters in a model, it is difficult to extend it to the analysis of spontaneous discourse. Furthermore, the ATN model is for comprehension and not production of speech. The preceding discussion has relied on the assumption that in production there are certain processing strategies that keep track of agreement, which may be equivalent to those used in comprehension; but there is a crucial difference. In production, there is an intention, a deep structure, a goal that the speaker holds, whereas this is the end product of comprehension. Models of production are not nearly so well advanced.

In the absence of a theoretical model, we can only seek additional empirical evidence that this morpheme ordering has some validity in other situations in which the discriminability rather than the complexity of morphemes comes into play. There are two tentative pieces of evidence. First, it will be recalled that there was a strange correlation between the relative decrease in contexts and the difficulty of the morpheme. The possibility exists that the aphasic subjects avoided contexts for morphemes they could not supply, but it is hard to imagine how such monitoring could be accomplished for these frequent and nonstylistic elements of speech. Instead, allow that the scorer may have failed to recognize some contexts of obligation, because of the disrupted nature of the speech train. I have argued above that the aphasic also has trouble recognizing contexts because of the lowered rate of speech (see table 7.7) and because of a possible rehearsal problem (Goodglass, Denes, and Calderon 1974). The scorer has less of a problem in dealing with a written transcript as he can check back to earlier or later parts of the discourse to identify obligatory contexts and hence to spot a place where a morpheme is missing but is normally required.

Suppose that one morpheme is usually cued by an immediately adjacent, salient item, such as a cardinal number preceding a noun in the case of the plural. The scorer might only miss 1% of such obvious contexts, and the aphasic subject might miss 5%. This would show up as a 1% decrease in frequency, and over 95% of the morphemes would be scored as supplied. A morpheme such as the past tense is often more remotely cued—by an adverb appearing several sentences earlier, for instance. More of these contexts might be missed— say 10% by the scorer and 20% by the patient in speaking. It is then apparent that the frequency decrease in comparison to normal speech would correlate highly with the difficulty the patient had in supplying that morpheme, because the basis of the problem is the same.

It would be more convincing to present, as a second piece of tentative evidence, that normal adults find some morphemes more difficult than others for this reason, but as table 7.5 shows, normal adults supply all the morphemes automatically. The demonstration requires a wider range of difficulty with an adult system of knowledge. Those conditions are met, albeit with additional confounding, in the adult learning English as a second language. Bailey, Madden, and Krashen (1975) have recently reported that adults learning English as a second language manifest an almost identical difficulty in ordering as that of the nonfluent aphasics, but unfortunately the two studies share only six morphemes in common. Nevertheless, the rank order correlation between the orderings is highly significant (rho = 0.95, p < 0.001). Krashen (1975) is confident that the difference between this ordering and the order in first language acquisition is a consequence of the brain's maturity, but I would look further than that for the explanation of the ordering itself.

Furthermore, I am reluctant to overlook the methodological differences among the studies. Bailey et al. used a set of questions and pictures known as the Bilingual Syntax Measure (BSM) (Burt, Dulay, and Hernandez 1973), designed to elicit the various inflections and functors in as natural a way as possible. This measure has been used extensively with children learning English as a second language, with the remarkable finding that they all learn English the same way regardless of their first language (Dulay and Burt 1973). As far as the data presently stand, everyone tested on the BSM has shown approximately the same ordering of difficulty with the items on the test. The test has also been employed exclusively with second-language learners. There is thus a fundamental question of test validity that has been ignored: to what extent is the BSM a representative sample of spontaneous speech? It would be a simple matter to administer the BSM to a child learning English as a first language and to check that the sample selected on the test is a reflection of normal spontaneous speech. The first language learner on the BSM should give again the first language order of acquisition. Until this check is performed it cannot be said with certainty that the ordering of difficulty in second language learners is not a characteristic of the Bilingual Syntax Measure rather than one of second language learning.

There is another way to collect data from normal adults that might result in a greater range of difficulty in morpheme production, that is, to collect speech from these subjects under conditions of a slow rate of speech and disrupted rehearsal. The problems arise in approximating those conditions. I have recently tried one method in which a subject has access to the microphone for only two of every ten seconds on the average, on a random schedule. Between access times, the subject must count backwards—hardly parallel to aphasia, but the usual method preventing rehearsal in verbal memory tasks. Despite this contrivance, no subject so far has had the slightest difficulty with grammatical agreements. There are many occasions when the subject repeats a phrase, but agreements in tense and number are perfectly preserved over time lapses of ten seconds or more. It is comforting to know that normal speech is so resistant and automatic; but synthetic agrammatism is not so easy to manufacture as I had hoped.

CONCLUSION

What, then, can we conclude about the differences in difficulty ranking for the same grammatical items in children and Broca's aphasics? The underlying problem for each is to recognize obligation, to know when to supply a morpheme. For the child, this is the acquisition of knowledge about his language and the world. He is slowly learning the multiple and varied contexts that require a morpheme, and this learning is governed by grammatical and semantic complexity. So his mastery of a form such as the copula awaits his mastery of the component forms that mark tense and number.

The aphasic patient already knows about such things as number and tense, as shown by his sophisticated use of adverbs and qualifiers as markers. For whatever reason, the usually automatic nature of the grammatical agreements in speech has been disrupted, and he fails to notice some contexts of obligation.

A full account of this problem requires a detailed model of adult speech production, rather than a model of linguistic competence.

REFERENCES

Bailey, N.; Madden, C.; and Krashen, S. D. 1974. Is there a "natural sequence" in adult second language learning? *Language Learning* 24:235–43.

Bever, T. G. 1970. The cognitive basis for linguistic structures. In *Cognition and the development of language*, ed. J. R. Hayes, pp. 297–352. New York: John Wiley & Sons.

Brown, R. 1973. *A first language: the early stages.* Cambridge: Harvard Univ. Press.

Brown, R. W., and Hanlon, C. 1970. Derivational complexity and order of acquisition in child speech. In *Cognition and the development of language*, ed. J. R. Hayes, pp. 155–207. New York: John Wiley & Sons.

Brown, R. W., and Herrnstein, R. J. 1975. *Psychology.* Boston: Little, Brown.

Burt, M. K.; Dulay, H. C.; and Hernandez, Ch. E. 1973. *Bilingual syntax measure* (restricted edition). New York: Harcourt, Brace, Jovanovich.

de Villiers, J. G., and de Villiers, P. A. 1973. A cross-sectional study of the acquisition of grammatical morphemes in child speech. *J. Psycholing. Res.* 2:267–78.

Dulay, H. C., and Burt, M. K. 1974. Natural sequences in child second language acquisition. *Language Learning* 24:37–53.

Fodor, J. A., and Garrett, M. 1966. Some reflections on competence and performance. In *Psycholinguistics Papers*, ed. J. Lyons and R. J. Wales, Edinburgh: Edinburgh University Press.

Goodglass, H. 1968. Studies on the grammar of aphasics. In *Developments in Applied Psycholinguistic Research*, ed. S. Rosenberg and J. Koplin. New York: Macmillan.

Goodglass, H., and Hunt, J. 1958. Grammatical complexity and aphasic speech. *Word* 14:197–207.

Goodglass, H.; Denes, G.; and Calderon, M. 1974. The absence of covert verbal mediation in aphasia. *Cortex* 10:264–69.

Goodglass, H.; Fodor, I. G.; and Schulhoff, C. 1967. Prosodic features in grammar: evidence from aphasia. *J. Speech Hearing Res.* 10:5–20.

Goodglass, H.; Gleason, J. B.; and Hyde, M. R. 1970. Some dimensions of auditory language comprehension in aphasia. *J. Speech Hearing Res.* 13:595–606.

Hakuta, K. 1975. Becoming bilingual at age 5: the story of Uguisu. Honors thesis. Harvard University.

Howes, D. 1964. Application of the word frequency concept to aphasia. In *Disorders of Language*, ed. A. V. S. de Rueck and M. O'Connor. Ciba Foundation Symposium. London: Churchill.

Jacobs, R. A., and Rosenbaum, P. S. 1968. *English transformational grammar.* Waltham, Mass.: Blaisdell.

Kaplan, R. M. 1975. Transient processing in relative clauses. Ph.D. dissertation, Harvard University.

Kendall, M. G. 1948. *Rank correlation methods.* London: Griffin.

Krashen, S. D. 1975. The critical period for language acquisition and its possible bases. *Ann. N.Y. Acad. Sci.*, 263:211–24.

Snow, C. E. 1972. Mother's speech to children learning language. *Child Devel.* 43:549–65.

Spreen, O. 1973. Psycholinguistics and aphasia: the contribution of Arnold Pick. In *Psycholinguistics and Aphasia*, ed. H. Goodglass and S. Blumstein, pp. 141–70. Baltimore: Johns Hopkins Univ. Press.

Wanner, E., and Maratsos, M. 1972. An augmented transition network model of relative clause comprehension. Unpublished manuscript, Harvard University.

8

COMPREHENSION OF COMPLEX SENTENCES IN CHILDREN AND APHASICS: A TEST OF THE REGRESSION HYPOTHESIS

Alfonso Caramazza and Edgar B. Zurif

The possibility of a relation between aspects of language acquisition and language breakdown has intrigued psychologists and linguists from time to time. A clear statement of such a relation appeared in Roman Jakobson's well-known monograph *Child Language, Aphasia, and Language Universals* (1968). What Jakobson suggested—now termed the regression hypothesis— may be stated as follows: The pattern of language dissolution in aphasics is similar, but in reverse order, to the pattern of language acquisition in children. Those aspects of language competence acquired last, or, more presicely, those that are most dependent on other linguistic developments, are likely to be the first to be disrupted consequent to brain damage; those aspects of language competence that are acquired earliest and are thus "independent" of later developments are likely to be most resistant to the effects of brain damage.

Acceptance of this regression hypothesis implies that language knowledge consists of a layered sequence of mental structures: at the "bottom" are the first acquired and more primitive; at the "top," the last acquired and those currently in use. This view in turn permits a number of brain-behavior interpretations. One possibility can easily be ruled out, namely, that an undifferentiated neural capacity for language varies inversely as a function of the extent of tissue damage; that these variations correspond in some fashion to different levels of neural maturation; and therefore, that these variations and the language skills they sustain correspond to differential levels of language development. The problem with this global "neural power" interpretation is that it ignores the contribution of the site of the lesion. Neural capacity for

The research reported here was supported in part by grants NS 11408 and NS 06209 to Boston University School of Medicine. Some of the material in this paper is taken from Dissociation of algorithmic and heuristic processes in language comprehension: evidence from aphasia, *Brain and Language* 3 (1976): 572–82. Reprinted here with permission of Academic Press, New York.

language is not neuroanatomically undifferentiated; rather, language impairments take different forms that are related to different areas of the brain.

Nor can these clinical forms, i.e., the different aphasic syndromes, be aligned with levels of language acquisition. Developmentally, semantic intentions appear in advance of their adequate syntactic expression. But it does not follow from this that the telegrammatic aphasic, whose speech can at least be understood, is at a more primitive stage than the aphasic whose speech, although marked by a variety of complex grammatical forms, contains incorrect lexical insertions and even neologisms (see also Chapter 5).

At most, then, the regression hypothesis would appear to apply only within specific aphasic syndromes, each of which may be considered to represent the differential breakdown of specific language components (semantic, syntactic, etc.). Within this framework, the hypothesis can be reinterpreted as follows: The critical aphasic variable in the development-dissolution equation is the severity of impairment within each syndrome, and any parallels between language acquisition and language breakdown will hold only between stages of development of specific language components and severity of disruption of like components—the latter associated with determined sites of damage.

We can contrast the stratificational view implicit in the regression hypothesis to one where knowledge structures are considered as "historical gestalts" (Piaget 1963). In this latter approach, earlier mental structures are not given an independent existence; rather, they are considered to be integrated and hence transformed into a single complex hierarchical structure. Here the relation between language acquisition and breakdown is seen as being less direct than that proposed by Jakobson. The hierarchical view suggests that when the adult language-processing apparatus is disrupted, those components that continue to function will do so in a *different* (though possibly related) way from the primitive or earlier modes of processing out of which they developed.

In this report, these rival empirical issues are examined within a particular linguistic context. Young children of various ages and patients presenting different aphasic syndromes were assessed on their ability to process center-embedded object-relative constructions of the type, "The cat that the dog is chasing is brown."

LINGUISTIC THEORY AND LANGUAGE PERFORMANCE

Central to the developmental-breakdown issue is Chomsky's (1965) competence-performance distinction. In its familiar, most general form it separates the tacit knowledge that a speaker has of his language from the psychological mechanisms that produce and interpret utterances.

There is little doubt that an adult native speaker has at his disposal the sort of knowledge that governs performance at the level of judgment and correction.

We recognize "colorless green ideas sleep furiously" as conforming to the structure of English even though the sequence is meaningless. We do so because, presumably, we have an algorithm or failure-proof device that, given a sequence of sounds conformable to its internal restrictions, assigns the sequence a correct structural description.

The problem with this notion of a linguistic device, however, is that it remains rather insulated from experimental disconfirmation. The failure to demonstrate a direct relation between various versions of linguistic theory (e.g., Chomsky 1957, 1965) and language performance (Fodor, Bever, and Garrett 1974) has led to the admonition that linguistic theory should not be taken as a process model (Chomsky 1965). Instead, the relation is held to be abstract and, as a corollary, impervious to prevailing psycholinguistic experimentation.

At present, therefore, linguistic theories can be taken only as rational reconstructions of the sorts of knowledge (and underlying cognitive processes) that form the data base upon which the theories themselves are constructed. In this sense, the relation between linguistic theory and tacit language knowledge is analogous to that between logic and the content of thought—and of like scope.

What is needed is evidence for the existence of finite, deterministic procedures that, in defining tacit language knowledge, actually subserve real-time comprehension and production; or, stated differently, evidence for a process grammar.

Evidence from Aphasia

Evidence that syntactic algorithms form an essential component of language use and are experimentally accessible (verifiable) stems from analyses of Broca's aphasia. Patients presenting this syndrome have a great deal of difficulty expressing themselves; their language output is characterized by distorted articulation, and, most strikingly, they produce a telegrammatic output in which syntax is restricted to simple declarative forms, articles and copula forms appear only infrequently, and verbs are most often uninflected. In contrast to this laborious and distorted output many such patients seem to know what they want to say and show relatively intact comprehension. Given this clinical description it is not unreasonable to invoke what might be termed a sufficiency principle: that language competence is at least equal to a patient's best level of performance and, granting the agrammatic patient's near-normal comprehension, that the patient does seem to retain his knowledge of language. Indeed, accepting that anterior damage spares the patient's tacit knowledge of his language, one current version (Lenneberg 1973; Fodor, Bever, and Garrett 1974) attributes the telegrammatic output solely to a neuromuscular problem: the strain of speaking is so great that the patient speaks asyntactically in order to economize effort.

Yet, several recent analyses of the Broca's metalinguistic performance cast doubt on this notion (Zurif, Caramazza, and Myerson 1972; Zurif and Caramazza 1976; Zurif, Green, Caramazza, and Goodenough, 1976). The metalinguistic data in the studies by Zurif et al. were gained by asking patients with agrammatic speech and control patients with no neurological impairment to judge how words in a written sentence "went best together" in that sentence. No vocal output was required; in fact, precautions were taken to limit even subvocal factors. The patients indicated their judgments simply by pointing to the words that they felt clustered best within the sentence. These judgment-derived word groupings served as input matrices for a clustering procedure (Johnson 1967) that generated, for each sentence separately, a graphic description in the form of a phrase-structure tree. The more often any two words of a sentence were judged to form a "constituent," the more compact was the node joining these two words.

The results of these studies indicate that whereas neurologically intact subjects respected surface-structure constraints in their judgments, the agrammatic aphasics coupled only the content words together. The aphasics attended inconsistently to grammatical morphemes and grouped them in a seemingly unprincipled fashion, such as linking an article with a verb. As a result, the aphasics' judgments violated the linguistic unity of the noun phrases of the sentences (provided by the structure-marking determiners) and also failed to account appropriately for copula forms. That the Broca's tacit knowledge of his language is limited in precisely the same manner as is his production points to a relatively autonomous syntactic component that when disrupted, limits language use and further suggests the likelihood that comprehension skills can be sustained largely by heuristic procedures of a nondeterministic nature. In effect, anterior brain damage appears to disrupt the full structural decoding of sentences independently of other cognitive operations.

Evidence from Language Development

The notion that syntactic operations can be dissociated from semantic inference systems also gains credence from some developmental psycholinguistic evidence. Specifically, there is evidence that a child only progressively masters syntactic algorithms for language comprehension. Thus young children comprehend sentences that are semantically constrained (nonreversible) but fail to comprehend sentences that do not have these semantic constraints (Bever 1970; Strohner and Nelson 1974). These results suggest that young children first use strategies that depend on semantic plausibility to assign a reading to a sentence and only later develop cognitive operations that are independent of semantic plausibility to assign grammatical (functional) relations to sentences (Macnamara 1972). In this view, heuristic procedures are a cognitive prerequisite to the formation of grammatical knowledge in the sense that language experience obtained through the use of heuristic procedures leads to the discovery of grammatical regularities in the language.

A TEST OF THE REGRESSION HYPOTHESIS: CENTER-EMBEDDED SENTENCE COMPREHENSION IN CHILDREN AND APHASICS

Cast in the above framework, the question asked was "What is the relation of algorithmic to heuristic procedures in the child acquiring language and in various forms of language dissolution?" To attempt to answer this question we compared comprehension performance for center-embedded sentences in children ranging in ages from 3 to 6 years old and in three types of aphasia— Broca's, Wernicke's, and conduction.

Broca's aphasia has already been described; very brief descriptions of the other two clinical varieties follow. Like Broca's aphasics, conduction aphasics show good auditory comprehension, but their spontaneous speech is unlike that of the Broca's. Although often restricted to brief bursts of speech, within these bursts the patients produce well-articulated sequences and a variety of syntactic patterns. An intriguing feature of this syndrome—which is considered to result from a posterior lesion involving the arcuate fasciculus—is that repetition is disproportionately impaired in relation to output and comprehension. Patients presenting Wernicke's aphasia—a syndrome usually depending upon a lesion in the posterior region of the first temporal gyrus of the left hemisphere—present impaired comprehension and speech that is termed paragrammatic. This latter clinical feature refers to an output marked by facility in articulation and by many long runs of words in a variety of grammatical constructions. But the output is informationally empty; indefinite noun phrases are often substituted for an appropriate noun, and when a noun with specific reference is chosen, it is often the wrong one.

Experimental Details

There were four types of sentences used in the experiments we carried out: three types of center-embedded object-relative constructions and a set of control sentences.

Type 1 center-embedded sentences were *nonreversible* (CE_S); that is, sentences of this type contained certain semantic constraints that did not permit the alternative pairing of noun phrases (NP) and verb phrases (VP). Consider in this respect, "The apple that the boy is eating is red." Clearly, in this sentence it must be the boy, not the apple that is doing the eating. Thus the first NP must be paired with the second VP.

Type 2 sentences were *reversible* center-embedded sentences (CE_R). In these sentences certain semantic constraints were relaxed and a correct interpretation depended on a knowledge of syntactic regularities of the language. An example of this sentence type is; "The boy that the girl is chasing is tall." In this case both the boy and the girl can do the chasing and both can be tall. A correct interpretation of this sentence requires that a correct pairing be made between "girl" and "chase" and "boy" and "is tall." Note that this sentence is not structurally ambiguous. Native speakers of English will assign only one meaning to this sentence.

Sentences of the third type were *improbable* but grammatically well formed (CE_I). An example of such sentences is, "The boy that the dog is patting is fat." This sentence violates neither syntactic nor semantic rules of English. Yet it is clearly deviant from the point of view of our knowledge of the world. It is usually boys that pat dogs and not vice versa. It remains the case, however, that adult speakers of the language can assign a correct interpretation to sentences of this type.

The fourth type of sentences were *control sentences* (C) of the form "The boy is eating a red apple." These sentences, like the CE sentences, have two underlying sentoids. In the example given above they would be (1) The boy is eating an apple and (2) The apple is red. Of course, the deep structure of the control and CE sentences are not the same.

The study made use of a sentence-picture matching task. And if we assume that a correct choice can be made on the basis of partial information, the nature of the distractor item becomes critical. This can be illustrated by an analysis of the sentence material used in the present research.

Consider the sentence "The cat that the dog is chasing is brown" in terms of its underlying propositions: (1) The dog is chasing a cat; and (2) The cat is brown. A correct pictorial representation of this sentence must depict both propositions correctly. Now, it is obvious that a distractor (incorrect item) can depict a change in either or both of these two propositions, making the whole picture an incorrect referent of the sentence. Thus, for example, focusing upon only one of the propositions, we can show a picture of a dog chasing a black cat rather than a brown one.

Of the many possible contrast types that could have been constructed for each sentence, we chose the following four: (1) a change in the complement (predicate adjective) of the matrix sentence; (2) an incorrect depiction of the main verb; (3) an incorrect depiction of both the main verb and the complement; and (4) a picture showing a reversal of matrix sentence subject noun (N_1) with embedded sentence subject noun (N_2). As an example of these contrasts for the sentence "The cat that the dog is chasing is brown," the four incorrect alternatives were: (1) a dog chasing a *black* cat; (2) a dog *biting* a brown cat; (3) a dog *biting* a *black* cat; and (4) a *cat* chasing a brown *dog*. On any one trial the correct pictorial representation of the auditorily presented sentence was paired with *one* of the four incorrect pictorial representations. The subject's task was to choose from the pair of pictures the one that represented the cognitive content of the spoken sentence.

It is quite obvious that in some of the conditions the subjects' choice need not have depended on his full understanding of the spoken sentence but could have been made on the basis of partial information. In the complement change condition (Condition 1), for example, all the subject needed to know to choose a correct match to the spoken sentence was that the cat is brown, not *black*. It is also apparent that the four distractor-type conditions require different levels of understanding in order for subjects to respond correctly. The important aspect to note here is the difference between the "reversal of N_1 with N_2" and the other three incorrect alternatives that feature lexical changes. The incorrect alternatives that represent changes 1, 2, and 3 each respect the syntactic relation that obtains between the matrix sentence and the embedded sentence. The locus of change for 4, however, is to be found in the syntactc relationship between the two underlying sentences. Thus, a proper test of syntactic understanding is possible only in the fourth picture-contrast condition.

The aphasic patients included in this study were classified on the basis of clinical examination and on the results of the Boston Diagnostic Aphasia Test (Goodglass and Kaplan 1972). Where possible, laboratory data (Brain scan and EEG) provided supporting evidence for lesion localization. There were five Broca's aphasic patients, five conduction aphasics, and five patients presenting Wernicke's aphasia. Five male patients chosen from the nonneurological wards of the Boston Veterans Administration Hospital served as control subjects. These patients were comparable in age and educational background to the aphasic patients.

The children studied were divided into four groups of fifteen subjects each. The median ages in months for each group were: 42 (3 year olds), 52 (4 year olds), 66 (5 year olds), and 76 (6 year olds).

The adult patients and the children were tested individually in a quiet room and were screened to insure that they understood the general testing requirements. Each subject received a different random order of the 32 test sentences: 2 sentences for each combination of the four sentence types (semantically constrained, reversible, improbable, and control) and the four distractor types (complement, main verb, main verb and complement, and subject-object reversal). The experimenter read each sentence in a clear voice at a conversational pace, and the subject was required to indicate his choice of the picture that captured the meaning of the sentence. The subject's response could be either verbal or simply a pointing gesture. Each response was recorded immediately.

Developmental Results and Their Implications

The age main effect is relevant to the question of what processes are operating at various ages. A comparison of adjacent age-group means (table 8.1) shows that performance improved substantially between 3 and 4 years and between 5 and 6 years but that little improvement seemed to take place between 4 and 5 years of age. Other investigators (e.g., Brown 1971) have already pointed out that in the acquisition of embedded constructions there is a much more rapid improvement in performance between the age of 3 and 4 than between 4 and 5 years. But the marked improvement in performance between the ages of 5 and 6 years has been ignored (Gaer 1969). And this has led to the false impression that the comprehension of center-embedded constructions as a function of age can be characterized by a smooth, positively increasing, negatively accelerating curve, and that this curve can be taken as characteristic of a single phase model of rule acquisition.

On the contrary, the rate of improvement with age observed here suggests the need for a two-phase model of the acquisition of center-embedding rules or for the acquisition of language comprehension strategies in general. To check this observation further, trend analyses on mean correct responses for age groups were carried out. Consistent with the qualitative observations stated earlier, both linear and cubic components were present ($p < 0.01$ and $p < 0.05$, respectively).

It seems, then, that in dealing with center-embedded sentences, a first set of strategies and rules is acquired between 3 and 4 years of age and that a reformulation and addition to these rules and strategies seems to take place between the ages of 5 and 6 years. Further details can be added: For the noun-phrase reversal condition, the 3-, 4-, and 5-year-old children performed essentially at chance level; however, for the other conditions—which could be dealt with on the basis of partial information—they performed at 70% to 95% level of accuracy. This pattern contrasts significantly with that of 6-year-old children who performed relatively accurately in all the distractor conditions (figure 8.1). Thus, whatever strategies the 3 to 5 year olds may be using in decoding the meaning of sentences, it is certainly not an algorithmlike syntactic

Table 8.1

Mean Correct Responses
for Age Groups (maximum
possible score $= 32$)

Age Group	Mean
3	22.20
4	25.67
5	26.80
6	29.33

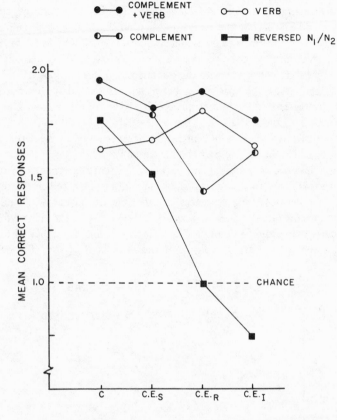

Fig. 8.1 Mean correct responses for distractor types at each age level (age x distractor type).
Post-hoc comparisons (Newman-Keuls—p. < 0.05)
Reversed N_1/N_2 type 3 4 5 6

processing device. Indeed, it seems that up to age 5 subjects are relying heavily on diagnostic indicators of a semantic nature to help them make their choice. It is only at age 6, during the second phase of development, that the child begins to use strategies that reflect the importance of syntactic cues.

An objection that could be raised is that the young subjects were incapable of making the proper discrimination, not because of the linguistic complexity, but because of some general difficulty with the distractor items. This objection, however, can be discarded on the basis of the results obtained in the sentence type x distractor type interaction. Thus, in figure 8.2, it can be seen that performance with the reversed Ns distractor item for control sentences was not any worse than for the other distractors. The difficulty only emerged when the sentences were center-embedded and especially when semantic and pragmatic constraints were removed (CE_R and CE_I). This would be expected if subjects could not decode the syntax and had no semantic cues to help them. Furthermore, in the case of CE_I sentences, performance was even worse than chance, suggesting that given the degree of co..plexity, subjects were choosing pictures that were consistent with their knowledge of the world.

To further assess the relationship between semantic and syntactic comprehension strategies within the two phases described above, a second analysis was restricted to those trials with the reversed N_1/N_2 condition. Only these sentences provide a measure of sentence comprehension that is relatively free of the subject's ability to use partial information.

Figure 8.3 presents mean-correct responses for sentence types as a function of age. In this figure there are two major outcomes to be noted. First, there is the contrast between CE_S sentences, on the one hand, and CE_R and CE_I sentences, on the other, at ages 3, 4, and 5. Whereas the 3 year olds performed more poorly than 4 and 5 year olds ($p < 0.01$) on CE_I sentences, they performed about as well ($p > 0.05$) on CE_R sentences, and better ($p < 0.05$) on CE_I

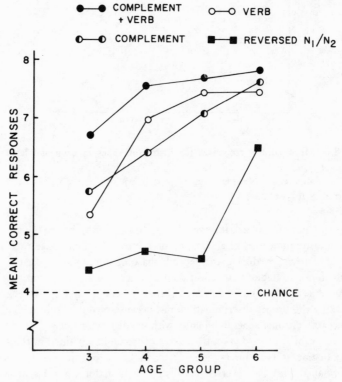

Fig. 8.2 Mean correct responses for distractor types at each sentence type level (sentence type x distractor type).

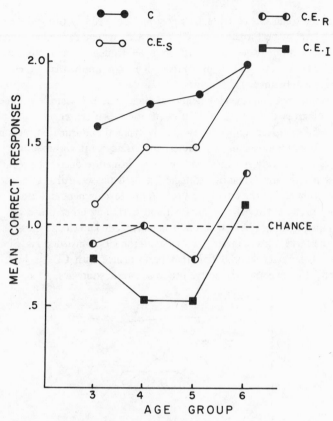

Fig. 8.3 Mean correct responses for sentence type at each age level (age x sentence type) for reversed N_1/N_2 data only.
Post-hoc comparisons (Newman-Keuls—$p < 0.05$)

C.E.$_S$	3	4	5	6
C.E.$_R$	3	4	5	6
C.E.$_I$	3	4	5	6

sentences. These contrasts lead to the conclusion that phase 1 can be characterized primarily, although not only, as semantic in nature. Thus, the increase in performance between age 3 and 4 for CE_S sentences appears due to an improved ability to utilize semantic constraints in these sentences. After all, when these constraints were reversed, (sentences CE_I), performance decreased. This suggests further that both semantic and pragmatic factors are important in deriving strategies for language comprehension.

Properties for phase 2 can be inferred from the change in performance between ages 5 and 6 years. In this age range there is a marked increase in performance for all types of sentences ($p < 0.01$), suggesting that the subjects now also use some sort of syntactic algorithm for decoding the sentences. Yet, from the level of performance for CE_R and CE_I sentences it would seem that this syntactic strategy was still not completely independent of semantic and pragmatic constraints. This, of course, does not imply that independence may never be obtained.

To summarize our developmental findings, phase 1 seems to reflect primarily an increased ability to deal with semantic cues in sentences, while phase 2 involves the increased ability to use purely syntactic information, presumably in some algorithmic fashion. Characterizing strategies in the first and second phases as respectively semantic and syntactic in nature does not preclude the use of syntactic and semantic strategies in both phases. All that is intended by this notion is that the rate of progress in the development and use of certain strategies predominates over others without excluding other processes. Thus, for example, it cannot be denied that some syntactic knowledge must be available to the 3 year olds in order to understand the CE_S constructions. Similarly, even in 6 year olds we still find that performance with CE_S is better than CE_R and CE_I, reflecting the active use of semantic strategies. At any rate, the

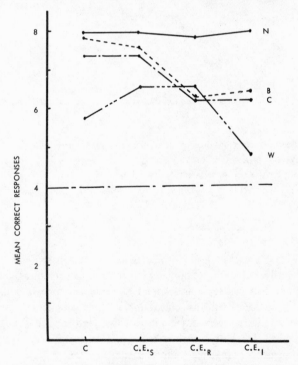

Fig. 8.4   Mean correct performance for each patient group (N = Normal, B = Broca's, C = conduction, and W = Wernicke's) as a function of sentence type (C.E.$_S$ = semantically constrained, C.E.$_R$ = reversible, C.E.$_I$ = improbable, and C = control).

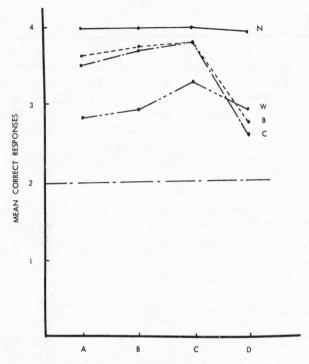

Fig. 8.5 Mean correct performance for each patient group (N = Normal, B = Broca's, C = conduction, and W = Wernicke's) as a function of distractor types (A = predicate adjective change, B = main verb change, C = predicate adjective and main verb change, and D = subject-object reversal).

child acquiring a language appears to proceed by first developing semantic strategies and then by using these strategies to construct algorithmic procedures for decoding the syntax of language (see Macnamara 1972).

Aphasia Results and Their Implications

The results relevant to our contention that brain damage may independently affect syntactic and semantic processes are charted in figure 8.4, which shows mean correct performance for each group of aphasics and the control group as a function of sentence type. There are a number of points to be noted in this figure. First, when semantic constraints were absent, as in the CE_R and CE_I sentences, performance for the conduction and the Broca's aphasics dropped substantially. This suggests that both Broca's and conduction aphasics are impaired in their capacity to algorithmically compute a full structural description of the CE sentences. Parenthetically, given the finding that the conduction aphasics performed in a very similar manner to the Broca's, it seems that, alongside the repetition deficit in conduction aphasia, there is an additional disruption to mechanisms of comprehension.

While it is of interest to note that the Wernicke's aphasics performed very differently from the other aphasic groups, we remain perplexed about the actual pattern of their performance; their general level of performance was quite high, but they seemed insensitive to either the syntactic (C vs. CE) or the semantic CE_S vs. CE_R and CE_I) factors manipulated in the experiment. (The good level of performance in the Wernicke's patients may have been due simply to a bias in the selection of patients; since patients had to have enough comprehension skills to be able to understand our instructions and perform the experimental task, we likely included only very mildly impaired, atypical Wernicke's aphasics.)

Figure 8.5 shows mean correct responses for the groups as a function of distractor types. As can be seen in this figure, Broca's and conduction aphasic patients performed quite accurately on distractor types that cued only lexical

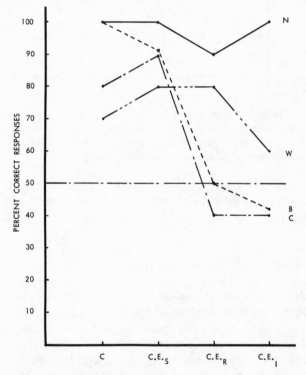

Fig. 8.6   Mean correct performance for each patient group (N = normal, B = Broca's, C = conduction, and W = Wernicke's) as a function of sentence type (C.E.$_S$ = semantically constrained, C.E.$_R$ = reversible, C.E.$_I$ = improbable and C = control) for the subject-object reversal distractor type only.

changes (83% to 92%). However, when the distractor type marked a syntactic change, performance over all sentence types dropped to about 68%. This provides further evidence for the notion that neither the Broca's nor the conduction aphasics have retained syntactic algorithmic processes. Clearly, then, these two patient groups were relying, just as the 3-, 4-, and 5-year-old children do, on partial cues to make the correct choice; when they had to rely on syntax, their performance was considerably impaired.

Consequently, a fair assessment of their comprehension skills, at least with respect to their ability to use algorithmic processes, can only be obtained by considering their performance on sentence types for the reversed N_1/N_2 distractor-type condition. Figure 8.6 depicts these data. Again, the conclusion is inescapable—Broca's and conduction aphasics seem relatively incapable of syntactic processing. Thus, for those sentences that were semantically constrained, performance was approximately at the 90% level; but it dropped to chance level when these semantic constraints were not avilable. As for the Wernicke's, their pattern of performance again remains uninterpretable.

It appears that the presumed dissociation between language production and comprehension does not hold for Broca's and conduction aphasics; the present analysis of their comprehension skills suggests that such patients are as impaired in comprehension as they are in production. The impairment, moreover, is specific: these subjects are unable to use syntacticlike algorithmic processes. Yet, of equal importance, they have retained the capacity to use heuristic procedures to assign a semantic interpretation to, at best, an incompletely represented syntactic organization. From the evidence at hand, these heuristics are based upon the semantic plausibility of the arrangement of lexical items (CE_S vs. CE_R sentences) and upon a sequential regularity whereby noun-verb surface arrangements can be mapped as actor-action relations (control sentences). These results have clear implications both for neurolinguistic and normal language-processing theories.

These data, together with previously reported metalinguistic data, suggest that Broca's and conduction aphasics are incapable of processing syntactic structure in an independent fashion (see also Saffran and Marin 1975; Scholes, Chapter 9). Granting this conclusion and granting also that Broca's aphasics show relatively intact comprehension, it would appear that heuristic procedures can assign meaning without the full participation of a grammar and that the grammar is normally used in a back-up fashion for those instances in which the input is insufficiently constrained for the efficient use of heuristic procedures.

ACQUISITION AND APHASIA: SUMMARY

1. All three aphasic groups are impaired in their syntactic knowledge. Children between the ages of 3 and 5 also do not have syntactic algorithms at their disposal. But 6-year-old children do.

2. The Wernicke's aphasics do not resemble any of the stages of language acquisition charted here.

3. Broca's and conduction aphasics seem to perform in a similar way to the younger children, but only in the sense that both groups cannot deal with syntactic information algorithmically. There are, however, important differences between these populations. Unlike the 3 to 5 year olds, the aphasics performed equally well on the C and CE$_S$ sentences, suggesting that they are not as dependent on an NVN-like strategy. Stated more generally, the aphasics seem to have a more efficient system for mapping meaning, one that allows operations on discontinuous constituents, i.e., embedding. This distinction is crucial since it shows that the strategies for inferring meaning from an utterance in the aphasic and the child need not be the same. Our results, then, support the hierarchical gestalt view of knowledge organization.

4. We have argued that the similarity in performance between the aphasic and the child may be misleading. That is, the differences that emerged seem to be important enough to be considered as possible counterevidence for the regression hypothesis. A more reasonable view is that language comprehension is to be seen as the result of a complex inferential process. The rules can be separated roughly into semanticlike and syntacticlike processes. Both kinds of inference rules operate at all levels of functioning, whether it be at the level of the young child, the adult, or the aphasic. The difference is to be found predominantly in the relative distribution of the use of each of these two sets of rules. The young child first develops semantic inferential rules consonant with his general cognitive development; as his general cognitive apparatus expands so do his semantic inferential strategies. In addition to the development of these semantic strategies, the child constructs a more rigorous inference system based on the syntactic regularities of his language. In the case of language breakdown, if syntactic knowledge is impaired the aphasic will have to rely primarily on his semantic inference system, a system that includes a lifetime of experience and knowledge. It seems unlikely that the inference processes used by the aphasic will strictly correspond to those used by the child. There will certainly be a similarity in performance, but, consonant with the hierarchical model, there is no point where complete correspondence obtains between the child's developing rules for mapping meanings and the residual functions the aphasic is using to infer meanings.

REFERENCES

Bever, T. G. 1970. The cognitive basis for linguistic structures. In *Cognition and the development of language*, ed. J. R. Hayes, pp. 297–352. New York: John Wiley & Sons.

Brown, H. D. 1971. Children's comprehension of relativized English sentences. *Child Devel.* 42:1923–36.

Chomsky, N. 1957. *Syntactic structures.* The Hague: Mouton.

———. 1965. *Aspects of the theory of syntax.* Cambridge, Mass.: M.I.T. Press.

Fodor, J. A.; Bever, T. G.; and Garrett, M. F. 1974. *The psychology of language: an introduction to psycholinguistics and generative grammar.* New York: McGraw-Hill.

Gaer, E. P. 1969. Children's understanding and production of sentences. *J. Verb. Learning Verb. Behav.* 8:289–94.

Goodglass, H., and Kaplan, E. 1972. *The assessment of aphasia and related disorders.* Philadelphia: Lea & Febiger.

Jakobson, R. 1968. *Child language, aphasia, and phonological universals,* trans. A. R. Keiler. The Hague: Mouton.

Johnson, S. C. 1967. Hierarchical clustering schemes. *Psychometrika* 241–54.

Lenneberg, E. 1973. The neurology of language. *Daedalus* 102:115–33.

Macnamara, J. 1972. Cognitive basis of language learning in infants. *Psychol. Rev.* 79:1–13.

Piaget, J. 1963. *The origins of intelligence in children.* New York: W. W. Norton.

Saffran, E., and Marin, O. 1975. Immediate memory for word lists and sentences in a patient with deficient auditory short term memory. *Brain and Language* 3:420–33.

Strohner, H., and Nelson, K. E. 1974. The young child's development of sentence comprehension: Influence of event probability, nonverbal content, syntactic form, and strategies. *Child Devel.* 45:567–76.

Zurif, E. B., and Caramazza, A. 1976. Psycholinguistic structures in aphasia: studies in syntax and semantics. In *Studies in neurolinguistics,* ed. H. Whitaker and H. Whitaker. New York: Academic Press.

Zurif, E. B.; Caramazza, A.; and Myerson, R. 1972. Grammatical judgments of agrammatic aphasics. *Neuropsychologia* 10:405–17.

Zurif, E. B.; Green, E.; Caramazza, A.; and Goodenough, C. 1976. Grammatical intuitions of aphasic patients: sensitivity to functors. *Cortex* 12:183–6.

9

SYNTACTIC AND LEXICAL COMPONENTS OF SENTENCE COMPREHENSION

Robert J. Scholes

INTRODUCTION

Comprehension and Production

Studies of both developmental linguistics and aphasia have traditionally and largely examined the production of linguistic signals. There are numerous problems in attempting to describe the linguistic capability of an individual by looking at his speech output. In the first place, the absence of a particular expression or construction in a given corpus says nothing about a person's ability to produce it; he may simply not have had occasion to produce it. Secondly, it is clear that an individual can produce utterances that are not properly in his domain of linguistic competence (e.g., the imitation of expressions in other languages). Nonetheless, the establishment of the milestones of language acquisition have been based largely on the emergence of increasingly complex types of utterances (see Lee and Cantor 1971), and few attempts have been made to plot a developing curve of comprehension ability (Carrow 1968). Similarly, studies of the comprehension of language in impaired populations are rare. Schlessinger (1970) and Bellugi and Klima (1972) have researched the ability of deaf subjects to comprehend syntactic aspects of sentences in signing, and some work on sentence comprehension in the hard-of-hearing has been done; but influential work is largely limited to the language *produced* by those whose hearing is impaired. In aphasiology, little more than lip service is paid to comprehension deficits. Terms such as *receptive aphasia* occur, but even here the defining characteristics are often features of the patient's speech (e.g., "In simple terms some patients produce many significant substantive words, primarily nouns but also action verbs and significant modifiers, whereas others use many relational words, adjectives, adverbs, modifying phrases, or cliches but lack the specific substantive word to complete the statement" [Benson 1967, p. 378]). The Boston Diagnostic Aphasia Examination (Goodglass and Kaplan 1972) utilizes several tests of auditory comprehension but does not

163

allow for autonomous syntactic or lexical deficits (i.e., the lexically impaired patient will score badly on all items). The common practice among aphasiologists of speaking of some patient's comprehension as being "disturbed" or "good" is not very informative to the linguist struggling with the linguistic complexities of sentence comprehension.

What follows is an attempt to show that the comprehension ability of both normal and language-impaired groups can be studied with results that relate directly to linguistics and that provide an informative and interesting characterization of language acquisition and debilitation. The data will be primarily those gathered by the author in a series of studies with several co-investigators. These data will be supplemented, where appropriate, with results from other published work.

Sentence Comprehension

In order to provide a framework for our discussion, let us establish a simple model of sentence comprehension. A sentence of a natural language consists of one or more *major lexical items* (MLI) (Chomsky and Halle 1968) embedded in a syntactic framework of relational and modificational formatives. MLI are, basically, nouns, verbs, and adjectives, and the syntactic formatives include such things as prepositions, pronouns, articles, and derivational or inflexional affixes. Strings of syntactic formatives and MLI constitute the superficial signals of the sentence.

It is generally agreed that sentence comprehension involves the process of converting signals to underlying, logical representations of sentences; i.e., deep structures.

The basis for considering deep structure as an isolable representation lies largely in the finding (by Jacques Mehler and others in the early 1960s; see Mehler 1963, 1964) that memory for sentences is best represented by the simple, active, affirmative, declarative (*kernel*, or *SAAD*) form of the sentence plus a "tag" containing the transformational processes the sentence has undergone in gaining its surface form. This claim was based on the finding that the kernel and its tag decayed in memory at different rates—that, for example, after some period of time both an active and a passive form of a sentence were remembered as having been presented in the active form; the interpretation being that the passive transformation "tag" has been forgotten. Other support came from the finding by Savin and Perchonock (1965) that the amount of "space taken up in memory [is] proportional to the number of transformational rules implicit in the surface structure of the sentence"—e.g., a sentence that is interrogative and passive takes up more space than one that is either interrogative or passive.[*]

---

[*] More recent work, however, suggests an alternative interpretation for the transformation effect on short-term memory (Scholes, Heilman, and Rasbury 1975; Scholes, Rasbury, Scholes, and Dowling 1976).

However it is done, it seems clear that for a sentence to be stored in a way that most directly relates to its meaning, the form of storage must be a representation in which the logical relationships and structure are expressed. For the purposes of this discussion we will simply assume that some kind of deep structure is recovered from the input signal and that it is this deep structure that forms the basis for sentence memory and any response (imitation, recall, verification, etc.) the subject makes.

Thus, the simplest model of sentence comprehension may be represented as in figure 9.1.

When we now ask how this comprehension analysis takes the incoming signals and derives the deep structure, certain basic facts must be considered.

1. The deep structure can be recovered solely on the basis of lexical information (i.e., MLI) when this information yields a unique structure. This is supported by the greater time required for the verification of passives than for the corresponding actives when either of the noun phrases can function as subject or object; when only one noun phrase can be the subject and only one the object, no latency differences are observed (Slobin 1966).

2. The deep structure can be recovered solely on the basis of syntactic information when the major lexical items are not glossed. No experiments have been done or need to be done to verify this point; it is clear because one can interpret such sentences as Lewis Carroll's "all mimsy were the borogroves," where the content words are empty.

3. Over at least some period of time, not only is the meaning of a sentence known, but the actual form in which it was heard (the superficial structure [SS]) is also known. Thus, this information must be retained through the comprehension process. Given, then, a sentence such as "That man is despised by nearly everyone he meets," the output of the comprehension strategy must include the information represented by the deep structure and also the information that the form in which the sentence was heard has undergone a number of transformations (passivization, pronominalization, etc.) (see Carroll 1971, p. 65 et passim, for discussion).

4. Although it would seem to follow from the third point that if one "knows" both the surface structure and the deep structure for a given sentence,

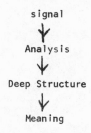

Fig. 9.1 Basic comprehension.

he must also "know" the rules that relate the two representations (that is, he must know the transformational rules that have been applied in the derivation) this is not necessarily the case. It will be seen later that there is some reason to suppose that transformational rules are applied only when a discrepancy between deep- and surface-structure information occurs.

To summarize the above points, the comprehension algorithm must yield the deep structure of the sentence, the associated surface structure of the sentence, and, in some cases, the transformational rules that relate the two; and it must be able to do this on the basis of lexical information, syntactic information, or both. The kind of rule that yields information on the basis of morphological (e.g., inflexions) and acoustic information is called an *inference* rule; the kind of rule that projects deep structures on the basis of distributional restrictions on lexical items is called a *projection* rule. A model of the comprehension process that fits the requirements listed above and operates with inference, projection, and transformational rules is shown in figure 9.2.

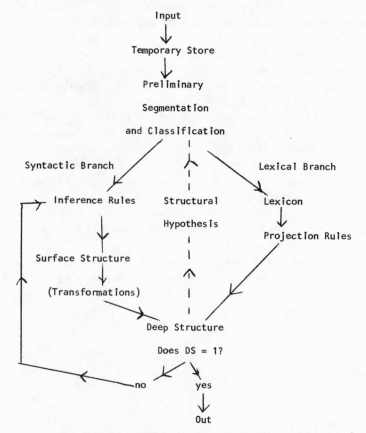

Fig. 9.2   The parallel process comprehension model.

One component of figure 9.2 that has not yet been discussed is the box labeled "structural hypothesis." This is a fairly complex component in which various kinds of predictions about the structure of the incoming sentences are applied.

One such prediction is that a sentence will most likely have an actor-action-(object) sequence. This prediction has been found (Bever 1970) to obtain in a variety of cases. It explains, for example, subject behavior with self-embedded constructions in which the first elements fit the predicted structure, e.g., "*The bird flies* bothered became morose." Subjects are largely unable to comprehend such strings since, their initial hypothesis having been confirmed and other potential structures having been rejected, they are unable to recover the alternative hypotheses when the primary one is shown to be false. Bever has also found evidence that these probabilistic strategies are acquired at a different rate from the basic grammar of the language.

Another type of structural hypothesis has to do with the frequency with which words are associated in context (an alternative phraseology would speak of the number of semantic features the words have in common, but since we are dealing primarily with the sequential processing of sentences, we will use the less abstract terminology). Jarvella (1970) and Rosenberg (1968, 1969) have shown that sentences like "The doctor cured the patient" (a) are more intelligible (using envelope-matched noise) than sentences like "The doctor liked the author" (b). Sentences like (a) are said to be *semantically well integrated* (SWI); those like (b), *semantically poorly integrated* (SPI), the idea being that *doctor/cured/patient* are more closely associated—better integrated (share more semantic features)—than *doctor/liked/author*. If a sentence frame such as "the doctor _____ the _____" is given, subjects will fill in *cured* and *patient* much more frequently than items like *liked* and *author*. That sentence (a) is significantly more intelligible under given signal-noise ratios than is sentence (b) suggests that semantic integration is part of the prediction that listeners make when hearing sentences. Such information, within the model given by figure 9.2, must necessarily come from projection rules operating on lexical information (in another framework, this is expressed in terms of word association of the syntagmatic, as opposed to paradigmatic, type).

Another obvious (but generally ignored in recent literature) source of information relevant to predicting sentence structure lies in acoustic signals probably best described as tone of voice. These signals may well be decomposed into various stress, intonation, and juncture phenomena, but the inability of research to separate out such components easily leads to an acceptance of the more general term. Note, for example, the way in which the first clauses of sentences (c) and (d) would be spoken; such "tone of voice" phenomena yield information regarding the imperative-declarative difference in the following two readings:

(c) You will wash your hands, young man, and stop arguing with me!

(d) You will wash your hands, young man, or you will not; I don't care.

Thus, the structural hypotheses are advanced in part on the basis of acquired information on the popularity of sentence types and structures, in part on the basis of semantic associations, and in part on the basis of normal "ways of saying" certain structures. There may well be other sources of such structural predictions, sources that may or may not properly be part of a general theory of sentence comprehension. A source that is probably not part of such a theory is information about particular modes of expression of specific individuals (I have a colleague whose normal speech behavior is to start one sentence, which turns out to be irrelevant to the message and which is halted somewhere, and then to come out with the sentence containing the message. I have learned never to listen to his first utterance, but to wait until the pause and re-start before paying attention). A source that probably ought to be considered, but that cannot be in any very rigorous way, is the listener's extralinguistic knowledge relevant to the message—such information as, say, knowing when and where the sentence is being said, as well as having experience about the real world that may or may not be exhaustively accounted for by such things as semantic features (for example, does the semantic information regarding the word *Pinkville* include the fact that it typically refers not to a place but to a criminal act?).

In his doctoral dissertation, Eric Wanner set forth the basic theoretical foundations for the study of sentence comprehension and recall (Wanner 1968). Wanner first presented arguments and experimental evidence to the effect that the form of sentences in memory is essentially that of the deep-structure propositions that underlie the given sentence. Given two sentences such as "The governor asked the detective to cease drinking" (e) and "The governor asked the detective to prevent drinking" (f), memory would then contain the following propositions for each sentence:

(e) The governor ask the detective
      the detective cease
      the detective drink
(f) The governor ask the detective
      the detective prevent
      someone drink

Retaining only such propositions, and not the grammatical facts that related them in the original sentences, we would then anticipate that in recall tasks of certain latencies, subjects would produce sentences from which the same propositions are recoverable, but they would not retain the relationships obtaining in the originals. For example, a subject might produce strings such as: "The detective ceased drinking because the governor asked him to" (g) and "The governor asked the detective to prevent anyone from drinking" (h), for (e) and (f), respectively.

If we assume that Wanner is correct in his assessment of the form of sentences in memory, we can then state the problem of explicating the process of comprehension in the following way: how does the listener recover the deep-structure propositions from a given input sentence? Given a scheme such as that in figure 9.1, we can ask, what are the required properties of a comprehension analysis.

Wanner defines and discusses three candidates for such a device: *anlaysis by synthesis*, the *finite transformer*, and the *lexical model*.

Analysis by synthesis is defined (p. 136) as follows: "The input sentence is stored temporarily and subjected to a rough preliminary analysis. The results of this analysis are passed to a synthetic component which consists entirely of a transformational grammar. The grammar in turn simply generates all the sentences which are consistent with the results of preliminary analysis. Since the grammatical operations involved in generating a sentence automatically provide it with a structural description, the sequence of grammatical rules which synthesize a successful match constitute the relevant output of the device." This description is schematized in figure 9.3 (Wanner's figure 4.1).

Wanner dismisses this proposal as a tenable psychological model of comprehension since there appears to be no psychologically valid way to delimit the number of structural descriptions that will be generated in the search for a match. Lacking such a limiting factor, there is no guarantee that the algorithm will terminate in a finite amount of time.

The *finite transformer* is described by Wanner (pp. 143–4) as follows: "Instead of using superficial information as a source of cues which govern the application of rules in synthesis, the *finite transformer* attempts to find a transformation whose structural result matches the input sentence ... whereupon the input is detransformed during *analysis*." Thus, "the synthetic component is entirely eliminated and the deep structure of any sentence is recovered by means of applying a sequence of inverse transformational rules." This description is schematized in figure 9.4.

Wanner's criticism of this proposal is that "it is vulnerable to dead-ended analyses ... which result because the superficial phrase structure analysis of the input is not strong enough to guarantee that the correct path through the inverse transformations will be chosen." Thus, for example, a sentence like "The baby was found by the lamppost" (1) matches the structural result of the

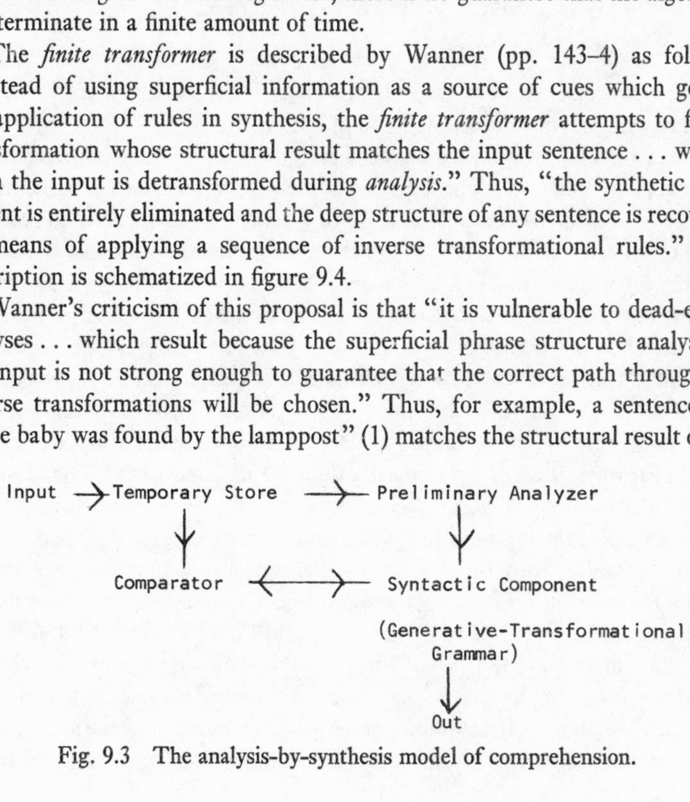

Fig. 9.3   The analysis-by-synthesis model of comprehension.

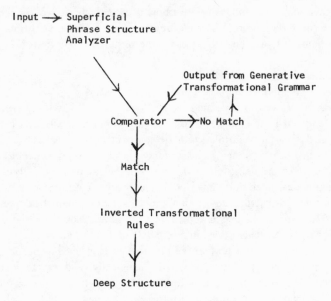

Fig. 9.4   The finite transformer.

inverse *passive* transformation and will thus result in the incorrect deep-structure analysis that the lamppost found the baby.

The last of the comprehension strategies, the *lexical model*, is characterized by Wanner as follows; "The input enters the temporary store sequentially, word by word. Each word is looked up in a lexicon of the type required by a transformational grammar (cf. Chomsky 1965). Such a dictionary specifies both the intrinsic semantic and syntactic properties of each word as well as information about the deep structure context in which each word can appear. . . . This lexical information passes to the component containing the 'constructional rules' [my 'projection rules'] which consists essentially of deformed versions of the selectional rules as defined by the grammar" (p. 149). To illustrate, among the "intrinsic semantic properties" of a word are the semantic features or sets of features that compositionally describe its "meaning." For example, a word such as *woman* is, semantically, a matrix of semantic features like [+ human], [+ female], [+ adult], and so on. Its ambiguity (compare "That woman is afraid of men" and "woman is afraid of man") is denoted, in this case, by the semantic feature specification that the item may or may not be a specific individual [+/− generic] (see Katz and Fodor 1963; Katz 1966). The "intrinsic syntactic properties" of a word are the syntactic contexts in which it may occur; for example, *woman* may be a noun phrase (in one of its readings), or the head of a noun phrase (in the other of its readings), which phrase may in turn be part of prepositional phrases, verb phrases, and so forth. Also, the transformational possibilities of the words are stated as such properties; for example, the fact that the verb *hit* can be passivized, while *seem* cannot:

(j) The boor was hit by him (he hit the boor).
(k) *The boor was seemed by him (he seemed a boor).

The constructional rules are the set of deep-structure contexts, specified in terms of abstract structures, in which each lexical item may occur. For example, the verb *see* takes a subject-noun phrase that must be animate, it requires a (expressed or understood) direct object that may be anything semantically, and it does not take an indirect object. Such facts can be expressed by a notation such as:

$$[\text{NP}_{\text{animate}}] \underline{\quad\quad} V \underline{\quad\quad} (\text{*Ind Obj})[\text{NP}_x]$$

Given, then, a sentence containing the three lexical items *mouse, cheese,* and *eat,* the syntactic features and projection rules associated with these items will show that only one logical (deep) structure is possible (i.e., *eat* requires an animate subject, *cheese* is not animate, but *mouse* is), and the semantic features will, with the appropriate rules applied to these matrixes in their deep-structure relations, yield a correct reading of the sentence. None of these operations requires information concerning the order of the lexical items in the superficial structure—that is, whether the actual utterance was active or passive is irrelevant.

For other sentences, the lexical model is insufficient. For example, given a sentence such as "The girl was kissed by the boy" (1), the semantic and syntactic constraints associated with *girl, boy,* and *kiss* are insufficient to yield the correct reading of the sentence. To get the correct reading, one must know that the sentence is a passive, and that, therefore, the correct deep structure is given by reversing the passive transformational rule—that is, if the passive transformation is something like

$$T_{\text{pas}}: NP_1 + V + NP_2 \Rightarrow NP_2 + \text{Aux} + V + \text{by} + NP_1,$$

then the deep structure is recovered by reversing the direction of the rule. The fact that the sentence is a passive is found by reference to the identification of the word *by* preceding the second noun phrase and an auxiliary preceding the verb. This kind of information is applied, in Wanner's characterization, by "inference rules." "It is the job of the component containing the so-called 'inference rules' to locate superficial cues which distinguish ... among competing ... deep structures" (p. 153).

It would appear that at least two distinct types of inference rule are required. In one case (the case under discussion above), the lexical information and projection rules do not yield a unique deep structure, and one must refer to the superficial structure of the sentence—for example, to the information that, owing to the sequence Determiner + Noun + Aux + Verb + by +

Determiner + Noun, the sentence is potentially a passive. Such a surface structure, given the information provided on the lexical analysis, yields the correct reading of such cases as reversible passives. In these, the lexical operations are clearly logically prior to the inference rules, and these latter rules are employed only when the prior analysis is nonunique.

There are, however, data to suggest that superficial structure analysis precedes lexical analysis. In experiments involving self-embedded sentences (sentences in which one clause is embedded within another, and both have the same general syntactic structures—e.g., "The corn the bird the hunter shot ate grew wild" (Bever 1968, p. 36, 37; see also Blumenthal 1967)) it was found that when the first sequence of words could be interpreted as a simple declarative sentence, the subject's comprehension of the whole sentence was essentially destroyed. For example, if one takes an embedded structure such as "The bird that flies bothered wouldn't touch the seeds" (m), and deletes the *that* (a perfectly permissible syntactic operation) to get "The bird flies bothered wouldn't touch the seeds" (n), the first three words can be taken as part of a simple declarative sentence ("The bird flies"). In such cases Bever's subjects did, in fact, take just such a line of analysis and treated the remaining words as a list of unrelated items. The thing to notice here is that if lexical operations in fact precede superficial analysis, such "garden path" tricks should not bother the listener. The semantic and syntactic features of the words *bird, fly, bother, touch,* and *seed* will, to be sure, yield a large number of potential deep structures (note that *fly, bother, touch,* and *seed* can all be either nouns or verbs); but there are a sufficient number of constraints here (e.g., *bother* doesn't *touch*) and on the superficial level (e.g., the inference rule that you can't string finite verbs) to yield a reading for the sentence. Consequently, the listener's inability to handle sentences of this type must be due to his hypothesizing a deep structure on the basis of superficial structure information (*viz.*, the hypothesis "subject + verb + object") that is not confirmed. Furthermore, when such a rejection of an hypothesis occurred, it would appear that little or no information had been placed in the lexical strategy since the subject was pretty much at a loss as to what the sentence was about. Therefore, it seems that there must be a set of "structural hypotheses" available to the comprehender. The set of available hypotheses is established not only on the basis of the grammar of the language (what are the "sentence types") but also on the basis of popularity (what sentence type is most likely given the environmental context). Which hypothesis is selected is probably based initially on the popularity criteria, and then, given some input, on a real-time superficial analysis of the sentence. Thus, the listener normally expects a sentence to have the structure "subject + verb + object," although he must keep in mind the other possible structures. When the first few words confirm his "most-popular-sentence-type" hypothesis, he rejects all other hypotheses and, consequently, is no longer able to refer to them when his selected hypothesis is dashed on the rocks of self-embedding.

Thus, in modeling a theory of comprehension, the components of the superficial structural analysis and those of the lexical analysis cannot be considered to be in series. This parallel syntactic and semantic processing is shown in a number of experiments (Mehler and Carey 1968; Mehler, Bever, and Carey 1968).

Further, it is clear that a sentence such as (o) "The cheese ate the rat" is "understood" by a listener as being deviant. If Wanner's model were to be taken literally and projection rules supposed to be logically and temporally prior to inference rules, the above sentence would be understood incorrectly as "the rat ate the cheese," and no awareness of its deviance would occur. To account for the listener's knowing the above sentence to be deviant and how to correct it (i.e., knowing what's wrong), one would have to assume that (a) the comprehender is aware of a mismatch between the outputs of the inference rules and projection rules and that (b) both rule component outputs must contain sufficient syntactic and lexical information to make such a match. That means that the inference rules cannot simply produce structural descriptions of the type

(((art) (noun)) ((verb) ((art) (noun))))

since such descriptions would be compatible with the projection-rule output and fail to produce the mismatch required to know the sentence to be deviant. One (probably too simple) way to get the mismatch would be to suppose that (at least) word shapes are retained through inference rules and that these shapes (or feature specifications) are also retained in the projection-rule operations. The projection rules would then specify a deep structure such as

(((art) (rat)) ((ate) ((art) (cheese)))),

which would then be matched with the structural description output of the inference rules.

The lexical model is shown, in at least one of its forms, in figure 9.2.

It remains, using the above assumptions, to explain the systematic variations in RT (reaction time) for reversible passives, and similar cases. This could be done by assuming that a transformation-inversion component is appended after the inference rules. It is applied if, and only if, the projection-rule and inference-rule outputs do not match, or if they result in multiple matches. This variation on the model is incorporated in figure 9.5.

Additional aspects of the modeling of comprehension and a variation in the selection of relevant literature can be found in an extensive review by John B. Carroll (1971).

Normally, full-sentence comprehension—i.e., knowing what the sentence means—is accomplished by the application of both lexical and syntactic analyses, and both are necessary. That the two types of analysis appear to be isolable through brain damage, maturation, or experimental manipulation suggests, however, that they operate in a parallel (rather than serial) fashion. At the very

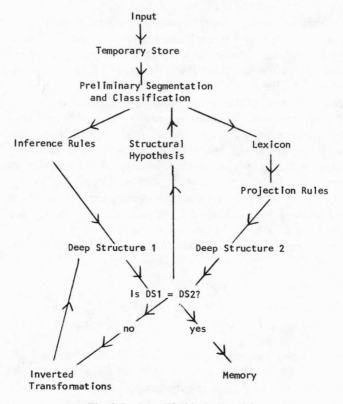

Fig. 9.5   A modified lexical model.

least, these facts clearly indicate that a single measure of "comprehension" is inadequate to any serious treatment of linguistic behavior.

Testing Sentence Comprehension

The primary criterion for a study of sentence comprehension is that the subject must be put into a situation such that his understanding of the linguistic stimulus is based solely and entirely on the information contained in the stimulus—in other words, looking around won't help. To achieve this we use a picture-identification task in which a sentence is presented to the subject and he is asked to point to (or otherwise indicate) one of a set of four pictures. The pictures all denote equally plausible (or implausible) events, and the subject's choosing correctly requires him to process the syntactic as well as the lexical content of the sentence. The major set of studies used a type of construction made famous by the MIT psychology group in the 60s (Mehler et al. 1967).

The sentences are constructed thus: (1) "They fed her dog biscuits." The interesting thing about structures like this is that in written form or in a "flat" reading they are quite ambiguous; this one could mean that biscuits were fed to some lady's dog or that dog biscuits were fed to some lady. The sentence is easily made unambiguous, however, by the appropriate application of pause and stress or by the insertion of a definite article, as in "They fed her the dog biscuits" and "They fed her dog the biscuits."

If, now, we present such sentences to a listener, showing him an appropriate pair of pictures denoting the events described by the sentences, and he fails to correctly pick the pictures, we can say that he has a comprehension deficit. The deficit is specific: it involves utilizing a syntactically generated formative, *the* (which comes from a feature [+ Definite] on the noun phrase; see Jacobs and Rosenbaum 1968) to parse the indirect- and direct-object constituents. In other words, we have isolated a purely syntactic deficit in comprehension.*

If our stimuli—sentences and pictures—had also included "They fed her the catfish" and "They fed her cat the fish," and if the subject had pointed to the picture corresponding to one of these when presented with a sentence about dog biscuits we could then claim a deficit in the comprehension of MLI.†

The experimental procedure followed in the studies to be described here utilized sentences constructed on the pattern illustrated above. For each sentence presentation, the subject was shown four pictures, corresponding to the sentence presented, a syntactically different sentence, and two lexically different sentences. For the aphasic population the sentences were read by the experimenter (Dr. Kenneth Heilman); for other populations they were presented from taped recordings.

Details of the experiments described below are provided in other publications referred to elsewhere in this chapter; here the results will be summarized and synthesized.

Following the summary of our research on the syntactic and lexical aspects of comprehension, some relevant work by others will be cited in an attempt to devise a model of language processing. This model will be limited largely to syntactic and lexical issues and will consider the hemispheric capacities of the brain as well as localizations within the dominant hemisphere. In particular, we will be interested in the role of normal audition in the acquisition of syntactic competence and in the relation of classical syndromes of aphasia (Broca's, Wernicke's, and conduction) to the syntactic and lexical aspects of language.

---

* *Asyntactic* is preferred over *agrammatic* (Goodglass and Berko 1960) because, in linguistics, a *grammar* is a complete theory of a particular language, including its syntax, semantics, and phonology. Other existing terms (e.g., *expressive aphasia, Broca's aphasia, nonfluent aphasia*) largely fail to maintain that linguistic theory has anything to do with language behavior.

† As with *asyntactism*, the only word that appears to maintain linguistic integrity and that describes someone who has lost the ability to process or store major lexical items is *alexical*.

THE INDIRECT-DIRECT OBJECT TEST

Methods

Fifteen different sentences are used in the Indirect-Direct Object Test. Ten of the sentences are unambiguous and are presented once each. Five of the sentences are ambiguous and are presented twice each, yielding a total of 20 trials per subject.* The types of sentences used are illustrated in the two example sets below:

Set	Reading	Sentence
1	A	He showed her baby the pictures.
1	B	He showed her the baby pictures.
1	X	He showed her baby pictures.
2	A	He showed her bird the seed.
2	B	He showed her the bird seed.
2	X	He showed her bird seed.

Five such sets were constructed. For each set, one sentence—the X reading —is ambiguous in that it is not clear which words of the predicate compose the indirect object and which words compose the direct object. The two unambiguous sentences in each set—the A and the B readings—make the parsing of the predicate clear by the location of the definite article.

Within the pair of unambiguous sentences in each set, one member has only the last noun as the direct object—the A reading. In the other member—the B reading—the last two nouns make up the direct object.

Each presentation of one of these stimuli is accompanied by an $8\frac{1}{2} \times 11$-inch paper containing four line drawings. One of the drawings corresponds to the sentence presented, one corresponds to the other reading within the set of sentences, and the other two drawings correspond to the A and B readings from a different set of sentences. For the ambiguous sentences, then, there are two pictures that are correct choices. Twenty different arrays of pictures are used, one page for each trial. Correct, incorrect, and inappropriate pictures are randomly arranged on each page and the inappropriate selections are chosen at random from the four other sets for each trial.

For the normal hearing populations the stimuli were presented through air

---

* The actual tests were slightly more involved than this description indicates. We also tested for the parsing of the indirect and direct objects when these were indicated by disjuncture (i.e., by pause and stress cues). The results for disjuncture—dealing more with acoustic than with syntactic cues for comprehension—are not relevant to the issue central to this chapter.

Only the ambiguous forms of the sentence sets used in the Indirect-Direct Object Test are given here; the unambiguous sentences are easily found by inserting a definite article before or after the penultimate word of each sentence: (1) The man showed the girls bird seed; (2) The man showed the boys horse shoes; (3) The man showed her girls hats; (4) The man showed her baby pictures; and (5) The man showed his friends lion tracks. A picture array appropriate to sentences from (2) or (4) is shown in figure 9.6.

from taped recordings (except for the aphasic population, where the experimenter read the sentences). For the hard-of-hearing subjects each audial presentation was accompanied by a visual presentation of the sentence typed on a 3 × 5 card. For any trial, a sentence is presented and an array of pictures is simultaneously shown. The subject is given unlimited time to respond. The 20 trials are run at a single session; the total time required is generally less than thirty minutes.

The subject populations that have been tested with this instrument to date including normal children aged 5 to 13 (nearly 200 of them), hard-of-hearing teen-agers, aphasic and nonaphasic stroke victims, and normal geriatrics.*

Fig. 9.6   Sample page of drawings (see note on p. 176).

---

* Other populations that have been studied are mentally retarded adolescents, deaf high school students, and dyslexic children. Analyses of the results for these groups had not been completed as of the date of submission of this chapter.

Results: By Populations

Sentence stimuli included both ambiguous and unambiguous cases. In this section, the results for the unambiguous cases will be presented; the ambiguous cases will be reported later.

Normal Children and Young Adults

Eleven college-age students and staff of the Communication Sciences Laboratory were tested. This group made no errors across lexical sets (i.e., responses in an entirely inappropriate set of pictures) and made 7 syntactic errors in the 110 trials (94%). There were no significant differences among sets of sentences or types of readings.

Twenty children (ten male, ten female) of each of the age groups 5-, 7-, 9-, 11-, and 13-year-olds were tested. All children were from regular classes of the University's P. K. Yonge Laboratory School. A systematically increasing ability to correctly respond was seen over the age groups. The 5 year olds performed at chance level (58%)—for nonpathological populations, we use 50% as chance since the lexically inappropriate responses appear to be irrelevant to the subjects' task; the 13 year olds were comparable to our college-age group (95%); and the intermediate-aged groups showed gradually increasingly correct scores between the two extremes (table 9.1). Lexical errors were minimal

Table 9.1

Average Percentage of Correct Responses to Unambiguous Sentences

Subject Group	% Correct
Normal, 5-year-olds	58.5
Normal, 7-year-olds	74.5
Normal 9-year-olds	86.0
Normal, 11-year-olds	90.0
Normal, 13-year-olds	95.5
Normal, 22-year-olds	94.0
Normal geriatric (69)	86.5
Nonaphasic stroke (60)	85.0
Hard-of-hearing (14.5)	61.5
Aphasic: Broca's	54.5
Aphasic: conduction	53.0
Aphasic: Wernicke's	16.0 (36.0)

NOTE: For the Wernicke's aphasics, the first figure represents overall correct responses; the figure in parentheses, the percentage correct within lexically correct responses.

(less than 1%) in all age groups. This population is reported in more detail in Scholes, Tanis, and Turner (1976).

Aged Normals

A group of twenty normal subjects averaging 69 years of age was tested. As expected, they made no errors across lexical sets, but did less well than young adults on the syntactic clues. Their percentage of correct responses, 86%, is nearly identical to that of the nonaphasic stroke victims of comparable age.

Seven nonaphasic stroke victims in their 60s got 85% of the responses correct and made no lexical errors.

Hard-of-Hearing Teen-agers

In a large study of the hard-of-hearing done for her doctorate in speech pathology, Martha Anderson used the Indirect-Direct Object Test with a population of hard-of-hearing people (−62dB in the better ear) who averaged 14.5 years of age. This group got 61% correct on the unambiguous sentences (no lexical errors) even though Dr. Anderson showed each sentence to each subject while it was played (Anderson 1974; Scholes, Tanis, and Anderson, ms).

Aphasics

Dr. Kenneth Heilman has used this test with aphasic patients (Heilman and Scholes 1976), dividing the population into Broca's, conduction, and Wernicke's aphasias on the basis of neurological examination. Broca's and conduction patients made few lexical errors (no worse than the normal young adults) but clearly showed that they could not comprehend the syntactic clue for the A and B readings, scoring just over 50% correct.

The Wernicke's patients, however, showed clear lexical noncomprehension. In 55% of the trials their response was to point to one of the two lexically inappropriate pictures. When they did point to one of the pair of lexically appropriate pictures, they got the correct syntactic form in only 36% of the trials.

Discussion: By Populations

Normal Children and Young Adults

Our "base-line" group of young adults clearly showed that the sentences and the visual representations of our test were quite comprehensible and plausible. While the subjects found some of the sentences "funny," they had no difficulty carrying out the task requested. The few errors that did occur were largely accounted for by a single person, who was generally on the low end of any verbal tests we ran.

The test appears to be a fairly sensitive and reliable indicator of syntactic development in children of elementary school age. Stayton's work (Stayton 1972) established that the marked form of the double-object predicate was not comprehensible to preschool children, whereas the unmarked (i.e., the *to* form) was well within the competence of most four year olds. Her work, then, establishes that the notions of dative and accusative (indirect and direct objects) are within the cognitive capacity of the preschooler, thus permitting us some confidence in our view that our research maps a purely syntactic aspect of development (see also Waryas and Ruder 1973; Waryas and Stremel 1973).

The absence of lexical errors in the children of any age group shows that the lexical aspect of comprehension is well established by the earliest age (5 years) studied (and, indeed, other work suggests that this may be the first thing accomplished by the child). Since the 5 year olds in our study performed at a chance level and the older children did well above chance, the ability to process syntactic formatives in comprehension appears to develop sometime between age 5 and puberty. Since the curve for our data appears to approach the asymptote at nine and since other linguistic skills and abilities are established at this age,* we may refine our claim thus: the acquisition of the ability to utilize syntactic formatives in comprehension occurs between 5 and 9 years of age.

It may be well to mention here one fairly large-scale study of language comprehension in children that appears to indicate earlier mastery of syntax than claimed here. This study (Carrow 1968) used a picture-selection task with an extensive set of morphological, syntactic, and semantic variables. Unfortunately, the study was not done seriously, and little confidence can be placed in it. For some distinctions, for example, a two-choice forced choice was used, while for others three choices were available; yet for all distinctions the age at which a 60% correct response was obtained is reported (60% correct is very different when chance is 33% and when chance is 50%). Age groups were not equaled; this and numerous other problems prevent Carrow's report from being usable.

---

* Palermo and Molfese (1972) review a sizable body of research studies in this regard. They cite, for example, medial and final position speech sound production and consonant cluster articulation; wholistic versus componential (i.e., phonemic) treatment of words; development of complex (transformational) syntactic abilities; control of the "minimal distance principle"; and control of both physical and psychological meanings of words.

Aged Normals

The results with geriatric, nonaphasic stroke victims, comparable to similarly aged nonstroke victims, suggest that a decreasing ability for syntactic comprehension is associated with normal aging and that the nondominant hemisphere does not participate in this diminishing ability.

The nonstroke geriatric group shows a lexical comprehension that is intact but a syntactic ability below that of younger normals. The lowered performance may be due to presbycusis (since the task involved hearing the sentences) (Bergman 1964) or it may indicate debilitation at a deeper level. In either case, it is clear that aging brings about communication deficits that are linguistically characterizable.

Hard-of-Hearing Teen-agers

Human beings who have been forced to acquire language through non-auditory modalities characteristically display an impoverished syntactic system. I. M. Schlessinger (1970) has shown that users of Israeli Sign Language have great difficulty in communicating syntactic relations such as "subject of the main verb," "object of the verb," and "indirect object" (but also see Bellugi and Klima 1972). Written English of the adolescent deaf shows abundant errors in the use of articles and in number agreement, verb tense and aspect, and other errors in the use of syntactic formatives (Myklebust 1965). Studies of the spoken language of the deaf has also revealed syntactic deficits (Brannon 1968; Cooper 1967; Power and Quigley 1973).

Studies of syntactic comprehension in hard-of-hearing subjects are rare. Wilcox and Tobin (1974) employed a repetition task to investigate syntactic patterns in ten hard-of-hearing children. The experimental group showed significantly lower means in each grammatical form than did the normal hearing controls. Power and Quigley (1973) studied deaf children's comprehension of the passive voice by requiring them to move toys to demonstrate the action of a sentence or to select a picture appropriate to an indicated action. They found that virtually all hearing children had mastered both the comprehension and production of the passive by age eight whereas many deaf children had not mastered this skill by age 18. Pressnell (1973) used the Northwestern Syntax Screening Test in a study of normal and hearing-impaired children aged 5 to 13. The hearing-impaired did less well on this test than normal controls, and there was significantly less improvement over ages in the hearing-impaired than in the normals.

If the absence of the hearing modality results in the acquisition of a syntactically impoverished form of language, then, we hypothesize, a significant (though not total) loss of hearing should result in an inability to handle some of the more complex aspects of syntax. The Indirect-Direct Object Test results support this hypothesis. This group, though shown the sentences, performed well below age level. It should be noted that this population wore hearing aids, received special training, and were normal enough to be in regular classrooms.

Aphasics

Syntactic aspects of comprehension or production in aphasics have been studied by a number of researchers. Goodglass and Berko (1960) demonstrated that in speech production, the difficulty in the articulation of a particular phonemic sequence was a function of the linguistic source of that sequence. In one case, the sequence [əz] was most difficult when its source was the possessive construction, easiest when it came from a plural marker, and of intermediate difficulty when the syntactic source was third person singular of the verb.

Zurif, Caramazza, and Myerson (1972) showed that anterior aphasics rank the word-relatedness of sentences in terms of MLI rather than (as normals do) the constituent structure of the sentence. For example, given "The baby cries," normal subjects would split it into "the baby" plus "cries"; the aphasics structured it as "the" plus "baby cries." This is consistent with the view that the anterior aphasias retain linguistic skills relevant to MLI, but have lost the syntactic component.

Von Stockert (1972) asked Broca's and Wernicke's patients to order constituents into meaningful sentences. He found that the Wernicke's case could put, for example, "is pretty," "from Boston," and "the girl" together correctly to make "The girl from Boston is pretty"; the Broca's aphasics could not. This is consistent with the view (Goodglass and Kaplan 1972) that syntactic abilities are lacking in Broca's aphasia.

Parisi and Pizzamiglio (1970) studied a range of syntactic skills in aphasics. Their finding that the Wernicke's aphasics did less well than the Broca's is neither surprising (given that Wernicke's aphasics lack the ability to handle MLI) nor interesting. Their tasks comprise a hodgepodge of syntactic, lexical, and semantic aspects of language. While their studies included indirect-direct object constructions (e.g., "The boy shows the cat the dog" vs. "The boy shows the dog the cat") and their method was a picture verification task, in the absence of a well-defined linguistic theory (i.e., a claim concerning what is and what is not syntactic) their results cannot be directly related to our own. Having only two pictures to choose from, as in the case of the two example sentences, allows no way to distinguish the patient who makes the wrong choice because he did not understand "cat" and "dog" from the patient who understood all the lexical items but had no way of using the ordering to parse the indirect and direct object constituency.

In our own work, the Wernicke's patient's inability to discriminate among sentences distinguished by major lexical items versus the Broca's and conduction patient's lack of difficulty with MLI discrimination but apparent absence of syntactic comprehension is the crucial point. Whether or not the Wernicke's cases also display a syntactic impairment is something this test does not show. The findings, however, support the view that there are autonomous lexical and syntactic components in the neurolinguistic model of language (as there are in the psycholinguistic model of comprehension) and that these components can be localized as posterior and anterior, respectively. At the very least, this work shows that dividing aphasias into "expressive" and "receptive" or utilizing a single dimension of comprehension is inadequate. It is unlikely that any aphasic syndrome retains full comprehension. This being the case, it ought to be clinically valuable to utilize tests such as the Indirect-Direct Object Test in diagnosis.

Summary Discussion of Results

Overall, it is clear that the picture-identification test of double-object sentences is highly sensitive to maturation and to various communicative disorders. The ability to utilize the determiner to correctly parse the components of predicates like those tested is acquired during the elementary school years; it is an ability that is significantly impaired by hearing loss and aphasia, and it reliably distinguishes at least two important aphasic syndromes.

In normals, this ability apparently developed to adult level by the age of 9, children aged 5 or less being unable to comprehend the construction (although, remember, they have mastered the "unmarked" form, e.g., "He showed seed to her bird," at the age of 3). Thus, this is probably a good measure of language acquisition for early elementary grade (K through 5) children.

While this ability is mildly impaired by aging (the normal and stroke-victim geriatric populations score at the 9-year-old level rather than the "young adult" level), this is not a significant loss and may well be associated with presbycusis. Since the test sentences were read in a normal fashion, the article that indicated the correct parsing of the predicate may well be relatively lower in amplitude than the major lexical content; in addition, hearing loss due to noise level (which is what we find in 25% of older Americans) generally affects higher frequencies most, and the fricative that begins the definite article is, essentially, a high-frequency speech sound.

Since a nondominant hemisphere stroke does not add any impairment to that found in normal aging, we can be confident that the ability we are measuring is well confined to a dominant-hemisphere linguistic ability.

Any of the three major syndromes of aphasia obviously impaired the ability to correctly utilize the syntactic cue for parsing the double objects. Broca's and conduction cases, however, have no difficulty in choosing the correct pair

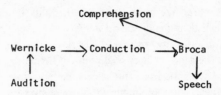

Fig. 9.7   A serial model.

of pictures (i.e., they can easily tell "boy's horse shoes" from "girl's bird seed") but they cannot distinguish between the two readings clued by the location of the article. Thus, the picture that emerges is that in terms of the major components of a linguistic theory the lexical operations are localized in the posterior portions of the left cerebral hemispheres, the syntax in the anterior portions. In comprehension, a loss of the anterior (Broca) area or access to this area (conduction) will result in an inability to understand the syntactic aspects of the meaning of a sentence. Loss of the Wernicke area results in an inability to understand that part of the meaning of a sentence that is conveyed by major lexical items.

The hard-of-hearing group shows a significant impairment in syntactic comprehension. Since, for these subjects (and only for these subjects) the sentences were simultaneously shown (typed on 3 × 5 cards) and heard, this impairment cannot be explained by an inability to hear the clue word. While it is a well-known aspect of the speech and writing of the hard-of-hearing that syntactic errors abound (see Myklebust 1965 for some examples), the relation between a congenital absence of normal hearing and the acquisition of language has not been formulated in neurolinguistic terms. The results of our research, together with that of other investigators, suggest that the acquisition of the syntactic component of human natural language is keyed to auditory acuity. If language must be acquired via a nonauditory modality, it will be a language noticeably lacking full syntactic competence.

LEXICAL AND SYNTACTIC COMPONENTS OF A NEUROLINGUISTIC MODEL OF APHASIA

Our research clearly shows that the Wernicke's patient has lost the lexical component of sentence comprehension (i.e., the projection rules) whereas the lexical ability of Broca's and conduction patients is intact, although they have lost the syntactic component of sentence comprehension (i.e., the inference rules). What we have not shown (in my opinion) is that the Wernicke's patient does or does not have an intact syntactic comprehension component.

If the Wernicke is asyntactic as well as alexical, sentence comprehension would appear to conform to a serial model (figure 9.7) which asserts that a disruption in the Broca area *or any area linking it to the auditory cortex* will result in asyntactism. While such a model would predict the random responses

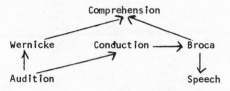

Fig. 9.8   A parallel model.

observed in this population on our test, it fails to conform to a number of other observations; *viz.*, those dealing with Delayed Auditory Feedback and recovery (see below).

If, on the other hand, we assume that the Wernicke's patient is not asyntactic (but that we simply have not done the experiment to show this), then a parallel model of comprehension (figure 9.8) would be indicated. This model would assert that the auditory cortex can be linked to the Broca area without necessarily involving the Wernicke area. This model would correctly account for the lexical comprehension observed in the anterior aphasias; in addition, it is consistent with recent work on Delayed Auditory Feedback (DAF) and with paraphasic to anomic "recovery" in some Wernicke's aphasics.

DAF produces various types and quantities of disfluencies in the normal speaker. These disfluencies are caused by delaying the subject's speech (generally by about a fifth of a second) to his own ears. The effectiveness of the delay depends on the subject's having an intact audition-speech feedback system; if the subject is mute or deaf or disinterested in his own speech (as in the case of schizophrenia) the delayed feedback will not be effective (Yates 1963). In a series of studies, we have looked at the affects of DAF on aphasics (Ory 1974; Heilman 1974). This work, preliminary and somewhat inconclusive, suggests that DAF is debilitating in all but the posterior aphasias; i.e., Broca's and conduction cases show that the delay is bothering them; Wernicke's cases don't seem to be troubled by the delay. These results indicate that the normal communicative feedback system (whose presence is required for the delay to be effective) is present in the conduction and Broca's cases, but not in the Wernicke's patients. This finding, should it prove to be reliable, would clearly support a model in which the Wernicke area is not a required link in the audition-to-speech neurological system.

A further indication of the "feedback loop" hypothesis comes from the fact that Wernicke's aphasics often "recover" from an earlier paraphasic behavior to a later anomia. In an early state, they will often produce words (especially nouns) in a distorted shape; for example, "Thridi" for *thirty*, "towt" for *town*. The behavior of the patient generally indicates that he is unaware of the error, and he acts as though his listener is simply not understanding him. Such behavior clearly supports the notion that the auditory feedback system, which should permit detection of the error by the patient,

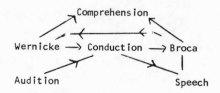

Fig. 9.9   The parallel model with production.

is not operational. In later stages of this syndrome, a pure anomia may appear (that is, speech with the major lexical items omitted or circumvented). This would suggest that the feedback system has recovered to the point that the patient is aware of the errors and chooses to not produce the erroneous form (note that the monitoring of "feedback" must be internal in this case). The early unawareness of the paraphasia complements the DAF hypothesis so as to support the notion that normal auditory feedback is not disrupted in Wernicke's aphasia. That is, the patient is apparently not monitoring his own speech during this paraphasic stage. When awareness later increases, the patient no longer "accepts" the incorrect forms. Detailed argument concerning the paraphasic and anomic stages of Wernicke's aphasia are given in Buckingham (1975).

To go even further afield, research on child language and psycholinguistic studies of sentence processing in normal adults suggest that major lexical items are identified for processing partly on the basis of phonological shape (Scholes 1970) and partly on the basis of syntactic clues (Scholes 1972). For example, the listener knows that *walk* is to be treated semantically as a verb if it appears in the frame "is ____ing," but as a noun if it occurs in the frame "the ____ is." If this is a true picture of sentence comprehension, then it follows that some syntactic processing must precede lexical processing (i.e., the sentence comprehender cannot figure out that the sentence refers to any specifically named things until he has isolated those names from the utterance). A comprehension model that would capture these claims would not only isolate the Wernicke/MLI component but would also treat it as a loop within the full model.

In addition it is, of course, clear that anterior aphasics do utter things (typically, "telegraphic"). A full neurolinguistic model must, then, allow for signals to be processed from the Wernicke area to the motor cortex for speech without having to go through the (destroyed or disconnected) anterior areas of language processing. A model that conforms to these observations is shown in figure 9.9.

A further note on lexical and syntactic competence in aphasia stems from a different set of studies. In looking at various aspects of short-term memory in aphasics, Dr. Heilman and I have employed the sort of "sentence following by

digit strings" stimuli first made famous by Savin and Perchonock (1965).*
In the course of these studies we found that the anterior aphasics did much
less well on recalling reversible sentences than on nonreversibles (i.e., sentences
in which either of two noun phrases could be subject or object—"the boy hit
the girl"—are more difficult than sentences in which the function of the noun
phrases is restricted by the nouns themselves—"The mouse ate the cheese")
Heilman, Scholes, and Watson (1976). The point of this finding, it seems to
me, is that it indicates that the aphasic patient whose MLI processing is intact
will appear to comprehend the syntax of a sizable number of utterances just
because the crucial information (as in the case of nonreversibles) is contained
in the nouns, verbs, and adjectives themselves. When, on the other hand, such
a patient is asked to indicate syntactic comprehension where the animateness
and such features of the MLI won't help, he will show significant impairment.
The fact that some syntactic information (like co-occurrence restrictions illustrated above) is part of the data inherent in MLI may, in fact, go far to account
for the "good comprehension" associated with Broca's and conduction
aphasias.

ACQUISITION OF SYNTAX AND LEXICON:
DOMINANCE AND AUDITORY FACTORS

The normal child clearly acquires the syntax of his language at a different
rate and in a different way than he acquires the major lexical items and their
meanings. Our studies of utterance imitations in 3- and 4-year-old children
(Scholes 1966, 1969, 1970) showed that these children omitted many more
function words than content words in their imitations. The children in these
studies deleted noncontent words from utterances when such words were real
or nonsense, but when the content words were nonsense and the function words
real (e.g., my tak kiled his klim) the strategy broke down and no content-function
word difference appeared in the deletions. We concluded, from that work, that
the child utilizes a "telegraphic" language because he has not yet acquired a
concern (or ability) for syntax. It is indeed fortunate for the child and his
environment that strings of uninflected content words convey far more
information of concern than a well-formed contentless syntactic frame (compare:
"Daddy go store" with "My ____ed to the ____"). But this circumstance is
probably not an accident; more likely, it is a reflection of the developing organism on which humans have learned to capitalize.

It appears that the development of syntax is tied to the development of
cerebral dominance, whereas the acquisition of the lexicon is not. Studies of

---

* Literature reviews and presentations of the results of our own research in this area can
be found in Scholes, Heilman, and Rasbury (1975); Scholes, Rasbury, Scholes, and Dowling
(1976); Heilman, Scholes, and Watson (1976); and Scholes (1974).

"split-brain" cases (Gazzaniga 1970; Sperry and Gazzaniga 1967) suggest that the nondominant hemisphere of the brain could handle the operations (acquisition, storage, and retrieval) necessary for using major lexical items but that it could not deal with the analytical operations necessary to syntax. The right hemisphere can match words to objects as long as no decomposition of the word is required, but cannot do this if some morphological analysis is required; for example, the right hemisphere can match the word and object *butter* but not *holder* (the latter requires analysis into *hold* plus *agent*). Dennis and Kohn (1975) and Dennis and Whitaker (1976), using adolescents who had had early hemidecortication, showed that individuals who had acquired language with the right hemisphere only could not comprehend sentences in which the comprehension required syntactic analysis (e.g., passives) but could handle sentences whose meaning is given essentially by the major lexical items and their sequence. Such adolescents could, for example, understand "The boy hit the ball" but not "The ball was hit by the boy." Individuals who had acquired language with only the left (dominant) hemisphere had no difficulty with lexicon or syntax.

Our studies of the acquisition of the ability to utilize syntactic cues to comprehend double-object constructions suggest that full syntactic ability is not gained until around the ninth year, whereas lexical skills are clearly mastered much before then.

Thus, since syntax appears to require dominance, it cannot develop beyond the normal development of dominance, and the predominant child must communicate with his environment in a language that is essentially lexical.

Equally important, it would seem, to the acquisition of full mastery of the syntactic component of language is the availability of normal human hearing acuity. Our own work, along with that of others, shows that a significant loss in hearing during the language acquisition years will result in an inability to handle syntax. Wilcox and Tobin (1974) found that hard-of-hearing children did less well than normal controls on several grammatical forms. Quigley (1973) found that deaf children could not handle passive sentences by age 18. Pressnell (1973) found that hearing-impaired children did less well on the Northwestern Syntax Screening Test than normals and did not improve significantly with age. Our work showed that teen-aged hard-of-hearing subjects had not learned to use the definite article to parse the double-object constructions.

Thus, two factors appear to be requisite to the acquisition of syntax: normal hearing and cerebral dominance (Scholes 1974).

RESPONSES TO AMBIGUOUS SENTENCES: STRATEGIES

Bever (1970) has shown that the comprehension of a sentence may be accomplished through the application of the grammar of the language or through a set of probabilistic *strategies*. The classical evidence for this distinction in children comes from Bever's studies of passive sentences. Bever found that children showed a definite and systematic increase in their ability to comprehend passive sentences up to the middle of the fourth year, at which time the ability dropped sharply before continuing to increase. This drop, Bever argued, was due to the application of a strategy based on probability: namely, that for any sentence having a sequence N-V-N, the first noun is the subject. Such a strategy would obviously lead to many correct solutions (and shortcut the complex operations of syntax) but would lead to errors in passive (and certain other) sentences.

Given ambiguous sentences such as those used in our study, with two equally acceptable responses to choose from, whichever response is chosen (since it can't be chosen on the basis of the structure of the sentence) must be based on such a strategy. In the case of our test instrument, a choice could also be made on the basis of (pragmatic) plausibility or even the clarity of the pictures, but this possibility is not supported in the absence of significant differences due to the sentence sets.

Overall, the subject populations in our studies to date tend to prefer the B-reading response to the ambiguous sentences; that is, they would tend to interpret "He showed her bird seed" as meaning "He showed her the bird seed." The mean percentage of B-reading responses is shown for each subject group in table 9.2.

As table 9.2 shows, there appears to be a systematic increase in the B-reading response in the normal children from youngest to oldest. Both the very young (5 year olds) and the college-age adults divide their responses nearly 50-50. I suspect that these two groups show similar results for very different reasons;

Table 9.2

Percentage of B-Reading Responses
Assigned to Ambiguous Sentences

Subject Group	% B-Reading Responses
Normal, 5 year olds	57
Normal, 7 year olds	65
Normal, 9 year olds	84
Normal, 11 year olds	81
Normal, 13 year olds	85
Normal, 22 year olds	47
Normal geriatric (69)	92
Nonaphasic stroke (60)	81
Hard-of-hearing (14.5)	72
Aphasic: Broca's	35
Aphasic-conduction	22
Aphasic: Wernicke's	58

the 5 year old (as shown by his chance responses to the unambiguous sentences) does not yet know that there are two meanings for such sentences, while the college student knows there are two readings, but he's too sophisticated to prefer either one. In between, we find a gradually increasing tendency to assign to the three nominal elements in a predicate (i.e., symbolically S(ubject) + V(erb) + N(ominal) + N(ominal) + N(ominal)) the structure S + V(N) + (N N). Why this interpretation should be preferred over the alternative S + V + (N N) + (N), I do not know. If it were to be accounted for by the plausibility of the meanings or the pictures denoting those meanings, then we ought to find significant variation among the five sentences used, and we do not.

The (N) (N N) strategy is strong in the older nonaphasics (stroke patients and normals). The hard-of-hearing group shows a fairly strong preference for this reading (quite a bit higher than the 5-year-old normals with whom they compare on syntactic comprehension). The aphasic groups differ considerably in their preference for this reading, with the Broca's and conduction groups showing a shift to the A-reading preference.

SUMMARY

In this chapter, we have been concerned with the comprehension of sentences by normal adults, normal and hearing-impaired children, and aphasics. A number of proposals for models of sentence comprehension were presented. It was shown that such models must account for the contribution of lexical co-occurrence restrictions, syntactic indicators of constituent structure, and predictive strategies employed by the language users to the task of fully understanding a given sentence. Such models must also be able to provide for comprehension in very fast time, and several models are rejected on this basis. They must allow for parallel operation of the various components in order to account for the partial comprehension of "telegraphic" utterances and sentences with nonsense major lexical items and for the incorrect comprehension of certain embedded sentences. Other models are rejected on these bases.

Using sentences having both indirect and direct object constituents in which the constituency of these is indicated by the syntactic formative *the* or in which the constituency is ambiguous, we have been able to construct a sentence comprehension task that isolates the syntactic, lexical, and strategic components of the comprehension of these structures. The results of the application of this test to varying ages of normal language users to hearing-impaired teen-agers, and to aphasic patients are presented. These results isolate the stages of the acquisition of the syntactic component of the comprehension of these sentences and show how the lexical, syntactic, and heuristic aspects are affected by maturation and debilitation.

REFERENCES

Anderson, M. A. 1974. Psycholinguistic abilities and academic achievement of hard of hearing, Ph.D. dissertation, Department of Speech, University of Florida.

Bellugi, U., and Klima, E. S. 1972. The roots of language in the sign-talk of the deaf. *Psychology Today* 6 (1):61–4.

Benson, D. F. 1967. Fluency in aphasia: correlation with radioactive scan localization. *Cortex* 3 (4):373–95.

Bergman, M. 1964. Effect of aging on hearing. *MAICO Audiological Library Series* 11:6.

Bever, T. G. 1968. *A survey of some recent work in psycholinguistics* (= IBM Report AF 19 [628]–5127), section 4, pp. 1–66.

————. 1970. The cognitive basis for linguistic structures. In *Cognition and the development of language*, ed. J. R. Hayes. New York: John Wiley & Sons.

Blumenthal, A. L. 1967. Observations with self-embedded sentences. *Psychonomic Science*, June.

Brannon, J. B. 1968. Linguistic word classes in the spoken language of normal, hard-of-hearing, and deaf children. *J. Speech Hearing Res.* 11:239–87.

Brannon, J. B., and Murry, T. 1966. The spoken syntax of normal, hard-of-hearing, and deaf children. *J. Speech Hearing Res.* 9:604–10.

Buckingham, H., Jr. 1975. The condution theory and neolinguistic jargon. *Comm. Sci. Lab. Quart. Prog. Rep.* 13:2.

Carroll, J. B. 1971. *Learning from verbal discourse in educational media: a review of the literature.* Princeton, N.J.: Educational Testing Service.

Carroll, L. *The Complete works of Lewis Carroll.* New York: Modern Library.

Carrow, Sister Mary Arthur. 1968. The development of auditory comprehension of language structure in children. *J. Speech Hearing Dis.* 33 (2):99–111.

Chomsky, N. A. 1965. *Aspects of the theory of syntax.* Cambridge, Mass.: M.I.T. Press.

Chomsky, N. A., and Halle, M. 1968. *The sound pattern of English.* New York: Harper & Row.

Cooper, R. L. 1967. The ability of deaf and hearing children to apply morphological rules. *J. Speech Hearing Res.* 10:77–86.

Dennis, M., and Kohn, B. 1975. Comprehension of syntax in infantile hemiplegics after cerebral hemidecortication: left hemisphere superiority. *Brain and Language* 2.4:472–82.

Dennis, M., and Whitaker, H. A. 1976. Language acquisition following hemidecortication: linguistic superiority of the left over the right hemisphere. *Brain and Language* 3 (3):404–33.

Fargo, N., and Armacost, R. W. 1968. *Bibliography: delayed auditory feedback.* Baltimore: Johns Hopkins Univ. School of Medicine.

Gazzaniga, M. S. 1970. *The bisected brain.* New York: Appleton-Century-Crofts.

Geschwind, N. 1972. Language and the brain. *Scientific American* 226 (4):76–83.

Goodglass, H., and Berko, J. 1960. Agrammatism and inflexional morphology in English. *J. Speech Hearing Res.* 3:257–67.

Goodglass, H., and Kaplan, E. 1972. *The assessment of aphasia and related disorders.* Philadelphia: Lea & Febiger.

Heilman, K. M. 1974. DAF and Wernicke's hypothesis. Paper delivered at the 2d annual meeting of the International Neuropsychological Society, Boston.

Heilman, K. M., and Scholes, R. J. 1976. The nature of comprehension errors in Broca's, conduction, and Wernicke's aphasics. *Cortex*, 12:258–65.

Heilman, K. M.; Scholes, R. J.; and Watson, R. T. 1975. Auditory affective agnosia (disturbed comprehension of affective speech). *J. Neurol. Neuros. Psychiatry* 38:69–72.

———. 1976. Short-term memory defects in Broca's and conduction aphasia. *Brain and Language* 3:201–8.

Jacobs, R. A., and Rosenbaum, P. S. 1968. *English transformational grammar*. Waltham, Mass.: Blaisdell.

Jarvella, R. J. 1970. Effects of syntax on running memory span for connected discourse. *Psychonomic Science* 19 (4):235–6.

Katz, J. A. 1966. *The philosophy of language*. New York: Harper & Row.

Katz, J. J., and Fodor, J. A. 1963. The structure of a semantic theory. *Language* 39:170–210; reprinted in Fodor, J. A., and Katz, J. J. 1964. *The structure of language*. Englewood Cliffs, N.J.: Prentice-Hall.

Lee, L. L. 1966. Developmental sentence types: a method for comparing normal and deviant syntactic development. *J. Speech Hearing Dis.* 31 (4):311–30.

Lee, L. L., and Cantor, S. M. 1971. Developmental sentence scoring: a clinical procedure for estimating syntactic development in children's spontaneous speech. *J. Speech Hearing Dis.* 36 (4):315–40.

Mehler, J. 1963. Some effects of grammatical transformations on the recall of English sentences. *J. Verb. Learning Verb. Behav.* 2:346–52.

———. 1964. How some sentences are remembered. Ph.D. dissertation, Harvard University.

Mehler, J., and Carey, P. 1968. The interaction of veracity and syntax in the processsing of sentences. *Perception and Psychophysics* 3:109–11.

Mehler, J.; Bever, T. G.; and Carey, P. 1967. What we look at when we read. *Perception and Psychophysics* 2:213–18.

Myklebust, H. R. 1965. *Development and disorders of written language*, vol. 1. New York: Grune & Stratton.

Ory, B. A. 1974. An investigation of the effects of delayed auditory feedback on aphasics. Master's Thesis, Department of Speech, University of Florida.

Palermo, D. S., and Molfese, D. L. 1972. Language acquisition from age five onward. *Psychol. Bull.* 78 (6):409–28.

Parisi, D., and Pizzamiglio, L. 1970. Syntactic comprehension in aphasia. *Cortex* 6:204–15.

Power, D. J., and Quigley, S. P. 1974. Deaf children's acquisition of the passive voice. *J. Speech Hearing Res.* 16:5–11.

Presnell, L. M. 1973. Hearing-impaired children's comprehension and production of syntax in oral language. *J. Speech Hearing Res.* 16:12–21.

Quigley, S. P.; Smith, N. L.; and Wilbur, R. B. 1974. Comprehension of relativized sentences by deaf students. *J. Speech Hearing Res.* 17:325–41.

Rosenberg, S. 1968. Association and phrase structure in sentence recall. *J. Verb. Learning Verb. Behav.* 7:1077–81.

————. 1969. The recall of verbal material accompanying semantically well-integrated and semantically poorly integrated sentences. *J. Verb. Learning Verb. Behav.* 8:732–6.

Savin, H. B., and Perchonock, E. 1965. Grammatical structure and the immediate recall of English sentences. *J. Verb. Learning Verb. Behav.* 4:348–53.

Schlessinger, I. M. 1970. The grammar of sign language and the problem of language universals. In *Biological and social factors in psycholinguistics*, ed. John Morton. Urbana: Univ. Illinois Press.

Scholes, R. J. 1966. Children's imitation and comprehension of English imperative constructions. *Word* 22:1, 2, 3, 163–89.

————. 1969. The role of grammaticality in the imitation of word strings by children and adults. *J. Verb. Learning Verb. Behav.* 8:225–8.

————. 1970. On functors and contentives in children's imitation of word strings. *J. Verb. Learning Verb. Behav.* 9:167–70.

————. 1972. Performance aspects of readjustment rules. Papers from the Eighth Regional Meeting of the Chicago Linguistic Society, pp. 558–66.

————. 1972. On sentence comprehension. *Comm. Sci. Lab. Quart. Prog. Rep.* 10:2.

————. 1974. Recent studies in neurolinguistics. *Comm. Sci. Lab. Quart. Prog. Rep.* 12:1 (includes "Syntax, cerebral dominance, and the primary linguistic system").

Scholes, R. J.; Heilman, K. M.; and Rasbury, W. C. 1975. Immediate recall of sentences plus digits: a new approach. *Language and Speech* 18:333–40.

Scholes, R. J.; Tanis, D. C.; and Anderson, M. W. Comprehension of double-object constructions in hard-of-hearing adolescents. Unpublished manuscript.

Scholes, R. J.; Tanis, D. C.; and Turner, A. 1976. Syntactic and strategic aspects of the comprehension of indirect and direct object constitutents by children. *Language and Speech* 19:212–23 (also in *Comm. Sci. Lab. Quart. Prog. Rep.* 12 (3) [1974]).

Scholes, R. J.; Rasbury, W. C.; Scholes, I.; and Dowling, C. 1976. Sentence comprehension and short-term memory: some developmental considerations. *Language and Speech* 19:80–7 (also in *Comm. Sci. Quart. Lab. Prog. Rep.* 12 (3) [1974]).

Slobin, D. I. 1966. Grammatical transformations and sentence comprehension in child and adulthood. *J. Verb. Learning Verb. Behav.* 5:219–27.

Sperry, R. W., and Gazzaniga, M. S. 1967. Language following surgical disconnection of the hemispheres. In *Brain mechanisms underlying speech and language*, ed. C. H. Millikan and F. L. Darley. New York: Grune & Stratton.

Stayton, B. 1972. The acquisition of direct and indirect objects in English. Unpublished manuscript, University of Kansas Bureau of Child Research.

von Stockert, T. 1972. Recognition of syntactic structure in aphasic patients. *Cortex* 8:3.

Wanner, H. E. 1968. On remembering, forgetting, and understanding sentences: a study of the deep structure hypothesis. Ph.D. dissertation, Harvard University.

Waryas, C. L., and Ruder, K. 1973. Children's sentence processing strategies: the double object construction. Working Paper #296, Parsons Research Center, University of Kansas.

Waryas, C. L., and Stremel, K. 1973. On the preferred form of the double object construction. Working Paper #287, Parsons Research Center, University of Kansas.

Wilcox, J., and Tobin, H. 1974. Linguistic performance of hard-of-hearing, normal, and deaf children. *J. Speech Hearing Res.* 17:286–93.

Yates, A. J. 1963. Delayed auditory feedback. *Psychol. Bull.* 60:213–32.

Zurif, E. B.; Caramazza, A.; and Myerson, R. 1972. Grammatical judgements of agrammatic aphasics. *Neuropsychologia* 10:405–17.

IO

TOKEN TEST MEASURES OF LANGUAGE COMPREHENSION IN NORMAL CHILDREN AND APHASIC PATIENTS

Harry A. Whitaker and Ola A. Selnes

The hypothesis that the language performance of aphasics represents a relapse to an earlier or more primitive stage in language development, currently known as the regression hypothesis, may be traced as far back as the writings of John Hughlings Jackson (1958). He used the term *dissolution*, which he adopted from Herbert Spencer, to describe functional retrogression in diseases of the central nervous system in general: "It is a process of undevelopment, it is a 'taking to pieces' in the order from the least organized, from the most complex and most voluntary, towards the most organized, most simple, and most automatic. . . . Hence the statement 'to undergo dissolution' is rigidly the equivalent of the statement 'to be reduced to a lower level of evolution'" (p. 46). He distinguished between *uniform* dissolution, in which the nervous system as a whole is affected, and *local* dissolution, in which only part or a single function of the nervous system is functionally reduced. It is worth emphasizing that Hughlings Jackson conceived of the principle of dissolution as one applying to diseases of the nervous system in general and not to aphasia in particular. Among the disease processes representing examples of dissolution, he mentions muscular atrophy, hemiplegia, *paralysis agitans*, epileptic seizures, chorea and aphasia, and the latter "well illustrated the doctrine of dissolution, and in several ways" (p. 49). In cases of total speechlessness, Hughlings Jackson notes that while voluntary language is lost, the patient may still be able to use "emotional language"—smiling, frowning, gesticulation, and sometimes singing. He also considers the fact that otherwise entirely speechless patients may use the words *yes* and *no* to support the dissolution hypothesis, because these two utterances, owing to their frequent use, represent automatic use of language. According to Hughlings Jackson, receptive language functions are somehow more

Some of the material in this paper is taken from Whitaker and Noll, Some linguistic parameters of the Token Test, *Neuropsychologia* 10 (1972): 395–404. Reprinted here with permission of Pergamon Press, Oxford, England.

automatic than expressive functions, and he therefore viewed preservation of the ability to understand speech in patients with severe expressive impairments as another example of the principle of dissolution. He was careful to emphasize, however, that while dissolution of a function through disease *in general* represents a reversal of the ontogenetic development of that function, there is no absolute correspondence between the two: "Scarcely ever, if ever, do we meet with a case of dissolution which we can suppose to be the exact opposite of evolution" (p. 47).

Freud, who in his small monograph on aphasia (1953) criticized most of the then leading authorities in the field of aphasia, had nothing but praise for Hughlings Jackson, and adopted his views on the evolution and dissolution of function without reservations:

> In assessing the functions of the speech apparatus under pathological conditions we are adopting as a guiding principle Hughlings Jackson's doctrine that all these modes of reaction represent instances of functional retrogression (*Rückbildung*) of a highly organized apparatus, and therefore correspond to previous states of its functional development. This means that under all circumstances an arrangement of associations which, having been acquired later, belongs to a higher level of functioning, will be lost, while an earlier and simpler one will be preserved (p. 87).

Freud's point of view thus represents an associative-strength theory: speech habits that are frequently used will be more resistant to brain damage than those less frequently used. This explains, according to Freud, why a second language is lost before the mother tongue, and why the words *yes* and *no* are so frequently preserved even in severe aphasics. (As an aside, it is not true that in aphasia a second language is always lost before the mother tongue; cases are on record of quite the opposite situation.) Similarly, a patient with agraphia, if capable of writing at all, is usually able to write his own name. The inability of patients with motor aphasia to produce their names is explained simply by the fact that we only rarely say our own names. Freud also mentions that a patient's last utterance before the onset of the disease is frequently preserved, and explains this in terms of the last utterance becoming associated with the traumatic insult, and being highly resistant. The importance of associations in the preservation of language is additionally illustrated by the commonly observed phenomenon that series of words, such as successive numbers, days of the week, etc., are better preserved than single words. He quotes a case in which a patient was unable to state numbers directly but could give a correct response by counting from one until he arrived at the requested number.

A significant contribution to the development of the regression hypothesis in its more current form is found in the works of Roman Jakobson; his monograph on child language and aphasia (1968) summarizes most of his views. Unlike Hughlings Jackson and Freud, Jakobson is chiefly concerned with demonstrating regularities in the phonological development of the child; his work probably represents the first linguistic investigation of the regression hypothesis. He provides several examples demonstrating that the relative chronological order of phonological acquisitions is fairly stable across different language groups; by citing data from other investigators on aphasic language, he argues that "the dissolution of the linguistic sound system in aphasics provides an exact mirror-image of the phonological development in child language. Thus, for example, the distinction of the liquids *r* and *l* is a very late acquisition of child language, and as Froeschels observes, it is one of the earliest and most common losses in aphasic sound disturbances" (p. 60). Jakobson gives several other specific examples of analogies between immature child language and aphasic language. Noting that in English the acquisition of the alveolar fricatives /s/ and /z/ precedes that of the interdental fricatives (/θ/ and /ð/), he quotes Head's observation that English aphasics lose the interdental fricatives earlier than the alveolar ones. Other examples include loss of secondary vowels prior to primary vowels, simplification of affricates to their corresponding plosives, and merging of the velar nasal with the alveolar nasal. Jakobson also cites some evidence that the order in which language is restored in aphasia closely parallels the development of child language (p. 62). According to Jakobson, then, the linguistic development of the child mirrors the regression of the aphasic, and the study of both processes is valuable in revealing the structural organization of language.

Several other investigators, regardless of their particular interpretation of aphasia, have subscribed to the regression hypothesis. This includes Goldstein (1948), whose view of aphasia as an impairment of abstract attitude differs somewhat from the classical interpretations. In a chapter entitled "Some Similarities between the Development of Language and Defects in Aphasics" (p. 44), he quotes some of Jakobson's data as well as personal observations illustrating the regression hypothesis.

Wepman and Jones (1962) present a summary of the most characteristic features of the language behavior of five types of aphasia (syntactic, semantic, pragmatic, jargon, and global) and attempt to correlate these with different stages of language development. It should be noted that they postulate "speechlessness" and "babbling-cooing" as *stages* in language development. This amounts to a claim that some aphasics have reverted to a prelinguistic stage. For example, the speech of jargon aphasics Wepman and Jones correlate with the stage of "babbling-cooing," although the former has phonological regularities, predictable from the native language of the adult.

Blumstein (1973) analyzed consonant production errors in three different types of aphasic patients (Broca's, conduction, and Wernicke's aphasia) and made a systematic description of the pattern of errors based on distinctive-feature theory. Her analysis showed that the types of errors are fairly uniform in each aphasic group and similar across groups. Substitution errors involving only one feature change were significantly more frequent than those involving more than one feature. Blumstein furthermore demonstrated that some features are more likely to be lost or substituted than others, and a hierarchical ordering of different features according to their "vulnerability" in aphasia closely resembles (in reverse order) the hierarchy that Jakobson (1958) proposed for the acquisition of these features.

Two authors who explicitly take exception to the view that the dissolution of language is mirrored in its development are Weisenburg and McBride (1973). While they agree that some clinical evidence suggests that "automatic" language is better preserved than volitional language, "there is no such regularity as to support a general rule that the most automatic and presumably the best established activities remain functioning longest. Both physiologically and psychologically considered, aphasia is a complex deterioration in which thoroughly established as well as newly organized activities are disturbed" (p. 436). In a footnote (p. 438) they state that "the behavior of the aphasic patient differs from that of the primitive man or of the child at any developmental level both as a whole and in specific responses." Weisenburg and McBride thus feel that too much of the language behavior of the aphasic is left unaccounted for by simply postulating that it represents a regression to an earlier developmental stage, and they argue for a more comprehensive set of hypotheses to characterize language disturbances in aphasia.

This brief review of the development of the regression hypothesis, besides attesting to its general popularity, illustrates that it has derived its support from different types of observations. Hughlings Jackson and Freud based their interpretations essentially on the amount of functionally intact language in aphasia, and Jakobson added to the credibility of the hypothesis by providing detailed information about the phonological development in the child. The most specific evidence in support of the hypothesis comes from the work of Blumstein, whose data, in conjunction with Jakobson's data, demonstrate that there is a remarkable degree of correspondence between the order in which the phonological system disintegrates in aphasia and the order in which it develops during acquisition of language.

Common to all the above investigations, however, is their focus on expressive language development and disorders. Far less work has been addressed to the receptive component of language. Part of the explanation for this is undoubtedly the notorious difficulty of constructing good tests for evaluating language comprehension. The development of the Token Test (De Renzi and Vignolo 1962), however, somewhat remedied this situation. The Token Test was designed to assess language impairment in aphasia and is very simple to administer. The test material consists of tokens varying in size, shape, and color, arranged in a predetermined order, and the patient's task is to move or touch these according to standardized oral commands given by the examiner. The motivation for the development of this test was twofold: to find a means for assessing milder forms of receptive dysfunction, which were difficult if not impossible to reveal by standard clinical methods; and to make the assessment as purely linguistic in nature as possible. With regard to the second purpose—the linguistic nature of the task—De Renzi and Vignolo made several important observations regarding linguistic complexity, novelty, and redundancy. Unusual syntactic constructions as well as rare words were excluded, and nonlinguistic clues inherent in many testing situations, such as the examiner-subject relationship or clues derived from the sociocultural nature of the test objects, were also minimized. The success of the Token Test in meeting these aims is well documented in the subsequent literature and needs little further discussion (Boller and Vignolo 1966; Orgass and Poeck 1966; Boller 1968; Noll and Berry 1969; Spellacy and Spreen 1969; Swisher and Sarno 1969; Needham and Swisher 1972). Evidently, the Token Test meets the following criteria for a satisfactory test of language perception: it is based upon objectively quantifiable responses; it reduces paralinguistic redundancies as much as possible; it makes minimal demands on nonverbal types of memory and is relatively easy to administer; in addition, it includes levels of increasing linguistic difficulty or complexity.

Most of the research reported so far in the literature has been almost exclusively concerned with adults, but Orgass and Poeck (1966) did test a group of normal children in the age group 5 to 14 years to make a preliminary assessment of the relationship between age and performance on the Token Test. They found, as expected, that the under-15-year-old group made significantly lower scores than the adult groups; no further analysis was done with the children's data. It is well established that children acquire linguistic skills over a considerable period of time (Slobin 1971; McNeill 1970; Menyuk 1972) and that some intricacies of syntax are not effectively learned until approximately 10 years (C. Chomsky 1969). Therefore, any test that uses linguistic complexity as the main variable ought to provide easily distinguished results when given to children, and analysis of data from children can also contribute to an understanding of general linguistic processing in adults. In addition, since the Token Test begins with simple commands and gradually increases in complexity and, hence, difficulty, it can serve as an effective measure of children's language development.

The Token Test has also been used to assess the degree of receptive language impairment in children with language disorders. Tallal (1975) studied a group of dysphasic children (N = 12, mean age 8:6 years) and a group of normal, matched controls. She found that while the performance of the dysphasics was significantly poorer than that of the controls on parts 2–5 of the test, the two groups showed a similar pattern in terms of frequency of errors. Both groups made only a few errors on the first parts of the test, but their scores progressively deteriorated toward the last parts. Comparing the total number of errors on parts 4 and 5 of the test, Tallal found that both the controls and dysphasics made slightly fewer errors on the last part. Tallal suggests that the high rate of errors on part 4 of the test pertains to problems with auditory retention or verbal memory, rather than grammatical complexity per se.

The purpose of the study to be reported here was not to put the regression hypothesis to a test, but rather to provide a norm for the performance of normal children at different age levels on the Token Test; however, the obtained data, in conjunction with data on the performance of aphasics, provide a basis for comparing the degree of receptive language impairment in aphasics with the degree of receptive language development in children and may thus shed some light on the regression hypothesis.

J. Douglas Noll administered the Token Test to a group of 252 normal children, 18 in each of the 6-month age groups from 5:0 years to 11:11 years, from the public schools around Lafayette, Indiana (reported in Whitaker and Noll 1972). There were 128 girls and 124 boys in the sample; on the basis of school records, only those children were tested who demonstrated achievement or intelligence scores (IQ) between approximately 95 and 110. No child with clinically deviant speech was included. The form of the Token Test used was similar, although not identical, to that described by Boller and Vignolo (1966). For example, *square* was substituted for *rectangle*. All items were scored as either right or wrong. No partial credit scoring was used; any variation in response from the explicit instructions was scored as an error.

Table 10.1 shows the obtained means, standard deviations, and maximum and minimum scores at each 6-month age level.

It can be seen that, as expected, there is a pattern of increasing tests scores with increasing age, although the curve begins to plateau at about 7:6–8:0 years. After 8:0 years there is relatively little change in scores; these mean scores

Table 10.1

Token Test Scores for Children
(maximum score = 62)

Age	Mean Scores*	Range*	SD
5:0–5:5	41.8	30–56	7.6
5:6–5:11	45.4	32–56	6.7
6:0–6:5	46.1	31–56	8.2
6:6–6:11	49.3	38–60	6.5
7:0–7:5	52.6	43–57	3.9
7:6–7:11	55.8	48–60	3.1
8:0–8:5	54.7	47–60	3.6
8:6–8:11	55.4	51–60	2.9
9:0–9:5	55.8	44–61	5.0
9:6–9:11	58.0	53–61	2.5
10:0–10:5	56.4	47–62	4.1
10:6–10:11	58.3	53–62	2.3
11:0–11:5	58.7	55–61	1.7
11:6–11:11	59.0	55–62	2.2

Table 10.2

Averaged Errors and Range of Errors
for Each Part of Token Test

Part	Average Number of Errors per Command	Range of Errors for All Commands
1	0.3	0–1
2	8.4	3–17
3	19.6	11–31
4	53.7	30–87
5	61.3	1–168

are similar to those obtained from normal adults as reported in previous research, e.g., Swisher and Sarno (1969). The variability also decreases with age, as can be seen by the progressively smaller standard deviation values, probably a ceiling effect.

The Token Test is arranged in five parts. In parts 1–4 all commands are syntactically the same: the imperative construction containing either one or two noun phrase (NP) objects; they vary from part to part in the adjectival content of the various NP objects. The ten commands in parts 1–4 are analogous to:

1. Part 1: Touch the red square.
   Part 2: Touch the big yellow circle.
   Part 3: Touch the green square and the blue circle.
   Part 4: Touch the little white square and the big red square.

Part 5, which has twenty-two commands, introduces different verbs and different NP structures in the predicates:

2. Part 5: Put the red circle on top of the green square.
   Instead of the white square, take the yellow circle.

Most children who make errors make more on each subsequent section, most in part 5. The average number of errors for each part and the range of errors from all 252 children is shown in table 10.2. The average number of errors per command was calculated by obtaining the total number of errors for each part from all 252 children and dividing by the number of items in each part. For example, there were 537 total errors on part 4, which contains 10 items, and thus 53.7 mean number of errors per command (537/10). Likewise, there were 1349 total errors on part 5, which contains 22 items, and thus 61.3 mean number of errors per command (1349/22). The values shown in table 10.2 for the range of errors for all commands were calculated by totaling all errors for each individual command within each of the 5 parts. For example, the range of 11–31 listed for part 3 (in table 10.2) means that no command in part 3 had fewer than 11 errors and no command had more than 31 errors. There were only 7 items that resulted in no errors from the total subject sample: items # 1, 2, 3, 7, 8, 9, and 10, all in part 1; all of the remaining 55 items in parts 1-4 resulted in some error responses, as indicated in the range of error tabulation. There were a few children who made more errors in part 4 than in part 5. The complexity-difficulty in part 4 is due to the amount of adjectival information in the object NPs; this fact apparently identifies those children who have greater difficulty with auditory retention or verbal memory, as opposed to structural complexity per se. The most important observation, however, is the range of errors in part 5, which almost totally overlaps the range of error scores in the other four parts of the Token Test. Obviously, the commands in part 5 are not all more difficult or complex than those in parts 1-4; therefore, the true picture of developmental receptive language ability is being obscured by simply counting up the total errors for that part of the test.

In analyzing the individual error scores of each child, it became apparent that certain instructions contributed more to error scores than others. It is plausible to assume that this is the case whenever the test is administered, but most of the published literature is not explicit regarding different error scores for different items. It was found that 8 of the commands in part 5 (out of 22) accounted for most of the errors. The total number of errors for these 8 commands ranged from 77 to 168 and thus did not significantly overlap the error scores for parts 1-4. The 8 sentences from part 5 that account for most of the errors are:

3. 43. Touch the blue circle with the red square (168 errors).
   44. Touch, with the blue circle, the red square (122 errors).
   45. Touch the blue circle and the red square (101 errors).
   51. Touch the white circle without using your right hand (77 errors).
   54. Touch the squares slowly and the circles quickly (77 errors).
   59. Together with the yellow circle, take the blue circle (81 errors).
   60. After picking up the green square, touch the white circle (99 errors).
   62. Before touching the yellow circle, pick up the red square (121 errors).

All but 1 of these commands use the verb *touch*; interestingly enough, parts 1-4 of the Token Test use the verb *touch* exclusively. Twelve of the remaining 14 commands in part 5 use three other verbs: *pick up*, *put*, and *take*. One of the remaining 14 uses *touch* in reference to the examiner, not the subject; only 1 of the 14 uses *touch* as in the sentences cited above in (3) or as in parts 1-4. The problem then is to explain this surprising fact: sentences (commands) using the verb *touch*, which all subjects had been previously exposed to in parts 1-4, suddenly become difficult to process. We can readily dismiss some of the possible hypotheses. Considering the number of morphemes, we find a range of 8 to 12 for the sentences in part 5; however, the number of morphemes for the above 8 sentences is unrelated to the number of errors and therefore this measure of complexity cannot be the basis for the higher number of errors. The Length-Complexity Index (LCI), a composite linguistic measure in which both sentence length and sentence complexity are rated according to a numeric weighting system, was calculated for these following Miner (1969); the LCI indexes ranged from 8 to 12 for the sentences in part 5 but again were unrelated to the number of errors for the 8 sentences in question and were therefore ruled out as the basis for the processing difficulty. Serial position was considered. Part 5 comprises commands numbered 41 through 62; of the low-error sentences, number 57 had 1 error, number 58 had 16 errors, and number 61 had 21 errors. In addition, since the 8 high-error sentences in question were dispersed throughout part 5, we conclude that serial position had little if any effect on the error scores. The basis for the higher error rate can be found, we believe, in the deep-structure linguistic differences in these sentences.

The verb *touch* has an implicit instrumental (INS) case associated with it as part of its meaning; thus, when one is admonished, "Don't touch that!" it means or implies, *with* some part of your body, usually your finger. The INS is often marked by the preposition *with* although it can take a verbal form as noted below. *Touch* also takes an agentive (AG) case, which is the "understood *you*" in the imperative sentence just cited, and an objective (OBJ) case, which in the usual sense is also the goal of the action of touching. *Touch* may also have an overt or explicit INS, which may replace the understood one; thus, we may have the warning "Don't touch that *with anything metallic* (or you may get a shock)!" in which the overt INS is emphasized. For the purposes of comparing the verb *touch* with the other verbs in the Token Test, it is not necessary to discuss other possible noun phrases that may collocate with it, such as locative or temporal phrases, since these are commonly allowed with the other verbs as well and therefore do not provide distinguishing criteria.

The semantic information just outlined may be represented in the following "formula" (cf. Fillmore 1968; Langendoen 1970):

4. TOUCH: AG, OBJ/goal, $\begin{Bmatrix} \text{INS-implicit} \\ \text{INS-overt} \end{Bmatrix}$ $\begin{Bmatrix} \text{LOC/source} \\ \text{implicit} \\ \text{(LOC/source} \\ \text{overt)} \end{Bmatrix}$

The braces indicate that one or the other INS must be part of the structure of sentences containing *touch*. We would then have at some deep-structure level roughly the following semantic information expressed:

5. You + touch + with your finger, etc. + the red circle
  AG   +   INS-implicit   +   OBJ/goal

and the surface structure representation of this command is:

6. Touch the red circle.

Again, the analysis of adjectives such as *red* is not germane to the comparisons between the various verbs and will therefore not be dealt with here; we also overlook the semantics of *circle* and *square*, noting only in passing that they "represent" the objects in question by describing their shape but are not actually the objects. One is requested to touch "the plastic object shaped like a circle," therefore, "circle," etc. It is conceivable that aphasics might be able to touch objects but not the abstract names of objects; thus, "Touch the red thing" might elicit a correct response, but "Touch the red circle" no response, parallel to Goldstein's observations on abstract attitude; however, this will not be explored in this paper. Using the same format, the semantic structure for the other verbs in part 5 of the Token Test will look like these:

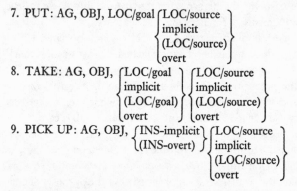

7. PUT: AG, OBJ, LOC/goal
$$\begin{Bmatrix} \text{LOC/source} \\ \text{implicit} \\ \text{(LOC/source)} \\ \text{overt} \end{Bmatrix}$$

8. TAKE: AG, OBJ,
$$\begin{Bmatrix} \text{LOC/goal} \\ \text{implicit} \\ \text{(LOC/goal)} \\ \text{overt} \end{Bmatrix} \begin{Bmatrix} \text{LOC/source} \\ \text{implicit} \\ \text{(LOC/source)} \\ \text{overt} \end{Bmatrix}$$

9. PICK UP: AG, OBJ,
$$\begin{Bmatrix} \text{INS-implicit} \\ \text{(INS-overt)} \end{Bmatrix} \begin{Bmatrix} \text{LOC/source} \\ \text{implicit} \\ \text{(LOC/source)} \\ \text{overt} \end{Bmatrix}$$

(Note that LOC = locative phrase; the parentheses indicate that the case is optionally chosen for the verb.)

Casual observation of these semantic structures suggests that PUT is the most complex to process in the usual situation since there are three obligatory cases associated with it. One cannot just "Put the red circle"; it has to be put *somewhere*, i.e., the LOC must be expressed overtly. But in the sentences using TAKE and PICK UP, the LOC phrases need not be expressed. The LOC which identifies the goal is implicit unless overtly expressed, just like the INS case for the verb TOUCH; thus, we have "Take the red circle," which means implicitly *to yourself*, but we can also have "Take the package from your office *to the laundry*," thus overtly stating the LOC/goal. PICK UP has an implicit INS just like TOUCH (in the Token Test this possible semantic variant is not used). The LOC/source for both TAKE and PICK UP is usually defined by the context. In the Token Test, of course, it is unequivocally defined, since all commands refer to the tokens in front of the subject. LOC/source for the other verbs is similarly represented. When the LOC/source is unclear, one usually specifies it in contrast to other items with which it may be confused; thus, "Take the one on the bottom shelf," etc.

Although both PICK UP and TOUCH may employ the overt INS, only TOUCH is so specified in the Token Test. We might make some additional observations about INS in order to fully appreciate the level of complexity being added in part 5. Overt INS may be paraphrased by a clause containing the verb USE, as in:

10. Touch the red square with the green circle.
11. Use the green circle to touch the red square.

Since negation usually requires a predicate that can be negated (disregarding constituent negation, which is irrelevant here), we thus find in command #51, a high-error item, that the implicit INS is negated—the subject is not supposed to use his dominant hand—but in order to accomplish this, the INS must be made overt and put into its clause form as well:

12. 51. Touch the white circle without *using* your right hand.

We note, in passing, that there are verbs which not only have an implicit INS like TOUCH but which do not allow an overt INS to be expressed, unlike TOUCH. That is, their meaning is strictly bound up with the implicit INS. We can see this by observing the drastically different results of attempting to alter the INS from implicit to overt in the one case and in the other (the asterisk indicates an utterance that is unacceptable in English):

13. Touch the red circle but use something else.
14. *Listen to the radio but use something else.

It is evident from the above discussion that there is potentially a great deal of linguistic complexity in the sentence commands of the Token Test, not all of which is utilized, of course. The basis for the high-error scores on the 8 sentences from part 5 seems to be the shift from implicit to overt INS. If the difficulty were only the overt INS, it would be hard to explain the high number of errors on command #45, a command identical to those of part 3 in which the highest number of errors was only 31. In order to properly execute these commands the subject must do two things: process the new information (the overt INS) and suppress the old information that was formerly predictable (if there is no overt INS, then TOUCH *must* have an implicit INS as part of its meaning). The children in our sample found this difficult to do. Simple conjunction, on the other hand (as in parts 3 and 4 of the Token Test), only *adds* new information; and in fact, the new information in conjunction is structurally identical to the old—the noun phrases are parallel in terms of the linguistic structure of the sentence. This is clearly not the case with the overt INS.

What is particularly interesting is the actual erroneous response to these commands, what the children actually did with the tokens; the responses suggest that the linguistic processing is in part a confusion between coordinated structures and overt instrumental structures and in part a misanalysis of the verb element of the command in such a way as to permit the coordination/INS confusion. A frequent error occurred when the subject, having been told to

"Touch the blue circle with the red square," moved the tokens in such a way that they were touching each other. That is, a subject will move both the blue circle and the red square toward each other until they "are touching." Such an error clearly implies a coordination in the sense of equating the two tokens; it also represents a confusion between the active verb TOUCH and the stative verbal TOUCHING; the verbal TOUCHING, of course, permits the conjoined noun phrases, as in

15. The blue circle and the red square are touching (each other).

The verbal TOUCHING is comparable to a class of words that we designate for convenience Approximators (APPROX); these are words like: NEAR (TO), FAR FROM, CLOSE TO, etc. These words are stative rather than active, i.e., one cannot command a person to " *be far from something" but can only observe whether or not such is the case. These words are symmetrical, i.e. the subject and object are interchangeable without changing the meaning, as seen in these examples:

16. The blue circle is touching the red square and vice versa.
17. The red square and the blue circle are touching.

These words also participate in the Each-Other rule, as noted in example (15).

To further increase the likelihood that subjects will confuse conjunction with other case relationships, we note that sentence #59 introduces yet another syntactic function represented by the word WITH. This is the Comitative case (COMIT).

18. Together with the yellow circle, take the blue circle.

COMIT, which implies accompaniment, is usually expressed with the word AND as normal conjunction:

19. Orpheus went to the underworld *with* Eurydice.
20. Orpheus *and* Eurydice went to the underworld.

Interestingly enough, while the children from whom these data were obtained found the COMIT form of conjunction to be quite difficult (81 errors overall) the sample of aphasic patients we report on below did not; however, the aphasics did find the other 7 high-error sentences in part 5 to be difficult.

The only remaining high-error scores on these 8 sentences that we have not accounted for are sentences #60 and #62. Although these sentences employ the verb TOUCH in the sense it was used in parts 1–4 of the Token Test, there are two further levels of complexity introduced by these sentence commands. For the first time in the Token Test the subject is required to process two verbs (which is comparable to the familiar two-stage command test for aphasia) and there is a constraint on temporal sequencing for each command. Thus, in #60, the subject must touch the white circle after picking up the green square and in #62 the subject must touch the yellow circle after picking up the red square; however, the words BEFORE and AFTER are used in these sentences such that the surface word order is the same as the temporal order of the action in one case (#60) and is the reverse of the temporal order in the other case (#62). It is not surprising that there are more errors on #62. These results are also consistent with a study of children's acquisition of the meaning of *before* and *after* (E. V. Clark 1971).

In order to compare the performance of the group of children with that of aphasic patients, data from two other studies were examined on a sentence-by-sentence basis. Wertz and Keith (personal communication) administered part 5 of the Token Test to a group of 108 aphasic patients. These patients were not, for the purpose of this use of the data, divided into different aphasic types, and therefore comparisons should be considered quite tentative. Nevertheless, comparison of the results of Whitaker and Noll's study with the Wertz and Keith data yielded a Spearman rank correlation coefficient of 0.60, which suggests similar processing difficulties in the two populations. One command that did not correlate well, as noted above, was #59, the comitative form of the conjunction ("Together with the yellow circle, take the blue circle"). The aphasics did much better on this one than did the normal children. For the aphasics, #59 was ranked seventh most difficult in part 5, and for the children it was sixteenth most difficult (out of 22 commands).

Poeck et al. (1974) administered part 5 of the Token Test to a group of aphasics and a group of brain-damaged non-aphasics (N = 100 for both groups). In analyzing their data, they specifically looked at whether or not the items identified by Whitaker and Noll (1972) as being most difficult for children were the ones producing most errors for the brain-damaged aphasic and non-aphasic patients. The rank ordering of the scores for the group of aphasic patients shows that the items pointed out by Whitaker and Noll as being most difficult were clustered, with the exception of items #59 and #44, in the lower half of the rank-ordered distribution. This was not the case for the brain-damaged non-aphasics. Comparison of the rank-ordered distribution of total error scores for both the children and the aphasic group on all items of part 5 resulted in a Spearman rank-order correlation coefficient of 0.63 (significant at the 0.01 level), indicating that the same items were in general easy or difficult for both groups. Among the items that did not correlate well, the commands #44, #49, and #59 were easier for the aphasic group, and commands #41 and #46 were easier for the children.

The distribution of errors for the two groups was, however, quite different. While the children made few errors on some of the commands on part 5 and many errors on others (range: 1–168), the distribution of errors for the aphasic group was narrower (range: 47–88). This explains why, as pointed out by Poeck et al., the critical items for the children accounted for only 37% of the total number of errors made by the aphasic group.

In a recent paper, Lesser (1976) raised a question about the linguistic analyses of the Token Test discussed in this chapter. Lesser first claimed that a reduction in auditory memory is a performance limitation characteristic of aphasia. She then claimed that because the Token Test in part measures verbal and nonverbal memory, such impairments in aphasic patients cloud linguistic interpretations such as those offered by us. The measure of verbal auditory memory that Lesser correlates with scores on the Token Test is a task of pointing to a series of objects in the correct sequence after an examiner has named them; the series is varied from two to eight objects. The scores on this test of verbal auditory memory were compared to Token Test scores by analyzing the sentences in the Token Test in terms of *units of information*, which in fact is no more than counting up certain words. For example, "Show me the *white square*" has two units of information, and "*Put* the *red circle on* the *green square*" has six units of information, according to Lesser. She also claims that six units of information is the maximum in the Token Test.

This system is clearly another surface structure taxonomy, analogous to the one by Miner just discussed. The asymmetrical distribution of errors in part 5 of the Token Test does not correlate with the asymmetrical distribution of Lesser's units of information; consequently, some other explanation is needed. Of course, this is not to deny that reduced verbal auditory memory may inpair performance on the Token Test by aphasics (as well as young children); the problem is that in its simple form of measuring the number of separate words that one can remember immediately, it cannot account for the observed scores on the Token Test. No one would be surprised to find that a patient whose verbal auditory memory was severely impaired obtained a low score on the Token Test.

The problem with simple counts of content words as a measure of the verbal memory component of a sentence can be illustrated by a common clinical observation. A sentence repetition task measures auditory verbal short-term memory, at least in part. In an unpublished study, we compared the ability of aphasic patients to repeat sentences of these two syntactic types:

1. I ordered a ham sandwich, a glass of milk, and a piece of apple pie.
2. The office is on the twenty-first floor of the Merchant's Bank Building.

We found four groups of aphasic patients: those who could repeat both types of sentence with equal ease, those who could not repeat either type, those who could repeat sentences of type 1 but not of type 2, and those who could repeat sentences of type 2 but not of type 1. Of the latter two groups, there were more patients who could repeat type 2 than type 1 sentences, in a ratio of about two to one. There was no apparent correlation between these latter two groups and their performance on a digit span test. Clearly, an index of complexity such as those proposed by Miner or Lesser will fail to predict the occurrence of the group of patients who could only repeat type 1 sentences. It would seem more plausible to seek an explanation based on the linguistic structure of these two sentence types, the first relying on coordination of noun phrases and the second relying on the collocation of adjectives in a partitive noun phrase.

Although the data presented above show relatively good agreement between the rank-ordered distribution of error scores for the group of children and that of two groups of aphasic patients, this obviously does not constitute strong support for the regression hypothesis. Obviously, to the extent that these sets of data agree, one may conclude that linguistic complexity (e.g., the overt INS) is a factor in language acquisition as well as in aphasia. Nonetheless, it is clear from other studies that children fail some items on the Token Test for different reasons (Tallal 1975), and the same is true for different types of aphasics. What may be concluded is that the Token Test, already demonstrated to be a useful instrument for detecting mild aphasic symptoms, is a potential instrument for assessing language acquisition. What remains to be investigated are the factors that, in addition to linguistic complexity, account for the similarities and differences in the acquisition and dissolution of language.

REFERENCES

Blumstein, S. E. 1973. *A phonological investigation of aphasic speech* (Janus Linguarum Ser. Minor, Nr. 153). The Hague: Mouton.

Boller, F. 1968. Latent aphasia: right and left "nonaphasic' brain-damaged patients compared. *Cortex* 4:245–56.

Boller, F., and Vignolo, L. A. 1966. Latent sensory aphasia in hemisphere-damaged patients: an experimental study with the Token Test. *Brain* 89:815–30.

Chomsky, C. 1969. *The acquisition of syntax in children from 5 to 10*. Cambridge, Mass.: M.I.T. Press.

Clark, E. V. 1971. On the acquisition of the meaning of *before* and *after*. *J. Verb. Learning Verb. Behav.* 10:266–75.

De Renzi, E., and Vignolo, L. A. 1962. The Token Test: a sensitive test to detect receptive disturbances in aphasics. *Brain* 85:665–78.

Fillmore, C. J. 1968. The case for case. In *Universals in Linguistic Theory*, ed. E. Bach and R. T. Harms. New York: Holt, Rinehart and Winston.

Freud, S. 1953. *On aphasia: a critical study*. London: Imago Publishing Co.

Goldstein, K. 1948. *Language and language disturbances*. New York: Grune & Stratton.

Jackson, J. H. 1958. *Selected writings of John Hughlings Jackson*, ed. J. Taylor, vols. 1 and 2. London: Staples Press.

Jakobson, R. 1968. *Child language, aphasia, and phonological universals*, trans. A. R. Keiler (Janua Linguarum, Ser. Minor, nr. 72). The Hague: Mouton.

Langedoen, D. T. 1970. *Essentials of English grammar*. New York: Holt, Rinehart and Winston.

Lesser, R. 1976. Verbal and non-verbal memory components in the Token Test. *Neuropsychologia* 14:79–85.

McNeill, D. 1970. *The acquisition of language*. New York: Harper & Row.

Menyuk, P. 1972. *The development of speech*. Indianapolis: Bobbs-Merrill.

Miner, L. E. 1969. Scoring procedures for the length-complexity index: a preliminary report. *J. Comm. Dis.* 2:224-40.

Needham, L. S., and Swisher, L. P. 1972. A comparison of three tests of auditory comprehension for adult aphasics. *J. Speech Hearing Dis.* 37:123-31.

Noll, J. D., and Berry, W. 1969. Some thoughts on the Token Test. *J. Indiana Speech Hearing Ass.* 27:37-40.

Orgass, B., and Poeck, K. 1966. Clinical evaluation of a new test for aphasia: an experimental study on the Token Test. *Cortex* 2:222-43.

Poeck, K.; Orgass, B.; Kerchensteiner, M.; and Hartje, W. 1974. A qualitative study on Token Test performance in aphasic and non-aphasic brain damaged patients. *Neuropsychologia* 12:49-54.

Slobin, D. I. 1971. *Psycholinguistics*. Glenview, Ill.: Scott-Foresman.

Spellacy, F., and Spreen, O. 1969. A short form of the Token Test. *Cortex* 5:390-7.

Swisher, L. P., and Sarno, M. T. 1969. Token Test scores of three matched patient groups: left brain-damaged with aphasia, right brain-damaged without aphasia, non-brain-damaged. *Cortex* 5:264-73.

Tallal, P. 1975. Perceptual and linguistic factors in the language impairment of developmental dysphasics: an experimental investigation with the Token Test. *Cortex* 11:205.

Weisenburg, T., and McBride, K. E. 1973. *Aphasia: a clinical and psychological study*. New York: Hafner Press.

Wepman, J. M., and Jones, L. V. 1962. Five aphasics: a commentary on aphasia as a regressive linguistic phenomenon. In *Disorders of communication*, ed. D. M. Rioch and E. A. Weinstein. Res. Pub. Ass. Nerv. Ment. Dis., vol. 42.

Whitaker, H. A., and Noll, J. D. 1972. Some linguistic parameters of the Token Test. *Neuropsychologia* 10:395-404.

I I

COMPREHENSION DEFICIT IN ACQUIRED APHASIA AND THE QUESTION OF ITS RELATIONSHIP TO LANGUAGE ACQUISITION

Eric H. Lenneberg
Kenneth E. Pogash
Alice Cohlan
and
Jacqueline Doolittle

The infant who begins to speak is building up language knowledge by a process of differentiation, as well as by a process of accretion. Relationships become clearer and clearer, thus leading to the understanding of new relationships (e.g., relations between relations). At the same time, the vocabulary and the repertoire of syntactic constructions increase, either by the addition of items of the kind already present in the child's competence or by the development of new categories of items. In general, the limits of the infant's knowledge of language recede in the course of language acquisition. Aspects or items beyond these limits are simply nonexistent as far as the child's language capacity is concerned.

In the adult patient with acquired aphasia, language operations that were functioning smoothly premorbidly are interfered with or blocked; neurophysiological processes are deformed through the destruction of tissue. (Metabolic disturbances, though, may bring about similar disturbances without gross anatomical changes.) There are indications that this kind of *language interference* may be distinguished from a state of partial or total *language ignorance*, i.e. absence of language knowledge. Our working hypothesis is that the aphasic patient and the young infant who fail to give the correct answer to a given test item may do so for quite different reasons. In some instances, the aphasic patient may be shown to have the necessary knowledge available to him to comprehend a certain word if the interfering conditions are minimized by appropriate manipulations on the part of the examiner. The language-learning child, however, cannot give the right answer to questions containing certain words, even when the experimenter optimizes test conditions, because the prerequisite knowledge is simply not there yet.

211

As is well known, the general expressive capacity of a patient is not well correlated with his capacity for language comprehension. A patient with speech apraxia (Broca's aphasia), anomia (amnestic aphasia), or fluent jargon aphasia may often be shown to have a surprising degree of comprehension of either spoken or written language. Thus, his state of language knowledge may be reflected better in his comprehension capacity than in his expressive capacity. In view of this, the observations reported on in this study are focused primarily on the patient's impairment of comprehension. This seems to be more relevant to language knowledge; it is also an area in which the examiner may exercise fairly direct control over what is to be tested, without having to rely on his intuition about what might be on the patient's mind and what he is trying to say.

OBJECTIVES OF THIS STUDY

In the present research, we have concentrated on a small set of words that denote certain relationships and attributes. The words (or concepts underlying the words) were chosen because there are indications that children experience varying degrees of difficulty with their correct usage, which suggests that certain cognitive processes must become operative before the words are correctly understood. Thus the material is particularly well-suited to comparing language acquisition and language loss.

Our principal objectives were: (1) to arrange the words tested for in terms of general difficulty for the patient group as a whole; (2) to see whether the order of difficulty is similar for all patients or whether each patient has his own peculiar types of difficulties with these words; (3) to see whether the patients' order of difficulty is the same as the order noted for children; and (4) to see if patients are consistent in their mistakes or, if not, what causes them to fluctuate.

The work reported here is of a preliminary nature. Its main value has been to suggest to its authors how a more ambitious investigation on the same topic should be designed.

METHODS AND MATERIALS

We examined eight stroke patients who had been admitted to Burke Rehabilitation Center, a Cornell-affiliated teaching hospital. All patients were at least four weeks past the acute onset of their illness, and all took part in a vigorous rehabilitation program including physical and occupational therapy, gymnastics, and speech therapy.

All but one patient had right-sided motor involvement of varying degrees. The exception (patient I.) was a 58-year-old multilingual, right-handed stockbroker with a history of hypertension of over ten years' duration and a number of prior episodes of transient ischemic attacks involving both right and left hemispheres. At the time of our examination, he had no unequivocal lateralizing signs (a questionable Hoffman sign on the left, and one observer thought he had an extensor plantar response on the right; stereognosis, graphesthesia, and two-point discrimination were equally poor for both sides). He could utter a few words and phrases with great effort, and his comprehension was grossly impaired. This condition came on suddenly (minutes) and remained unchanged from the day of onset to the end of our contact with him three months later.

Four of the remaining patients (D., F., R.D., and S.) had varying degrees of right somatosensory impairments. None seemed to have visual-field defects in confrontation tests. One right-handed patient (C.) with complete right hemiplegia involving face, arm, and leg had only transient aphasic symptoms. Four weeks after the stroke no expressive and only mild receptive difficulties were demonstrable by our methods.

Our work-up of the patients was basically that of Goodglass and Kaplan (1972), although the content of the tests was partly altered to fit our special interests. Estimates of impairment of comprehension and expression and their rank-order correlation are shown in figure 11.1. For a characterization of the

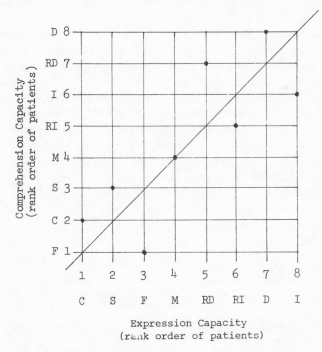

Fig. 11.1   Rank order correlation of expression and comprehension capacity of the eight patients studied; all rank orders based on relevant tests of the Goodglass and Kaplan battery. Letters are patients' initials.

Table 11.1

Characterization of Eight Patients' Expressive Symptomatology

Symptom	C.	D.	F.	I.	M.	R.I.	R.D.	S.
Normal speech production	x							
Apraxic blockage		2		3		2	1	
Articulation disorder				1		1	1	1
Voice disorder			1					
Fluent jargon					3			

NOTE: x = present; 1 = mild; 2 = moderate; 3 = marked.

eight patients' symptoms of expressive disorders, see table 11.1. Comprehension was tested further by a Token Test adapted from that of De Renzi and Vignolo (1962). In addition, the patient had to signal yes or no to a number of questions, some referring to objects and situations before them, others referring to more remote situations than the here and now. The items composing the actual test are evident from table 11.2.

All patients were seen at least twice—once in the morning before the start of the day's program, and once in the afternoon or early evening, toward the end of their day; most patients were seen more often. Some were observed over a period of four weeks.

In most instances, the entire test was administered twice, and items on which a patient failed were rechecked as often as necessary to satisfy the examiner that the item was really beyond the patient's capacity. Special attention was paid to all variations in a patient's performance, and an effort was made to discover the factors responsible for these fluctuations. Once he had formulated an hypothesis about why a particular patient had difficulties with the test as a whole or with given items from it under certain circumstances, the experimenter went back to the patient in an attempt to provide further evidence for his hypothesis. It soon became clear that much of the variation could be accounted for by just a few variables and that in some instances these could be manipulated experimentally at the bedside. At least some of these variables were operative in every patient's performance. We therefore incorporated them as far as possible, into our methodology, and systematic manipulation of at least some of them became part of the protocol. The following variables emerged:

1. order of presentation, including catastrophic reaction
2. size of the stimulus universe
3. environmental context (including social and physical factors)
4. verbal context
5. number of items in commands or questions
6. tendency to perseverate
7. patient's state: mood and/or fatigue
8. patient's state: arousal or attention

9. unaccounted for fluctuations (unaccounted for successes and failures on the same item—i.e., occasional impairment)

We tried to gain some insight into the relative importance of these variables by the following means. Items that were missed in one testing session became the first items tested in subsequent sessions. If it was noted that a patient regularly became increasingly confused as the session went on, we systematically shortened subsequent sessions, in some instances to the point where we would ask a patient to do just a few things at a time or merely "ask him a couple of questions in passing." The number of stimuli confronting the patient during a task was an important variable, particularly in the Token Test; for example, the command to the patient might remain the same (e.g., "Put the circle on the square") while the number of tokens in front of the patient could be varied from only two to as many as sixteen. Variables 3 and 4 were studied in the following way. For example, if understanding of the concepts *more* or *less* was to be tested, we elicited an answer to the question "Is a dollar seventy-five more money than twenty-seven dollars?" and also showed the patient two unequal piles of pennies and asked, "Does this pile have more pennies than that?" The physical context of the latter question might help the patient to demonstrate his knowledge of the concepts *more* and *less*, while the remoteness of the former question might lead him to an erroneous answer. Similarly, one might say to the patient: "Mr. Smith has a son and a daughter; Mr. Brown has seven children. Does Mr. Smith have more children than Mr. Brown?" Or: "I see from the chart that you have a son and a daughter."—pause—then, "I have seven children myself. Tell me, do you have more chilrden than I do?" The latter test question is put within a tangible social context for the patient; the interest is in whether this helps him to organize his thoughts and answer. If his answer is correct in the latter situation, we have evidence that he can comprehend the concepts *more* and *less* and that his mistakes in the former situation are due to a different aspect of the task. Variable 4 was also studied by comparing answers in the Token Test with answers to yes or no questions in a purely verbal context. For instance, the response to "Watch: did I drop the square *after* I dropped the circle?" was compared with the response to "Tell me: does spring come *after* summer?" If a patient fails on "Show me a large green square," it is necessary to see whether he knows the individual concepts involved. To manipulate variable 5, we tested separately knowledge for each word in relative isolation as well as in combination with other words. In order to rule out a memory deficit, the longer commands were repeated as often as the patient was still trying to follow them. Patients who had demonstrated preservation of reading ability were allowed to read the command on a card, and the card was left in view until the patient had finished (this was the case with patient M.).

Documentation for the next three variables had to be more uneven. Assessment of a patient's fatigue, mood, arousal, and attention depends on the examiner's subjective judgement. The invocation of these variables remains a most unsatisfactory explanation. Arousal, especially, is not easily manipulated, but we shall describe below some situations that provide bona fide evidence in support of this explanation. Finally, it is possible that what appear to be erratic alternations between periods of apparent understanding and periods of hopeless confusion are reflections of the observer's inability to determine precisely the underlying causes.

Although the tests we have used have been standardized and yield numerical scores, we did not evaluate our patients in these terms. From the outset there was no intention of comparing *groups* of patients with one another, and therefore statistical parameters and pooled numerical data were of little use to us. In this study we were interested in the specific performance on particular items by each patient under certain specifiable experimental circumstances. The only relevant statistic is the comparison of error scores, item by item, for every patient under various conditions. At this stage of our work, we considered the patient to have given evidence of knowing the meaning of an item if he made no more than one mistake in a single session consisting of at least six trials, or no mistakes in four trials on different occasions. In some instances, judgment of intact comprehension could be based on the patient's performance on a coherent block of items. For example, if all questions were concerned with the adjectives for color and size and if the patient did not make a single mistake on the ten possible questions, each dealing with one of these words, we construed this as evidence for knowledge of the meaning of these words. We found that these criteria were easy to apply because in short blocks of time (about ten minutes), a patient seemed always quite consistent—at that moment he either seemed to know what the right answer was or he was obviously confused. This procedure deviates from common practice in experimental psychology, where one bases oneself strictly on numerical scores and tries to ignore the correlated, more general behavior of one's subject. The neurological examination, however, is based on the procedure we have followed here. We find that with a minimum of practice and experience with patients, one learns to make judgments of a patient's competence with a high degree of interobserver reliability. Numerical treatment of scores allows the use of sample statistics, thus revealing trends and deviations from random models. However, it is based frequently on unwarranted assumptions about the invariant nature of unity and scales, and it may sometimes obscure the specific mechanisms for wrong answers.

RESULTS

A survey of our test results is given in table 11.2. Each cell has three figures. The first indicates the number of times the patient gave evidence of understanding the item (by one of the criteria mentioned above); the second indicates the number of times the patient failed to reach the criteria for knowing the item. (In other words, these figures do not refer to individual responses, but to the performance on a subtest of several questions.) The third figure is a weighted score for the patient's total performance with respect to that item: 1 means no evidence of incomprehension throughout our contact with the patient; 2 means that the patient gave evidence of knowing the meaning of the item more often than he gave evidence for not knowing it; 3 means that he showed himself wrong more often than right; and 4 means that there was no evidence ever that the patient understood the meaning of the word.

In order to rank the inherent difficulty of each item, we computed the the average weighted score for each row. In order to rank the patients in terms of their difficulty with our tests, we computed the average weighted score for each column. These averages formed the basis of the rank orders shown in table 11.3.

If the degree of difficulty with an item is due to something like "inherent complexity" and is thus an invariable property of that item (much the way its phoneme sequence is), then one might expect the severity of a patient's condition to correlate with the number and type of items he can master; a mild disorder would interfere only with the most difficult items, and a severe disorder would impair comprehension of most or all items. The only independent measures we have of the patients' condition derive from the Goodglass and Kaplan scores shown in figure 11.1. We may, however, ask whether the rank order of difficulty (left-most column of table 11.3) plotted against the rank order of patients' comprehension impairment (top row) produces an ordered scale of patient performance. Table 11.3 suggests that such scaling is, in fact, possible, the upper left quadrant of the matrix is free from errors, whereas the right lower quadrant shows a heavy accumulation of mistakes. (The scale is not perfect, but neither is the scoring method. Also, the unequal number of items tested for in individual patients introduced some artifacts, as in the case of patients C. and S. The trend is nevertheless clear.) This indicates that the scale of relative difficulty was the same for all patients, and that there is something inherent in the various words and concepts that accounts for this difficulty. Since the patients' understanding of the various words was tested by different methods, testing artifact alone can scarcely account for these results. Notice also that the rank order of patients calculated from our tests agrees rather well with the rank order based on Goodglass and Kaplan tests.

In addition to the test scores tabulated, it may be of value to present here a few summary comments on each patient's general performance.

C.: Confusion when presented with all tokens at once, and improved performance when only a few tokens are in view; understands when mistakes are pointed out and makes appropriate corrections.

D.: Global aphasia; the two successful performances due to unexplained fluctuation.

Table 11.2

Survey of Results of Comprehension Tests for Eight Patients

Items	C.			D.			F.			I.		
Small/large	2	0	*1*				1	0	*1*	9	3	*2*
Square/round	2	0	*1*	0	1	*4*	1	0	*1*	3	4	*3*
Top, on, over	3	0	*1*	0	1	*4*	1	0	*1*	6	3	*2*
Under	2	1	*2*	0	1	*4*	1	0	*1*	5	3	*2*
In, into/out							1	0	*1*	2	0	*1*
Next, by, beside	3	0	*1*	0	1	*4*	1	0	*1*	0	4	*4*
Between	2	1	*2*	0	1	*4*	1	0	*1*	6	4	*3*
Right/left				0	1	*4*	7	2	*2*	10	5	*2*
Before/after	8	1	*2*	0	2	*4*	1	0	*1*	7	17	*2*
Together, same time				0	2	*4*	1	0	*1*	1	0	*1*
First/then				1	1	*2.5*	1	0	*1*	1	1	*2.5*
Numbers:							1	0		1	0	
More/less, fewer	5	1	*2*	2	2	*2.5*	8	5	*2*	5	4	*2*
Any							1	0		1	0	
Every, all										0	5	
And/or				0	1	*4*	1	0	*1*	1	0	*1*
Both/either				0	1	*4*	1	0	*1*	1	0	*1*
Same as	2	1	*2*	0	1	*4*	9	2	*2*	5	4	*2*
Comparative:												
Larger/smaller	3	0	*1*	0	1	*4*	1	0	*1*	1	0	*1*
Blue	3	0		0	1		1	0		2	1§	
Red	3	0		0	1					2	1§	
Green	3	0	*1*			*4*	1	0	*1*	1	0	*1.7*
Yellow				0	1							
Black/White	2	0		0	1		1	0				
Rank order by number of errors	4			8			1			6		

NOTE: Left figure in column = number of times test was administered and patient reached criterion of knowing the item. Middle figure = number of times that test was administered and patient gave evidence of failure. Right figure = weighted score for item: *1* = always correct; *2* = more correct than wrong; *3* = more wrong than correct; *4* = always wrong; blank = no evidence. Rank orders of items and patients based on the average weighted scores computed for rows and columns respectively.

F.: Identifies *right/left* on own body but has difficulty in deciding *right/left* with respect to an object in front; *same as* causes difficulty only when the entire set of tokens is in view; failure on *more/less* due to unexplained fluctuation.

I.: Goes through whole test battery once without mistake; when battery is repeated immediately (for confirmation or detection of possible weaknesses) makes mistake on every item (catastrophic reaction); makes mistakes on *yes/no* questions involv-

M.			R.I.			R.D.			S.			Rank Order of Difficulty
1	0	1	2	0	1	1	0	1	1	0	1	2
1	0	1	2	0	1	1	0	1	1	0	1	7
1	0	1	6	8	2	1	3	3	6	2	2	10
1	0	1	7	6	2	1	3	3	6	2	2	12
			2	0	1	2	1	2	1	0	1	1
1	0	1	1	3	3	1	3	3	3	0	1	16
2	1	2	8	6	2	2	3	3	5	2	2	17
1	0	1	3	1	2	0	4	4	8	3	2	12
1	0	1	11	13	3	6	4	2	15	18	3	14.5
1	0	1	2	0	1	2	1	2	1	0	1	6
1	0	1	2	0	1	2	0	1	1	0	1	3
			1	0		2	0		2	0		*
3	3	2.5	1	0	1	1	2	3	4	1	2	12
1	0		1	0		2	0		2	0		†
						2	1		1	0		‡
1	0	1	2	3	3				1	0	1	8.5
1	0	1	2	0	1				3	0	1	8.5
5	3	2	3	2	2	5	2	3	4	2	2	14.5
1	0	1	3	0	1	4	2	2	3	0	1	4
1	0⎫		3	0⎫		2	0⎫		1	0⎫		
			3	0		1	0		1	0		
1	0⎬	1	2	0⎬	1	2	0⎬	1	1	0⎬	1	5
			2	0		1	0					
1	0⎭		3	0⎭		2	0⎭		1	0⎭		
2			5			7			3			

* Excluded—selection of patients tested biased.
† Excluded—difficult to test.
‡ Excluded—insufficient observations.
§ In test where all were wrong.

ing *more/less* but points correctly to heaps of more or less pennies; answers *yes/no* questions involving *before/after* correctly when they refer to events in patient's day, but makes mistake when *before/after* refers to manipulation of tokens. Mistakes, in general, become more frequent as test goes on, despite initial success and regardless of item. Intervals between questions or commands improve chances for success and, conversely, shortening the pauses between questions worsens performance. Unexplained fluctuations in performance of *same as* and *right/left*.

Table 11.3

Guttman-Type Scale for Comprehension Tests

		Patients							
Items		1 *F.*	2 *M.*	3 *S.*	4 *C.*	5 *R.I.*	6 *I.*	7 *R.D.*	8 *D.*
1	In, into/out	1		1		1	1	2	
2	Small/large	1	1	1	1	1	2	1	
3	First/then	1	1	1		1	2.5	1	2.5
4	Larger/smaller	1	1	1	1	1	1	2	4
5	Colors	1	1	1	1	1	1.7	1	4
6	Together, same time	1	1	1		1	1	2	4
7	Square/round	1	1	1	1	1	3	1	4
8.5	And/or	1	1	1		3	1		4
	Both/either	1	1	1		1	1		4
10	Top, on, over	1	1	2	1	2	2	3	4
12	Under	1	1	2	2	2	2	3	4
	Right/left	2	1	2		2	2	4	4
	More/less	2	2.5	2	2	1	2	3	2.5
15	Before/after	1	1	3	2	3	2	2	4
	Same as	2	2	2	2	2	2	2	4
	Next, by, beside	1	1	1	1	3	4	3	4
17	Between	1	2	2	2	2	3	3	4

NOTE: Patients (columns) are rank ordered by success on comprehension tests; items (rows) are rank ordered by degree of difficulty they caused the patients. Entries are the weighted scores taken from table 11.2.

M.: Can read rather well, but has severe auditory incomprehension and totally unintelligible jargon aphasia. *Same as* correct on *yes/no* questions when subject matter is some concrete circumstance; mistakes when subject matter is tokens. Points correctly to the pile that has *more* pennies, but makes mistake on *yes/no* question, "Is 23 more than 35?" Understands *between* correctly with regard to objects of daily use but makes mistakes with regard to tokens. Patient has repeatedly been observed (by different investigators) to have sudden moments (30 to 60 seconds long) of clear auditory comprehension and fluent, well-formed, coherent, and appropriate utterances. These occur only after periods during which the patient appears to be absorbed mentally in a silent task. Also, the first word of any utterance tends to be phonemically better constructed than subsequent words. There is anosognosia for all failures.

R.I.: About half of all mistakes due to perseveration; on two separate days patient completed the test of the day without mistakes and then, immediately afterwards, got all items wrong (catastrophic reaction). Understands well any adjective used singly, but in any concatenation of adjectives none is understood; this cannot be attributed to memory because the question is repeated throughout the patient's attempt to answer it (or to follow the command). Chances for mistakes increase with every successive task. Begins to make mistakes when more than three tokens or more than five objects are in view. After a mistake on a question with many words, the next two or three questions, even though short and within patient's proven capacity, are invariably wrong. Makes mistakes on *before/after* when subject matter is tokens, but answers *yes/no* correctly when *before/after* refers to events in patient's day.

R.D.: Perseveration accounts for one third of mistakes. Mistakes may be minimized either by reducing number of tokens in view or by confining task to only two alternatives (*in* vs. *under*; *large* vs. *blue*; etc.). As either the number of alternatives (even though patient has been shown to understand each concept involved) or the number of tokens in view increases, mistakes multiply. Concatenation of adjectives results in failures on all items involved (despite mnemonic facilitation). Patient is often heard during the test to give himself an instruction as if he were repeating to himself what the experimenter had just demanded of him, but the patient's version differs from the experimenter's; further, the patient's response is incorrect for either the original or the modified demand. Temporal concepts give trouble in commands for performance but are apparently understood in questions that require a *yes/no* answer; the opposite is the case for quantitative concepts.

S.: Mistakes when too many tokens in view; concatenated adjectives cause total incomprehension; a difficult task, even when preceded by a long run of entirely correct answers, frequently elicits catastrophic reaction with total incomprehension for the rest of the testing session. *Before/after* is understood in context of patient's day, but not in connection with token manipulation. Identifies *right/left* correctly on own body, but not with regard to objects in front; some fluctuations in performance seem erratic.

Table 11.4

Incidence of General Psychological Variables Observably Affecting Patients' Performace on Comprehension Tests

Variable	C.	D.	F.	I.	M.	R.I.	R.D.	S.
Order of presentation and catastrophic reaction			x			x	x	x
Size of stimulus universe	x		x	x			x	x
Environmental context			x	x			x	x
Verbal context	x			x			x	x
Number of words in command				x		x	x	x
Perseveration						x	x	
Physiological state: I. mood and fatigue						x		
Physiological state: II. arousal and attention					x			
Unaccounted for fluctuations (sporadic impairment) (%)	15	15	30	14	95	20	0	0
Irrecoverable loss: permanent impairment (%)	20	85	0	16	0	0	8	0

NOTE: Figures in bottom rows are percentages of total number of errors made by patients. They may help us to form an idea of the relative importance of general cognitive factors accounting for aphasic incomprehension.

Table 11.4 summarizes these observations and gives an idea of how much of the patients' variance in performance may be attributable to the variables enumerated earlier. More exact quantification was not possible in the present preliminary study. However, the two bottom rows give percentages of total occurrence of errors and thus reveal the relative importance of psychological factors in determining success and failure on these language tasks. Note that none of these factors belongs to any aspect of the formal structure of language.

DISCUSSION

In spite of some obvious methodological shortcomings in this study (the different number of tests run on each patient and the lack of quantifiable observations on some important variables), some interesting issues emerge.

We have already noted that the scalability of the mistakes suggests that there is a gradient of difficulty inherent in the words and concepts used in this study. Insofar as patients had difficulties, they tended to have difficulties with the same words. We must now ask, what is the source of this difficulty?

Linguistic Structure as a Source of Patients' Difficulties

When we study the rank order of item difficulty, certain semantic and logical criteria for groupings become apparent. This is most obvious in the case of color terms. A patient either knew them all or knew none. Particularly telling is the case of patient I.: six of his tests included two, and one of the tests included three, color terms. The two times he made mistakes, he not only got both colors wrong but was also wrong on all other items of those tests.

The logical connectives *and*, *or*, *both*, and *either* posed the same degree of difficulty for the patient group as a whole, and this was also the case for some of the spatial prepositions (*on*, *over*). This, together with the behavior on the colors, suggests a logicosemantic or linguistic source of the patients' difficulties. On the other hand, the ordering of the items in table 11.3 also leaves many questions unanswered. There is no logical or semantic reason why *in* should be so different from *on*; why *more* and *less* should be so different from *larger* and *smaller*; why the color and size predicates should be more different from each other than from colors and the comparatives *larger* and *smaller*; etc. One gets the impression that the linguistic and logical nexus is not the only source of the relative difficulty experienced by patients. This idea is reinforced when we turn our attention to syntactic aspects. Naturally, the items used could not be tested for in a syntactic vacuum; nor could syntactic complexity be held constant in the formulation of questions and demands. We shall show that the test results might here and there have been influenced by syntactic complexity, although, once again, this could only have been a small contributory factor in the patients' performance.

Consider the following tasks. A blue square and a red circular token are placed in front of the patient; the test consists of the following commands: "Point to the square token"; "Point to both the square *and* the round tokens"; "Point to the blue token"; "Point to *both* the square *and* the red tokens"; "Point to *either* the blue *or* the red token"; "Point to the round token"; "Point to *either* the square *or* the round token"; "Point to *both* the blue *and* the red tokens"; and so on, making use of all twelve possible combinations of the words *square, round, blue, red, and, or*. Patients R.I. and I. were both capable of giving entirely correct answers to all of these questions. However, if they were faced with four tokens, round and square blue ones and round and square red ones, and asked to "Point to the square, blue token," they became confused, sometimes to the point of eliciting catastrophic reaction for the next half-dozen questions. One is tempted to attribute this failure to the difference in syntactic structure between "square blue token" and "square and blue tokens." However, at least one of the patients seemed to have less trouble (than with square blue) with "Point to the big, square token" in a different situation, where the relevant attributes were size and shape. Moreover, even if it had not been for this inconsistency, any explanation for the experienced difficulty on purely syntactic grounds would tend to be rather *ad hoc*. Also from the syntactic point of view, we must conclude that psycholinguistic factors alone are insufficient to explain the difficulties.

Nonlinguistic Cognitive Factors as a Source of Patients' Difficulties

A survey of table 11.4 and the perusal of our additional comments on patients' behavior in the previous section strongly suggest a number of disturbing or "nuisance" factors that are quite unrelated to either the formal or the semantic structure of language. The patient is easily disturbed by (1) the simultaneous impingement of spatially coexisting stimuli, such as many tokens confronting him all at once, and (2) by stimuli that reach him sequentially one after the other. In other words, there is disturbance in the spatial as well as in the temporal domain. The first type may be related to what has been called *simultanagnosia*. The patient in this instance has no difficulty in recognizing a tree drawn on a card or a bird drawn on another card. However, when he is shown a card in which the two pictures are combined, with the bird sitting in the tree, he cannot recognize either. This has been studied recently in our laboratory by K. Flekköy, who has demonstrated that some brain-damaged patients may become confused even when the bird is cut out from his empty background and moved on to the tree, the operation being performed in full view of the patient. When the figures are separated again, the gestalt of each becomes recognizable; when the bird is returned to the tree and the patient is asked one minute later what it is, he can no longer name either of the two objects. To the onlooker it seems as if the two simultaneously presented patterns and the need to interrelate them produce internal interferences that confuse the patient. This may also be the reason why dyslexia is such a common clinical finding with left-hemisphere lesions. The simultaneously presented words cause confusion. (N.B.: Our one patient [M.], whose reading ability was well preserved, despite auditory incomprehension and jargon aphasia, characteristically had no trouble in this respect; she performed as well with many as with few tokens in view, which suggests that the spatial difficulty is dissociable from the temporal difficulty.)

The temporal disturbance has a number of different manifestations, though they are probably all interrelated. In the most severe case, the patient may only comprehend one relatively short item at a time, and the demands or questions directed at him must be preceded and followed by quiet. Any kind of stringing up of words confuses him, even if we make sure that we do not tax his memory by means of frequent repetitions. Ideally, one explains a task to a patient with this problem by gesture or silent demonstration and lets the demand simply consist of a laconic "red"; "both"; "small"; etc., with the implication that he is to hand you the respective token(s). It may be a sign of a lesser degree of involvement if a patient can successfully point to "the square and the blue tokens," even though he fails on "the square, blue token." Perhaps the difficulty in the latter case is that the sequentially presented adjectives must both be brought to bear upon simultaneously coexisting attributes in a single object. This conjecture is, of course, difficult to prove.

Perseveration could be interpreted in a similar vein: a disturbance in the sequential order of physiological processes. A patient is asked to do something; when he is given a further command, his response is still dominated by the mental activity originated by the preceding question. There is something wrong in the temporal structure of his neurological activities (such as a defect in inhibitory mechanisms that should ordinarily dampen the action at the end of its course). A first process (patient's response tendency to question 1) that should have been arrested by a second process (the inhibitory action) is abnormally prolonged because the second process has become inoperative. Self-excitatory processes are allowed to go unchecked, thereby disturbing the system in a nonadaptive, pathological way. This view is further encouraged by a scrutiny of jargon aphasia. The patient's self-initiated activity underlying speech is no longer regulated by the normally existing balance between excitatory and inhibitory mechanisms; the jargon is a release phenomenon due to lack of inhibition and the correlated neuronal processes produce proactive and retroactive interference with other activity patterns. One is reminded of patients with chorea of ballism: in perfect repose all involuntary movements disappear. But the moment the patient initiates movement or tries to exercise control over the musculature in the maintenance of posture, involuntary movements appear, often spreading over the entire body. They are self-initiated release phenomena due to an interference with a normal system of checks and balances.

While spatial disturbance seems to be caused by interference of simultaneously ongoing neuronal processes, in temporal disturbance the disorder appears to be due to interference of sequentially appearing activity patterns. In the first case, simultaneously occurring (in parallel) processes get into each other's way; in the second case, subsequent processes (in series) get into each other's way. It is true that these are highly speculative interpretations—not facts. However, the symptoms themselves and their observable (and experimentally controllable) antecedents are objective enough observations, and they clearly point to neuropsychological mechanisms that are much more general than linguistic processes pure and simple. They are general neuropsychological nuisance factors.

Other psychological factors are indicated by the patients' capacity to point correctly to their own right or left body parts while they cannot point to the experimenter's right or left, nor arrange objects to the right or the left of other objects in front of them. These are mental transformations (unrelated to language) that seem to go beyond the patient's cognitive capacity. K. Goldstein (1948) used to analyze patients' behavior in terms of what he called the capacity for abstract attitude. This notion has fallen into disrepute because of the patent difficulty in providing objective definition of the concept *abstract*. Nevertheless, one cannot help but notice that comprehension of words and concepts is frequently facilitated by a corroborative environment and interfered with if the task is stripped of all supportive environmental clues (as is the case in the Token Test). Whatever may lie behind this phenomenon, the interfering factor is clearly not a purely linguistic, but a general, cognitive one.

We may note in passing that the various psychological nuisance factors discussed here may also be seen to be at work in a great variety of other diseases that interfere with intellectual functioning—for example, general dementia—without affecting language. How and why these same factors combine to interfere with langauge, particularly in the case of certain left-hemisphere lesions, remains a mystery. To state that the lesions destroy the language centers is simply to give the mystery a label, not an explanation.

Purely Physiological Factors as a Source of Patients' Difficulties

We have only indirect evidence that purely physiological factors must play a powerful role in many aphasic symptoms. The sudden changes in level of performance noticeable in a great variety of aphasic patients seem most commonly related to a patient's physiological state, including arousal level (as evidenced by autonomic functions), fatigue, blood-sugar level, pathological fluctuations in temperature, etc. It is not at all uncommon for a patient with metabolic disease to behave like a classic aphasic in the morning, appear to have undergone a miraculous change at noon time, and be severely aphasic again in the late afternoon. Thus the degree of language knowledge is masked during the aphasic states, and both comprehension and expression may become blocked. With improved systemic conditions, the language capacity reemerges; the cognitive system organizes itself again to become a competent language-machine.

The advantage of using aphasic patients who are not too severely affected lies in the insight they give into the effect of different *degrees* of involvement of the language function. When one arranges the patients in terms of severity of the condition, one gets the impression that the same nuisance factors discussed above take an ever-increasing hold on cognitive and language processes. These factors (or rather the pathology that causes them) disturb the organism ever more, distorting and interfering with its normal function and the interrelation between its subfunctions. The nuisance factors do not cause "pieces of language knowledge to be destroyed and lost." They merely cause misfirings. Our investigations show how the nuisance factors may sometimes be experimentally checked, and when this happens, the continued presence of (or the reactivated) language knowledge may be demonstrated. Under certain conditions of limited insult to the brain, the mechanism for understanding the meaning of the words *under*, *blue*, *square* is not irretrievably destroyed in the aphasic patient, but may be made to function temporarily if the system is artificially shielded—for example, from the disturbing intrusion of too much stimulation by too many tokens in view. This, of course, works only under highly contrived or specialized circumstances, and the reappearing language capacity still bears many hallmarks of abnormal function; and if the disease is serious enough, language capacity may be so severely affected that it is, for all practical purposes, irreversibly abolished.

COMPARISON WITH LANGUAGE ACQUISITION

The aphasic disturbances brought out in our investigations have some commonalities with certain difficulties encountered by children. In our laboratory, we have observed that children of less than three years of age may still have difficulty with the phrase *next to*, whereas words like *on*, *under*, *in*, and *out* are well established. Comprehension of color words is difficult for some young children, and in an earlier study the senior author found that children usually either understand the meaning of all of the common words for color or understand none. This is reminiscent of what we found in this study of aphasic patients. Thus we do not contest Roman Jakobson's (1968) notion that one can occasionally find symmetries between language acquisition and language loss due to aphasia. However, there are also very important discrepancies in the types of mistake made by children and by aphasics. Certainly the *general* order of difficulty that appeared in the present study is not paralleled by the *general* order of difficulty encountered by normal children. Moreover, a closer look at the type of mistake made by children and by aphasics shows that there are differences here, too; for example, the semantic overgeneralization seen in children is never seen in the same form in patients (in aphasics one finds circumlocution), and when the patients make mistakes they seem to be confused and to be acting randomly, whereas children go through a stage at which the underlying concept of the word is related to but different from that of adult usage. Much more importantly, the psychological nuisance factors described above, all due to a malfunctioning brain, are essentially absent from healthy children's behavior. No child's discourse becomes confused by either a multiplicity of simultaneously presented physical stimuli or by a succession of demands. Children do not perseverate the way patients do, and it never happens that a healthy child is speech-incompetent at one time of the day and competent at another.

These considerations suggest that language is most likely a hierarchical structure built up of relations and relations of relations corresponding to physiological processes and processes that operate on these processes. Thus a hierarchy of subtlety and lability comes into being. During development and acquisition the hierarchy is built up from the bottom, so to speak; how could it be otherwise? On the other hand, the most labile processes—the top of the hierarchy—are most susceptible to a wide variety of disturbing factors. It is not surprising, therefore, that the most subtle aspects of language may well suffer in the course of disease. But the disease need not be thought of as acting first on the top of the hierarchy and then upon successively lower strata in any systematic way. Disease acts on tissue, and there is so far no evidence whatever that the tissues are ordered hierarchically in the sense that language is; there is even less reason to believe that if there were a tissue hierarchy, it would in some way be isomorphic with the functional hierarchy postulated by linguistic science. (For example, that the most complex syntactic or semantic structures are elaborated by specific cell assemblies in a special cerebral focus; that the next level of complexity is elaborated by a different focus; and so on, each linguistic level corresponding to separate tissue.) Hierarchies that are of concern to linguists might be of a physiological nature (sequences and interdependencies of processes may involve many tissues at all levels—cutting horizontally through any anatomic hierarchy; while anatomically differentiated structures have their own physiological peculiarities, each making its own contribution to the modulations of neuronal activity patterns as a whole, language processes may still involve many different loci all at once). However that may be, the partial symmetries that do exist between language acquisition and aphasic language decay are not likely to be attributable to any common causal factors or, for that matter, to any essential symmetries between language acquisition processes and language interference processes.

REFERENCES

DeRenzi, E., and Vignolo, L. A. 1962. The Token Test: a sensitive test to detect receptive disturbances in aphasics. *Brain* 85:665–78.

Goldstein, K. 1948. *Language and language disturbances.* New York: Grune & Stratton.

Goodglass, H., and Kaplan, E. 1972. *The assessment of aphasia and related disturbances.* Philadelphia: Lea & Febiger.

Jakobson, R., 1968. *Child language, aphasia, and phonological universals.* The Hague: Mouton.

12

AUDITORY LANGUAGE COMPREHENSION IN THE RIGHT HEMISPHERE FOLLOWING CEREBRAL COMMISSUROTOMY AND HEMISPHERECTOMY: A COMPARISON WITH CHILD LANGUAGE AND APHASIA

Eran Zaidel

INTRODUCTION

The core of this chapter is a synopsis of continuing studies on the structure and scope of auditory language comprehension in the nondominant right hemisphere. The experiments are part of a research program, conducted in Roger W. Sperry's psychobiology laboratory at the California Institute of Technology, on hemispheric specialization for higher functions from the special vantage points of the chronic disconnection and hemidecortication syndromes (Sperry 1968; 1974; Bogen 1969). We have focused on the evidence of three experimental subjects: two selected commissurotomy patients and one patient who had dominant (left) hemispherectomy at age 10, when already pubescent.

These studies of the commissurotomy patients were made possible largely by the introduction of a new method for presenting continuous lateralized visual stimuli to a single hemisphere (Zaidel 1975a). The technique permits free ocular scanning of the visual stimulus and self-monitoring of the subjects' own manual performance. In this manner it is possible to directly compare the positive performance of right with left hemispheres automatically matched for age, sex, education, etc. This approach avoids the methodological problems associated with inference from deficit in populations with unilateral lesions.

This work was supported by National Institute of Mental Health award MH 57381 to the author and by NIMH Grant MH 03372 to Professor R. W. Sperry. Thanks are due to Drs. Joseph Bogen, Harold Gordon, Charles Hamilton, and R. W. Sperry, to Dahlia Zaidel, and to the editors for numerous helpful comments on drafts of the manuscript. I am also grateful to Dr. Marlene Oscar-Berman, Dr. E. Carrow, and Mr. John McGintey (the latter from the Southwest Educational Laboratory) for providing unpublished data that was incorporated in this chapter. Carole E. Johnson has provided valuable assistance in collecting and analyzing the data. Testing of children was made possible through the generous cooperation of Mrs. D. Urner of the Polytechnic School, Pasadena, and Mrs. Nan Hatch of All Saints Day Care Center in Pasadena.

In such populations diaschistic effects are commonly present and difficult to determine, and the problems of matching right- and left-lesioned subjects on the crucial variables (e.g., nature, location, and size of lesion) are often formidable. To be sure, the disconnection syndrome has its special limitations, most notably the absence of processes that are inherently interhemispheric in the intact brain. But in this respect our data are on a par with those of any classical psychological experiment that infers normal function from observations made under extreme and well-controlled constraints.

We may view the disconnected right hemisphere as a nonstandard model of natural language that can help elucidate, by contrast, the normal linguistic process. Like child language and aphasia, the right hemisphere offers a model of the language process in *partial structuration*, where "deep structure" is closer to the surface and is consequently more easily observable and manipulable. In fact, comparisons with children and with diverse aphasics provide two independent (language) performance metrics for evaluating linguistic competence in the right hemisphere. These are (1) developmental or age scores and (2) percentile ranks relative to aphasics. In this way it is possible to compare directly not only the left and right hemispheres but also performances across individuals and tasks.

A description of right-hemisphere language is of obvious importance to the issues of first-language acquisition and residual language in aphasia following a circumscribed left-cerebral insult. To the extent that the right hemisphere participates in the acquisition and use of language, the question should be raised whether the concept of a developmental *stage* in first-language acquisition reflects complex interhemispheric interactions and is not applicable to either hemisphere in isolation? More generally, what is the ontogenesis of language lateralization in the brain? Lenneberg (1967) hypothesized that language lateralization to the left hemisphere is complete by the end of the critical period for first-language acquisition, around the age of 13 or at puberty. The studies summarized below present data on the ontogeny of language lateralization to the left that are pertinent for evaluating Lenneberg's hypothesis and for clarifying the role of the right hemisphere in first-language acquisition.

The preceding questions may be recast as follows: is the developmental hypothesis true of the right hemisphere? In its strict form the developmental hypothesis says that the linguistic competence of the right hemisphere can be characterized as equivalent to that of a child of some particular age; and furthermore, that language development in the right hemisphere follows the sequence of stages of first-language acquisition. It is immediately clear from numerous studies of the commissurotomy patients that the developmental hypothesis does not apply *uniformly* to the total linguistic system of the right hemisphere. For example, it has been repeatedly shown and conclusively established (e.g., Sperry et al. 1969) that auditory language-comprehension is superior to speech capacity in the disconnected right hemisphere, whereas no such difference is observable in normal children possessing comparable levels of auditory language comprehension. We ask, therefore, whether a weaker version of the developmental hypothesis applies to the right hemisphere, i.e., whether it applies at least to auditory language comprehension in the right. In other words: is auditory language comprehension in the right hemisphere the same as some particular stage in the development of children's comprehension?

Second, the question arises as to the role of the right hemisphere in compensating for aphasia incurred by a left-sided lesion in adults. Does right-hemisphere language follow the pattern of some classical aphasia subtype? If so, is this because it possesses some compensatory language structures that are anatomically homologous to those impaired in the particular aphasic syndrome? Or, conversely, is the performance of the right hemisphere similar to that of some aphasics because it is only competent to support (and therefore resembles) those very functions that are spared in the given aphasic syndrome?

If the right hemisphere does in fact support language in some aphasics, then a delineation of its "developmental" and "aphasic" status could clarify the relation of aphasia to first-language acquisition. The possible relation of language acquisition to language breakdown is, of course, the theme of this volume. To what extent, for example, is the ontogenetic regression hypothesis for aphasia true? According to that hypothesis (Spreen 1968) aphasia represents a linguistic deterioration or regression from normal adult competence to an earlier developmental stage of the individual. Furthermore, as language is recovered, the aphasic is said to go through all stages of the child acquiring language for the first time.

To recapitulate the plan of this chapter: we will present developmental and aphasic profiles of one isolated and two disconnected right hemispheres on tests of pictorial concepts and of the phonological, semantic, and syntactic components of auditory language comprehension. The data will permit us to reassess the course of language development in the right hemisphere and the ontogeny of language lateralization to the left. We will then be in a position to suggest that neither the developmental hypothesis (even in its weaker form) nor Lenneberg's hypothesis are correct as they stand. It will also emerge that the right hemisphere can and is likely to support much of auditory language comprehension in aphasia. Given the developmental status of the right hemisphere, it follows that the ontogenetic regression hypothesis must also be neurologically untenable.

THE EXPERIMENTS

Technique and Paradigm

Commissurotomy subjects were individually fitted with scleral contact lenses for prolonged unilateral visual presentation (figure 12.1) on their

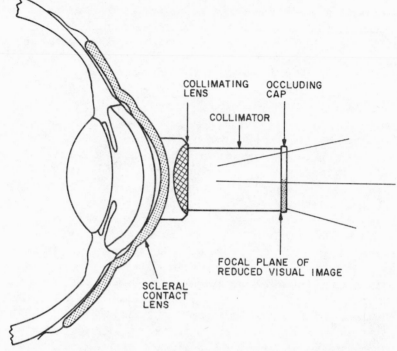

Fig. 12.1   Contact lens with mounted collimator and occluding screen for prolonged lateralized visual presentations.

dominant, right eye. The contact lens technique is a variation on the collimator method for presenting stabilized retinal images, the main difference being that a half-field occluder rather than the viewed image itself is stabilized. The lenses have a triple curvature with corneal and limbal clearance, with a point of contact above the limbus, and with good scleral anchoring. For added stability, negative pressure is applied by means of a manometer to the solution between the lens and the eye, so that the lens follows the subject's eye movements faithfully with an error tolerance of less than 1° for eye movements of ±15°. A small collimating tube is attached to the lens in a fixed position along the optical axis. A powerful collimating lens (f = 10 mm) is embedded in the tube and focuses at the end of the tube, where the half-field occluder is positioned. It enables the subject to focus on a reduced image (projected very close to his eye) of a stimulus board place in his lap. The collimator then presents an enlarged image of the stimulus at normal size and distance with the retinally stabilized occluding screen superimposed on the spatially stationary stimulus image so that one visual half field is constantly blanked out. In this manner, free ocular scanning and manual manipulation of the lateralized stimulus are possible together with self-monitoring by the subject of his own performance on the stimulus board (figure 12.2).

In order to insure unilateral hemispheric processing of auditory stimuli, the following paradigm was used in most of the testing. The stimulus message is spoken aloud by the experimenter while the subject views an array of (usually four) pictures presented to only one hemisphere. The subject then responds by pointing with the hand controlled by the viewing hemisphere to the one picture that best corresponds to the auditory stimulus. The remaining decoy picture alternatives are chosen to make precisely the phonological, semantic, or syntactic distinctions at issue. Fortunately, there exist a variety of standardized developmental psycholinguistic and aphasia tests—such as the Peabody Picture Vocabulary Test—that use precisely this same paradigm, requiring no verbal response. Henceforth, we shall refer to this testing procedure as the Peabody paradigm.

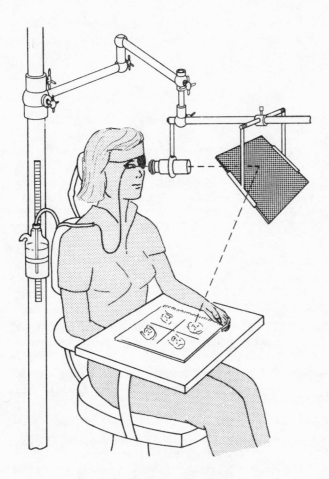

Fig. 12.2 The experimental setup.

This paradigm overcomes some of the limitations imposed by the early method of fleeting tachistoscopic presentations, but it may have introduced new biases of its own. The use of pictorial associates may seem to favor the right hemisphere. On the other hand, the selection of a correct answer by the successive rejection of close alternatives may bias task performance against the right hemisphere so that its observed performance may be regarded as a low limit of its actual competence in more natural communication contexts.

An attempt was made to minimize the opportunity for left-hemisphere interference during right-hemisphere performance, so that generally no overt "cross-cueing" was observed in lateralized testing. A few correct but delayed pointing responses were discounted. Characteristically, the commissurotomy patients could not name or verbally describe stimuli presented in the left visual half field (LVF) even though they could point to them promptly and correctly in response to auditory stimuli. In general, one observes in the long-term disconnection syndrome a similar verbal naïveté in the patients regarding their left-sided deficits or right-hemisphere experiences to that observed immediately following surgery.

Subjects

We will compare in some detail the linguistic behavior of the left and right hemispheres of two selected commissurotomy patients, N.G. and L.B., each of whom was fitted with a contact lens for prolonged lateralized presentations. The performance of the disconnected right hemispheres will also be compared with the isolated right hemisphere of a 15-year-old female, R.S., who had undergone dominant (left) hemispherectomy for a late tumor at age 10. Her control is a 17-year-old male, D.W., who had undergone nondominant (right) hemispherectomy at age 8, with onset of symptoms at 6.

The case histories are summarized in table 12.1. N.G. and L.B. had both undergone similar surgeries for ameliorating intractable epilepsy (Bogen, Fisher, and Vogel 1963). These two "split-brain" patients vary noticeably in their IQs, in the age at which the first epileptic seizures occurred, and in the age at which surgery was performed. Both are also believed to have a minimum of extracallosal damage relative to others in the series studied at Caltech; in both these patients the postoperative course was particularly smooth.

R.S. was an apparently normal right-handed girl until the age of 7:6, when persisting frontal headaches, drowsiness, and vomiting began, eventually followed by right-sided convulsions. On her eighth birthday a craniotomy was performed for the removal of a left intraventricular ependymoma. Following surgery she did quite well, walking with a cane, talking, and writing, until at the age of 10, when she was already pubescent, headaches recurred and a right homonymous hemianopia appeared. She then had a left hemispherectomy,

Table 12.1
Summary of Case Histories

Patient	Sex	Reason for Surgery	Surgery	Age at Surgery	Years Postop at Testing	Age at Onset of Symptoms	IQ History*	
							Preop	Postop
N.G.	F	Intractible epilepsy	Complete cerebral commissurotomy: single-stage midline section of anterior commissures, corpus callosum (and presumably psalterium), massa intermedia, and right fornix. Surgical approach by retraction of the right hemisphere	30	9	18	Wechsler-Bellvue 76(79, 74) at age 30	WAIS 77(83, 71) at age 35
L.B.	M	Intractible epilepsy	As above, but massa intermedia was not visualized and fornix spared	13	7	3:6	WISC 113(119, 108) at age 13	WAIS 106(110, 100) at age 14
R.S.	F	Glioma	Left (dominant) hemispherectomy including caudate nucleus and upper portion of thalamus. Partial tumor removal via a left parietal incision at age 8	10	3	8	Kuhlman-Anderson 100 at age 8	WISC 56(63, 55) at age 13
D.W.	M	Intractible epilepsy	Right hemispherectomy presumably sparing basal ganglia and thalamus. Frontal topectomy at age 6:11	7:9	9	6:7	Stanford-Binet 125 at age 3:6	WISC 67(80, 60) at age 16:6
G.E.	F	Glioma	Right (nondominant) hemispherectomy partially sparing basal ganglia. Partial removal of right precentral tumor 4 months prior to hemispherectomy	28	6	28	—	WAIS† 89(99, 77) at age 29 WAIS‡ 88(105, 68) at age 34

* WISC and WAIS scores are expressed: full-scale IQ (verbal IQ, performance IQ).
† Smith (1969).
‡ Gott (1973).

including the removal of the caudate nucleus and upper portion of the thalamus. R.S. has a right parieto-occipital lesion incurred by the installment and revision of a ventriculocardiac shunt. Progressively worsening aphasia just before the hemispherectomy suggests that little or no functional right-hemisphere takeover of language functions had occurred earlier.

R.S. is mildly dysarthric and has no functional reading, writing, or arithmetic. She is moderately anomic with good recognition of her deficit. The majority of her naming errors are semantic associates of the same class as the stimulus, e.g., "submarine" for "ship." Some verbal or semantic paraphasias occur in responsive naming but rarely in free speech. Literal paraphasias or neologisms are rare. Sentence repetition breaks down after 3 items and shows a strong semantic focus, a prevalence of concrete and egocentric interpretations, as well as a tendency to perseverate. Metalinguistic tasks, such as defining words or performing sentential transformations to request, are particularly difficult. R.S. is dysfluent and agrammatic, but her speech possesses a relative variety of syntactic form and excellent intonation, which she uses to advantage as a syntactic cue.

D.W. was left-handed prior to surgery, as are two of his brothers. But preoperative intracarotid amobarbital injection showed language lateralization to the left, remaining hemisphere. Today he is dyslexic, dysgraphic, and dyscalculic and has poor but *phonetic* reading; spelling and misspelling contrast with the very limited *sight* vocabulary of R.S. Both D.W. and R.S. show a parietal syndrome of visuospatial deficit. In addition to her visuospatial problems R.S. has a selective difficulty in handling color names. Both symptoms may be due to her posterior right lesion.

Pictorial Concepts

The Peabody paradigm described above presupposes the ability of each hemisphere to semantically associate verbal and pictorial stimuli. Partly to verify this assumption, two semantic tests—the Visual Reception and the Visual Association subtests of the Illinois Test of Psycholinguistic Abilities (ITPA) (Kirk, McCarthy, and Kirk 1968), which require neither verbal presentation nor verbal response, were administered unilaterally to the patients. The ITPA was designed after Osgood's behavioral model of the communication process (Kirk and Kirk 1971). In it, three dimensions are hypothesized: (1) processes—receptive (decoding), central organizing (association), and expressive (encoding); (2) levels of organization—representational (symbolic) and automatic; and (3) channels of communication (input-output modalities)—visual-motor and auditory-vocal. The Visual Reception and Visual Association subtests represent the receptive and associative processes, respectively, at the representational level of the model.

ITPA Visual Reception

On this subtest the subject is shown a single picture of a simple object or scene on one page, which is then replaced by a response page with four variously related response pictures. The subject is required to point to the option that "goes best with," i.e., depicts the same semantic relation as, the stimulus ("find one here"). The data is summarized in table 12.2.

It is clear from table 12.2 that either hemisphere has the ability to recognize different pictorial representations of semantic concepts. Such concepts must, therefore, somehow be stored abstractly, i.e., independently of any specific sensory representation. In effect, the test requires the subject to match two exemplars of the same semantic concept, relation, or propositional function even when they are perceptually dissimilar. Thus the test investigates a single elementary but fundamental semantic relation, namely, that of "hyponymy" or class inclusion. Some of the decoys are perceptually more like the stimulus than the correct answer and some are distantly related to it semantically. All the concepts possess a natural linguistic label (e.g., "bridge," "windy," or "reflections") so that verbal mediation is possible. The data show that the right hemisphere is at least able to construct or synthesize the meaning of the more general superordinate from exemplars or co-hyponyms, i.e., instances, of it. Furthermore, it can do so while ignoring the strong distracting perceptual similarity of some decoys. It follows that Levy et al.'s characterization (1972) of the right hemisphere as "perceptual" and the left as "semantic" should be qualified.

Table 12.2

Results and Statistical Analysis of the ITPA Visual Reception Test (maximum score = 40)

	N.G.			L.B.			S.W.	R.S.
	FV*	LH	RH	FV	LH	RH	LH	RH
RS	24	10	17	36	27	13	25	19
PLA	7:4	4:4	5:10	>10:10	8:5	5:0	7:9	6:2
CPLA	9:0	—	—	>10:1	—	—	8:8	5:2
SS	30	—	—	47	—	—	34	44
Statistical comparisons	$\{$	$t = 4.58$ $p < 0.002$	$t = 2.48$ $p < 0.02$		$t = 3.36$ $p < 0.002$	$t = 4.58$ $p < 0.002$	$t = 1.77$ $p < 0.1$	

NOTE: The psycholinguistic age (PLA) is derived from the raw scores (RS) of 1000 children 2–10 years old. A subject's composite psycholinguistic age (CPLA) indicates the age of an average child who achieves the same total raw score (RS) on the *whole* ITPA. The scaled score (SS) is a transformation of the raw score with a mean of 36 and a standard deviation of 6.

* FV = free vision score; L(R)H = left-(right-) hemisphere score. Statistical comparisons of free vision to left-hemisphere raw scores and of left-hemisphere to right-hemisphere raw scores use 2-tailed t-tests for correlated means.

Comparison with normal adults of similar ages shows a severe deficit in either hemisphere, but in no case is the performance of the right hemisphere below that of a 5-year-old child. The superiority of bilateral (free vision) to unilateral left- or right-hemisphere scores in both commissurotomy patients suggests a possible interhemispheric interaction of bilateral involvement on this test. In comparing with each other the unilateral left- and right-hemisphere scores, the most noteworthy result is the superiority of N.G.'s right over her left hemisphere.

ITPA Visual Association

Part 1 of the test contains 20 items in which the subject is required to select from among four pictures the one that most meaningfully *relates* to a stimulus picture. In this test the "language-free" sampling of the semantic relation studied in the Visual Reception subtest is extended to a variety of other semantic relations, such as "used for" or "part of." The second part of the test consists of visual analogies. The subject views pictures in which two objects have a certain relationship (e.g., a gun and a holster). He or she must then choose one out of four other objects (e.g., bullet, letter, pencil, picture) that similarly relates to a new given object (an envelope).

The results (table 12.3) show again that age estimates for the right hemisphere are all above 5 years of age. As in the Visual Reception subtest, N.G.'s right-hemisphere score was higher than that of her left, although the difference is not statistically significant. And again, the free vision performance of the two commissurotomy patients was superior to unilateral performances, suggesting bilateral cooperation even in the absence of direct cortical connections through the commissures. This interpretation (as opposed to deficits due to lens artifacts) is reinforced by the relatively high score of the patient with dominant hemispherectomy (R.S.) and the relatively low score of the one with nondominant hemispherectomy (D.W.); both show almost the same age scores.

Phonology

Auditory Discrimination

Developmental Analysis. The subject had to select, by pointing, one picture named orally from a set of four pictures whose names differ from the stimulus name in only one phoneme (Goldman, Fristoe, and Woodcock 1970). Only monosyllabic CVC (Consonant-Vowel-Consonant) or CV words that are acquired early were used, and they were classified by distinctive-feature analysis. Each decoy varies from the target picture in one to three of the following

Table 12.3

Results on the ITPA Visual Association Test (maximum total score = 42; maximum score for part 1 = 22)

	N.G.			L.B.			D.W. R.S.	
	FV	LH	RH	FV	LH	RH	LH	RH
RS total	24	16	17	32	29	18	22	20
RS part 1	19	13	17	20	18	13	20	17
RS part 2	5	4	3	20	11	11	2	3
PLA	7:2	5:0	5:3	>10:3	9:4	5:6	6:6	6:0
CPLA	9:0	—	—	>10:1	—	—	8:8	5:2
SS	32	—	—	38	—	—	29	41
Statistical comparisons	$t = -2.471$ $p < 0.02$	$t = -0.879$ $p < 0.5$		$t = 3.816$ $p < 0.002$	$t = 1.4031$ $p < 0.2$		$t = 1.289$ $p < 0.5$	

NOTE: Notations as in table 12.2. Statistical Comparisons are for total raw scores.

Table 12.4

Results on the Auditory Discrimination Test

	N.G.			L.B.			D.W. and R.S.†		
	% Correct	Estimated Mental Age	Percentile Relative to Chronological Age Group*	% Correct	Age	Percentile	% Correct	Age	Percentile
LH									
Training (max. = 64)	100	—	—	100	—	—	100	—	—
Quiet (max. = 30)	90	5:3	6	100	‡	63	100	‡	65
Noise (max. = 30)	83	‡	80	80	19:3	47	87	‡	79
RH									
Training	81	—	—	95	—	—	97	—	—
Quiet	77	4:4	<1	97	7:7	20	93	5:7	10
Noise	37	3:10	<1	73	9:9	17	43	4:0	<1
Differences between LH and RH	Quiet $t = 1.4389, p < 0.2$			Quiet $t = 0.9999, p < 0.5$			Quiet $t = 1.44, p < 0.2$		
	Noise $t = 4.4741, p < 0.002$			Noise $t = 2.1125, p < 0.05$			Noise $t = 3.8901, p < 0.002$		

SOURCE: Goldman, Fristoe, and Woodcock 1970.

* Values of percentile rank norms have been calculated to the midpoint of each raw score interval.

† LH data refer to D.W., who has only a left hemisphere. He is compared to R.S., who has only a right hemisphere. Her scores appear under RH.

‡ Larger than maximum mean score for any age group.

phonetic features: voicing (+, −), stop (plosive, continuant, nasal), and place of articulation (bilabial, labiodental, linguadental, lingua-alveolar, linguapalatal, linguavelar, glottal). Two sets of words were presented on a prerecorded tape: one set in quiet, and the other against background noise. A pretest ascertains without phonetic competition the availability of the vocabulary and the pictorial representations used in the test. It is generally believed that the ability to distinguish between speech sounds is age related, reaching its ceiling during the eighth year (Goldman, Fristoe, and Woodcock 1970).

The data (table 12.4) and error analysis (table 12.5) show that the right hemisphere is inferior to the left, but this difference is only significant on the *noise* subtest. This suggests that the normal right hemisphere does not specialize in phonetic analysis of the input auditory signal in noisy everyday situations, perhaps because it is generally not an efficient separator of signal from noise. Nevertheless, our data do qualify the claim on the basis of visual rhyming experiments (Levy 1974, p. 161) that "there is no evidence whatsoever that the right hemisphere can analyze a spoken input into its phonetic components."

Distinctive-feature analysis of the errors reveals a difference between the performance of the right hemisphere and that of children in the Quiet subtest, but a rather close correspondence in the Noise subtest. As in normal subjects (Goldman, Fristoe, and Woodcock 1970), the nasals account for the majority of right-hemisphere errors in the Quiet subtest, while the nasals and voiced continuants account for the majority of errors in the Noise subtest. In general, the presence or absence of a given phonetic feature is more significant for normal subjects than for the right hemisphere, whose performance resembles that of children more than that of adults in this respect. With one minor exception, the right hemisphere, like normal subjects, found plosives easier to discriminate than continuants and the presence of nasality or voicing harder to recognize than their absence. Right-hemisphere confusions involving words that differ

Table 12.5

Percentage of Total Errors by Speech Sound Category: Comparison between Mean Left Hemisphere, Mean Right Hemisphere, and Mean of Children 5 to 9 years old

		Voiced Plosives	Unvoiced Plosives	Voiced Continuants	Unvoiced Continuants	Nasal
	Voicing	+	−	+	−	+
	Stop	+	+	−	−	+
	Nasal	−	−	−	−	+
LH	Quiet	0	0	100	0	0
	Noise	0	0	47	20	33
RH	Quiet	20	0	10	20	50
	Noise	18	16	23	16	27
Children	Quiet	13	21	22	10	34
(5:9–9:0)	Noise	14	14	29	16	27

in one phonetic feature reveal that nasality is most likely to be confused, voicing next, then stops; place of articulation is easiest to distinguish. Thus the somewhat rudimentary auditory-discrimination competence that can be displayed by the right hemisphere does not point to distinctive phonetic analyzers in it, but suggests, by analogy with children, an ontogenetically immature mechanism.

Aphasiological analysis. Discriminating between Paired Words—Subtest 2 in the Auditory Disturbances category of Schuell's Minnesota Test for Differential Diagnosis of Aphasia (Schuell 1965a, 1965b)—is essentially a test for phonemic discrimination using common words. Table 12.6 shows scores of the patients' left and right hemispheres on this test and their percentile ranking relative to aphasics with left-hemisphere lesions. The aphasic group consisted of 157 patients with diverse etiologies and severity of deficits. Yet these aphasics made surprisingly few errors on this test, with a mean of 1.23 errors and a standard deviation of 2.11 errors (Schuell 1965b). Thus, the performance of the right hemisphere is quite comparable to that of aphasics on this test; like most aphasics the right hemisphere does seem to have a rudimentary competence for phonetic analysis. This was also demonstrated by the right hemisphere's performance on the Auditory Discrimination Test (above), but the mechanisms involved are still unclear.

Dichotic Listening

In this section I will attempt to integrate briefly the published findings on children, patients with unilateral brain damage, and my own data on the commissurotomy patients on a dichotic listening task involving pairs of the synthetic or natural stop consonant CVs (/ba/, /da/, /ga/, /pa/, /ta/, /ka/). It will be shown that from the point of view of hemispheric dominance and interaction, the physiological mechanisms in the three groups (children, aphasics, and the disconnected or isolated right hemispheres) during dichotic speech perceptions are fundamentally different. It is suggested that these

Table 12.6

Percentage of Unilateral Correct Responses and Percentile Ranks Relative to Unselected Aphasics on the Word Discrimination Test (A. 2) of the Minnesota Test for Differential Diagnosis of Aphasia

	N.G.		L.B.		D.W. vs. R.S.	
	% Correct	Percentile	% Correct	Percentile	% Correct	Percentile
LH	100	72	100	72	100	72
RH	92	36	100	72	100	72

SOURCE: Test and aphasic data from Schuell 1965a and 1965b.

differences are also reflected in normal monotic or binaural perception of natural speech in these groups.

The dichotic results with normal right-handed adults (Shankweiler and Studdert-Kennedy 1967; Studdert-Kennedy and Shankweiler 1970) are clear and consistent. There is a more accurate report of CVs reaching the right ear than the left (the right-ear advantage), and each ear score in the dichotic condition is much inferior to its near perfect monotic score. The right-ear advantage is commonly interpreted as a hemispheric laterality effect whose size is a function of the degree of left-hemisphere specialization for the stimulus material. Three independent assumptions are commonly made in this interpretation. First, it is claimed that the left hemisphere specializes in processing the linguistic stimuli (Kimura 1961). Second, it is believed that the ipsilateral signal from the left ear to the left hemisphere is suppressed at a subcortical level (Kimura 1967). Finally, the transcallosal signal from the ipsilateral (left) ear is said to compete or interfere with the contralateral (right) ear signal at the level of the left cortex while being dominated by this more direct right-ear signal (Sparks and Geschwind 1968).

Split brains. Two studies were carried out with the commissurotomy patients. The first experiment elicited verbal (hence, left-hemisphere) responses. The results show a massive right-ear advantage in the dichotic CV condition (Zaidel 1976a). Invariably the patients respond with only one sound and subsequently deny that they have ever heard two different syllables. Contrary to normal subjects, the right-ear report of both the disconnected and isolated left hemispheres is nearly as accurate in the dichotic as in the monotic control condition. Two conclusions follow. First, the hypothesis of ipsilateral suppression (independent of cross-callosal interaction) is reconfirmed directly on this task (cf. Milner et al. 1972). Secondly, the difference in amount of suppression between the normal and split brain suggests that in the intact brain the neocortical commissures mediate the transfer of the effectively competitive left-ear signal to the left hemisphere via the right hemisphere.

Furthermore, it turns out that left-ear suppression in the commissurotomy patients is three times greater in pairs that differ in two phonetic features (left ear = 7% correct) than in pairs differing in one feature alone (left ear = 20% with either voice or place sharing).* The view that the feature of place of articulation is linguistically more coded than that of voicing was not supported by our data to date, i.e., equal laterality effects were observed for pairs differing in one or the other feature.

---

* In normal adults the corresponding left-ear scores are 22% correct and 17% correct for pairs differing in place and voicing, respectively, as against 11% for double contrast pairs. Of course, the commissurotomy patients are much more accurate in their right ear reports than are normal subjects.

In order to directly tap the right-hemisphere, a second experiment was designed in which each of the same dichotic pairs was immediately followed by a randomly lateralized tachistoscopic presentation of three consonants aligned vertically. The subject then had to point to the consonant he had heard (best) with the hand controlled by the viewing hemisphere. The results reveal a chance-level performance in the left visual half-field (i.e., right hemisphere) presentations. On the other hand, a massive right-ear advantage was again exhibited by the left hemisphere (right visual half field).

It would seem, therefore, that during dichotic listening to the CV pairs the right hemisphere serves merely as a passive relay (Springer 1971) of the auditory cross-callosal signal prior to linguistic-feature extraction. This demonstrates not only that the perception of stop consonants is heavily lateralized to the left hemisphere but also that language processing per se can take place without such phonetic discrimination. The right hemisphere seems to possess a limited capacity for discriminating phonetic features, and so its language comprehension must involve more continuous or pattern-driven auditory mechanisms.

Unilateral brain damage.   Figure 12.3 compares the dichotic performance of the disconnected and isolated left hemisphere on the stop consonants CV task (verbal report study) to that of normal children (Berlin et al. 1973), adults (Shankweiler and Studdert-Kennedy 1970; Berlin et al. 1973; Berman et al. 1975), and left- or right-brain-damaged patients (Berman et al. 1975; Berlin et al. 1974), as well as cases with complete left and right hemispherectomies (presumably for infantile hemiplegia) (Berlin et al. 1974). As yet there is no definitive theoretical analysis of the proper laterality measure, and consequently different researchers use different laterality and performance measures. Some consider two responses to each dichotic pair, whereas others consider first responses only. Still other researchers count only single correct responses, i.e., ones in which only one member of the dichotic pair was reported correctly so that a uniform accuracy level of 50% is reached. Line mn in figure 12.3 represents that 50% accuracy level and all scores are projected onto it along lines of equal laterality measure (f). Since our patients always report only one member of the dichotic pair, their scores were adjusted in figure 12.3 by assuming chance guessing reports of the second member.

We note that the accuracy level of left-brain-damaged patients (LBD) is lower than that of right-brain-damaged patients (RBD), who are in turn less accurate than normal subjects (Berlin et al. 1974; Berman et al. 1975). This is consistent with left-hemisphere specialization on this task. Second, the RBD show equal (Berman et al. 1975) or greater (Berlin et al. 1974) laterality effects than do normal subjects, whereas LBD show a strong reversed dominance (i.e., left-ear advantage). Rather than attribute both to a generalized "lesion effect" (Schulhoff and Goodglass 1969), we can interpret the increased right-ear advantage in the RBD as partial release from cross-callosal (left-ear) inter-

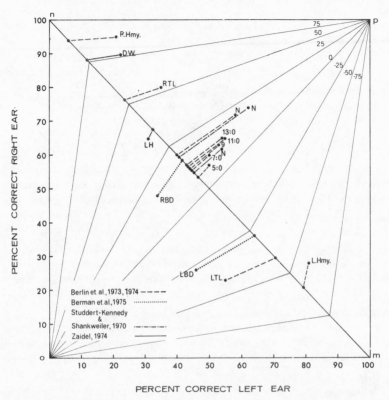

Fig. 12.3   Summary of laterality effects on dichotic stop consonant CV tasks. Laterality measure is $f = (Rc - Lc)/(Rc + Lc)$ if $Rc + Lc \leq 100\%$ and $f = (Rc - Lc)/(Re + Le)$ if $Rc + Lc \geq 100\%$ where $Rc(Re) =$ percent of correct (incorrect) right ear responses (Marshall, Caplan, and Holmes 1975). Line mn denotes a uniform 50% accuracy line and traverses the whole range of f from -100% to $+100\%$ with equal distances representing equal ranges of f. Lines parallel to mn represent points of equal accuracy. The lines connecting O and P and intersecting mn denote points of equal laterality index. N = normal subjects; 5:0 = 5-year-old children; RBD = right-brain-damaged patients; RTL = right temporal lobectomies; R.Hmy = cases of right hemispherectomy; LH = mean left-hemisphere score of our patients on verbal report; D.W. is our right-hemispherectomy patient.

ference. Unlike Sparks et al. (1970) one might also attribute the reversed ear advantage in LBD to a long-term shift of language to the right hemisphere. In another connection Berlin et al. (1973) found that subsequent testing of a patient who had undergone a left temporal lobectomy showed a constant level of right-ear reports but progressively improving left-ear scores. The low level of accuracy for dichotic listening in the LBD group (figure 12.3) is also consistent with the hypothesis of language shift to the right following insult to the language area in the left hemisphere. According to that hypothesis, compensatory auditory mechanisms in the right hemisphere partially take over phonetic analysis, albeit at a reduced efficiency.

Thus, on the dichotic task the disconnected right hemisphere does not show the compensatory potential shown by the connected right hemisphere following a left aphasiogenic lesion. Nevertheless aphasics, just like the disconnected right hemisphere, do fail to use phonetic feature information (Berman et al. 1975) and therefore reveal no shared feature advantage.

Children.   If we take the size of the right-ear advantage as a measure of the degree of hemispheric dominance on the nonsense CV task, then the data from Berlin et al. (1973) show early (as young as age 5) and fairly constant left-hemisphere specialization (figure 12.3). In contrast, using a similar task, Bryden and Allard (1975) found a much later and more gradual development of ear asymmetry reaching significance only at age 12. Paradoxically, some studies using different dichotic tasks (e.g., digit-pair recall in Geffner and Hochberg 1971) even show a developmental *decrease* in right-ear advantage.

We propose to conjecture and interpret these divergent laterality effects in dichotic listening of children in terms of the interplay between (1) relative hemispheric specialization and (2) efficacy of the cross-callosal signal. First, we posit a wide individual variation in cerebral dominance, its time of onset, rate of development, and degree of final asymmetry. Laterality effects in dichotic listening are apparently very sensitive to small task variations that can erase or even reverse an observed ear advantage.

Second, it is conceivable that function-specific cross-callosal connections mature at different rates and because of changes in myelinization (Yakovlev and Lecours 1967) are not in synchrony with the rate of ontogenesis of relevant functional lateralization. If, therefore, during a certain developmental time span cross-callosal transfer is enhanced (with progressing myelinization) more than hemispheric specialization for a given task, then an actual decrease in ear advantage may be observed in dichotic listening due to increased suppression. In any case, it is clear that children's dichotic listening performances on speech perception do not resemble unilateral hemispheric processors. Thus, arguments from functional asymmetry are insufficient to account for the changes of dichotic listening in children; shifting interhemispheric dynamics must be invoked as well.

Our findings on unilateral auditory discrimination in the disconnected and isolated hemispheres together with the following data on substantial lexical comprehension in the right hemisphere suggest that the perception of meaningful words is less lateralized than that of single phonemes. It is, then, only natural to assume that the right-ear advantage for phonemes also sets in earlier. This contrasts with Bryden and Allard's prediction (1975). Of course, it is possible that the level of linguistic function in the mature right hemisphere as characterized in the commissurotomy syndrome does not reflect the end point or an arrest of progressive development. Rather, it may represent a loss of phonemic discrimination skills that the right had possessed at earlier stages of development, i.e., a regression from a state in which the right hemisphere was less differentiated and specialized and when it shared with the left more potential for linguistic analysis.

Semantics of the Lexicon: The Peabody Picture Vocabulary Test

Developmental Analysis

Previous reports (e.g., Gazzaniga and Sperry 1967), based largely on correct blind tactual retrieval with the left hand of the commissurotomy patient in response to the examiner's verbal description, have indicated a capacity for auditory language comprehension in the right hemisphere. But the consistent upper limits of this ability were never determined systematically. To fill in that gap, form A of the Peabody Picture Vocabulary Test (Dunn 1965) was administered in the standard manner using the half-field occluder first to the left and then to the right visual half field of N.G. and L.B., and in free vision to R.S. (Zaidel 1976b).

Table 12.7

Performances by Patients on the Peabody Picture Vocabulary Test (150 items)

Patient	Condition	Raw Score	Mental Age	IQ	Percentile Rank
L.B.	LVF-LH (right hemisphere)	103	16:3	94*	34*
L.B.	RVF-RH (left hemisphere)	115	>18	106*	66*
L.B.	FV (both hemispheres)	130	>18	121*	89*
N.G.	LVF-LH (right hemisphere)	82	11:0	71*	2*
N.G.	RVF-RH (left hemisphere)	87	12:5	78*	8*
N.G.	FV (both hemispheres)	91	13:2	82*	14*
R.S.	FV (right hemisphere)	66	8:1	68	1
D.W.	FV (left hemisphere)	92	13:7	86	18

NOTE: RVF-RH (LVF-LH) = right (left) visual half-field presentation with right (left) hand pointing; FV = free vision.

* IQ and percentile estimates for these patients obtained by assuming the maximum chronological age of 18:5.

It has been argued (e.g., Moscovitch 1973) that the evidence for substantial auditory language comprehension in the disconnected right hemisphere is in conflict with cases of receptive aphasia due to unilateral left-sided lesions, where the right hemisphere seemingly fails to take over the lost ability. We will show that this alleged conflict between the commissurotomy and aphasia data is more apparent than real.

As may be expected (table 12.7) scores obtained with right visual half-field and right-hand (RVF-RH) presentations (left hemisphere) exceed the respective LVF-LH scores, but the difference is relatively small, and right hemisphere performance is surprisingly high with a mean mental age equivalent of 11:9 and a mean verbal IQ estimate of 78 as compared with an age greater than 14:8 and an IQ of 90 for the left hemispheres. These Peabody verbal IQ estimates are very close to the full scale WAIS IQ in those patients for whom both IQ measures were available in free vision. Thus, the disconnected and isolated right hemispheres are seen to have access to a substantial auditory vocabulary and to fairly diverse and complex pictorial representations of the meanings of words in terms of common experiential situations.

Furthermore, the performance of both hemispheres shows essentially the same dependency on word frequency (figure 12.4) that is also exhibited by normal and aphasic adults and normal children. This is somewhat surprising if we take word frequency to reflect the effects of linguistic experience. It may also seem redundant to duplicate identical lexical structures in each hemisphere.

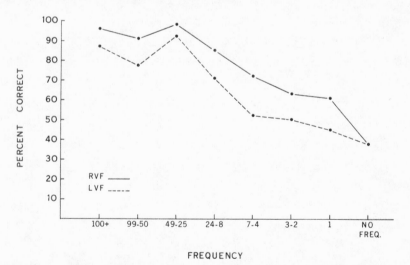

Fig. 12.4   Mean percentage of correct responses for the left and right hemispheres (RVF and LVF, respectively) as a function of word frequency (per million, Thorndike and Lorge 1944) on the picture vocabulary tests. Chance guessing score is 25% correct responses.

One may speculate that the two hemispheres share a dictionary or some vocabulary storage and retrieval mechanisms—perhaps at subcortical levels.

A preliminary analysis was also undertaken to determine whether the right hemisphere is selectively deficient in decoding verbs and action-name infinitives as compared with proper nouns. To that end the performance of the right hemispheres was scored on predetermined lists of 18 actions or verbs and 18 nouns constituting subsets of the Peabody Picture Vocabulary Test and matched pairwise for frequency and age of acquisition (Zaidel 1976b). No significant difference was found in right-hemisphere ability to comprehend verbs and action names (67% correct responses) as compared with nouns (68%). Based on this limited and, perhaps, biased (low-frequency) sample, the contention that the right hemisphere cannot comprehend verbs as well as it can comprehend nouns (Gazzaniga and Sperry 1967) is not supported (see also Gordon 1973).

Aphasiological Analysis

A wide scatter in the scores of the right hemispheres belies analogy with any one aphasic group; but on the average, the performance of the right hemisphere comes closest to that of Wernicke's aphasics. When the Peabody scores of the right hemispheres are compared to those of the five classial diagnostic aphasic groups—Broca's, anomic, Wernicke's, conduction, and global aphasics (Goodglass, Gleason, and Hyde 1970)—we find that the mean raw score of the right hemisphere (83.67) is somewhat lower than the mean of all the aphasics sampled (98.21). Smith and Burklund's adult case of dominant hemispherectomy (Burklund 1972, Table 3A) also obtained a raw score of 98 one year postoperatively. A similar parallel between the right hemisphere performance (Zaidel 1976b) and that of unselected aphasics (consecutive admissions) (Schuell, Jenkins, and Landis 1961) obtains for the Ammon Full Range Picture Vocabulary Test (1948) as well as for the auditory comprehension subtests from the Boston Diagnostic Aphasia Examination (Goodglass and Kaplan 1972) and the Minnesota Test for Differential Diagnosis of Aphasia (Schuell 1965a). On these two aphasia batteries, for example, the mean right-hemisphere score ranged from the 35th to the 61st percentile rank relative to unselected aphasics (Zaidel 1976b). Aphasics as well as the disconnected and isolated right hemispheres make very few errors on these tests.

On the Word Discrimination subtest of the Boston Examination the disconnected right hemispheres show the same pattern of deficits for specific semantic word categories (Zaidel 1976b), as do both fluent and nonfluent aphasics (Goodglass, Klein, Carey, and Jones 1966), i.e., object name errors < geometric form errors < actions < colors < numbers < letters. Thus, the parallel between the auditory vocabulary of the disconnected right hemisphere and that of aphasics extends at least to some primitive semantic structures of the lexicon.

Multi-Reference Phrases

Given the substantial auditory vocabulary of the right hemisphere, the question occurs whether this competence e...nds to phrases consisting of sequences of words from the right-hemisphere lexicon. We therefore administered the Token Test for aphasia (De Renzi and Vignolo 1962), since it provides just such a set of simple reference phrases or proper descriptions. Severe deficits on the Token Test have been consistently associated with aphasic disorders following left-sided lesions, irrespective of diagnostic type (Poeck, Kerschensteiner, and Hartje 1972), whereas right-sided lesions show little (Swisher and Sarno 1969) or no (Boller 1968) deficit relative to control subjects.

In the test an array of ten or twenty small plastic chips ("tokens") is presented to the subject who is asked to carry out oral instructions by manipulating a few chips. The chips come in five colors, two sizes and two shapes; and the instructions occur in sets of increasing complexity, e.g., "Touch the small red circle," and "Put the yellow square under the green circle." The last part of the test is linguistically the most complex and includes varied syntactic constructions. To eliminate position cues, the display was rearranged randomly before every instruction, and the tokens were painted on identical plaques to avoid ipsilateral somesthetic feedback.

The disconnected and isolated right hemispheres exhibited a severe deficit on this test comparable to aphasics, while the corresponding left hemispheres were essentially normal (figure 12.5). Since no developmental norms for the complete Token Text exist for children under 5, the test was also administered to twenty-six 4 and 5 year olds. The norms obtained show that the mean right

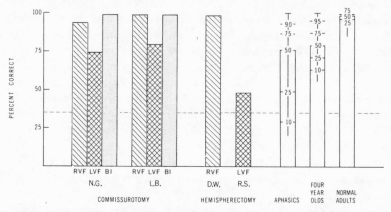

Fig. 12.5   Unilateral weighted scores on Spreen and Benton's version of the Token Test (1968) and percentile ranks relative to adult normal and aphasic subjects (Spreen and Benton 1968) and children (Zaidel 1977). Weighted scores allow partial credit and permit the reference phrases to occur in any order. Unilateral pass-fail scores are lower both absolutely and relative to aphasics.

hemisphere score was like that of 4:6 year olds, and there is a significant rank order correlation of mean item difficulty between the 4 year olds and the right hemispheres ($r_s = 4.66$, $p < 0.05$) on the last part of the test (Zaidel 1977).

The mean rank order correlation between the right hemisphere and aphasics, on the other hand, was not significant ($r_s = 0.314$, $p > 0.05$), so that the two groups seem hampered by different aspects of the task. The right hemisphere is poorer than aphasics in retaining the order of the adjectival modifying phrases; it has more reference (color, size, shape) than particle (prepositions, conjunctions, adjectives, etc.) errors in the last part of the test, whereas the reverse is true for aphasics. It seems in general less sensitive than aphasics to linguistic parameters and more sensitive to memory variables of the task, with better performance in part 4 than in part 5 of the test—in contrast to aphasics. Nevertheless, the right hemisphere seems to share with aphasics a basic limitation in short-term verbal memory that may account for poor performance on the Token Test by precluding rehearsal of the reference phrases.

To summarize: The right hemisphere is especially incompetent to understand Token Test instructions because they include too many nonredundant items that must be remembered in the correct order without any help from the context.

Grammar and Syntax

There is no single test for auditory comprehension of syntactic structures that utilizes pointing responses to a pictorial array of alternative choices and has adequate developmental as well as unilateral brain-damaged norms. Consequently, a variety of special-purpose tests, each with either developmental or aphasiological norms, were administered unilaterally using the contact lens system to the commissurotomy patients (Zaidel 1973). We will illustrate the general results with findings from Carrow's Test for Auditory Language Comprehension (1973), for which developmental norms and some preliminary aphasic data are both available.

According to the manual, "The test consists of 101 plates of line drawings."

The pictures represent referential categories and contrasts that can be signaled by form classes and function words, morphological constructions, grammatical categories, and syntactic structure. The form classes and function words tested by the instrument are nouns, verbs, adjectives, adverbs, and prepositions. Morphological constructions tested are those formed by adding "er" and "ist" to free morphs such as nouns, verbs, and adjectives. Grammatical categories that are evaluated involve contrasts of case, number, gender, tense, status, voice, and mood. Syntactic structures of predication, modification, and complementation are also tested. Most of the lexical items used in the Test are those learned early in the language development sequence. Inclusion of these items ensures that the

Table 12.8

Percentage of Unilateral Error Responses by Category, of Total Percentage Correct Responses, and Age Estimates on the Fifth Edition of Carrow's TACL

	N.G.						L.B.						D.W. vs. R.S.					
	% Wrong				% Correct	Mental Age	% Wrong				% Correct		% Wrong				% Correct	
	Lex.	morph.	gram.	syntax.														
Category	I	II	III	IV	Total	Estimate	I	II	III	IV	Total	Age	I	II	III	IV	Total	Age
LH	4	11	14	17	91	6:10	4	22	7	8	93	6:10	1	0	5	25	95	6:11
RH	23	22	36	33	71	5:0	1	0	9	8	96	>6:11	8	11	21	33	84	6:4
Difference between LH and RH	t = 3.9061, p < 0.002						t = 0.8096, p < 0.5						t = 3.7148, p < 0.002					

NOTE: Ceiling effect at 6:11. Statistical comparisons between left and right hemispheres use 2-tailed t-tests for correlated means.

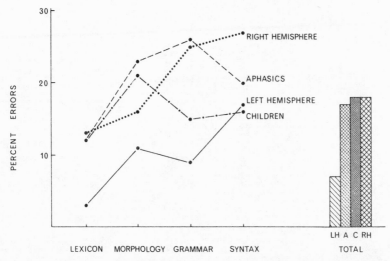

Fig. 12.6   Error scores on the four parts of Carrow's TACL: comparison between mean left- and right-hemisphere scores of our patients (LH and RH, respectively), 70 kindergartners (denoted C, from Carrow 1973 and Mr. John McGintey, Southwest Educational Development Laboratory, Austin, Texas, 1975, personal communication), and 18 aphasics with mild-to-moderate comprehension defects (denoted A and provided by Carrow 1975, personal communication).

words used in testing linguistic structures be tested first as separate items; failure on subsequent items then indicates lack of knowledge of the grammatical form and not lack of knowledge of the lexical form used. (Carrow 1973, pp. 6–7)*

The data (table 12.8) indicate that the right hemisphere can make diverse grammatical and syntactic discriminations even under conditions of minimal redundancy. In all cases the right hemisphere attained a mental age equal to or above that of 5 years on this test. Developmental norms for the test show a ceiling effect around age 7 and the superiority of L.B.'s right hemisphere relative to his left, is, therefore, not significant. This evidence for substantial syntactic competence in the disconnected right hemisphere supersedes previous negative conclusions (Gazzaniga and Hillyard 1971) that "little or no syntactic capability exists in the right hemisphere."

In figure 12.6 the mean performance of the right and left hemispheres of our patients are compared with those of children (kindergartners and first graders—Carrow 1973; John McGintey 1975, personal communication) and with aphasics who exhibit mild or severe comprehension disorders tested

---

* It should be pointed out that Carrow's characterization of grammatical categories as distinct from sentential syntactic structures is rather arbitrary, as is the very limited sample of "syntactic structures" used in her test.

Table 12.9

Mean Percentage of Correct Responses and Rank Orderings of Difficulty on Each Category of Carrow's TACL by Patient Group

| | Unilateral | | | | Moderate Aphasics | | | | Severe Aphasics | | | |
| | LH | | RH | | Before Therapy | | After Therapy | | Before Therapy | | After Therapy | |
	% Error	Rank	% Error	Rank	% Error	Rank	% Error	Rank	% Error	Rank	% Error	Rank
Form classes and function words (68)												
nouns (30)	14	17	7	1	3	1	1	3	34	3	17	1
adjectives (19)	0	2.5	16	7	20	10	6	7	56	10	44	15
color (3)	0		0		13		0		40		24	
quality (7)	2		4		13		7		40		29	
quantity (8)	16		24		30		28		86		45	
direction (1)	50		33		48		7		67		29	
verbs (8)	2	6	18	8	14	7.5	5	6	43	4.5	32	10
adverbs (1)	13	15	13	5	26	13.5	0	1.5	53	8	29	7.5
demonstratives (2)	0	2.5	21	10	24	12	7	8.5	73	18	43	13.5
prepositions (6)	1	5	19	9	12	5	4	4.5	5	1	43	13.5
interrogatives (2)	15	18	39	17	43	18	39	18	80	19.5	64	20

Morphological constructions (8)												
noun + *er* (2)	6	9	22	11	26	13.5	18	13	47	6	29	7.5
verb + *er* (2)	0	2.5	10	2	22	11	21	14	67	17	29	7.5
[noun + *er* masculine (1)	13	15	25	12.5	—	—	—	—	—	—	—	—]
adjective + *er/est* (2)	5	8	11	3	11	4	11	11	43	4.5	21	3
noun + *ist* (2)	16	19	50	20.5	35	15	29	16	53	8	21	3
Grammatical categories (25)												
gender and number-pronouns (5)	11	12.5	46	18.5	14	7.5	13	12	57	12	40	11
number-noun (4)	9	10	25	12.5	15	9	9	10	57	12	50	16.5
number-verb (2)	34	22	50	20.5	46	19	43	19	80	19.5	41	12
tense-verb (6)	10	11	30	15.5	41	17	31	17	63	16	50	16.5
voice-verb (4)	11	12.5	46	18.5	40	16	27	15	57	12	54	18
status-verb (4)	3	7	13	5	5	2	7	8.5	32	2	25	5
Syntactic structure (10)												
[imperative mood* (2)	0	2.5	13	5	—	—	—	—	—	—	—	—]
predication:												
N-V agreement (2)	28	21	29	14	13	6	4	4.5	60	14.5	29	7.5
complementation (1)	25	20	57	22	57	20	50	20	53	8	57	19
modification (2)	13	15	30	15.5	9	3	0	1.5	60	14.5	21	3

* Ranks of left and right hemispheres include this item, but their rankings without it were used for correlation with the aphasic groups.

Table 12.10

Spearman Rank Order Correlation Coefficient of the Mean Right Hemisphere with the Mean Left Hemisphere and with Aphasics (pre- and posttherapy) on Twenty-three Structures of the TACL

RH vs.	LH	Mild-to-Moderate Aphasics		Severe Aphasics	
		Pre	Post	Pre	Post
r_s	0.6900	0.6885	0.6082	0.5217	0.5076
p	<0.1	<0.01	<0.01	<0.01	<0.05

NOTE: All comparisons are statistically significant.

before and after speech therapy (Carrow 1975, unpublished data). A more detailed comparison between right-hemisphere performance and the aphasics' performance is presented in tables 12.9 and 12.10. (Unfortunately a comparable rank order of item difficulty is not available for the children.) It is noteworthy that there is a mild but significant correlation between the mean scores obtained by the left and right hemispheres. Furthermore, the right hemisphere correlated higher with mild than with severe aphasics and higher on posttherapy than on pretherapy testing. This is what we may expect if the undamaged right hemisphere does in fact compensate for deficient language in a chronically lesioned left hemisphere. On this interpretation the data suggest that pathological inhibition in the severely aphasic actually prevents the remaining right hemisphere from assuming its full potential.

There are some universal factors affecting the performance of normal children and adults as well as of pathological cases. For example, all experimental groups including children (Carrow 1971) found adjectives of quantity and position ("few," "left," "third," etc.) harder to comprehend than the prepositions sampled. Similarly, the structural contrast of active-passive voice was particularly difficult universally.

Extensive additional tests of comprehension of grammar and syntax in the disconnected or isolated right hemisphere (Zaidel 1973) indicated a nonsignificant Spearman rank order correlation of the mean scores of the right hemispheres with children ($r_s = 0.4498$) and a moderately significant correlation ($r_s = 0.6035$) with aphasics—higher with Wernicke's than with Broca's aphasics. It should be noted that many items in the TACL test vocabulary rather than grammar, so the competence measure of the right hemisphere (mean age estimate >6:3) may be overestimated. Indeed, the same right hemispheres scored somewhat lower (mean age estimate 4:0, Zaidel 1973) on the Northwestern Syntax Screening Test (Lee 1971), which, like the TACL, uses the Peabody paradigm but does not test for vocabulary.

Unlike the aphasics, who are more sensitive to the linguistic variables of the task (Zaidel 1973, 1977) such as form class or grammatical marking, the right hemisphere seems more limited by perceptual constraints such as length, order, and redundancy, implicating a short-term auditory verbal memory deficit in the right. Consequently, the right hemispheres scored least well on such items as subject-object and direct-indirect object relations, in contrast to aphasics (Goodglass 1968).

No doubt there are important limitations to right-hemisphere syntax, and it is likely that the right hemisphere "understands" many sentences by using lexical and semantic cues as well as the pragmatic context of the utterance. Nevertheless, the TACL demonstrates the ability of the right hemisphere to distinguish "minimal grammatical pairs," that is, to reject the decoy response pictures, each of which differs from the stimulus in precisely the grammatical structure in question. In fact, the Peabody paradigm used here allows minimal linguistic or visual redundancy and hence probably underestimates the ability of the right hemisphere to understand spoken phrases in the normally redundant conversational context.

Recapitulation

The preceding experiments may be recapitulated from the point of view of normal interhemispheric interaction by noting four patterns of unilateral LH (left hemisphere) or RH as compared with FV (free vision) performance of the commissurotomy patient. (1) $FV = LH > RH$. This is the most common result for all tests (e.g., on the Token Test, Zaidel 1977), and it confirms the usual left-hemisphere specialization for language. (2) $FV = RH > LH$. This occurs very rarely for supposedly linguistic tasks, but it exists, as in N.G.'s scores on the ITPA Visual Reception and Association tests for pictorial concepts. (3) $FV > LH > RH$. This occasional result (e.g., in the picture vocabulary tests, provided the unilateral deficits are not attributable to apparatus limitations) reflects interhemispheric interaction in free vision in spite of callosal disconnection. (4) $FV = XH < YH$ where either $X = L$, $Y = R$ or conversely. This result can be interpreted to reflect inhibition exerted by the X hemisphere on free vision performance, which is released when YH is allowed to act alone. Although we have not previously mentioned this result in our brief synopsis patient L.B. did exhibit it on the ITPA Visual Sequential Memory Test (Zaidel 1973). There, his free vision score was equal to his unilateral right-hemisphere score (18/50 for an equivalent age of 6:6), while his unilateral left-hemisphere score was dramatically superior (at 35/50 or better than a 10:5 child).

THE ARGUMENTS

Speech versus Comprehension

There is no doubt that the ability of the disconnected right hemisphere to produce appropriate speech is, if present at all, remarkably lower than its ability to comprehend spoken words. Indeed, the inability to verbalize about stimuli exposed in the left visual half field has come to serve as a control for adequate lateralization of the stimuli. As argued in the introduction, this refutes the application of the stronger form of the developmental hypothesis to the right hemisphere: the linguistic competence of the right hemisphere cannot be characterized uniformly (for all language functions) as corresponding to a given stage in first language acquisition. This appears to be simply because no normal child exhibits a similar receptive lexicon together with a comparable central speech disability for eliciting the same vocabulary items.

The physiological reality of a model of language that combines substantial comprehension with an apparent absence of speech is of some theoretical importance. It refutes the *logical* necessity of some models in which language development is viewed as a sequence of "shifting influence[s] between [the] mutually dependent, but different, underlying [receptive and expressive] processes" (Chapman 1974, attributed to Bloom 1974). Similarly, it follows that motor (constructive) theories of speech perception (Liberman et al. 1967) are not physiologically necessary to account for comprehension, at least on the phonetic and lexical levels.

Our studies, in addition to neuropsychological analyses of cases of hemispherectomy for postinfantile lesions and intracarotid amobarbital testing of adult patients, indicate that speech is much more lateralized than is auditory language comprehension and that the ontogenies of cerebral specialization for the two functions have quite different natural histories (Kinsbourne 1975). Lesions to either side of the brain during the first few years of language development disrupt speech with almost equal probability; the deficits are temporary and are largely expressive rather than receptive (Lenneberg 1967). Even among adults, receptive aphasia appears to be more common in the older age group (Kinsbourne 1975). Brown and Jaffe (1975) have in fact raised the possibility that lateralization of receptive speech increases at a much slower pace than lateralization for speech expression and that it extends into adulthood. Given the superior comprehension vocabulary of the right hemisphere, our data qualify this hypothesis by restricting it largely to the individual's auditory comprehension lexicon qua single words. The reasons for more complete speech lateralization to the left hemisphere are unclear at present. Kinsbourne (1975) speculates that while the neural demands of early language can be met without lateral specialization, there is some change in language use at about the fifth year of life that requires lateral asymmetry as its neural substrate, but he does not elaborate any further. Our data do demonstrate that brain mechanisms underlying comprehension and speech are neurophysiologically different in a fundamental way. Speech is apparently more compatible with unified intrahemispheric control resulting in an all-or-none hemispheric specialization. Comprehension, on the other hand, allows for bilateral development, and, plausibly, interhemispheric interaction.

Methodology of Testing Language Comprehension

It should be noted that in the foregoing experiments we have used rather strict criteria to ascertain the comprehension of a spoken word. The criteria are specified by the experimental paradigm outlined in the introduction. This picture-selection paradigm is intended to allow only minimal redundancy so that the word itself or an unambiguous pictorial representation of what it stands for serves as the only linguistic or contextual cue for response. This implicates internal representation in the comprehension process, but that is as it should be: comprehension is a process operating on internal representations. The general and yet unsolved problem is to specify with some precision the effect on the comprehension process of extralinguistic parameters such as the relation of the perceptual representation of the referent (the picture) to its linguistic reference (the word). Some further methodological issues associated with this paradigm are discussed in Huttenlocher (1974), Chapman (1974), and Baird (1972).

The paradigm may also be complicated by errors due to visual artifacts in the optical system, such as lost focus and displaced vision. Further, it may not be valid to assume that the artifacts are random or symmetric with respect to the two hemispheres. On the contrary, it was our impression during testing, for example, that relatively low acuity hampered performance in the right visual half field (left hemisphere) more than in the left half field (right hemisphere). Thus, in general, the data should be taken as suggestive of qualitative patterns in performance rather than as specifying precise quantitative results.

Refutation of the Developmental
Hypothesis for Right-Hemisphere Comprehension

There is at present no comprehensive account of the normal developmental sequence in auditory language comprehension. Specific syntactic structures cannot serve a priori as indices of development. This is because their availability as a function of age may be neither a continuous function nor monotonically increasing. In particular, it would be invalid to infer order of acquisition of a set of structures from their rank order of difficulty at some given age. Conse-

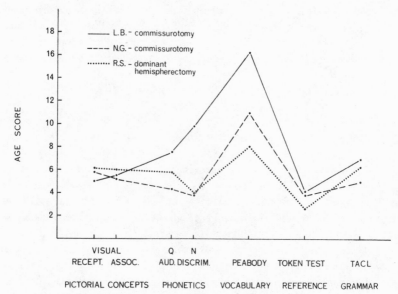

Fig. 12.7   Age profiles of the disconnected and isolated right hemispheres on language tests sampled.

quently, no attempt is made to correlate in detail the performance of the right hemisphere with that of children on particular language structures. Rather, the developmental status of the right hemisphere is analyzed on the basis of total test scores. It turns out that these scores for all the language abilities sampled above are monotonically increasing functions of age and will serve simply as age indices.

We show, first, that the right hemispheres studied here do not have the same age scores for all language functions sampled. Next, we argue that when the pattern of right-hemisphere performance on a given test is compared with that of children who obtain similar total scores, there emerges consistently a two-sided result: a *moderate* quantitative correlation between the error patterns of both groups together with definite *qualitative differences* in sensitivity to task variables. For example, the perceptual limitations of the right hemispheres and the linguistic deficit of aphasics lead to similar Token Test scores (Zaidel 1977), for somewhat different reasons.

The pattern of right-hemisphere performance on the selected tests of auditory language comprehension sampled here (figure 12.7) refutes at once the "developmental hypothesis." It is not the case that right-hemisphere auditory comprehension can be characterized uniformly as the receptive competence of a child of a given age. For, by any account, there is no normal stage in the development of language comprehension such that a child may possess both the vocabulary of a 12 year old and the apparent syntax of a 6 (TACL, table 12.8) or a 4 (NSST, figure 12.7) year old. This means that lateralization of language to the left does not occur at the same age or to the same degree for all components of the comprehension system.

The comprehension of single lexical items does seem to be surprisingly well developed in the right hemisphere. This could be part of an adaptive specialization in the right toward contextual orientation to the environment—nonverbal as well as verbal. It is certainly tenable on the basis of our data to accept the "age five hypothesis" about lateralization of language to the left (Krashen 1975) and simply regard auditory vocabulary as exempt from both strong left specialization and dependency on the critical period for first-language acquisition.

It may be objected that the exceptionally high Peabody Picture Vocabulary Test scores recorded for these right hemispheres actually reflect (1) nonuniform standardization procedures across the tests (e.g., the normative group for the Peabody test may well represent lower outdated cultural norms), and (2) noise within the accepted variability limits established for these tests.

To check these possibilities, representative tests from our sample were administered individually to each child of a first grade in a private school in Pasadena. Altogether, eleven children were tested (seven boys and four girls). Their mean age when tested was 7:2 (range 6:9–7:8, standard deviation 4 months) and their mean Stanford Binet IQ was 122 (range: 106–136, standard deviation 9.06). Instead of the long TACL, Lee's shorter but comparable

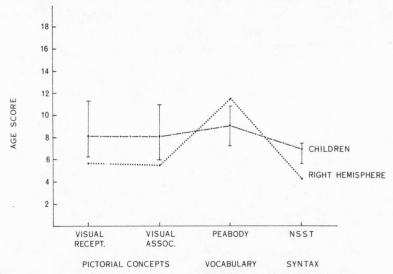

Fig. 12.8 Comparison between the mean age profiles of the right hemispheres and eleven 7-year-old children on selected auditory language comprehension tests.

Northwestern Syntax Screening Test (NSST, Lee 1969) was administered to assess the comprehension of grammatical and syntactic structures. The NSST, like the TACL, was inspired by and modeled after Fraser, Bellugi, and Brown's test of children's imitation, comprehension, and production of grammatical and syntactic structures (1963). Indeed, the NSST and Carrow's TACL both elicited similar right-hemisphere performances.

The results are shown in figure 12.8. The children scored slightly above their age norms, as may be expected from their above average IQ. The children also scored slightly higher on the Peabody Picture Vocabulary Test than on the other tests, but their performance is still approximately uniform. There is a clear and significant interaction of experimental group (children vs. the right hemispheres) by test (the Peabody vs. the NSST for example). In order to illustrate the magnitude of this cross-test difference in relation to variability in the children's performance, right-hemisphere scores on the four tests were plotted as Z-scores on a normal approximation to the children's mean raw score distribution (figure 12.9). There is a difference between the Peabody and the NSST of more than 3.5 standard deviation units in mean right-hemisphere performance relative to the children's scores.

This pattern of selectively high right-hemisphere score on the Peabody test also characterizes language *acquisition* in the isolated right hemisphere. A recent retest of patient R.S. (dominant hemispherectomy) three years after the data above were recorded disclosed a dramatic improvement in Peabody score, from a raw score of 66 and a mental age of 8:1 to a raw score of 84 and a mental age of 11:9, but no change in Token Test score. This would bring the mean age equivalent of the right hemisphere for Peabody vocabulary to 13:0, further accentuating the conclusions reached above.

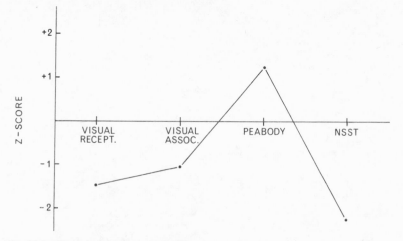

Fig. 12.9   Z-scores of mean right-hemisphere performance on selected tests relative to 7-year-old children.

It also appears that the age profile characteristics of the right hemispheres cannot be accounted for by reduced intelligence. This is revealed by unilateral scores obtained for our patients on Raven's Coloured (children version) and Standard Progressive Matrices—a common intelligence test that requires no verbal responses, a minimum of verbal instruction, and no praxis beyond pointing (Raven 1958, 1962). Right-hemisphere IQ estimates ranged from 74 to 93 (mean 81), and estimates for the left ranged from 74 to 103 (mean 85) (Zaidel, Zaidel, and Sperry 1977). It may be concluded that each hemisphere can solve Raven items of substantially equal overall difficulty. As D. Zaidel and Sperry have shown for a modified tactile form of the children's version (1973), the right hemisphere is indeed slightly superior on Raven's Coloured Matrices, but the left shows a small advantage on the Standard test for adults. Significantly, age estimates for either hemisphere on the two tests show considerable discrepancy; mean left-hemisphere scores are 9:4 on the standard test but > 10:4 on the colored version. Similarly, on the average, the right hemispheres scored 8:10 on the standard and > 10:7 on the colored test. It follows that the two hemispheres contribute differentially to total performance at a given developmental stage, and their relative contribution would seem to vary with age as well as with subtle task differences.

The Ontogeny of Language Lateralization

With the exception of individual lexical items, the level of competence of the preponderance of comprehension skills in the right hemisphere appears to congregate in the age period of 3 to 6. Thus, the following modified model of the ontogenesis of language lateralization to the left emerges. Until the age of about 4 or 5, the two hemispheres develop substantially parallel competence for language skills. At that point the competence for some components, such as speech, declines in order to permit left-hemisphere specialization for fine motor programming and better control of the speech apparatus. Other components, such as the auditory (or reading) lexicon, continue to develop in the right hemisphere, albeit at a reduced rate relative to the left, employing uniquely right-hemispheric processes, i.e., pattern recognition as opposed to feature extraction. The development of other components—notably at the phrase and sentence level—may be substantially arrested or even regressed. These components may, in turn, develop structural idiosyncracies that reflect the progressive differentiation of general perceptual structures in the right hemisphere.

That may be why the error patterns of the right hemisphere on, say, Carrow's test for the comprehension of grammatical and syntactic structures or on the Token Test diverge in important ways from the performance of children who obtain the same total scores. For example, kindergartners score lower than our patients' right hemispheres on the morphology subtest of the TACL but better on the grammar or syntax subtest. Similarly, results on the Token Test showed that 4-year-old children, like some aphasics but unlike the right hemisphere, seem to have particular difficulty in interpreting the linguistic particles that occur in the last part of the test. Both children and aphasics are hampered more by linguistic complexity and less by memory load and order information, compared to the right hemispheres.

Since our data pertain to the mature disconnected right hemisphere we can only conjecture about its role in first-language acquisition. The data do suggest early equipotentiality up to the age of about 5. During that period the right hemisphere may have a special role in the recognition of auditory and visual linguistic patterns (as in sight reading). Later specialization may assign it an important role in evoking experiential associations of word meanings without precise semantic specification. Still, it is not clear whether these relatively rich lexical semantics of the right hemisphere are used in cooperation with left-hemisphere language processing or whether they only serve the (nonverbal) cognitive needs of the right. We have not yet encountered a linguistic task in which the right hemisphere excels while the left fails, although on rare occasions (such as the ITPA Visual Reception) both disconnected hemispheres show a marked deficit, which suggests normal interhemispheric interaction on those tasks.

Right-Hemisphere Support of Language in Aphasia

Ideas about right-hemisphere participation in language have a long and distinguished history. As early as 1874 Hughlings Jackson believed that the right hemisphere normally subserves automatic speech but that it is even more actively involved in lexical decoding, especially in understanding speech (Joynt and Goldstein 1975). Henschen (1896) believed that the right hemisphere could act as a partial substitute for a damaged left hemisphere in the hearing and speaking of words. The right hemisphere, he wrote, was less able to take over the functions of reading and writing. Goldstein (1948) and Russell (1963) believed that disconnection of the nondominant temporal lobe increases the severity of impairment of speech comprehension in a person already rendered aphasic by a left-hemisphere lesion. Both Espir and Rose (1970) and Kriendler and Fradis (1968) believe that the right hemisphere plays a special role in recovery of receptive abilities in aphasia due to left-hemisphere lesions. Nielsen (1946) discussed the interfunctional and interindividual variability in right-hemisphere support of language in aphasia, and Lansdell (1969) and Milner (1974) have pointed out some consequences of the location and extent of left lesion to this language shift. Milner's data are based on unilateral sodium amytal injections to temporal lobe epileptics, while Nielsen's evidence was based mainly on patients who, after recovering partially or completely from aphasia precipitated by left-hemisphere damage, were apparently again rendered aphasic by new right-hemisphere lesions.

Before we can evaluate our evidence for right-hemisphere support of language in aphasia we discuss the extent to which (1) our small patient-sample characterizes the commissurotomy syndrome in general and (2) the disconnected or isolated right hemispheres offer insight into normal right-hemisphere competence in the intact adult brain in spite of possible early epileptogenic lesions or some postsurgical functional reorganization. Support for the generality of our data comes from the striking similarity in pattern and microstructure of auditory language comprehension in the right hemispheres of our commissurotomy and dominant hemispherectomy patients. For example, all had relatively superior auditory lexicon but poorer syntax and inferior decoding of non-redundant, context-free references, in spite of the many clinical and behavioral differences between them. This is particularly striking since, as was pointed out earlier, N.G. and L.B. were chosen for testing not only because of their relative freedom from extracallosal damage but also because of their widely differing IQs, general language abilities, and ages at time of surgery and onset of seizures. Furthermore, cases of dominant hemispherectomy for postpubescent lesions (Burklund 1972) as well as adult patients with late left-hemisphere lesions under temporary left-sided anesthesia due to left internal carotid sodium amytal injection (Milner et al. 1964) all show the same gross pattern of language abilities as the disconnected right hemisphere. On the contrary, early massive unilateral lesions, as in infantile hemiplegia, usually result in near complete takeover of all language functions more or less uniformly by the residual hemisphere (Basser 1962).

The experiments above have demonstrated a rough parallel between the pattern of auditory language competence in the right hemisphere and that in a heterogeneous aphasic population. The parallel occasionally extends to close quantitative agreement in total test scores between the means of our patients and those of unselected patients—especially in tests, like the Token Test, that are sensitive to the presence of aphasia without regard to clinical subtype. And this is just as true for tests that seem to tap the upper limits of auditory language comprehension in the right (e.g., Peabody Picture Vocabulary Test) as for tests tapping its lower limits (e.g., Token Test).

Some parallels between the performance of the disconnected and isolated right hemisphere and the performance of left-brain-damaged aphasics apparently reflect universal linguistic patterns such as dependency on word frequency—a feature that holds for the vocabularies of children as well. Nevertheless, the microstructure of right-hemisphere language competence more often agrees neither with the mean aphasic pattern nor with that of any classical aphasic type. The differences are rather consistent and show that aphasics as a group are more sensitive to linguistic complexity (such as the use of prepositions and connectives or the occurrence of sentential transformations—Zaidel 1973, 1977), while the right hemisphere seems relatively more affected by perceptual and memory load. (Concerning memory deficits in the disconnection syndrome, see D. Zaidel and Sperry 1974.) This conclusion also applies to *speech* in the isolated right hemisphere of R.S., which does not resemble any of the clinically identifiable types of aphasia (Zaidel 1975b).

In attempting to integrate our findings with aphasiological data the following model emerges: (1) there are large individual differences in the right-hemisphere language competence of normal dextrals and in its ability to take over language processing following a left aphasiogenic lesion, and (2) right-hemisphere compensation in aphasia is crucially dependent on the locus, severity, and age at onset of the lesion (Lansdell 1969; Milner 1974; Hécaen 1976). Nielsen (1946) in fact stated that the right hemisphere is likely to support comprehension of spoken language to a much greater degree than emissive speech and other functions. He added that auditory, motor, or visual function may transfer to the right independently of one another and to different extents across individuals. It is possible, then, that a limited left lesion would spare the inhibition of language development in the right and thus disrupt language behavior more than an extensive left-sided lesion, which would release the inhibition and lead to reliance on substantial right-hemisphere language competence. It follows from this model that pure word-deafness with a left lesion reflects a rare state of cerebral dominance or interhemispheric balance in some individuals whose right hemisphere cannot support auditory language-comprehension as it more commonly would. In sum, we may argue that the disconnected or isolated right hemisphere exhibits an idealized (certainly not complete) compensatory process of "backup system," free of the acute or diaschistic effects and function-specific deficits that often accompany focal lesions.

Refutation of the Aphasia-as-Regression Hypothesis

We have shown that the regression hypothesis is false for aphasics as a group because the developmental hypothesis is false for the disconnected or isolated right hemisphere, provided that the disconnected right hemisphere exhibits the linguistic ability of the right hemisphere in the intact normal brain and that the right hemisphere supports some language processing in aphasia. To be sure, the regression hypothesis was refuted only for those aphasics whose auditory language comprehension is supported by their right hemispheres. It is quite likely, as mentioned above, that in some aphasics with a relatively smaller lesion in the left language area, the linguistic competence of the right hemisphere remains unfunctional. Our data are irrelevant to these patients, and for them the regression hypothesis may still hold.

We have used the regression hypothesis in aphasia as an anchor for considering the developmental hypothesis in right-hemisphere language. But it should be pointed out that the ontogenetic regression hypothesis, recently revived by Jakobson (1941, 1968), has a long history (reviewed by Spreen 1968) that is independent of the problem of hemispheric specialization. Most current aphasiologists argue against the hypothesis directly on the basis of aphasia data (e.g., Jenkins et al. 1975), but Wepman and Jones (1964) have nevertheless extended the hypothesis to the classification of the aphasias by drawing a parallel between their five types of aphasia (global, phonetic jargon, pragmatic [semantic jargon], semantic [amnesic], and syntactic [expressive grammatical]) and five stages of development in children (speechlessness, babbling and cooing, fortuitous speech, substantive symbols, and grammar). Wepman and Jones argue that recovery from aphasia follows these stages as well. Our data are not consistent with this view.

A POSTSCRIPT ON LINGUISTIC COMPETENCE, DEVELOPMENTAL STAGES, AND THE REGRESSION HYPOTHESIS

It emerges that in a strict sense the disconnected right hemisphere of a typical right-hander is not a model for the *total* linguistic behavior of any real person, be he a normal adult, a child, or a brain-damaged aphasic. Nevertheless, the right hemispheres of our patients represent a physiological realization of a partial or potential (even when unfunctional) natural language system. Its selective competence constitutes an idealized model of natural language in the sense of being free of some linguistic constraints, such as those imposed by the speech-encoding system on the auditory decoding component or by grammar on the lexicon, both of which are traditionally considered universal. In this sense we can say that the right hemisphere is a sufficient model of natural linguistic competence*—that is to say, a *possible* realization of linguistic performance. It is a *nonstandard* model since language in the right cerebrum is supported by the general perceptual and cognitive structures of that hemisphere, which is apparently better suited for nonverbal interactions with the natural environment using context sensitive, redundant, concrete, and associative pattern-matching processes rather than analytic feature-extraction, as in the left hemisphere.

---

* This, I believe, is the only heuristically viable sense of "linguistic competence" as distinct from "linguistic performance" (Chomsky 1965), i.e., a physiologically or behaviorally grounded idealization of the natural language apparatus.

Consequently, the language system in the right hemisphere is more constrained by informational redundancy, length, and memory than by abstract linguistic variables, such as grammatical or transformational complexity (Zaidel 1973). More generally, the right hemisphere seems more sensitive to semantic and pragmatic rather than phonetic and syntactic parameters. The evidence for this view consists not only of auditory language comprehension in the disconnected right hemisphere but also of speech in the isolated right hemisphere. Indeed, R.S.'s responsive speech shows a highly semantic focus, a concrete and ego-centric bias, and a particular difficulty with metalinguistic tasks such as defining words of performing sentential transformations to request (Zaidel 1975b).

The main question that has concerned us in this chapter can then be restated as follows: Is the commonly observed developmental sequence of first-language acquisition a necessary feature of linguistic competence models in general and of the disconnected right hemisphere in particular? We have seen that this is not the case, and to that extent any realization of right-hemisphere competence, as perhaps following rehabilitation in aphasia, need not conform to any stage in language acquisition nor need it redevelop in the natural sequence. In other words, the regression hypothesis is false for aphasia in general.

Any regression theory of skill dissolution or acquired deficit, such as in aphasia, presupposes some general properties of the developmental stage theory, whose sequence the impaired system is claimed to trace or mimic in reverse. Most notably it is required that more advanced stages of development incor-porate or subsume the skills acquired at earlier stages so that a permanent record is available at any time of the complete developmental sequence. This assumption has been explicitly incorporated in Piaget's model of intellectual development and is commonly referred to as integration (e.g., Piaget 1971). Implicit here is the requirement that integration apply not only to the initial stage of skill aquisition but equally well to routine use of mature skills. Similar assumptions are made, for example, in claiming that hypnotic age regression is real.

The central issue underlying and transcending the regression hypothesis is the unsolved problem of cortical representation of developmental change. This itself is a special case of the outstanding problem of cerebral representation of cognitive function in general. The regression hypothesis implies that the cortical representation of cognitive development consists of progressive elabo-ration and differentiation (but not duplication) of already established structures so that the original cortical representations of the base skills remain constant and functional throughout. Given this hypothesis, any cortical damage to a given cognitive structure will, therefore, affect all subsequently developed structures. Were the regression hypothesis confirmed, it would lend consider-able support to "integration" in developmental stages and to its representation in terms of hierarchic or progressive cortical elboration. But none of these ideas are supported by our present data.

CONCLUSION

The disconnected right hemisphere (commissurotomy) seems mute, and the speech of the isolated right hemisphere (hemispherectomy) is severely aphasic. Both, however, can have substantial auditory language comprehension and reveal a similar pattern of receptive competence. They can recognize pictorial representations of diverse semantic relations and possess a surprisingly rich auditory-picture vocabulary. Nevertheless, the right hemisphere has poor phonetic discrimination and may employ alternative word-decoding mechanisms that rely on whole-pattern recognition or template matching rather than feature analysis, as in the left hemisphere. The right hemisphere can process grammatical or syntactic structures at both the word and phrase levels, but it fails to analyze correctly long, nonredundant sentences in which order is important or the context is not helpful. Its limitation may be attributed to a restricted (perhaps as small as a three-item) short-term verbal memory.

When right-hemisphere competence is expressed in terms of mental age scores on the phonetic, semantic, and syntactic components of auditory language comprehension, there results a widely fluctuating level of performance with a peak in auditory vocabulary (Peabody) and a minimum in nonredundant multireference phrases (Token Test). It follows that the linguistic competence in the right hemisphere is not like that of a child of any particular age. In other words, the developmental hypothesis is unsubstantiated for the right hemisphere. It further follows that the ontogeny of language lateralization in the brain is not the same for all language functions; speech and comprehension differ most in their cerebral history, but there is also a neurological separation between phonetic and auditory mechanisms in word comprehension and between syntactic and lexical structures. Excluding speech and the comprehension lexicon, however, our data are consistent with the hypothesis of early language-lateralization to the left, at about 5 years of age.

Could it be that the concept of a developmental stage (in first-language acquisition) also does not apply to the left hemisphere alone? That is, perhaps each stage in the acquisition sequence reflects complex interhemispheric interaction. This view would be supported by evidence of left-hemisphere deficits in the commissurotomy or hemispherectomy syndromes in addition to right-hemisphere competence cited above. While our data are consistent with that view, it is difficult to tease out true left-hemisphere deficits from poorer scores, owing to ceiling effects on the standardized tests used here or to artifacts attributable to the instrumentation and to the effects of reduced intelligence. It may very well be that only the acquisition stages are necessarily interhemispheric but that the mature left hemisphere can support basic language alone once acquired. Indeed, D.W., a patient who had undergone dominant hemispherectomy at 7:9 (onset of symptoms at 6:7), presents some permanent language disabilities, especially in reading and writing. At the same time, G.E., a patient whose nondominant, right hemisphere was removed at age 28, shortly after onset of symptoms, does not exhibit any of the same focal disabilities.

Right-hemisphere competence described above is better regarded as a description of what linguistic processing the right hemisphere *can* support under optimal conditions rather than what linguistic analysis it actually undertakes in the normal brain with intact commissures, or what language compensation it can provide following left-hemisphere lesions to the dominant language area. Our data are nevertheless compatible with substantial support, especially of auditory comprehension, by the right hemisphere in aphasia. Both on the Token Test, showing poor right hemisphere scores, and on the Peabody Picture Vocabulary Test, showing much higher scores, the mean right-hemisphere score of our patients is close to that of a heterogeneous aphasic population. To the extent that the right hemisphere does support some language in some aphasics, it follows from our refutation of the developmental hypothesis that aphasics themselves cannot be said to simply regress to some earlier stage of language acquisition. That is, the regression hypothesis for aphasia has not been substantiated by the present results. Frequent discrepancies in the micropatterns of linguistic competence between the right hemisphere and aphasics were documented above. This is what we might expect when the right hemisphere is no longer free to operate by itself but is, instead, engaged in cooperation with the residual linguistic functions of the left hemisphere, i.e., when the right is subject to normal and pathological left-hemisphere inhibition.

The linguistic competence we have attributed to the right hemisphere seems subject to the general cognitive style of that hemisphere. This style apparently involves synthetic, unitary whole-pattern processes that operate best in redundant cross-modal contexts and provide diffuse contextual orientation to the environment—nonverbal as well as verbal. This is perhaps best illustrated by right-hemisphere dominance for Thurstone's first visual closure factor: the ability to perceive an apparently disorganized or unrelated group of parts as a meaningful whole, i.e., the capacity to construct a whole picture from incomplete or limited material, as in various gestalt completion tests. The left hemisphere, on the other hand, seems to employ a complementary cognitive style involving analysis by feature extraction, and precise, sequential algorithmic processes. This latter style is illustrated by left-hemisphere dominance (Zaidel 1973) for Thurstone's second visual closure factor: the ability to hold a configuration in mind despite distraction, i.e., the capacity to see a given configuration that is hidden or embedded in a larger, more complex pattern, as in many embedded figure tests. The linguistic analog here is left hemispheric specialization for phonetic, syntactic, perhaps also metalinguistic analyses. The conjecture is that these differences in hemispheric cognitive styles are quite general and apply to a wide range of human behavior from perceptual mechanisms to personality structure.

REFERENCES

Baird, R. 1972. On the role of chance in imitation, comprehension, and production of test results. *J. Verb. Learning Verb. Behav.* 11:474–7.

Basser, L. S. 1962. Hemiplegia of early onset and the faculty of speech with special reference to the effects of hemispherectomy. *Brain* 85:427–60.

Berlin, C. I.; Cullen, J. K., Jr.; Lowe-Bell, S. S.; and Berlin, H. L. 1974. Speech perception after hemispherectomy and temporal lobectomy. Paper presented at the Speech Communication Seminar, Stockholm, Aug. 1–4.

Berlin, C. I.; Hughes, L. F.; Lowe-Bell, S. S.; and Berlin, H. L. 1973. Dichotic ear advantage in children 5 to 13. *Cortex* 9:393–401.

Berman, M. O.; Zurif, E. B.; and Blumstein, S. 1975. Effects of unilateral brain damage on the processing of speech sounds. *Brain and Language* 2:345–55.

Bloom, L. 1974. Talking, understanding, and thinking. In *Language perspectives: acquisition, retardation, and intervention*, ed. R. L. Schiefelbusch and L. L. Lloyd. Baltimore: University Park Press.

Bogen, J. E. 1969. The other side of the brain. I. Dysgraphia and dyscopia following cerebral commissurotomy. *Bull. L.A. Neurol. Soc.* 34:73–105.

Bogen, J. E.; Fisher, E. D.; and Vogel, P. J. 1965. Cerebral commissurotomy: A second case report. *J. Amer. Med. Assoc.* 194:1328–9.

Brown, J. W., and Jaffe, J. 1975. Hypothesis on cerebral dominance. *Neuropsychologia* 13:107–10.

Bryden, M. P., and Allard, F. 1975. Dichotic listening and the development of linguistic processes. In *Hemispheric asymmetries of function*, ed. M. Kinsbourne. Cambridge: At the University Press, forthcoming.

Burklund, C. W. 1972. Cerebral hemisphere function in the human: fact versus tradition. In *Drugs, development, and cerebral function*, ed. Lynn W. Smith. Springfield, Ill.: Charles C Thomas.

Carrow, E. 1971. Comprehension of English and Spanish by pre-school Mexican-American children. *Modern Language Journal* 55:299–306.

———. 1973. *Test for auditory comprehension of language*, 5th ed. Austin, Texas: Learning Concepts.

Chapman, R. S. 1974. Discussion summary: developmental relationship between receptive and expressive language. In *Language perspectives: acquisition, retardation, and intervention*, ed. R. L. Schiefelbusch and L. L. Lloyd. Baltimore: University Park Press.

Chomsky, N. 1965. *Aspects of the theory of syntax*. Cambridge, Mass.: M.I.T. Press.

Czopf, J. 1972. Über die Rolle der nicht dominanten Hemisphäre in der Restitution der Sprache der Aphasischen. *Arch. Psychiat. Nervenkr.* 216:162–71 (English summary).

De Renzi, E. and Vignolo, L. A. 1962. The Token Test: a sensitive test to detect receptive disturbances in aphasics. *Brain* 85:665–78.

Dunn, L. M. 1965. *Expanded manual for the Peabody Picture Vocabulary Test*. Circle Pines, Minn.: American Guidance Service.

Espir, M. L. E., and Rose, F. C. 1970. *The basic neurology of speech*. Oxford: Blackwell.

Gazzaniga, M. S., and Hillyard, S. A. 1971. Language and speech capacity of the right hemisphere. *Neuropsychologia* 9:273–80.

Gazzaniga, M. S., and Sperry, R. W. 1967. Language after section of the cerebral commissures. *Brain* 90:131–48.

Geffner, D., and Hochberg, I. 1971. Ear laterality performance of children from low middle socioeconomic levels on a verbal dichotic listening task. *Cortex* 7:193–203.

Goldman, R.; Fristoe, M.; and Woodcock, R. W. 1970. *Test of auditory discrimination.* Circle Pines, Minn.: American Guidance Service.

Goldstein, K. 1948. *Language and language disturbances.* New York: Grune & Stratton.

Goodglass, H. 1968. Studies in the grammar of aphasics. In *Developments in applied psycholinguistics research*, ed. S. Rosenberg and J. E. Koplin. New York: Macmillan.

Goodglass, H.; Gleason, J. B.; and Hyde, M. R. 1970. Some dimensions of auditory language comprehension in aphasia. *J. Speech Hearing Res.* 13:395–606.

Goodglass, H., and Kaplan, E. 1972. *The assessment of aphasia and related disorders.* Philadelphia: Lea & Febiger.

Goodglass, H.; Klein, B.; Carey, P.; and Jones, K. 1966. Specific semantic word categories in aphasia. *Cortex* 2:74–89.

Gordon, H. 1973. Verbal and non-verbal processing in man for audition. Ph.D. dissertation, California Institute of Technology. *Dissertation Abstracts International*, 1973, 33, 6106B (University Microfilms No. 73-14, 306).

Gott, P. S. 1973. Cognitive abilities following right and left hemispherectomy. *Cortex* 9:266–74.

Hécaen, H. 1976. Acquired aphasia in children and the ontogenesis of hemispheric functional specialization. *Brain and Language* 3:114–34.

Henschen, S. E. 1896. Klinische und anatomische Beiträge zur Pathologie des Gehirns. In *Beobachtungen von 1887 an Uppsala.* Stockholm: Almquist and Wiksell (cited in Joynt and Goldstein 1975).

Huttenlocher, J. 1974. The origins of language comprehension. In *Theories in cognitive psychology: the Loyola symposium*, ed. R. L. Solso. Potomac, Md.: Lawrence Erlbaum.

Jakobson, R. 1968. *Child language, aphasia, and phonological universals*, trans. A. R. Keiler. The Hague: Mouton (first published in German in 1941).

Jenkins, J. J.; Jimenez-Pabon, E.; Shaw, R. E.; and Sefer, J. W. 1975. *Schuell's aphasia in adults*, 2d ed. Hagerstown, Md.: Harper & Row.

Joynt, R. J., and Goldstein, M. N. 1975. The minor cerebral hemisphere. In *Advances in Neurology*, vol. 7, *Current reviews of higher nervous system dysfunction*, ed. W. J. Friedlander. New York: Raven Press.

Kimura, D. 1961. Cerebral dominance and the perception of verbal stimuli. *Canad. J. Psychol.* 15:166–71.

———. 1967. Functional asymmetry of the brain in dichotic listening. *Cortex* 3:166–78.

Kinsbourne, M. 1971. The minor cerebral hemisphere as a source of aphasic speech. *Arch. Neurol.* 25:302–6.

———. 1975. Mechanisms of hemispheric interaction in man. In *Hemispheric disconnection and cerebral function*, ed. M. Kinsbourne and Lynn W. Smith. Springfield, Ill.: Charles C Thomas.

Kirk, S. A., and Kirk, W. D. 1971. *Psycholinguistic learning disabilities: diagnosis and remediation.* Urbana: Univ. of Illinois Press.

Kirk, S. A.; McCarthy, J. J.; and Kirk, W. D. 1968. *The Illinois Test of Psycholinguistic Abilities*, rev. ed. Urbana: Univ. of Illinois Press.

Krashen, S. D. 1975. The critical period for language acquisition and its possible bases. In *Developmental psycholinguistics and communication disorders*, ed. D. R. Aaronson and R. W. Rieber. *Ann. N.Y. Acad. Sci.*, vol. 263.

Kriendler, A., and Fradis, A. A. 1968. *Performances in aphasia: A neurodynamical, diagnostic, and psychological study.* Paris: Gauthier-Villars.

Lansdell, H. 1969. Verbal and nonverbal factors in right hemisphere speech. *J. Comp. Physiol. Psychol.* 69:734–8.

Lee, L. L. 1971. *Northwestern Syntax Screening Test.* Evanston, Ill.: Northwestern Univ. Press.

Lenneberg, E. H. 1967. *Biological Foundations of Language.* New York: Wiley.

Levy, J. 1974. Psychobiological implications of bilateral asymmetry. In *Hemisphere function in the human brain*, ed. S. J. Dimond and J. Graham Beaumont. London: Elek.

Levy, J.; Trevarthen, C.; and Sperry, R. W. 1972. Perception of bilateral chimeric figures following hemispheric deconnexion. *Brain* 95:61–78.

Liberman, A. M.; Cooper, F. S.; Shankweiler, C. P.; and Studdert-Kennedy, M. 1967. Perception of the speech code. *Psychol. Rev.* 74:431–61.

Marshall, J. C.; Caplan, D.; and Holmes, J. M. 1975. The measure of laterality. *Neuropsychologia* 13:315–22.

Mempel, E.; Srebrzyńska, J.; Sobczyńska, J.; and Zarski, S. 1963. Compensation of speech disorders by nondominant cerebral hemisphere in adults. *J. Neurol. Neuros. Psychiatry* 26:96. Abstract.

Milner, B. 1974. Hemispheric specialization: scope and limits. In *The neurosciences: third study program*, ed. F. O. Schmitt and F. G. Worden. Cambridge, Mass.: M.I.T. Press.

Milner, B.; Branch, C.; and Rasmussen, T. 1964. Observations on cerebral dominance. In *Ciba Foundation Symposium on disorders of language*, ed. A. V. S. de Reuck and M. O'Connor. Boston: Little, Brown.

Milner, B.; Taylor, L.; and Sperry, R. W. 1967. Lateralized suppression of dichotically presented digits after commissural section in man. *Science* 161:184–5.

Moscovitch, M. 1973. Language and the cerebral hemispheres: reaction-time studies and their implications for models of cerebral dominance. In *Communication and affect: language and thought*, ed. P. Pliner, L. Krames, and T. Alloway. New York: Academic Press.

Nielsen, J. M. 1946. *Agnosia, apraxia, aphasia: their value in cerebral localization*, 2d ed. New York: Hoeber.

Piaget, J. 1971. The theory of stages in cognitive development. In *Measurement and Piaget*, ed. D. R. Green, M. F. Ford, and G. B. Flamer. New York: McGraw-Hill.

Raven, J. C. 1958. *Standard progressive matrices.* London: H. K. Lewis.

———. 1962. *Coloured progressive matrices,* London: H. K. Lewis.

Russell, W. R. 1963. Some anatomical aspects of aphasia. *Lancet* 1:1173–7.

Schuell, H. 1965a. *The Minnesota Test for Differential Diagnosis of Aphasia.* Minneapolis: Univ. of Minnesota Press.

————. 1965b. *Differential diagnosis of aphasia with the Minnesota Test*. Minneapolis: Univ. of Minnesota Press.

————. 1966. Some dimensions of aphasic impairment in adults considered in relationship to investigation of language disturbances in children. *Brit. J. Dis. Comm*. 1:33–45.

Schuell, H.; Jenkins, J.; and Landis, L. 1961. Reationship between auditory comprehension and word frequency in aphasia. *J. Speech Hearing Res*. 4:30–36.

Schulhoff, C., and Goodglass, H. 1969. Dichotic listening, side of brain injury, and cerebral dominance. *Neuropsychologia* 7:149–60.

Shankweiler, D., and Studdert-Kennedy, M. 1967. Identification of consonants and vowels presented to left and right ears. *Quart. J. Exp. Psychol*. 19:59–63.

Smith, A. 1966. Speech and other functions after left (dominant) hemispherectomy. *J. Neurol. Neuros. Psychiatry* 29:467–71.

Sparks, R., and Geschwind, N. 1968. Dichotic listening in man after section of neocortical commissures. *Cortex* 4:3–16.

Sparks, R.; Goodglass, H.; and Nickel, B. 1970. Ipsilateral versus contralateral extinction in dichotic listening resulting from hemisphere lesions. *Cortex* 6:249–60.

Sperry, R. W. 1974. Lateral specialization in the surgically separated hemispheres. In *The neurosciences: third study program*, ed. F. O. Schmitt and F. G. Worden. Cambridge, Mass.: M.I.T. Press.

————. 1968. Hemisphere deconnection and unity in conscious awareness. *Am. Psychol*. 23:723–33.

Sperry, R. W.; Gazzaniga, M. S.; and Bogen, J. E. 1969. Interhemispheric relationships: the neocortical commissures; syndromes of hemisphere deconnection. In *Handbook of clinical neurology*, ed. P. J. Vinken and G. W. Bruyn, vol. 4. Amsterdam: North Holland Publishing Co.

Spreen, O. 1968. Psycholinguistic aspects of aphasia. *J. Speech Hearing Res*. 11:453–66.

Spreen, O., and Benton, A. L. 1969. *Neurosensory center comprehensive examination for aphasia, edition A. Manual of instructions*. Neuropsychology Laboratory, University of Victoria, British Columbia.

Springer, S. P. 1971. Ear asymmetry in a dichotic detection task. *Perception and Psychophysics* 10:239–41.

Studdert-Kennedy, M., and Shankweiler, D. 1970. Hemispheric specialization for speech perception. *J. Acoust. Soc. Amer*. 48:579–94.

Thorndike, E. L., and Lorge, I. 1944. *The teacher's workbook of 30,000 words*. New York: Teachers College Press.

Wepman, J. M., and Jones, L. V. 1964. Five aphasias: a commentary on aphasia as a regressive linguistic phenomenon. In *Disorders of communication*, ed. D. M. Rioch and E. A. Weinstein. Baltimore: Williams & Wilkins.

Yakovlev, P. I., and Lecours, A. R. 1967. The myelogenetic cycles of regional maturation of the brain, pp. 3–70. In *Regional development of the brain in early life*, ed. A. Minkowski. Oxford: Blackwell.

Zaidel, D., and Sperry, R. W. 1973. Performance on the Raven's colored progressive matrices test by subjects with cerebral commissurotomy. *Cortex* 9:34–39.

————. 1974. Memory impairment following commissurotomy in man. *Brain* 97:263–72.

Zaidel, E. 1973. Linguistic competence and related functions in the right cerebral hemisphere of man following commissurotomy and hemispherectomy. Ph.D. dissertation, California Institute of Technology. *Dissertation Abstracts International*, 1973, 34, 2350B (University Microfilms No. 73-26, 481).

————. 1975a. A technique for presenting lateralized visual input with prolonged exposure. *Vision Research* 15:283-9.

————. 1975b. The case of the elusive right hemisphere. Paper presented at the 13th Annual Meeting of the Academy of Aphasia in Victoria, British Columbia, Oct. 7.

————. 1976a. Language, dichotic listening, and the disconnected hemispheres. *Proc. Conf. on Human Brain Function*, Sept. 1974, ed. D. O. Walter, L. Rogers, and J. M. Finzi-Fried, U.C.L.A., *Brain Information Service*, pp. 103-10.

————. 1976b. Auditory vocabulary of the right hemisphere following brain bisection or hemidecortication. *Cortex* 12:191-211.

————. 1977. Unilateral auditory language comprehension on the Token Test following cerebral commissurotomy and hemispherectomy. *Neuropsychologia* 15:1-18.

Zaidel, E.; Zaidel, D.; and Sperry, R. W. 1977. Left and right intelligence: unilateral visual performance on Raven's Progressive Matrices following brain bisection or hemidecortication. In preparation.

13

THE DEVELOPMENT AND DEMISE OF VERBAL MEMORY

Laird S. Cermak

The relationship between proficiency of language use and memory for verbal material has recently been emphasized by a growing number of information-processing theorists (Atkinson and Shiffrin 1967; Craik and Lockhart 1972; Cermak 1975). These theorists view verbal memory as a by-product of the extent to which an individual "analyzes" the information he is asked to retain. The belief is that the greater the extent to which an individual analyzes the information, i.e., the more features of the verbal information he can detect and encode, the greater the probability of retrieval. This analysis could potentially encompass such distinctive characteristics of the information as its visual, phonemic, and semantic features. It is further theorized that any conditions that prevent analysis of the features of verbal information will reduce the probability that the individual will be able to retain the information (Cermak 1975).

This dependence of memory upon feature analysis puts the child at a distinct disadvantage. Since the child has not had the opportunity to build up an extensive repertoire of past linguistic experience, he is not able to detect as many "distinctive" features of new verbal information as an adult. Also, the child's strategy for memorization may not place as much emphasis on studying the material for these distinctive features, since he may be less aware of the relationship between analysis and retrieval than his adult counterpart. The effectiveness of the child's memory system will increase, of course, as he gains more experience with verbal information and begins to realize the relationship between feature analysis and verbal memory. The greater his linguistic skills become, the more likely it is that the child will be able to analyze incoming verbal information effectively and retain its feature representations in memory.

The adult who has suffered damage to his central nervous system through

. The research reported in this chapter was supported in part by National Institute of Alchohol & Alchohol Abuse Grant AA 00187, National Institute of Child Health and Human Development Grant HO 09508, and National Institute of Neurological Diseases and Stroke Grant NS 06209 to Boston University School of Medicine.

disease, stroke, alcohol abuse, or aging may, like the child, suddenly find himself at a disadvantage when attempting to incorporate new verbal material into memory. While this type of patient, i.e., an amnesic, might retain such ostensible linguistic skills as the ability to communicate and pass vocabulary tests, he may be less able to "utilize" his language to effectively analyze new verbal information. Like the young child he may not be as efficient in detecting the many distinctive features of verbal information that provide the normal adult with a mechanism for retention. It could be that the difficulties amnesics experience attempting to analyze new information are similar to those experienced by the child learning to utilize his linguistic facility to improve his memory. In the case of the child the deficit appears to exist because the tools of analysis have not yet been fully developed; in the case of the amnesic the deficit may exist because the individual is unable to "use" these tools effectively during his analysis of new verbal information.

The suggestion that parallels exist in children's and amnesics' information-processing abilities is a relatively new one, and it warrants a more complete investigation. Unfortunately, comparative studies performed with amnesics and children have not yet been undertaken. However, by looking at the results of some highly similar tasks found in the separate literatures on these two populations, some tentative conclusions about parallels can be reached. Naturally, definitive conclusions drawn from such comparisons have to await more direct testing. The parallels are, nevertheless, quite intriguing, and the commonality of their interpretations forms the basis for the present chapter.

Having now set the stage for an investigation of the parallels between amnesics' and children's information-processing abilities, a brief description of the course of this inquiry is in order. This chapter will begin by exploring the extent to which results from free-recall studies are similar in these two populations. This will be followed by a discussion of whether or not amnesics and children share similar encoding strategies when attempting to memorize lists. Next, an examination of the "rate" at which children and amnesics perform feature analysis of verbal information will be presented. Finally, the author will propose a theoretical framework within which the results from both studies in the development of memory and studies with amnesics can be encompassed.

FREE RECALL

The existence of developmental levels in children's ability to freely recall lists of words, pictures, or objects has been documented with increasing frequency in recent years (Mandler and Stephens 1967; Vaughn 1968; Cole, Frankel, and Sharp 1971; Rosner 1971). Most of these reports have attributed increases in the ability to recall this type of information to improvements in the child's strategy of organizing the information during the initial presentation of the list. Tulving (1968) has shown that the probability of recalling a list actually increases as a function of the extent to which the subject initially organizes the list, especially when that organization is based upon characteristics inherent within the material itself. This ability to organize a list on the basis of categories represented by the items in the list has been shown to increase with age (Bousfield, Esterson, and Whitmarsh 1958). Young children are less able to *chunk*, i.e., organize in memory, by category, and more prone to retain the list by contiguity, than are adults (Wallace 1970). What this may mean is that children mature as they become increasingly capable of detecting the features that tie information in a list together into a common semantic domain (e.g., animals, vegetables, etc.) and of storing the products of this analysis in chunks.

A parallel has been found in amnesics' attempts to freely recall lists of words. Cermak and Butters (1972) have analyzed Korsakoff patients' recall following presentation of a list of categorizable words and found that it did not show any of the patterns of chunking on the basis of category-inclusion usually found in normal adult recall. Instead, as has been shown to be true of very young children, the contiguity of the items during list presentation was a more salient determiner of these patients' retrieval protocol than was category inclusion. It appeared that the Korsakoff patients simply did not rely upon their analysis of the semantic features of the items when chunking them into storage.

When no obvious semantic characteristics exist within a list of words, adult subjects ordinarily impose some form of subjective organization upon the list (Tulving 1962). They may, for instance, rehearse the material in chunks of three or more contiguous items. Rundus and Atkinson (1970) have developed a technique that allows a means of observing this subjective organization in progress. By instructing the subject to rehearse aloud during the presentation of a list, the extent to which subjects chunk during their rehearsal of the list can be monitored. Using this technique Rundus and Atkinson found that adults generally rehearse not only the word presently before them but several words previously presented in the list as well. This strategy of rehearsal develops gradually. It is present in sixth graders, less so in fourth graders, and practically nonexistent in second graders (Ornstein, Naus, and Liberty 1973). In fact, second graders rehearse only one word at a time—that being, of course, the word presently before them. Interestingly enough, Korsakoff patients also employ this rather underdeveloped rehearsal strategy (Cermak, Naus, and Reale 1976). They, too, limit their rehearsal to the one word being presented. As a consequence, it is not too surprising that young children and amnesic patients do not organize a list based on semantic class inclusion. It may be that neither group employs rehearsal strategies that are consonant with grouping items on *any* basis.

PHONEMIC AND SEMANTIC ENCODING

There is some evidence that a child's and a Korsakoff patient's, difficulties with analysis of words in a list may actually go beyond mere strategy of rehearsal. By utilizing a procedure called the false recognition technique developed by Underwood (1965), Felzen and Anisfeld (1970) have demonstrated that young children do not analyze individual words in the list to the same extent as older children and adults do. Their procedure involved presenting a list of words, one at a time, to a child who was instructed to indicate when a word was repeated in the list. Included in the list were words that bore systematic relationships to preceding words. When a child "falsely" recognized one of these words as being a "repeat," it was taken as an indication that a prior word had been encoded on a level equal to, but not greater than, the level of the relationship shared by the falsely recognized word and that word. Felzen and Anisfeld found that third graders falsely recognized many more rhyming words and highly associated synonyms as repeats, than did sixth graders. It appeared from these results that the older subjects were capable of a greater degree of semantic analysis than the younger children, since the sixth graders made fewer acousti-cally based errors than did the second graders. Bach and Underwood (1970), who have reported the same result, concluded that either second graders encode words only on a phonemic level while sixth graders perform semantic analysis or else both groups encode the words on the same level but the younger children prefer to "rely" on the lower, phonemic, level to retain and retrieve the material. Put differently, the younger children's encoding deficit might still represent a strategy difference rather than an inability to analyze semantic properties of words. However, in this case the strategy involves analysis of a single item rather than the chunking of several items. It may even be that the younger children's chunking deficits are an outgrowth of this more basic strategy of relying on a phonemic rather than semantic representation of the word in memory (see also Hasher and Clifton 1974).

A similar interpretation was offered by Cermak, Butters, and Gerrein (1973), who found that amnesics' performance on the false recognition test paralleled the second graders' performance. The Korsakoff patients' impressive number of phonemic errors on this task suggested that they also rely more upon a phonemic analysis of the information than upon a semantic analysis. The patients may have performed some rudimentary semantic analysis of the verbal material, but this analysis did not appear to be utilized any more by these patients than by young children during the storage and retrieval of verbal information.

Another technique that has been frequently used to investigate a subject's ability to analyze and store semantic features of verbal information is a variant of the Peterson and Peterson (1959) distractor technique developed by Wickens (1970). In this technique, the subject views three words briefly (usually 2 seconds), then performs a 15-second counting task (to prevent rehearsal of the triad), and finally tries to recall the three words (usually 10-second recall interval). Wickens has shown that after three or four such trials, during which all the words are drawn from the same semantic category (e.g., either animal or vegetable terms), normal adult recall drops from 95% to approximately 40% correct. This decrement is attributed to the influence of the proactive interference (PI) that is generated by the preceding, similarly analyzed, items. However, if after four such trials, a word triad is presented containing words from a new category, interference from the preceding category is no longer effective, and the subject's recall increases to approximately 85–90% correct. Presumably, this increase only occurs when the subject detects and "encodes" (i.e., analyzes and stores) the difference in class inclusion. If for any reason the subject does not detect the category shift, then no increase in performance will occur. Consequently, one might expect that young children and amnesics would be less likely to show increased performance following a category shift than would normal adult subjects if, indeed, they perform "less" semantic analysis on verbal information. Thus, this technique can be used to determine what types of encoding children of various ages are capable of performing and upon what types of encoding amnesics tend to rely.

Acting upon this premise, Zinober, Cermak, Cermak, and Dickerson (1975) employed Wickens's technique with children of several different age groups. They found that third and fifth graders were able to use taxonomic categories as encoding dimensions, as evidenced by their increased recall following a shift in these categories (figure 13.1). Second graders, however, were less able to benefit from the shift (Cermak 1974; Kail and Schroll 1974). Evidently, such taxonomic categories become more and more salient for use as encoding

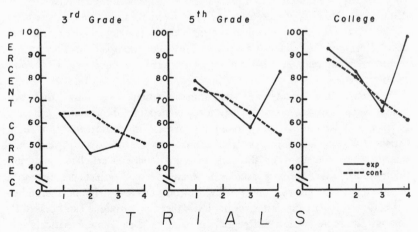

Fig. 13.1   Percentage of correct responses for third and fifth graders following a shift in taxonomic categories.

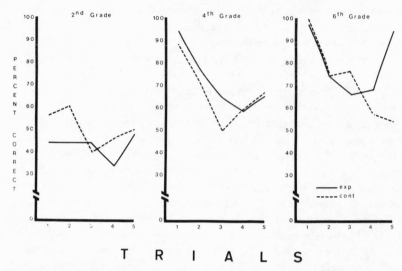

Fig. 13.2 Percentage of correct responses for second, fourth, and sixth graders following a shift in evaluative connotation categories.

dimensions as children get older. Developmental trends have also been observed for the processing of the evaluative connotation of words. Cermak, Sagotsky, and Moshier (1972) found that sixth graders could successfully use connotation as an encoding "tool," but only a few of the fourth graders and none of the second graders used this feature of words (figure 13.2). When sense impression words (e.g., "round" words, such as *ball* or *wheel* vs. "white" words, such as *snow* or *chalk*) were used, only the college-age subjects showed a release of PI (Zinober et al. 1975). Apparently, analysis of verbal information on the basis of the sense impression it conveys is not relied upon by children until the development of their linguistic skills is fairly near completion. The precise period of such development has not yet been determined, but it must be beyond the fifth grade.

On exactly the same type of task, amnesic patients have shown that they cannot even use taxonomic categories as encoding dimensions. Cermak, Butters, and Moreines (1974) found no increase in performance for these patients following a shift in class from animals to vegetables, or vice versa; nor was there an increase when the shift involved tools and articles of clothing (figure 13.3). In fact, the only instance in which Korsakoff patients demonstrated increased performance was following a shift from consonant trigrams to number triads (figure 13.4). This latter result shows that the technique can be used to demonstrate some level of differential encoding in these amnesic patients but this level is less than that achieved even by the second graders, who at least use taxonomic categories in encoding.

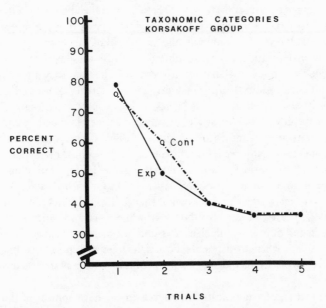

Fig. 13.3 Percentage of correct responses for Korsakoff patients following a shift in taxonomic categories.

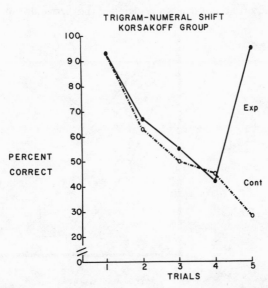

Fig. 13.4 Percentage of correct responses for Korsakoff patients following an alpha-numeric shift.

Since amnesic patients perform so little semantic encoding during the course of the experimental procedure just described, it follows that the rate at which these patients forget information on any given trial of the distractor task might also be faster than it is for normal subjects. Because these patients rely extensively upon their phonemic analysis of verbal information, they are quite likely to be more susceptible than normals to any interference generated during a distractor interval filled with verbal tasks such as counting backwards. This is because fewer differential features exist between phonemic encoding and counting than between semantic encoding and counting. Consequently, differential analysis, and eventually retrieval is made more difficult. This hypothesis has been validated by Cermak, Butters, and Goodglass (1971), who found a much faster rate of forgetting for Korsakoff patients than for normals across retention intervals varying from 0 to 18 seconds (figure 13.5). DeLuca, Cermak, and Butters (1975) have further pointed out that while Korsakoff patients' phonemic encoding in and of itself is sufficient to maintain a memory trace across an interval of 20 seconds when no distraction occurs, its high susceptibility to the effects of interference places the patient at a distinct disadvantage as soon as distraction does occur.

Several studies have indicated that levels in the development of the ability to maintain a memory trace across a distractor interval also exist in children. Older groups of children (mostly sixth graders) display slower rates of forgetting than younger children (mostly third graders). Perhaps, as has been suggested this is because the older children have developed a reliance upon their encoding of semantic features that permits a bridging of the distractor gap. The younger

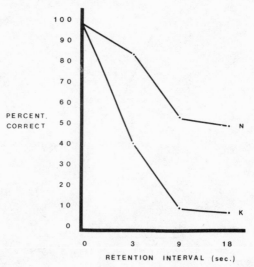

Fig. 13.5   Percentage of correct responses for Korsakoff patients following varying intervals of distractor activity.

children, on the other hand, might rely more heavily on their easily disrupted phonemic analysis of the verbal material.

SPEED OF INITIAL PROCESSING

Thus far, encoding efficiency has been described solely in terms of the "extent" to which subjects analyze incoming information. We have seen that the development of verbal memory involves the acquisition of semantic analysis abilities (or, at the very least, reliance on these abilities) and that the loss of these abilities (or of a reliance on these abilities) underlies memory disorders. An alternate way to study a subject's encoding efficiency is to investigate the "speed" with which he performs the processing that is within his encoding capabilities. In the case of amnesic patients and young children, this means studying the speed at which they can process the visual and phonemic features of words. It has been suggested that semantic analysis may even depend, to some extent, upon the completion of these visual and phonemic analyses (Sperling 1960; Cermak 1972; Craik and Lockhart 1972). Thus, a retarded "rate" of visual and phonemic analysis might have some effect on the "extent" to which information is eventually analyzed. With this possibility in mind, two areas of research on amnesic's and children's rate of processing can be explored. The first is primarily concerned with the investigation of the rate at which children and amnesics can perform phonemic analyses, and the second with the rate at which these two populations can accomplish analysis of the visual features of visually presented verbal information.

Posner and Mitchell (1967) have developed a technique that allows an estimation of the time it takes for a subject to process the "name" of stimuli such as single letters (a phonemic analysis). The procedure basically involves giving subjects differential processing instructions during the performance of a reaction-time task. Under Level 1 instructions the subject is told to press a key marked "same" whenever two simultaneously presented letters are visually identical (e.g., A, A) and to press the "different" key when the letters are not identical (e.g., A, B or A, a). Under Level 2 instructions, the subject is told to press the "same" key when the two letters have the same name (e.g., A, A or A, a) and "different" when they do not (e.g., A, B). Posner and Mitchell have shown that normal adult subjects take longer to respond under Level 2 instructions than they do under Level 1. This difference in reaction time is indicative of the additional time needed to analyze the phonemic features of letters once their visual features have been identified. Hoving, Morin, and Konick (1974) have shown that it takes more time for children to process the phonemic features of information than it does for adults, and that the amount of time needed to make these analyses decreases as children get older. Thus, it appears that the "speed of processing" phonemic features of verbal information is age dependent. As might be anticipated, deficits on this task have also been documented for Korsakoff patients (Cermak, Butters, and Moreines 1974). Specifically, it was found that, while Korsakoff patients were able to perform the visual identity match (A, A) as fast as normals, they performed all tasks under Level 2 instructions slower than normals. Apparently these patients had lost the rapid information-processing abilities they must once, at some point in their lives, have had.

The task that has most often been used to study the rate at which the visual features of information can be processed is the backward masking task (Sperling 1963). In this task a stimulus is presented briefly (10–50 msec) followed by a second stimulus which, if presented soon enough after the first, effectively erases, or masks, the first stimulus. By varying the delay of this masking stimulus, the length of time that it takes the subject to analyze the visual features of the first stimulus can be estimated. The point at which both stimuli can be identified represents the time interval needed for processing the visual features of the first stimulus. Gummerman and Roberts (1972), Welsandt, Zupnick, and Meyer (1973) and Blake (1974) have all shown that the rate at which visual features of information can be analyzed decreases as a function of increasing age. These investigators found that the interval between the presentation of the target stimulus and the masking stimulus had to be longer in order for younger children to identify the target than it had to be for the older children. Oscar-Berman, Goodglass, and Gorenstein-Cherlow (1973) have found that Korsakoff patients also needed more interstimulus interval time between the target and the masking stimulus than normals. Apparently, then, it takes longer for both Korsakoff patients and young children to analyze visual features of information than it takes normal adults. Thus, given that the speed at which *both* visual and phonemic features can be analyzed is somewhat slower for these two populations than it is for normal adults, it is not surprising to find that each is at a disadvantage when higher-level analyses are demanded by the task.

CONCLUSION

This chapter began with the observation that young children and amnesics are less able to remember than are older children or adults. It has been pointed out that this deficit is largely due to inefficient strategies of organization during the early stages of information processing. Efficient strategies, which are developed by children as they continue to mature, appear to be unavailable to the amnesic. This lack of efficient strategy goes beyond the level of organization within lists of words to the level of individual item analysis. Indeed, it appears that young children and amnesics may rely upon their phonemic analysis of individual items (rather than their semantic analysis) to a far greater extent than do normal adults. A shift from reliance on this easily disrupted code to reliance on a more permanent semantic code increases with age, but it, too. appears to be lost in the amnesic. Unfortunately, amnesics and young children are even inefficient in their encoding of the phonemic features of words, as demonstrated by the fact that they process these features more slowly than do normal adults. This inefficiency probably results in a more rapidly decaying trace for amnesics and young children and, perhaps, in a weaker base upon which to build semantic analyses. It may be that the changes in encoding strategy that occur as children mature accompany increases in the rate at which visual and phonemic features can be analyzed. The return to a reliance on phonemic encoding seen in Korsakoff patients may, in part, represent a slowing of these same abilities. Assuming all this to be true, one is left with the theory that children increase their potential for memorizing verbal information as they develop effective feature-analysis strategies and increase the speed with which they can perform these analyses. Conversely, Korsakoff patients may lose their ability to memorize verbal information when they lose these analytic skills Naturally this theory cannot, and should not, be accepted as the sole explanation for the development and demise of memory. However, it might very well provide a viable framework for future research on these two aspects of memory.

REFERENCES

Atkinson, R. C., and Shiffrin, R. M. 1967. Human memory: a proposed system and its control processes. Technical Report No. 110, Stanford University.

Bach, M. I., and Underwood, B. J. 1970. Developmental changes in memory attributes. *J. Ed. Psychol.* 61:292–6.

Blake, J. 1974. Developmental change in visual information processing under backward masking. *J. Exp. Child Psychol.* 17:133–46.

Bousfield, W. A.; Esterson, S.; and Whitmarsh, G. A. 1958. A study of developmental changes in conceptual and perceptual associative clustering. *J. Genet. Psychol.* 92:95–102.

Cermak, L. S. 1972. *Human memory: research and theory.* New York: Ronald Press.

———. 1973. Reply to "Does the Wickens STM technique tap encoding in young children?" *J. Exp. Child Psychol.* 15:362–4.

———. 1975. *Psychology of learning: research and theory.* New York: Ronald Press.

Cermak, L. S., and Butters, N. 1972. The role of interference and encoding in the short-term memory deficits of Korsakoff patients. *Neuropsychologia* 10:89–96.

Cermak, L. S.; Butters, N.; and Gerrein, J. 1973. The extent of the verbal encoding ability of Korsakoff patients. *Neuropsychologia* 11:85–94.

Cermak, L. S.; Butters, N.; and Goodglass, H. 1971. The extent of memory loss in Korsakoff patients. *Neuropsychologia* 9:307–15.

Cermak, L. S.; Butters, N.; and Moreines, J. 1974. Some analyses of the verbal encoding deficit of alcoholic Korsakoff patients. *Brain and Language* 1:141–50.

Cermak, L. S.; Naus, M. J.; and Reale, L. 1976. Rehearsal and organizational strategies of alcoholic Korsakoff patients. *Brain and Language* 3:375–85.

Cermak, L. S.; Sagotsky, G.; and Moshier, C. 1972. Development of the ability to encode within evaluative dimensions. *J. Exp. Child Psychol.* 13:210–19.

Cole, M.; Frankel, F.; and Sharp, D. 1971. Development of free recall learning in children. *Dev. Psych.* 4:109–23.

Craik, F. I. M., and Lockhart, R. S. 1972. Levels of processing: A framework for memory research. *J. Verb. Learning Verb. Behav.* 11:671–84.

DeLuca, D.; Cermak, L. S.; and Butters, N. 1975. An analysis of Korsakoff patients' recall following varying types of distractor activity. *Neuropsychologia* 13:271–80.

Felzen, E., and Anisfield, M. 1970. Semantic and phonetic relations in the false recognition of words by third- and sixth-grade children. *Develop. Psychol.* 3:163–8.

Gummerman, K., and Roberts, C. R. 1972. Age, iconic storage, and visual information processing. *J. Exp. Child Psychol.* 13:165–70.

Hasher, L., and Clifton, D. 1974. A developmental study of attribute encoding in free recall. *J. Exp. Child Psychol.* 17:332–46.

Hoving, K. L.; Morin, R. E.; and Konick, D. S. 1974. Age-related changes in the effectiveness of name and visual codes in recognition memory. *J. Exp. Child Psychol.* 18:349–61.

Kail, R. V., and Schroll, J. T. 1974. Evaluative and taxonomic encoding in children's memory. *J. Exp. Child Psychol.* 18:426–37.

Mandler, G., and Stephens, D. 1967. The development of free and constrained conceptualization and subsequent verbal memory. *J. Exp. Child Psychol.* 5:86–93.

Ornstein, P. A.; Naus, M.; and Liberty, C. 1973. The development of rehearsal strategies in free recall. Paper presented at Psychonomic Society Meeting, St. Louis.

Oscar-Berman, M.; Goodglass, H.; and Gorenstein-Cherlow, D. 1973. Perceptual laterality and iconic recognition of visual materials by Korsakoff patients and normal adults. *J. Comp. Physiol. Psychol.* 82:316–21.

Peterson, L. R., and Peterson, M. J. 1959. Short-term retention of individual verbal items. *J. Exp. Psychol.* 58:193–8.

Posner, M. I., and Mitchell, R. F. 1967. Chronometric analysis of classification. *Psychol. Rev.* 74:392–409.

Rosner, S. R. 1971. The effects of rehearsal and chunking instructions on children's multitrial free call. *J. Exp. Child Psychol.* 11:93–105.

Rundus, D., and Atkinson, R. C. 1970. Rehearsal processes in free recall: a procedure of direct observation. *J. Verb. Learning Verb. Behav.* 9:99–105.

Sperling, G. 1960. The information available in brief visual presentations. *Psychol. Mono.* 74, no. 498.

Tulving, E. 1962. Subjective organization in free recall of "unrelated" words. *Psychol. Rev.* 69:344–54.

———. 1968. Theoretical issues in free recall. In *Verbal Behavior and General Behavior Theory*, ed. T. R. Dixon and D. L. Horton. Englewood Cliffs, N.J.: Prentice-Hall.

Underwood, B. J. 1965. False recognition by implicit verbal responses. *J. Exp. Psychol.* 70:122–9.

Vaughn, M. E. 1968. Clustering, age, and incidental learning. *J. Exp. Child Psychol.* 6:323–34.

Wallace, W. P. 1970. Consistency of emission order in free recall. *J. Verb. Learning Verb. Behav.* 9:58–68.

Welsandt, R. F.; Zupnick, J. J.; and Meyer, P. A. 1973. Age effects in backwards visual masking. *J. Exp. Child Psychol.* 15:454–61.

Wickens, D. D. 1970. Encoding categories of words: an empirical approach to meaning. *Psychol. Rev.* 77:1–15.

Zinober, J. W.; Cermak, L. S.; Cermak, S. A.; and Dickerson, D. J. 1975. A developmental study of categorical organization in short-term memory. *Develop. Psychol.* 11:398–9.

14

THE DEVELOPMENT AND BREAKDOWN OF SYMBOLIC CAPACITIES: A SEARCH FOR GENERAL PRINCIPLES

Howard Gardner

The recent interest in child development has its origins largely in a desire to improve the educational process; analogously, much of the research on mental breakdown, or dissolution, has been motivated by a hope that such processes can be reversed or that victims of various breakdowns might be helped. Yet there has also been a growing realization that understanding the processes of development and breakdown may be highly illuminating—indeed, essential— for a comprehensive appreciation of behavior and thought in the intact normal adult. Processes of development and breakdown are continuous and unceasing; many aspects of normal functioning can more clearly be identified and observed while unfolding during childhood or unraveling under conditions of brain damage; the organization of the components of an "end-state," or "mature behavior," is better understood when the steps leading toward that end-state or the process of its decomposition have been elucidated. For such reasons the traditional interest in aiding normal children or brain-injured adults has been reinforced by a new conviction: understanding these populations may be a prerequisite of understanding other subject groups.

Perhaps because of the diverse origins of the disciplines of developmental psychology and neuropsychology, few scholars have focused on populations in the process of development as well as populations undergoing some form of breakdown. And, for the most part, those who have focused upon these complementary processes have done so at some remove from the rich and sometimes contradictory data in these disparate domains. It is scarcely an exaggeration to maintain that those authorities who have pondered the relationship between development and breakdown have seen breakdown essentially as "development in reverse"—the running backwards of the film of growth, perhaps more rapidly

Preparation of this paper and part of the research reported herein was supported by the Spencer Foundation, the National Institute of Neurological Diseases and Stroke (Grant NS 11408 04), and the National Institute of Education (Grant G 003 0169).

in the processes of focal diseases, more slowly in the cases of dementing processes. Embracing this position in more or less explicit terms are such prominent
social scientists as Roman Jakobson, Heinz Werner, Arnold Pick, and Jean
Piaget. Indeed, of scholars writing during the first part of this century, only
Lev Vygotsky and his colleague, Alexander Luria, have to my knowledge
seriously contemplated asymmetries between the processes of breakdown and
development. For a time these scholars stood virtually alone in investigating
the roles assumed by specific brain structures in governing various capacities.
Only recently has the potential of this approach for illuminating the relationship
among specific symbolic capacities been more widely recognized.

Valuable insights about "normal performance" can certainly be gained from
studying either of the groups referred to above, without confronting the actual
relations between development and breakdown. For instance, the study of
children learning numbers (Piaget 1965) and the investigation of aphasic
patients attempting to communicate (Goodglass and Geschwind 1976) have
yielded rich data for the construction of models of normal processing. Yet,
once one realizes that data from these disparate sources might provide contradictory information, the necessity for comparing breakdown and development
becomes more pressing.

Consider one example. Suppose that data from development suggest that
learning to name and recognize numerical symbols is a more difficult task
than learning alphabetic symbols. One might infer that numerical processes
pose greater difficulties for all populations. However, data from studies of
dissolution might reveal an opposite picture: that skills involving numerical
symbols prove more robust in the case of brain damage than do skills entailing
alphabetical symbols. Unless one embraces the extreme position that none of
these data is relevant to the processes of symbolic understanding, a different
challenge must be confronted. One must ask, what features of the processing
of numerical symbols make this realm more difficult to acquire and yet, once
acquired, make it more solidly entrenched than other forms of symbolic
knowledge? And what is the relationship among different symbolic operations
in the normal individual? In my view, such questions must be faced; the reward
will be a firmer understanding of processes of development, breakdown, *and*
normal functioning. After all, aspects of development and breakdown occur at
all times; even the question of when to speak of development, when of breakdown, is a vexed issue, on the philosophical (Harris 1958) as well as the biological
(Bonner 1952) plane.

Relinquishing the level of theory, one confronts a horrifyingly complex,
messy, and contradictory set of data. Studies abound in each area, with the
number burgeoning monthly. Seldom are the same tasks and methods employed
within one area, let alone across the domains of development and breakdown;
clinicians dominate neuropsychology, and experimentalists dominate developmental studies—yet there is a broad range of investigation within each domain

as well. Complicating the picture further is the reasonable continuity in development across different ages and populations, as contrasted with scant uniformity in the area of breakdown. Scores of diseases and conditions of dissolution exist; it is presumptuous to equate dementing diseases with one another, let alone to extend generalizations about dementia to other cortical or subcortical disorders.

The researcher intent upon extracting viable generalizations from these perplexing areas faces a dilemma. One horn is excessive particularization; if one attempts to take into account every detail of every study in every domain, all generalizations will fall by the way. The other horn is Olympian distance; if one attempts to survey studies from too high a perspective, the possibilities for meaningful statements vanish, with only trite truisms remaining.

In the hope of evading these equally unpalatable extremes, I have attempted to define an area that is sufficiently focused to allow consideration of actual data and at the same time broad enough to stimulate generalizations of some power. For the most part I have concentrated on areas of research with which I am personally familiar, populations with which I have worked. In what follows I will sketch this area; review suggestive studies at each of a number of levels; indicate domains where genuine parallels seem to obtain between development and breakdown and also domains wherein the processes seem to work independently or antagonistically. Finally, I will assess whether this enterprise has achieved its goal: the elucidation of normal psychological processing.

The area investigated in the studies below may be termed *human symbolic functioning*. The term *symbol* is used broadly, and in a nontechnical sense, to refer to any element that can denote or express a concept, idea, or feeling; symbols may be combined into symbol systems, which can be utilized by individuals conversant with the rules governing their use. The studies under review probe various symbol systems employed by various individuals for the purposes of communicating information: words, diagrams, works of art, numbers, letters, and so forth. The research centers on the extent to which individuals can employ and interpret these symbols in a referential manner as well as on their capacities to master a new symbol or symbol system. For the most part the relevant populations are children without any special talents or disabilities and once-normal individuals who have suffered focal brain damage, and hence the loss of discrete functions, as the result of a stroke. However, in certain instances other populations—for example, individuals with dementing disease—are also considered.

THE NAMING OF OBJECTS

A basic symbolic capacity is the ability to name a physical object. Of interest, accordingly, are the factors that contribute to relative ease in naming.

Numerous studies confirm that familiar and frequently encountered objects (and other entities) are more easily named than those that are rarely encountered and infrequently used in the language (Oldfield 1966). Accordingly, the factor of frequency can be said to operate in both the realms of development and dissolution, rendering the familiar more readily accessible than the infrequent or the strange.

It is worth noting, parenthetically, that under selective conditions—for instance, in certain forms of anomia—the less familiar name may be more readily available than the more familiar (Kaplan 1973). Should this observation be validated, the resulting picture of the naming process would be considerably complicated. It might be necessary, for example, to stipulate that, in addition to familiarity, the distinctness of a figure against a ground contributes to ease of naming. On this model, words or names that stand out because of their distinctiveness (due in part to their unusualness) would under certain circumstances be more readily accessible. One would then need a model that could predict the interaction of distinctiveness with familiarity.

But can factors other than "that old debbil frequency" be isolated? Based on some clinical observations, we hypothesized that depicted objects that were relatively small, tangible, firm to the touch, and perceptible by more than one sensory modality would prove easier for brain-damaged patients to name than depicted objects of equal familiarity that were relatively large, difficult to hold, and that appealed primarily to one (usually the visual) sensory modality. On this hypothesis, of the elements in the environment, *tree* or *pebble* should prove easier to name than *cloud* or *lake*. Similarly, of household objects, *table* or *clock* should prove easier to name than *wall* or *carpet*.

Studies with aphasic patients confirmed that the former, "operative" nouns were easier to name than the latter, "figurative" objects (Gardner 1973). This trend proved true independent of the superordinate category of the word or its frequency. Parallel findings emerged when the same test was run with 3- and 4-year-old preschoolers (Gardner 1974a). That the results were not determined primarily by the degree of imagery associated with each element is borne out by the fact that *all* the objects were presented in pictorial form; a separate analysis confirmed that the representations of the figurative objects were no more ambiguous for a group of normal controls than were those of the operative elements. Finally, as a dramatic refutation of a simple picturability account, the same effects were observed when brain-injured patients were required to read long lists of unrelated words, whose frequencies matched but whose referents differed in their degree of operativity. Even under conditions in which a visual depiction was no longer available, operative objects proved easier to "read aloud" (Gardner and Zurif 1975).

In the case of actual naming performance, then, the factor of operativity seems to prevail in both the developmental and the breakdown process. But what of errors and misnamings found amongst the two groups? Here a more complex picture emerges (Gardner 1974a). Relative to the aphasics, the children gave a much larger proportion of "don't know" responses. They more frequently failed to recognize the name on multiple choice, were more likely to misname based on a visual misidentification (e.g., confusing a depicted banana with a depicted boat), were more likely to describe an element rather than give its name (a broom was called "something you sweep with"), and were more prone to offer "baby talk."

For their part, the aphasic subjects were more likely to produce misordered approximations to the principal sounds of the target word (a literal paraphasia), to perseverate on a wrong response, or to produce a nonsensical or totally irrelevant response. Here each population reflects its most salient behavioral characteristics. In the case of the aphasic patients, their difficulty in producing sounds in the correct order emerged; as for the children, their insensitivity to precise task demands, relative unfamiliarity with the rules of pictorial representation, and favoring of certain idiolects colored their response patterns. Here, then, is evidence that performances in a developing population can be distinguished from performances by patients with impaired mental capacities.

It should not be inferred that the children's misnaming differed totally from those of the aphasics. In the case of children 36% of incorrect respons were either synonyms or metonyms (part for the whole or whole for the part); the figure for aphasics was 32%. Thus, in both cases, about one third of the responses are close to the correct answer, departing in one or another direction from the degree of specificity demanded in the task.

This finding—a loosening of the usual bounds of word meaning—has recently been reinforced by further investigations. For instance, studying the naming errors of preschool children, Anglin (1975) found repeated evidence of errors of overextension and underextension. The child first learns words of intermediate specificity (*dog*) within a semantic domain and only later learns more general (*animal*) and more specific names (*terrier*). A related pattern of misnamings and misunderstandings had been uncovered in a series of studies on the comprehension of unfamiliar words by aphasic patients (Gardner and Ling 1976). Here errors of a metonymous nature (substituting, say, *wrist* for *arm* or *head* for *eye*) were far more likely than, say, confusions of the object with its usual location, with other objects drawn from the same category, or with an object customarily used with the one denoted. Further principles seem to emerge: errors in naming are particularly likely to incorporate elements having a part-whole relationship to a target or to result from choosing terms on a level of specificity other than that being sought.

These studies suggest one other possible difference across the populations. Young children, incapable of such logical operations as multiple classification, fail to appreciate that an object can "belong" to two categories—for example, *collie* belongs to the classes *dog* and *animal*. The ability of some brain-damaged adults (cf. Goldstein 1948) to classify objects on more than one level, however, means that, at least potentially, they should be able to provide names and to understand several levels of generality. Should this prove to be the case, one would expect the individual's overall cognitive capacity to modulate his symbolic behaviors—and misbehaviors (cf. Gardner, Strub, and Albert 1975).

THE NAMING OF CULTURALLY VALUED SYMBOLS

Clearly related to the naming of physical objects, yet somewhat distinct, is the ability to name (or "read aloud") symbols valued by the culture. Whereas every society spawns a language rich in object names, only literate cultures value the naming of squiggles that denote sounds (letters of the alphabet) or numerical arrays (numbers).

The nature of the two classes of symbol is not identical. A letter is an arbitrary construct whose significance derives solely from its place amidst the meaningful units of language—morphemes. Numbers, in contrast, have meanings whether considered alone or in combination. The possibility therefore arises that the processes involved in the naming and decoding of these symbols may not be isomorphic with one another and may indeed reflect different neural mechanisms.

One simple way to tap processing of numbers and letters requires subjects to name such written symbols. Groups of preschool children and focally brain-damaged patients were required to name various letters and numbers as well as sundry objects and colors (Gardner 1974a). By far the easiest symbols for aphasic patients to name were numbers, with letters, animals, and colors following in that order—virtually the opposite profile obtained with children. For them, colors and animals were by far the easiest to name; letters proved of intermediate difficulty; numbers were the most challenging. Indeed, a double dissociation obtained between the two populations: only one child performed better on letters and numbers than on animals and colors; only six of twenty-two aphasics performed better on animals and colors. Moreover, a comparison of means documented numbers as the category most difficult for children and easiest for aphasic patients.

Finally, it is worth noting that, as in the study of object naming, the pattern of errors differed across groups. Children made numerous responses that belonged to the same category as the correct response, indicating some recognition of the existence of a category long before they could differentiate its members. Aphasic patients were more likely to produce responses bearing no direct relation to the stimulus. In one sense, the children's difficulties with numbers are not surprising, since this culturally valued realm is generally introduced well after, say, animals. Yet, the particular difficulty with numbers, coupled with its relative robustness in organic patients, merits further analysis.

When encountering numbers, the child has at least two behavioral schemes on which to draw. He may simply name the usual configuration (as is done with letters) or he may count on his fingers. Initially, these conflicting schemes may interfere with each other, giving rise to a delayed mastery (though not a delayed recognition) of the realm. However, the double representation of numbers—as vocal and as tactile patterns—eventually yields a dividend. For the individual in whom focal brain damage thwarts one means of naming numbers, access to the numerical realm is still retained by means of a supplementary channel—hence the well-documented (Benson and Geschwind 1969) superior preservation of number naming and processing in certain cases of focal brain disease.

THE PROCESSING OF COMPLEX SYMBOLS

Although the complexity of naming symbols should not be minimized, naming numbers and letters remain among the most elementary tasks in the semiotic realm. Once the purely referential function of such symbols has been mastered, however, the possibility exists for more subtle operations upon them. We turn now to research that taps some of these "higher-level" symbolic functions, and to the neurological concomitant of these capacities.

Sensitivity to Artistic Style

Contact with a work of art often elicits, in the first instance, a recognition of the subject matter, plot, or theme of that artifact. One may, however, overlook this "literal aspect" and focus instead on properties generally deemed of greater esthetic significance—for instance, composition, balance, rhythm, or style.

In a series of studies (see Gardner 1972a) I have examined the capacity to attend to the style of a work of art. At issue is sensitivity to those properties that allow the grouping together of works produced by the same artist, despite manifest differences in subject matter. Children in the preadolescent years exhibit a strong tendency to focus upon the subject matter, size, or dominant color of a work of art; there is rarely a tendency to group works by style. And, even with some training, this task continues to pose a challenge for many youngsters (Gardner 1972b).

In the absence of verbal facility, it is difficult to confirm that children or aphasic subjects understand the requirements of the task. We have devised nonverbal variations of the task in which a patient is trained to point to works that exhibit a common style. Our findings to date indicate that brain-damaged patients have a greater proclivity than matched hospital controls to group together works by subject matter or dominant color. Sensitivity to style therefore emerges as somewhat brittle in cases of focal brain disease.

Of greater interest, however, is the finding that the location of the lesion influences an individual's style-detection capacity (Silverman and Gardner 1976). Specifically, individuals having damage to the right hemisphere score less well on a test of style sensitivity than subjects with correlative degrees of damage in the left hemisphere. In a similar vein, right-hemisphere-damaged (RHD) patients evince a greater tendency than left-hemisphere-damaged patients to categorize works by their dominant subject matter. Apparently the right hemisphere plays a crucial role in that sensitivity to fine detail and texture that is of paramount importance in style detection. It might be argued that RHD patients resemble children. In terms of absolute performance on the task, this is true. However, the best evidence suggests that entirely different mechanisms are at work. Brain-damaged adults may well be perceptually unaware of fine details in a work. Children's behaviors reflect, on the other hand, the ignoring of stylistic cues, rather than any lack of perceptual sensitivity (Gardner 1972b).

Sensitivity to Pictorial and Linguistic Metaphor

As part of our interest in artistic symbolization we have also investigated the capacity to recognize connections among objects or symbols drawn from domains usually considered separate from one another. This capacity involves the mental operation of *metaphor*: equating objects A and B on some property X, which has not been embodied in the classification systems customarily employed within the culture with reference to A and B.

Metaphor sensitivity is limited among young children who center upon the literal and pragmatic meanings of words. A study now in progress with brain-injured patients indicates that they also avoid figurative meaning: indeed, RHD patients seem so reluctant to recognize the connotations of words that some even refuse to take the test (Gardner and Denes 1973)! It is true that both young children and brain-damaged patients produce interesting verbal comparisons, but these seem most parsimoniously explained as unintentional semantic overextensions.

We have recently attempted a direct comparison of these populations by administering a test in which subjects must match a metaphoric phrase with one of four pictorial depictions (Winner and Gardner 1977). In a sample item, the subject hears the phrase, "A heavy heart can really make a difference." He must then choose one of four randomly ordered pictures and give a reason for his choice. One of the pictures is always a metaphoric (hence, "correct") representation of the sentence—e.g., a person crying. A second picture is a literal representation of the sentence (e.g., a person carrying a large red heart and staggering under its weight). A third picture is a depiction of the object exemplifying the adjective (a 500-pound weight). The fourth illustrates the noun (a plain heart). Subjects are also asked to explicate a subset of the items at a time when pictures are not available for inspection.

Kindergartners—the youngest subjects tested—display a marked tendency to select the literal picture; metaphoric pictures, although second in order of preference, are selected less than half as often. Almost no pictures representing the adjective or nouns only are picked. When given a second choice, subjects select either the metaphoric or the adjectival pictures. Second and fourth graders are more likely to choose the metaphoric pictures, but the literal pictures run a close second. And even subjects who made metaphoric choices often gave literal explanations, suggesting that the ability to appreciate the metaphor emerges earlier than the ability to provide an adequate explanation *in words*. This décalage parallels similar findings in other studies of metaphoric understanding (Winner, Rosenstiel, and Gardner 1976).

The responses of brain-damage patients constituted an instructive comparison. Aphasic patients with left-hemisphere lesions resembled normal controls in that they usually selected the metaphoric pictures. However, like young children, they encountered difficulties in presenting adequate verbal explanations for their choices. Often they lapsed into a concrete mode of justification that relied on repetitions of the words in the metaphor and hence resembled a literal explication. Patients with right-hemisphere lesions, on the other hand, presented the opposite pattern of responses. Asked to choose one of four pictures, they were as likely to choose the literal depiction as the metaphoric one; in this respect they bore a certain resemblance to demented individuals and very young children. However, when asked for verbal explications of the figure of speech, such patients were usually able to offer quite adequate explanations, even of items on which they had previously selected the literal depiction.

These results suggest a double dissociation in metaphoric capacity depending upon site of lesion. Patients with left hemisphere pathology are likely to exhibit preserved metaphoric sensitivity when a pictorial mode of response is available, but not in the case of verbal explication; patients with right-hemisphere pathology only exhibit preserved metaphoric sensitivity when a linguistic mode of explication is avilable, reverting to a literal response in the pictorial condition. And the two patient populations therefore resemble in different ways, the responses of young children. That is, the LHD patients resemble young children in the poverty of their verbal explications, while the RHD patients resemble young children in the literalness of their pictorial responses. As we move to a more complex linguistic capacity, the relations between responses of children and adults become more intricate and multifaceted.

THE LEARNING OF A NEW SYMBOL SYSTEM

The above-mentioned studies focus on the mastery of skills within a given symbol system. Of qualitatively greater magnitude is the mastery of an entire symbol system. The ability to learn a full symbolic code distinguishes humans from other animals, thereby making possible the various specific capacities described in this essay.

When the normal adult is asked to acquire a new symbol system—be it Vietnamese or a hitherto unfamiliar branch of mathematics—he or she will characteristically translate portions of the new symbol system into one already known. But for at least two human populations such a translation proves impossible: young children who have not yet fully mastered any symbol system, and brain-injured adults, whose prior symbol systems *seem to have been vitiated* and who must accordingly undertake "from scratch" a bootstrap operation of symbol learning.

We have recently had the opportunity to conduct a fine-grained comparison of the steps through which members of these populations pass on the way to acquiring a new symbol system. In young children, we have observed a maturing capacity to produce representational drawings—the evolution from a stage of simple scribbling, through the creation of familiar geometric shapes, to the phase wherein objects, events, and scenes can be depicted in a readable manner. As part of our neuropsychological research, we have devised an auxiliary or substitute form of visual communication (termed VIC); this symbol system is designed to aid severely aphasic patients in communicating about events and feelings of significance to them. And we have followed aphasic patients from their first quasi-random manipulations of the VIC cards to the point at which they achieve a measure of fluency in the system.

Details of these twin symbol-acquisition processes have been the subject of another study (Gardner 1976). Most germane here is the finding that in their drawings, young children pass through steps that bear suggestive parallels to those through which aphasic patients pass in mastering visual communication (cf. Gardner, Zurif, Berry, and Baker, 1976). To be sure, there are also striking differences in the processes, and these will be brought out later. However, what is of interest is that fact that even in such seemingly disparate symbol systems, and with such decisively different populations, it nonetheless proves possible to isolate a set of eleven steps that seem to characterize the child's acquisition of representational drawing as well as the adult's learning of a new mode of communication.

It must be stressed that this list is idealized: the earlier steps are not always easily distinguished from one another; behavior reflecting more than one stage is sometimes discerned; and evidence for the latter stages among aphasic patients is sketchy at best. Moreover, the parallels we have discerned tell only part of the story; there are also distinctive differences between the two symbol-acquisition processes.

Some of these differences are essentially mechanical. For example, the young child may have difficulty manipulating the pen, even as the aphasic (and often apractic) patient may experience some difficulty controlling the movement of his limbs. (Neither of these motor difficulties seems to have appreciably affected

Table 14.1

Steps in the Acquisition of a New Symbol System

Step	Normal Child Drawing	Aphasic Adult Learning VIC
1. Use of primitive bodily schemes	Puts marker in mouth	Places symbol card in mouth
2. Use of more neutral, less oral, schemes	Touches marker on end of paper	Clutches the symbol cards
3. Detection of potentially symbolic events	Attends to strokes made by the marker	Notes the ideographs and attends to detail
4. Appreciation of referential relation	Produces recognizable forms that depict objects "in the world"	Cards matched to objects that they depict
5. Sensitivity to a string of symbols	Produces several symbols denoting several objects	Appreciates a series of symbols denoting a series of objects
6. Appreciation of relations among symbols	Pictures now exhibit a sense of composition; objects arranged in a coherent array	Appreciates simple syntactic and semantic relations; possesses a "language frame" into which utterances can be fed
7. Medium used to communicate to others	Drawings modified to be more readily comprehended	Knowledge possessed by other communicators taken into account
8. System used in increasingly productive way	Drawings now include new schemes and combinations of schemes	New parts of speech incorporated into utterances
9. Interest in properties of the medium	Explores design properties of the medium—what can and cannot be expressed in drawing	Attempts to express new meanings; experiments with symbolic play
10. Achieving effects and stylization	Works become recognizable as products of a particular individual; certain visual effects favored	Evolves characteristic way of aligning cards and expressing utterances
11. Medium used to express one's feelings and ideas to others	Expresses one's own feelings in such a way that others can appreciate them	Use of symbols to express messages of personal significance

the above stage sequence.) Other differences reflect personality variables. Whereas nearly all children seem highly motivated to gain mastery of the major symbol systems of the cultures, many brain-damaged patients exhibit little motivation to master VIC, particularly in the absence of some immediate and potent reinforcement. The lack of motivation might in certain instances reflect the patient's realization that progress is slow and difficult. Yet it seems more likely to be a sequela of sizable injury to the brain: the individual's motivation is lowered generally, in realms where he can still cope as well as in those in which he is deficient. Perhaps also a product of this meager motivation is a corresponding willingness to remain in the situation even if it appears to be unproductive. Whereas the young child may, at a moment's notice, simply abandon the task, the aphasic individual is likely to remain within the therapeutic session despite unconcern or even obvious discomfort.

Clearly, then, there are important differences among our populations, and within the specific stages defined above. These differences help to explain why nearly every 4 year old has attained pictorial representation, while many adult aphasics experience much difficulty in mastering VIC. Despite these differences, however, the parallels observed seem worth considering. For they suggest that even in the case of symbol systems that differ substantially from one another, individuals must pass through a series of ordered steps en route to a competent mastery.

Certain problems entailed in the parallel also need to be mentioned. Thus the comparison of composition in drawing to syntax in language is at best rough; by the same token, the kinds of originality, sensitivity to style, and awareness of medium possible in one medium differ markedly from analogous features in the other (Gardner, Howard, and Perkins 1974).

Of great moment, too, are the particular strengths that each subject population brings to the symbol-learning task. The major forte of the brain-injured individual is his past experience. He has been involved in learning situations before; even though this one may be unfamiliar, even though he has forgotten much, he may still cling to the adapative notion that there is something to be learned and that he should be able to utilize cues to master the task. Although this faith may cause him to focus on certain irrelevant cues, the central point nonetheless remains. His general learning in the past, those cognitive operations of which he is still capable, and those strategies evolved to master specific tasks may all stand him in good stead in what is, after all, just another learning situation. Only to the extent that certain inappropriate prior strategies are invoked can earlier experiences serve as a nonproductive handmaiden in the acquisition of VIC.

If the brain-damaged patient's ally is experience, the child's advantage is youth. The child houses a healthy and growing brain that seems uniquely— and perhaps only temporarily—equipped to master new symbol systems. Indeed, one genius of the brain of early childhood may be its skill at discerning syntactic regularities, patterns, and features, among such diverse systems as pictorial representation, natural language, numerical language, and, in the case of certain youngsters, music and mathematics as well.

The child is at the same time superlatively alert to the demands of communication—after all, his initial relation to his parents features considerable communication of a nonsymbolic variety—and so the symbols learned are quickly placed in the service of bearing information. As suggested by studies of later language learning, this proclivity for acquiring new symbol systems may well decline after adolescence (Lenneberg 1967). And so even if the brain of the adult were somehow perfectly normal (but devoid of other mediating symbol systems), the acquisition of a symbol system might pose considerable difficulty.

In the foregoing we have sampled freely from diverse realms of symbolization. And we have contrasted the performances of two "less-developed" groups—the young child and the brain-damage adult— with the "higher-level" performances of a normal adult population. Our findings have undermined the once-prevalent notion that development and breakdown simply mirror one another. After all, in any number of studies, young children differ qualitatively from brain-injured adults. At the same time, our review challenges the equally unproductive position that no interesting parallels obtain between the two processes. Indeed, as a result of the kinds of investigations described here, it should prove possible to put Ribot's law to a strong test: to discover in just which areas breakdown mirrors development, and in which areas it does not.

Two tasks remain. First, we must review the generalizations suggested by the raft of studies reviewed here, as well as those studies by other investigators which, while not explicitly reviewed, speak to our central question. (After all the formulations are hardly worth propounding if they could be undermined by a more thorough culling of the extant literature.) Second, returning to our initial inquiry, we must consider whether studies of development and breakdown of symbol use inform our understanding of those normal (or idealized) processes of functioning so prized by empirically oriented social scientists.

One cluster of studies supports the classical view of symbolic breakdown as a simple reversal of the order of acquisition observed in development. These studies document the contribution of such factors as *operativity*, *frequency*, and the like, factors that contribute to ease of learning in early childhood, even as they allow continued competence despite brain injury in later life. One might speculate that these early forms of knowledge—involving many "associations," embedded in diverse sensory-motor schemes—are broadly represented in the brain; owing to such wide and redundant representation they prove relatively impervious to focal injury (Gardner 1973).

Also supporting the classical generalization are certain "primitive behaviors" discerned among both young children and brain-injured adults. Among these would be the tendency to focus on the figure, or subject matter, of a work of art; to gloss a metaphoric expression literally rather than in its intended, extended meaning; and at a still more primitive level, to place the symbol-bearing vehicle in one's mouth, or one's hands, or upon an available flat surface.

So far, then, we encounter support for a reciprocal relation between development and breakdown. The picture quickly clouds, however, as we encounter abilities which evolve relatively late, but which, once established, become entrenched and relatively resistant to brain injury. For instance, numerical symbols prove difficult to learn initially, perhaps because of a tendency to confuse members of the class with one another; once this category of symbols has been mastered, however, its wealth of associations—tactile as well as visual and auditory—contributes to its relative robustness. Perhaps, once acquired, the numerical processes are reorganized so that they dominate simpler concepts that once reigned supreme.

A related category of injury-resistant behaviors are those which, whenever learned, tend to be so often rehearsed that they become "over-learned." Such skills as reading nouns for meaning, playing a musical instrument, learning a poem, may take many months to master; once learned, however, they are frequently practiced under different conditions and eventually become routinized or automatized. Easily aroused under diverse situations, these well-rehearsed activities may prove more resistant to brain injury than others which, while learned at an earlier period of life, are only evoked in certain circumstances or are only associated with a limited number of schemes.

Certain capacities initially learned within one context may, by acquiring thereafter a "functional autonomy," persist in form even when the functions originally served are not longer evident. Examples here would include the ability to appreciate certain grammatical operations (Luria 1970) and sensitivity to different types of utterances (Boller and Green 1973). As suggested by von Stockert (1972), individuals may retain these capacities, originally learned in the course of ordinary conversation, despite significant language impairment. The challenge confronting the researcher is to document this persistence, perhaps by use of an alternative symbol system.

Another factor contributing to differences in the two populations is the degree of affect or motivation linked to a specific domain. A study of humor comprehension has revealed, for instance, that brain-damaged patients find sexual themes particularly amusing, while cartoons depicting animals and children are generally not appreciated (Gardner, Ling, Flamm, and Silverman 1975). One might expect the opposite picture among young children, who are known to prefer literary materials dealing with animals and who are unlikely to appreciate sexual innuendo. In this context, it is worth recalling that one of the most persistent abilities in brain-damaged individuals is the capacity to swear. Once again, this capacity reflects an affective domain that is of limited relevance to young children.

Also relevant are those characteristics that color the symbolic performance of each population. With children, for instance, one may expect baby talk, visual confusions based on lack of familiarity with the manner of depiction, and failure to understand the implicit demands of a task. Among brain-damaged adults, there is increased likelihood of perseverative responses (relatively rare among children), linguistic paraphasias (a particular function of injury to the language system), and profound difficulties in spatial and constructional tasks, found among patients with pathology in the minor hemisphere.

Let me cite a final differentiating feature. The young child possesses a healthy brain having enormous learning powers. Even if a sizable portion of that brain should be sacrificed, the prognosis for substantial recovery of function—the reestablishment of damaged capacities—would remain excellent until puberty. The brain-damaged patient, for his part, faces a less sanguine picture. First of all, specific abilities, being more focally organized, are more likely to be seriously impaired. Then, too, the chances that other areas of the brain can compensate for the injured capacity are more remote. The sole hope is that abilities that *have* been spared may somehow be drawn upon as a prosthetic—an alternative means—through which the impaired capacity can again be realized. In that he at least possesses other well-developed lifelong capacities, the brain-damaged patient is in a better position than is the young child, who is unlikely to possess any over-learned, or "substitute" capacities whatsoever.

In order to effect a comparison between our two groups, we have had to generalize about the consequences of brain damage. Yet, as the above notes have repeatedly documented, each variety of brain damage entails its own pattern of declines as well as its profile of spared capacities. This specificity of neural representation ensures that, at best, there can be but a rough correspondence between the symptom picture in various focal diseases and that encountered in ordinary childhood. True, certain focal pathologies bear interesting affinities to certain isolated disorders of childhood; thus, there are developmental as well as adult versions of the Gerstmann syndrome, suggestive parallels between alexia and dyslexia. Yet only in general dementing diseases such as Alzheimer's disease is one likely to encounter a pattern of breakdown that actually mirrors a large proportion of the processes of development during childhood (Gardner 1975, chapter 7). For only in such disorders may a hierarchical structure of abilities be gradually decomposed, leaving a residue of more primitive capacities, free once again to regulate the behavior of the hapless individual.

What lessons about normal symbolic functioning can be drawn from our review? A first point is that the processes that precede the more complex form of symbolic functioning do not completely disappear. Such tendencies as literal interpretation of meaning or oral exploration of potentially symbolic vehicles will reemerge under conditions of pathology. Moreover, as numerous studies of regression, fatigue, and other brain-altering states have revealed, these processes can even be demonstrated in otherwise normal individuals once more sophisticated behaviors have (at least temporarily) been swept aside.

In addition to indicating which behaviors remain present beneath the surface, studies of symbolic development and breakdown help specify the constituents of mature behaviors, even as they challenge our common-sense notions of the organization of skills in the normal mind. The determination, for example, that an individual can efficiently read numbers while losing the capacity to decode words and letters undermines any assumption that all "symbol reading" is of a piece (Gardner 1974b). Assumptions that metaphoric capacity functions similarly across symbol systems are also refuted by our findings. It may be that even the most sophisticated cognizer must pass, at least in elliptical form, through some of the steps the young child goes through (Flavell and Draguns 1957). And so a fuller understanding of the steps of development involved in skill organization provides clues about the kinds of processes that may be occurring—if more rapidly and in a less explicit and a piecemeal fashion—in all individuals.

Our review of the steps entailed in learning a new symbol system may also yield implications concerning normal functioning. When invading a new area of knowledge, most individuals attempt to utilize already existing symbol systems, even though such aids are unlikely to prove totally adequate. It is indeed possible that individuals of every age and degree of sophistication who tackle a new code must pass through some of the stages discerned amongst our children at the drawing board and our brain-damaged patients at the VIC table.

Work with the two populations has also yielded some unanticipated dividends. Novel concepts like the operativity of an element; useful analytic tools like the double dissociation of two cognitive skills (Teuber 1955); bizarre behavioral patterns like the spontaneous tendency to correct sentences with communicatively irrelevant syntactic errors but not those with errors of semantic force (Davis, Foldi, Gardner, and Zurif 1977)–these and many other instances can be further probed in normal subjects, once their presence has become known through their emergence in an immature or pathological population.

While this list of applications and implications could be expanded, the general point should be clear. The avenues of research outlined here are proving their fruitfulness. It seems fair to think of both research traditions as persistent and stimulating gadflys. The respective findings help to sharpen and, in some cases, to challenge unexamined assumptions about the nature and organization of skills in the normal individual. Such clinical syndromes as pure alexia or transcortical aphasia and such developmental phenomena as a failure to conserve quantity or an insensitivity to artistic style—all these help to fix and place in proper perspective the accomplishment of the competent adult.

To be sure, not all insights about normal processes must await the findings from the classroom or the hospital. Far from it; all the aforementioned insights might conceivably have resulted from experiments with normal subjects or even from careful introspection. But the point is that such insights do *not* magically arise. Indeed, if they did, all questions of psychology would long ago have been solved. Unexpected but compelling behaviors and syndromes force us to rethink our categories and enable us to construct a more comprehensive and veridical model.

In conclusion, it is worth recalling a lesson made clear by one of the first students of these populations. As Sigmund Freud repeatedly stressed, none of us is completely normal. By the same token, neither the child nor the organic patient is entirely devoid of normal characteristics. We must reaffirm our link to the child that we were and the patient we may become. Close study of these groups devastates our unexamined condescension, even as it provides valuable clues concerning central and yet mysterious human behaviors.

REFERENCES

Anglin, J. 1975. The child's first terms of reference. Unpublished paper.
Benson, D. F., and Geschwind, N. 1969. The alexias. In *Handbook of clinical neurology*, ed. G. W. Bruyn and P. J. Vinken, vol. 4. Amsterdam: North-Holland Publishing Co.
Boller, F., and Green, E. 1972. Comprehension in severe aphasics. *Cortex* 8:382–94.
Bonner, J. T. 1952. *Morphogenesis*. Princeton: Princeton Univ. Press.
Davis, L.; Foldi, N.; Gardner, H.; and Zurif, E. 1977. Repetition in the transcortical aphasias. Submitted for publication.
Flavell, J., and Draguns, J. 1957. A microgenetic approach to perception and thought. *Psychol. Bull.* 54:197–217.
Gardner, H. 1972a. Style sensitivity in children. *Human Development* 15:325–8.
———. 1972b. The development of sensitivity to figural and stylistic aspects of paintings. *Brit. J. Psychol.* 63:605–15.
———. 1973. The contribution of operativity to naming in aphasic patients. *Neuropsychologia* 11:213–20.
———. 1974a. The naming of objects and symbols by children and aphasic patients. *J. Psycholing. Res.* 3:133–49.
———. 1974b. The naming and recognition of written symbols in aphasic and alexic patients. *J. Comm. Dis.* 7:141–53.
———. 1975. *The shattered mind*. New York: Knopf.
———. 1976. The acquisition of first symbol systems. *Studies in the Anthropology of Visual Communication* 3:22–37.
Gardner, H., and Denes, G. 1973. Connotative judgements by aphasic patients on a pictorial adaptation of the semantic differential. *Cortex* 9:183–96.
Gardner, H., and Ling, P. K. 1976. Comprehension of low-frequency words in aphasia. Unpublished research.
Gardner, H., and Zurif, E. 1975. "Bee" but not "be"; oral reading of single words in aphasia and alexia. *Neuropsychologia* 21:113–26.
Gardner, H.; Howard, V.; and Perkins, D. 1974. Symbol systems: a philosophical, psychological, and educational investigation. In *Media and Symbols*, ed. D. Olson. Chicago: Univ. of Chicago Press.
Gardner, H.; Strub, R.; and Albert, M. 1975. An unimodal deficit in operational thinking. *Brain and Language* 2:333–44.
Gardner, H.; Ling, P. K.; Flamm, L.; and Silverman, J. 1975. Comprehension and appreciation of humor in brain-damaged patients. *Brain* 98:399–412.
Gardner, H.; Zurif, E.; Berry, T.; and Baker, E. 1976. Visual communication in aphasia. *Neuropsychologia* 14:275–92.

Goldstein, K. 1948. *Language and language disturbances*. New York: Grune & Stratton.

Goodglass, H., and Geschwind, N. 1976. Language disorders (aphasia). In *Handbook of perception*, ed. E. Carterette and M. Friedman. New York: Academic Press.

Harris, D., ed. 1957. *The concept of development*. Minneapolis: Univ. of Minnesota Press.

Kaplan, E. 1973. Personal communication.

Lenneberg, E. 1967. *Biological foundations of language*. New York: Wiley.

Luria, A. R. 1970. *Traumatic aphasia*. The Hague: Mouton.

Oldfield, R. C. 1966. Things, words, and the brain. *Quart. J. Exp. Psychol.* 18:340–53.

Piaget, J. 1965. *The child's conception of number*. New York: W. W. Norton.

Silverman, J., and Gardner, H. 1976. Style sensitivity in organic patients. Unpublished research.

Teuber, H. L. 1955. Physiological psychology. *Ann. Rev. Psychol.* 6:267–96.

von Stockert, T. 1972. Recognition of syntactic structure in aphasic patients. *Cortex* 8:323–34.

Winner, E., and Gardner, H. 1977. The comprehension of metaphor in brain-damaged patients. *Brain*, in press.

Winner, E.; Rosenstiel, A.; and Gardner, H. 1976. The development of metaphoric understanding. *Develop. Psychol.* 12:289–97.

III

A NEUROANATOMICAL
PERSPECTIVE

The following contribution by LeMay and Geschwind charts anatomical asymmetries in adults, and where available, lateral differences in newborns and children. As the authors themselves point out, it is unclear what implications, if any, these neuroanatomical data have for process models of language acquisition and disruption. Nonetheless, the measurements at least suggest that different forms of cerebral organization can be related to certain developmental language disorders and to different patterns of adult aphasia—particularly to the differences shown by aphasic right- and left-handers. Indeed, when the data from newborns and children are considered, the measurements even provide neuroanatomical support for the likelihood of a biologically determined left-hemispheric predisposition for language.

15

ASYMMETRIES OF THE
HUMAN CEREBRAL HEMISPHERES

Marjorie LeMay

and

Norman Geschwind

Until very recently the predominant view in the literature was that the human hemispheres were symmetrical or that the asymmetries seen were insufficient to account for the remarkable functional differences between the hemispheres, particularly those relating to the development and adult use of language. Since 1968, however, there has been a major revival of interest in asymmetries, and a large body of data has accumulated which document their presence. These demonstrations have depended on three types of evidence: (1) gross anatomical asymmetries observed in brains studied at post-mortem; (2) gross asymmetries inferred from routine arteriographic or pneumoencephalographic studies; and (3) gross asymmetries observed by computerized x-ray scanning techniques. The following material is a reivew of significant cerebral asymmetries noted in the past, some new material mainly concerning asymmetries discernible by new x-ray scanning techiques, and a discussion of the possible functional significance of the asymmetries. We will be presenting in this chapter primarily data on asymmetries observed in adults, as well as, when these are available, measurements on lateral differences in newborns and children. We do not yet have information which definitely relates these asymmetries to differences in cognitive or emotional behavior in individuals, to normal or abnormal development, or to the patterns of disorders after lesions. We hope, however, to indicate some of the directions that research may take to show the presence or absence of relationship of these asymmetries to behavior.

Meaningful comparative measurements of the cerebral hemispheres have been difficult to obtain because of variability in the morphology of brains and

The work discussed here has been supported in part by Grant NS 06209 from the National Institutes of Health ɩɔ the Aphasia Research Center, Boston University School of Medicine, and also by a grant from the William F. Milton Fund of Harvard University.

311

the necessity of making the measurements when the brain is in an abnormal state—either outside the body or after the injection of substances into the body to make parts of the cerebrum visible for measurements. Boyd (1861) found the left hemisphere to be heavier than the right and also noted some decrease in weight of the brain with age. Studies since then have reported that the right hemisphere is on the average heavier than the left (Knudsen; Wagner; Thurman; Braune; Wilde; Broca). The differences reported in the weights of the hemispheres are small. Although Braune (1891) and Wilde (1925) found the right cerebral hemisphere to be heavier than the left, they found that the weight of the left cerebellum to be greater than that of the right. Braune, besides noting the left cerebellar hemisphere to weigh more than the right, found curved cerebellar impressions in the left occipital bone in 53.8% of 91 skulls. In 12 cases he found the right cerebellum to weigh more than the left, and in none of these was there a history of left-handedness. Melley (1944), in a study of the brains of 450 neuropsychiatric cases, noted an inverse relationship between the weights of the hemispheres and ventricular size.

Comparative measurements of the lengths of the cerebral hemispheres have been made mostly by anthropologists measuring the asymmetry of skulls. The differences in lengths of the hemispheres in adults are small. Hadziselimovic and Cus (1964) and Hrdlicka (1907) found the fronto-occipital lengths of the internal surfaces in skulls to be on the average slightly greater on the left than the right, while right preponderance was found in 75.5% of 729 ancient Egyptian skulls reported by Hoadley in 1927. The right hemicranial fossa was usually found to be longer than the left in the skulls of the Galloway anthropological collection in Uganda (Gundara and Zivanovic 1968). The left cerebral hemisphere is, however, usually longer in fetal, newborn, and children's brains. In 11 brains of newborns and children, Connolly (1950) found the left hemisphere to be longer than the right in 7, the right longer in 3, and the right and left hemispheres to be equal in 1. On photographs of 49 fetal and newborn brains,* we found the hemispheres to be equal in length in 17, the right longer in 8, and the left longer in 24.

Although the differences in the lengths of adult human hemispheres are small, variations in the size of local areas in the brain occur regularly and are often striking. Anthropologists have noted local impressions on the inner table of the vault caused by pressure from the brain. The forward or backward extension of one cerebral hemisphere beyond the other is commonly referred to as "fronto-petalia," "occipito-petalia," etc. In their study of 297 East African skulls in Uganda, Gundara and Zivanovic found the greatest impressions in the parietal and occipital regions. The commonest combination of impressions

---

* These brains were obtained from the Southard Unit of the Eunice Shriver Kennedy Center for Mental Retardation in Waltham, Mass., and from the Yakovlev Collection at the Armed Forces Institute of Pathology in Washington, D.C.

Table 15.1

Widths and Protrusions of Hemispheres

| | Width* of Hemispheres | | | | | | Protrusions† of Hemispheres | | | | | |
| | frontal | | | occipital | | | frontal-petalia | | | occipito-petalia | | |
	left wider	=	right wider	left wider	=	right wider	left anterior	=	right anterior	left posterior	=	right posterior
Right-handers												
M	11	17	54	50	17	12	9	53	37	90	33	10
F	4	20	68	51	14	14	5	77	25	95	27	14
	15	37	122	101	31	26	14	130	62	185	60	24
Left-handers												
M	5	11	14	7	8	14	8	19	6	22	7	6
F	5	9	5	4	8	9	4	16	5	13	8	6
	10	20	19	11	16	23	12	35	11	35	15	12
Newborns and children	0	2	4	3	2	2	1	12	3	18	16	3

NOTE: Comparison, on x-ray computerized tomographic scans, of the width of the frontal and occipital portions of the brains studied, and of the expansion anteriorly and posteriorly of the frontal and occipital lobes, respectively, on each side.
* Left wider means left (frontal or occipital) region is wider than right; = means right and left (frontal or occipital) regions are equally wide. Right wider means right is wider than left.
† Frontal-petalia: right anterior means right frontal lobe protrudes further forward than left. Occipito-petalia: right posterior means right occipital lobe protrudes further back than left.
The totals in each group are not equal since in some cases it was not possible to determine the data from the scan. Thus the relative widths of the frontal lobes could be accurately ascertained in the scans of 174 right-handed patients, but the degree of occipital-petalia could be ascertained in 269 cases.

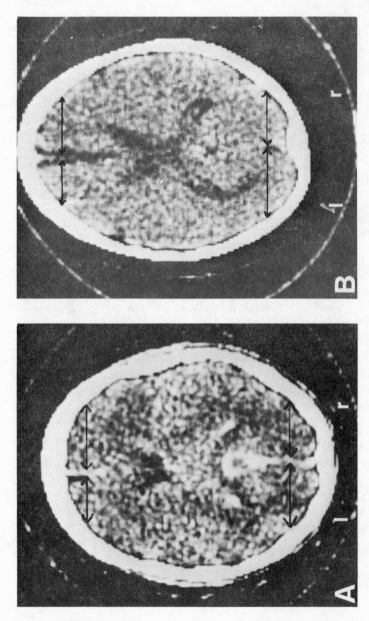

Fig. 15.1 Computerized Axial Tomograms. The central arrows mark the inter-hemispheric region. Note the wider *Rt* frontal and *Lt* posterior parietal-occipital areas. *A*. Patient with normal sided ventricles. There is a slight left occipito-petalia. *B*. Patient with slightly enlarged ventricles secondary to generalized atrophic changes. Note the left occipito-petalia and the slight right frontal-petalia.

was that caused by right fronto-petalia (the right frontal pole protruding further forward than the left) with left parieto-petalia and left occipito-petalia. Inglessis (1919) found that in 200 coronally sectioned brains, 10.5% showed asymmetry in the frontal part of the brain and 90.5% showed asymmetry in the occipital portion. In 11 brains, the left frontal lobe was larger than the right, and in 8 brains the right was larger. In 161 brains the left occipital area was larger and in 16 brains the posterior portion of the right hemisphere was larger. Inglessis (1925) noted less of a preponderance of the left hemisphere in women than in men.

With the use of computerized x-ray tomography (Hounsfield et al. 1973) it is now possible, without injecting foreign substances into the body, to compare in living persons the configuration of the inner tables of the right and left sides of the skull and the size of various areas of the brain.

Table 15.1 shows comparisons of the widths of the right and left cerebral hemispheres near the frontal and occipital poles, and also comparisons of the protrusions of the poles into the adjacent vault. These data were taken from computerized axial tomographic (CAT) studies of 63 left-handed and 269 right-handed patients over 10 years of age, and 37 children, 10 years of age and younger. None of the patients had evidence of localized supratentorial disease. A few patients had obstructive hydrocephalus secondary to lesions below the tentorium. In right-handed patients the right frontal lobe is commonly wider than the left, the left parietal-occipital region is wider than the right, and there is a left occipito-petalia. The frontal lobes usually project forward equally; if not, the right frontal lobe is much more apt to cause a pressure defect on the bone than is the left (figure 15.1). In left-handers the occipital portions of the brains tend to be more nearly equal in width and more often show an equal extent posteriorly than do the brains of right-handers. Left occipito-petalia is also common in fetal and newborn brains (figure 15.2).

VENTRICULAR ASYMMETRIES

The shape of the cerebral ventricles correlates to some extent with the shape and size of the skull (Bailey 1936; Berg and Lonnum 1966), and the ventricles also show predictable asymmetries throughout life. The ventricles are somewhat smaller in individuals under the age of 20. Thereafter, there appears to be gradual widening of the third ventricle (Engeset and Lonnum 1958), but in patients without intracranial disease there is little increase in size of the lateral ventricles until the seventh or eighth decade (Bruijn 1959; Burhenne and Davis 1963; Knudsen 1958; Last and Thompsett 1953; Reitmann 1951).

In numerous studies the left lateral ventricle has been shown to be significantly larger than the right (Bruijn 1959; Burhenne and Davis 1963; Harvey 1910, 1911; Knudsen 1958; Last and Thompsett 1953; Lodin and Kohler

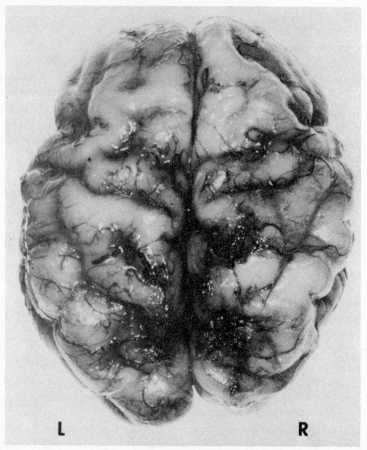

Fig. 15.2   Photograph of superior surface of a 32-week-old fetal brain showing a slight right frontal petalia and a more striking left occipito-petalia.

1957; Reitmann 1951). In a study of ventricular volumes in normal brains, Knudsen found the left ventricle larger than the right in 48% of cases and the right lateral ventricle larger in only 15%. Most comparisons of the lateral ventricles have been made by measurements across the roofs of the central portions of the venctricles (the "cellae media" or "ventricular span") or by measurements from the superior end of the septum pellucidum to the narrowest point along the caudate nucleus (figure 15.3). Table 15.2 shows the septal-caudate distances measured on successive pneumoencephalograms in individuals showing ventricles considered to be normal or having generalized atrophic changes. Patients with localized disease were excluded from the study. The study contained measurements from pneumoencephalograms of 90 females and 354 males. No difference was noted between ventricular asymmetries of males and females, and therefore the sexes were not separated.

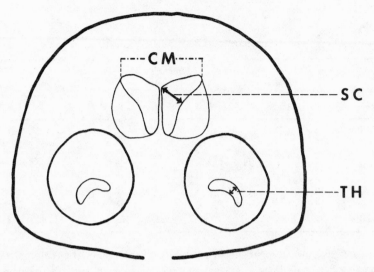

Fig. 15.3 Diagram of ventricular measurements made in brow-up pneumoen-cephalograms. CM = Cella media = width of bodies of the lateral ventricles. SC = Septal-caudate line = narrowest distance between the superior margin of the septum pellicidum and the caudate nucleus. TH = Width of top of temporal horn.

There is a physiological increase in width of the ventricular system during the first year, particularly anteriorly. Differences in the size of the lateral ventricles, the left generally being slightly wider than the right, are noted mainly after the first year (Lodin 1968). Eight of the patients in table 15.2 were less than a year old.

The occipital (McRae et al. 1968; Last and Thompsett 1953) and temporal portions of the lateral ventricles are also usually larger in the left hemisphere.

Table 15.2

Asymmetries of the Bodies of the Lateral Ventricles

	Septal-Caudate Measurements		
Age	R > L	=	L > R
0–10	9	5	9
11–20	5	5	14
21–30	7	6	22
31–40	19	16	50
41–50	23	25	67
51–60	17	20	59
61–70	10	5	35
70	2	5	9
Total	92	87	265

Table 15.3

Pneumoencephalographic Asymmetries

Age	Cella Media			Septal-Caudate Line			Temporal Horns		
	<40	41–50	<51	R > L	=	L > R	R > L	=	L > R
0–10	9	2		4	2	5	3	2	5
11–20	14	4		6	1	10	1	7	10
21–30	19	8	3	5	6	16	3	5	21
31–40	18	5	1	2	2	17	4	5	14
41–50	4	11	2	1	3	13	3	4	9
51–60	10	10	5	2	4	19	7	5	13
60	15	24	21	5	7	45	11	12	40
Total	89	64	32	25	25	125	32	40	112

Table 15.3 shows comparison of the width of the tips of the temporal horns and septal-caudate lines in a separate study made on pneumoencephalograms of patients without localized supratentorial disease.

McRae et al. reported some correlation between length of the occipital horns and cerebral dominance. They studied 100 consecutive air studies. Eighty-seven patients were right-handed; in these, the occpital horns were longer on the left in 52 (60%) and of equal length in 26 (30%); the right horns were longer in 9 (10%). The other 13 patients were left-handed or ambidextrous, and their occipital horns were longer on the left in 5 (38%); equal in 4 (31%); longer on the right in 4 (31%).

GYRAL ASYMMETRIES

The extreme variability of the cerebral gyri and sulci makes significant surface asymmetries difficult to detect. The most striking asymmetry of the hemispheres is in the region of the Sylvian fissures and adjacent parietal and temporal lobes. Eberstaller (1884) and Cunningham (1892) described the left Sylvian fissure as longer than the right. Cunningham also measured the angle formed by the Sylvian fissure and a line drawn through the anterior end of the fissure at right angles to the longest anterior-posterior diameter of the hemisphere. He found this angle to be significantly smaller on the right. A more acute angle is found on the right because the posterior end of the Sylvian fissure, labeled the "Sylvian point" by anatomists, is commonly higher on the right than the left, a difference that is present in fetal brains as early as the 16th week (LeMay and Culebras 1972). This difference in the heights of the posterior ends of the Sylvian fissures is more obvious on coronal sections (figure 15.4). A study of such coronal sections of brains of persons without neurological disease by LeMay and Culebras showed the Sylvian point to be

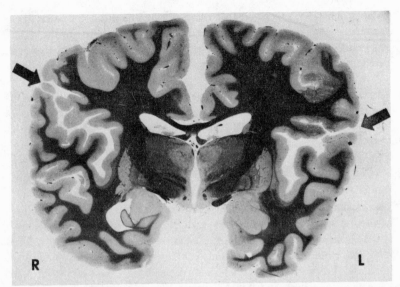

Fig. 15.4 Coronal section through a human brain at the posterior ends of the Sylvian fissures. The Sylvian point (arrows) is commonly higher on the right than the left.

higher on the right in 14 of 18 cases. Rubens (1975) found the posterior end of the right Sylvian fissure to angle sharply upward in 25 of 36 adult brains.

In most lower primates the Sylvian fissures are relatively longer, and their posterior ends relatively higher than in man (Ingalls 1914). Lowering of the Sylvian fissure in the course of evolution is associated with an increase in size and number of the convolutions in the parietal lobes. The postcentral gyrus, especially its lower portion, is wider on the left than the right, and there is a greater degree of fissuration on the left between the central sulcus and the posterior end of the Sylvian fissure (Connolly; Cunningham). In left-handers the posterior ends of the Sylvian fissures are more often nearly equal in height. A determination of the relative levels of the posterior ends of the Sylvian fissures can be made by cerebral arteriography (Hochberg and LeMay 1974). Table 15.4 shows a comparison of the positions of the ends of the Sylvian fissures in 106 right-handed and 28 left-handed persons.

Table 15.4

Relative Positions of Posterior Ends
of Sylvian Fissures

	Right Higher	=	Left Higher
Right-handers	71	27	8
Left-handers	6	20	2

Stankevich (1938) reported that the cortex of the inferior parietal region (Broadman areas 39 and 40) was greater in extent on the left than the right in 5 of 7 brains. Gurevich and Khachaturian (1936) found the cortical area of the superior parietal region to be greater on the left. In two patients, one known to be left-handed, the superior parietal lobule was greater on the right.

Asymmetries are also observed in the temporal lobe. Heschl's gyrus lies in the central portion of the temporal operculum. The superior surface of this operculum lying behind Heschl's gyrus and anterior to the posterior end of the Sylvian fissure is known as the planum temporale. Pfeifer (1936) stated that the left planum was larger than the right but gave no statistical data. Geschwind and Levitsky in 1968 found the planum temporale to be larger on the left in 65% of 100 adult brains, equal in 24%, and larger on the right in only 11%. These asymmetries were statistically significant at less than the 0.001 level. They found the length of the outer margin of the planum temporale to be 3.6 ± 1.0 cm on the left and 2.7 ± 1.2 cm on the right (p < 0.001). These findings have been confirmed by Wada et al. (1969, 1975), Witelson and Pallie (1973), and Teszner (1972). In addition, these authors have shown the same asymmetry in newborn and fetal brains. In Wada's series of adult and infant brains there was a complete absence of the right planum in approximately 10%, and the right planum was larger than the left in 10%. A larger right than left planum was found more often in the female than the male brain. Asymmetries are also evident in surface gyri. The superior temporal gyrus is more often wider on the right than the left (Hyde 1973). The superior temporal sulcus, just below the superior temporal gyrus, is usually continuous, but a break in this sulcus occurs more frequently in the left hemisphere than in the right (Connolly).

FRONTAL AREA

In spite of overwhelming evidence by CAT studies that the right frontal lobe is wider and that the right frontal pole protrudes more often anteriorly on the right than on the left, the anatomical differences responsible for these findings are not obvious, and the differences themselves are less obvious on inspection of the brains at post-mortem or on coronal sections. In a study (1938) of the cytoarchitectonic structure of the frontal lobe Konovova reported that although the cortical surface areas of the right and left frontal lobes are nearly equal, the variability of the gyral pattern is almost twice as great on the left, and this is particularly true of the lower anterior and opercular portions of the lobe. Cunningham found distinct variabilities of the gyral patterns of the frontal operculum. He pointed out that a single anterior ramus of the Sylvian fissure is more frequently seen on the right. More commonly, two separate anterior rami are present, particularly in the male and in the left hemisphere.

In some brains two anterior limbs extend from the Sylvian fissure by a single stem. This pattern is also more commonly seen on the left side, but more often in females. Wada and colleagues (1975) measured on photographs the opercular portion of the third frontal gyri in 100 adult and 85 infant brains and found the right side to be more often larger than the left. In approximately 10% of the brains the left opercular area was larger. There was no striking difference in this relationship between adult and fetal brains or between the sexes.

OCCIPITAL AREA

Minor asymmetries of cerebral sulci have been noted in the occipital lobes (Connolly 1950; Cunningham 1892), but the most striking differences are in the size and shapes of the right and left posterior parietal and occipital regions. These are shown very clearly in adults by the computerized tomography of the skull (table 15.1). Although the occipital asymmetries are not as apparent in the CAT scans in infants, left occipito-petalia is commonly present in the infant brain.

MEDULLA OBLONGATA AND SPINAL CORD

Significant asymmetries have also been noted in the medulla oblongata and the spinal cord. Yakovlev and Rakic (1966) in fetal and neonatal brains and Kertesz and Geschwind (1971) in adult specimens have found that the bundles of descending nerve fibers in the left pyramid of the medulla are larger and cross to the opposite side (before descending into the spinal cord) at a higher level than those of the right pyramid in 87% and 73%, respectively, of the cases studied. Examination of the cords in the fetal and newborn specimens showed the right ventral pyramidal tract to be larger than the left in 69.4% of the cases.

VENOUS CHANNELS

Differences in width of the posterior parietal-occipital regions can be quite accurately judged by the posterior end of the sagittal sinus and the transverse sinuses. These venous channels are shown during cerebral angiography but can also often be seen on plain skull films by impressions on the inner table of the vault. In post-mortem studies of 18 brains from patients who had arteriograms shortly before death, the position of the sagittal sinus to the right and a lower transverse sinus on the left accurately predicted the width of the posterior portion of the brain in 17. Table 15.5 shows the position of the lower end of the sagittal sinus in 129 consecutive cerebral angiograms. It is apparent that the

Table 15.5

Asymmetries of Venous Sinuses

Right-handers	Position of Lower End of Sagittal Sinus			Height of Transverse Sinus		
	To right of midline	midline	To left of midline	Right above left	=	Left above right
Male	35	22	9	32	18	10
Female	27	20	10	26	9	11
Total	62	42	19	58	27	21

posterior end of the sagittal sinus usually lies to the right and that the right transverse sinus is usually higher. These results reflect the presence of a smaller occipital brain mass on the right side than on the left. In left-handed individuals it has been shown (Hochberg and LeMay 1975) that the transverse sinuses are more often equal in position or that the left is higher than the right.

The main flow of blood in the sagittal sinus, which is usually to the right may well result from the position of the lower end of the sinus, which is also usually to the right. This direction of flow apears to be established by the time the embryo is 20 mm in length (Streeter 1915). Hemispheric asymmetries in the position of the posterior ends of the Sylvian fissures, the right commonly being higher than the left, have been seen at least as early as the 16th gestational week (LeMay and Culebras 1972). It would seem logical that differences in hemispheric size in the parietal region could be responsible for the position of the sagittal sinus. Since these anatomical findings are also related to handedness, it would seem likely that the predictability for handedness is established early in fetal life.

The draining veins of the surfaces of the two hemispheres tend to be similar (Hochberg and LeMay 1974; Matusubara 1961). DiChiro correlated the superficial venous drainage with cerebral dominance as determined by Wada tests (Wada and Rasmussen 1960). In 34 patients with left-hemisphere dominance, he found the vein of Labbe to be prominent on the left in 18 and prominent on the right in 2. In 9 patients with right-hemisphere dominance for speech, the vein of Labbe was found to be prominent on the right in 6 and on the left in 1.

SIGNIFICANCE OF ASYMMETRIES

Obviously, gross asymmetries in themselves provide little information. If there are true functional asymmetries between the hemispheres, these probably result from the greater extent of certain cortical areas on one side. Specific cortical areas could be defined either by a characteristic cellular architecture (cytoarchitecture) or by a characteristic pattern of connections. In the human brain it is difficult to obtain detailed evidence of the patterns of connection of different regions. One will therefore have to rely on cytoarchitectonic studies. This is probably not a serious shortcoming, since evidence in subhuman primates suggests that areas of distinctive cellular architecture usually have connection patterns differing from those of bordering areas. Architectural areas therefore probably defined functional units in most, if not all, cases.

It is of course possible that gross asymmetries might not correspond to any differences in the sizes of cytoarchitectonic areas. Thus, it is conceivable that the gross asymmetries are the result of mechanical factors relating to the shape of the skull or the configuration of the blood vessels of the brain. Individual cortical areas on the two sides could be of equal size but simply be folded differently. It is clear, therefore, that there will be unequivocal evidence of significant anatomical asymmetries only when it has been shown by cytoarchitectonic mapping that some areas are larger on one side than on the other.

One region in which there is good evidence for cytoarchitectonic asymmetry is the planum temporale. As noted earlier, Pfeifer (1936) had asserted that the left planum was typically larger than the one on the right, but von Bonin (1962) treated this claim with skepticism. Geschwind and Levitsky (1968), however, confirmed Pfeifer's assertion statistically, and their results have not only been confirmed in three other series, but it has been shown that the asymmetry is present in the brains of infants and newborns.

Von Economo and Horn (1930) demonstrated that the larger size of the left planum is the result of the greater extent of the auditory association areas TB and TA on the upper surface of the left temporal lobe. Even this carefully done study does not, however, settle the issue as to whether there is asymmetry of cytoarchitectonic areas. One could still argue that although there was a greater extent of TB on the left planum, part of the TB on the right side might not be on the planum but might extend vertically along the supramarginal gyrus bounding the posterior end of the right Sylvian fissure. In other words, it is still necessary to trace the full extent of each of these areas to prove that they are really larger on the left.

Although definite cytoarchitectonic information is still lacking, one can at this time offer some speculations as to which cortical areas are larger. It seems reasonable from the data we have that the posterior cortical speech regions are larger on the left; the longer left Sylvian fissure and the longer left planum would be compatible with a greater extent of Wernicke's area. The longer left Sylvian fissure would also probably lead to a greater size of the speech regions in the parietal operculum. This speculation is concordant with the finding of LeMay and Culebras that the left parietal operculum is larger than the one on the right, and also with their demonstration that the posterior end of the left Sylvian fissure lies lower than the one on the right. On the other hand, the greater posterior extent of the left Sylvian fissure suggests that the left posterior parietal region, behind the Sylvian point, is smaller than the corresponding region on the right. This asymmetry in length may, however, be compensated for by the greater width of the left parieto-occipital region and the frequent left occipito-petalia (table 15.1).

We do not know at this time the cause of the widening of the right frontal lobe as seen on the CAT scans. This remains a problem for further investigation.

It should be noted here that asymmetries may be present in subcortical gray masses as well as in cortex. Sinclair and Hightower (1954), while studying the brain from a young girl who had died of a nonneurological disease, dissected the caudate and lentiform nuclei and found their weights on the right to be 13.6 gm and on the left 11.9 gm. There was no significant difference in weights between the right and left thalami (11 gm and 10.9 gm). Obviously one must be cautious in drawing conclusions from this single specimen.

Assuming that true cytoarchitectonic asymmetries are found, what conclusions could be drawn concerning their functional significance? Since no studies have yet been done relating cytoarchitectonic asymmetries to functional differences, one must rely on some of the correlates of the gross differences. It is clear that certain patterns are associated with right-handedness, e.g., a higher right Sylvian fissure and wider left occipital lobe. These patterns are also seen in newborns and children, most of whom are, of course, future right-handers.

For reasons that should be obvious from the previous discussion, clear-cut functional conclusions cannot be stated, but certain tentative inferences can be drawn. First, asymmetries are in general present at birth or in early childhood or even in utero. This suggests that these anatomical differences are not related to postnatal experience and are very probably genetically determined. Second, the asymmetries in the brain are not absolute, but are distributed along a spectrum. One can contrast this with certain asymmetries elsewhere in the body. Thus, the liver is on the right and the spleen on the left, and only in very rare instances is the pattern reversed. On the other hand, the asymmetries in cortical regions come in all degrees. The left planum may be much larger than the right, or only moderately larger; the two sides may be equal or the right may be larger. Since there is continuous variation it is possible that these correspond to varying degrees of dominance of a function rather than to absolute dominance. Third, asymmetries tend to be less striking in left-handers. Thus, consider the width of the occipital regions (the following percentages are calculated from the data in table 15.1. The percentages of right-handers in whom the left occipital region is wider than the right, in whom the widths are equal on the two sides, and in whom the right is wider than the left are 64, 20, and 16, respectively. In left-handers, the corresponding percentages are 22, 32, and 46. The trend noted here and also seen in several other instances is for the left-handed group to contain a higher percentage of brains without asymmetry (32% vs. 20% for the right-handers). Furthermore, among the left-handers the percentage of right larger areas and left larger areas differs by a smaller amount than is the case with the right-handers. (For occipital width the absolute difference between these percentages is 24% for the left-handers and 48% for the right-handers.) Furthermore, if one takes the ratio of the number of cases on the side showing the greater asymmetry to the number of cases on the other, one finds that the value of this ratio is greater in the right-handers than the left-handers. Thus, in right-handers the ratio of percentages of left-wider occipital regions to that of right-wider is 64:16, i.e., 4:1, while for left-handers the ratio of right-wider to left-wider is 46:22, i.e., 2:1.

These three features of the left-handed group—(1) a larger percentage without asymmetry, (2) a smaller value of the absolute value of the difference between the groups showing right asymmetry and left asymmetry, and (3) a smaller ratio between the numbers showing greater asymmetry on one side to the numbers on the other side—are seen in the measurements of all the adult groups in table 15.1 and in the data in table 15.4. The same trend is seen in the data on asymmetries of the occipital horns of the ventricles in the report of McRae et al. (1968) quoted earlier in this paper.

These data suggest that left-handers probably have a different type of brain organization from right-handers and that dominance is probably on the average less marked in them than in the right-handers. These conclusions are compatible with many of the known functional data on left-handers. To give a simple example, in right-handed aphasics 99% or more of the cases have left-hemisphere lesions, whereas in left-handers about 60% have left-hemisphere and 40% right-hemisphere lesions.

One can speculate further about the asymmetries. It is conceivable that some of the patterns may account for certain childhood disorders. Thus, a child with Sylvian fissures of equal height and a small planum temporale on both sides might on the average develop language abilities more slowly than a child with a higher right Sylvian fissure, a large left planum, and a small right planum. Similarly, the patterns seen may be relevant to recovery in adults. One might guess that a patient with an equally large planum and parietal operculum on the two sides might recover well from aphasia after a left-posterior lesion, because the large right side may compensate for loss of the left. On the other hand, a patient with a large left- and small right-posterior speech region might recover poorly after destruction of the left side.

It is of some interest to consider here the rates of spontaneous recovery from aphasia. Luria (1972) records that in patients with penetrating brain wounds in one of the primary speech areas of the left hemisphere, severe aphasia was present in the initial period in nearly all cases. On reexamination some months later the aphasia had disappeared or improved markedly in about one quarter of the cases. Several factors might account for such recovery, i.e., it is likely that cases with small areas of destruction would show superior recovery. Luria's evidence, however, supports the view that much of the recovery was the result of individual differences. Thus, left-handers and right-handers with left-handed relatives showed a higher rate of recovery than pure right-handers without familial sinistrality. It is possible that those individuals who recover better than others with similar lesions may show anatomical patterns of asymmetry such as those described in the preceding paragraph. The figure of 25% good recovery is of the same magnitude as the number of brains with equal plana or with a right larger planum.

Although at this stage of our knowledge one can only speculate in a crude manner, it seems likely that the correlation of behavioral studies of normal children and of aphasics with the patterns of asymmetry in the brain will open an entirely new chapter in the study of the higher functions.

REFERENCES

Bailey, P. 1970. Variations in the shape of the lateral ventricles due to differences in the shape of the head. *Arch. Neurol. Psychiat.* 35:932.

Berg, K. J., and Lonerun, A. 1966. Ventricular size in relation to cranial size. *Acta Radiologica* 4, New Series Diagnosis: 65–78.

Boyd, R. 1861. Tables of the weights of the human body and internal organs in the sane and insane of both sexes at various ages arranged from 2114 post-mortem examinations. *Phil. Trans.* 151:241–62.

Braune, C. W. 1891. Die Gewichtsverhältnisse der rechten zur linken Hirnhälfte beim Menschen. *Arch. Anat. Physiol., Anat. Abstr.* 253–70.

Broca, P. 1885. Data reported by Topinard, P. *Elements d'anthropologie générale*, p. 591. Paris. A. Delabraye and E. Lecrosnier.

Bruijn, G. W. 1959. *Pneumonencephalography in the diagnosis of cerebral atrophy.* Utrecht. Drukkerij H. J. Smits Oudegracht.

Burhenne, H. J., and Davies, W. 1968. The ventricular span in cerebral pneumography. *Amer. J. Roentgen* 90:1176–84.

Connolly, C. J. 1950. *External morphology of the primate brain.* Springfield, Ill.: Charles C Thomas.

Cunningham, D. J. 1892. *Contribution to the surface anatomy of the cerebral hemispheres.* Dublin: Royal Irish Academy.

DiChiro, G. 1962. Angiographic patterns of cerebral convexity veins and superficial dural sinuses. *Amer. J. Roentgen.* 87:308–21.

Eberstaller, 1884. Reported 1892 by Cunningham, D. J. *Contribution to the surface anatomy of the cerebral hemispheres.* Dublin: Royal Irish Academy.

Engeset, A., and Lonnun, A. 1958. Third ventricles of 12 mm width or more. *Acta Radiologica* 90:5–11.

Geschwind, N., and Levitsky, W. 1968. Human brain: left-right asymmetries in temporal speech region. *Science* 461:186–7.

Gundara, N., and Zivanovic, S. 1968. Asymmetry in East African skulls. *Amer. J. Physical Anthrop.* 28:331–8.

Gurevich, M. O., and Khachaturian, A. A. (1936). Reported 1960 by Yakovlev, P. I., in *Mental Retardation*, ed. P. W. Bowman and H. V. Mautner, p. 17. New York: Grune & Stratton.

Hadziselimovic, H., and Cus, M. 1964. Konfiguracija lobanjskebazecovjeka u odonsu na izgled njenog okcipitalnog dijela. *Revue de la Société Anthropologique Yougoslav* 1:41–55.

Heidrich, R. 1955. Planimetrische Hydrocephalus Studien. In *Sammlung Zwangloser Abhandlungen aus dem Gebiete der Psychiatrie und Neurologie* 12, Halle (Saale).

Hoadley, M. F. 1929. On measurement of the internal diameters of the skull in relation: (1) to the prediction of its capacity, (2) to the "pre-eminence" of the left hemisphere. *Biometrik* 21:85–123.

Hochberg, F. H., and LeMay, M. 1974. Arteriographic correlates of handedness. *Neurology* 25:218–22.

Hounsfield, G.; Ambrose, J.; Perry, J.; and Bridges, C. 1973. Computerized Transverse Axial Scanning. *Brit. J. Radiology* 46:1016–51.

Hrdlicka, A. 1907. Measurements of the cranial fossae. *Proc. U.S. Natl. Mus.* 32:177–232.

Hyde, J. B.; Akesson, E. J.; and Berinstein, E. 1973. Growth of the superior temporal gyri in man. *Experientia* 29:1131.

Ingalls, N. W. 1914. The parietal region in the primate brain. *J. Comp. Neurol.* 24:291–341.

Inglessis, M. 1919. Einiges über Seitenventrikel und Hirnschwellung. *Arch. f. Psychiat.* 74:159–68.

———. 1925. Untersuchungen über Symmetrie und Asymmetrie der Menschlichen Grosshirnhemisphären. *Ztschr. f.d.ges. Neurol. Psychiat.* 95/96:464–74.

Kertesz, A.,and Geschwind, N. 1971. Patterns of pyramidal decussation and their relationship to handedness. *Arch. Neurol.* 24:326–32.

Knudsen, P. A. 1958. *Ventriklernes Storrelsesforhold i Anatomisk Normale Hjerner fra Voksne*, Copenhagen theses. Odense: Andelsbogtrykkeriet.

Kohler, M. 1957. Encephalographische Befunde bei Kindern mit besonderer Berucksichtigung der Mikroventrikulie und der Peripheren Liquorräumen. *Kinderarztl. Prax.* 25:87–97.

Konovora, G. P. (1938). Reported 1960 by Yakovlev, P. I., in *Mental Retardation*, ed. W. Bowman and H. V. Mautner, p. 17. New York: Grune & Stratton.

Last, R. J., and Thompsett, D. H. 1953. Casts of cerebral ventricles. *Brit. J. Surgery* 40:525–42.

LeMay, M., and Culebras, A. 1972. Human brain morphologic differences in the hemispheres demonstratable by carotid angiography. *New England J. Med.* 287:168–70.

Lindgren, E. 1952. A pneumographic study of the temporal horns with special reference to tumors in the temporal region. *Acta Radiol. Suppl.* 95:378–81.

Lodin, H. 1968. Size and development of cerebral ventricular system in childhood. *Acta Radiol.* 7:385–92.

Loken, A. 1959. Discussion in: The clinical value of the x-ray diagnosis atrofia Cerebri, by P. E. Hammerberg and T. Fog. *Acta Psych.Neurol. Scand. Suppl.* 137:83–4.

Luria, A. R. 1972. *Traumatic aphasia*. The Hague: Mouton.

McRae, D. L.; Braunch, C. L.; and Milner, B. 1968. The occipital horns and cerebral dominance. *Neurology* 18:95–98.

Matusubara, T. 1961. An observation on cerebral phlebograms with special reference to the changes in the superficial veins. *Nagoya J. Med. Sci.* 23:86–94.

Melley, A. 1944. Application d'une méthode de corrélation à la capacité ventriculaire dans différentes affections neuropsychiatriques. *Conf. Neurol.* 6:57–64.

Pfeifer, R. A. 1936. Pathologie der Hörstrahlung und der Corticalen Horsphäre. In *Handbuch der Neurologie* 6, ed. Bumke and Foerster, pp. 533–626. Berlin: Springer.

Reitmann, F. 1951. Evaluation of air studies. *Dis. Nerv. Syst.* 12:44–6.

Rubens, A. 1975. Personal communication.

Sinclair, J. G., and Hightower, N. 1954. Handedness and the corpus striatum. *Texas J. Sci.* 6:215–6.

Stankevich, I. N. (1938). Reported 1960 by Yakovlev, P. I., in *Mental Retardation*, ed. P. W. Bowman and H. V. Mautner, p. 17. New York: Grune & Stratton.

Streeter, G. L. 1915. The development of the venous sinuses of the dura mater in the human embryo. *Amer. J. Anat.* 18:145–78.

Teszner, D. 1972. Etude anatomique de l'asymétrie droite-gauche du planum temporale sur 100 cerveaux d'adultes. Doctoral thesis, University of Paris.

Thurman, J. 1866. On the weight of the brain and the circumstances affecting it. *Ment. Sci.* 120:43.

von Bonin, J. 1962. In *Interhemispheric relations and cerebral dominance*. ed. V. Mountcastle, pp. 1–6. Baltimore: Johns Hopkins Press.

von Economo, C., and Horn, L. 1930. Ueber Windingsrelief, Masse und Rindenarchitektonik der Supratemporalfläche, ihre individuellen und ihre Seitenunterschiede. *Z. Neurol. Psychiat.* 130:683–757.

Wada, J. 1969. Interhemispheric sparing and shift of cerebral speech function. *Excerpta Medica*, International Congress Series 193:296–7.

Wada, J., and Rasmussen, T. 1960. Intracarotid injection of Sodium Amytal for lateralization of cerebral speech dominance. *J. Neurosurg.* 17:266–82.

Wada, J. A.; Clarke, R.; and Hamm, A. 1975. Cerebral hemispheric asymmetry in humans. *Arch. Neurol.* 32:239–46.

Wagner, N. 1864. *Massbestimmungen der Oberfläche des Grossen Gehirns.* Cassel, Trummer and Dietrich. Gottingen: Georg-August University.

Wilde, J. 1926. Ueber das Gewichtsverhältniss der Hirnhälften beim Menschen. *Latvijas Univ. raksti* 14:271–88.

Witelson, S. F., and Pallie, W. 1973. Left hemisphere specialization for language in the newborn: neuroanatomical evidence of asymmetry. *Brain* 96:641–6.

Wolff, H., and Brinkmann, L. 1940. Das "normale" Encephalogramm. *Dtsch. Ztschr. Nervenheilk.* 151:1–25.

Yakovlev, P. I., and Rakic, P. 1966. Patterns of decussation of bulbar pyramids and distribution of pyramidal tracts on two sides of the spinal cord. *Trans. Amer. Neurol. Assoc.* 91:366–7.

CONTRIBUTORS

Sheila E. Blumstein: Department of Linguistics, Brown University; and Aphasia Research Center, Department of Neurology, Boston University School of Medicine

Alfonso Caramazza: Department of Psychology, The Johns Hopkins University

Laird S. Cermak: Aphasia Research Center, Department of Neurology, Boston University School of Medicine, and Boston Veterans Administration Hospital

Alice Cohlan: Department of Psychology, Cornell University

Jill G. de Villiers: Department of Pyschology and Social Relations, Harvard University

Jacqueline Doolittle: Department of Psychology, Cornell University

Howard Gardner: Aphasia Research Center, Department of Neurology, Boston University School of Medicine, and Boston Veterans Administration Hospital

Norman Geschwind: Departments of Neurology, Beth Israel Hospital and Harvard University Medical School; and Aphasia Research Center, Department of Neurology, Boston Veterans Administration Hospital

Jean Berko Gleason: Department of Psychology, Boston University; and Aphasia Research Center, Department of Neurology, Boston University School of Medicine

Harold Goodglass: Aphasia Research Center, Department of Neurology, Boston University School of Medicine, and Boston Veterans Administration Hospital

Jane M. Holmes: Aphasia Research Center, Department of Neurology, Boston University School of Medicine

David Ingram: Department of Linguistics, The University of British Columbia

Marjorie LeMay: Departments of Radiology, Massachusetts General Hospital and Harvard University Medical School

Eric H. Lenneberg (1921–1975): At the time of his death, Professor of Psychology, Department of Psychology, Cornell University

Kenneth E. Pogash: Department of Psychology, Cornell University

Robert J. Scholes: Communication Sciences Laboratory, Department of Speech, Program in Linguistics, Department of Psychology, and Center for Neurological and Behavioral Linguistic Research, University of Florida

Ola A. Selnes: Department of Psychology, University of Rochester

Paula Tallal: John F. Kennedy Institute, The Johns Hopkins University School of Medicine

Harry A. Whitaker: Department of Psychology, University of Rochester

Eran Zaidel: Division of Biology, California Institute of Technology

Edgar B. Zurif: Aphasia Research Center, Department of Neurology, Boston University School of Medicine, and Boston Veterans Administration Hospital

329

INDEX

Phonological processing: in aphasia, 5; auditory feedback in, 185; in infants, 16–18; levels of, 14; methods of studying, 68–70, 238–41; used in forming fricatives and affricates, 67; used by linguistically deviant children, 64, 82–3

Phonology: nature of deviant, 63–65; systems of, in aphasia, 87

Piaget, Jean, 268, 292

Pick, Arnold, 138, 292

Piercy, M., 47

Pizzamiglio, L., 182

Poeck, K., 199, 207

Pogash, K. A., 104

Poppen, R., 30

Posner, M. I., 285

Possessive case, 111, 112, 116–17, 118–19

Posterior aphasia, 6, 8. See also Aphasia; and other types of aphasia

Power, D. J., 181

Pressnell, L. M., 181

Primates, 319, 323

Process grammar, 147. See also Grammar; Transformational grammar

Progressive tense, 111; used by aphasics, 114; used by children, 113–14

Property detectors of speech, 18–21

Quigley, S. P., 181

Rapid auditory processing, 49–52, 58

Raven, R. C., 33

Raven's Coloured Progressive Matrices Test, 33, 43, 263

Reading: and brain damage, 96; children with problems in, 28, 31; decoding of, 91, 94; dyslexia and, 88–9, 224; and hard-of-hearing individuals, 179, 181–2, 184, 188; perception of, 91

Receptive aphasia, 163, 248, 258. See also Aphasia; and other types of aphasia

"Regression" hypothesis of aphasia, 109, 231, 270; dissolution of language and, 101; history of, 195–6; Jackson's description of, 195–6; Jakobson's theory of, 87–8, 95, 110, 145–6, 196–7, 226, 267; reading breakdown and, 87–96; refutation of, 266–8; a test of, 149–59; Token Test and, 195–8, 209

Repetition method of testing, 34–6, 36–7, 38, 39, 41–2, 45, 46, 49–50

Residual aphasics, 8. See also Aphasics; and other types of aphasics

Ribot's law, 101, 109, 114, 303

Right-ear advantage (REA), 57–8, 244, 246; interpretation of, 243

Right-handers: cerebral organization of, 315, 318, 324, 325; recovery from aphasia in, 326. See also Left-handers

Right hemisphere of the brain, 11, 299; and aphasia, 231, 248, 250–1, 264–6; auditory language comprehension in, 229–31, 241–59, 260–3, 264–6, 267–70; auditory memory in, 257; auditory vocabulary of, 250; decoding of verbs by, 249; developmental hypothesis for, 230; dichotic listening and, 244; experiments concerning, 231–58; grammatical discriminations in, 253, 256; inter-hemispheric interaction and, 230, 234; language acquisition and, 230, 259–63, 264; language shift to, 245; linguistic competence of, 230, 258; as a model of natural language, 230, 258, 266, 267–8; phonemic discrimination of, 247; semantic structures and, 249–50; speech production and, 258, 322; style-detection capacity and, 298; syntactic discrimination of, 253, 256, 257. See also Brain; Cerebral hemispheres; Cerebral hemispheric asymmetries; Left hemisphere of the brain

Roberts, R. C., 286

Rose, F. C., 264

Rosenbaum, R. S., 137, 175

Rosenberg, S., 167

Rosenthal, W. S., 30–1

Rubens, A., 319

"Rule of e," 91–2

Rundus, D., 279

Russell, W. R., 264

Sagotsky, G., 282

Same-Different method of testing, 30, 37–8, 41–2, 45, 46, 47, 52–3

Savin, H. B., 164, 187

Schlanger, B. B., 111n

Schlessinger, I. M., 181

Scholes, R. J., 187

Schuell, H., 242, 249

Schulhoff, C., 135

Semantic encoding, 280–6

Semantic processes: in aphasics' speech, 146, 148–9, 158, 159, 222–5; constraint in, 153, 154, 155, 157; in children's speech, 156–7; cues in, 156; pictorial representations of, 237, 238; in sentences, 167, 170, 171, 172, 223

Semantics, 4, 5; of lexicon, 247–50. See also Semantic processes

Sentences: acoustic signals and, 167, 183; ambiguous, 188–90; center-embedded, 150–1; comprehension of complex, 145–59; comprehension and production of, 163–90; deep structure of, 164–6, 168, 170, 171, 172; digit strings in, 187; embedded, 105, 149–51,

Library of Congress Cataloging in Publication Data

Main entry under title:

Language acquisition and language breakdown.

    Includes index.
    1. Aphasia—Congresses. 2. Children—Language—
Congresses. 3. Psycholinguistics—Congresses.
I. Caramazza, Alfonso. II. Zurif, Edgar B. [DNLM:
1. Language development. 2. Language disorders—
Etiology. 3. Asphasia—Complications. WL340 L287]
RC425.L36   618.9′28′552   77-4789
ISBN 0-8018-1948-2